Game AI Pro 360

Game AI Pro 360
Guide to Architecture

Edited by
Steve Rabin

CRC Press
Taylor & Francis Group
Boca Raton London New York

CRC Press is an imprint of the
Taylor & Francis Group, an **informa** business

CRC Press
Taylor & Francis Group
6000 Broken Sound Parkway NW, Suite 300
Boca Raton, FL 33487-2742

Printed on acid-free paper

International Standard Book Number-13: 978-0-367-15104-1 (paperback)
International Standard Book Number-13: 978-0-367-15107-2 (hardback)

Visit the Taylor & Francis Web site at
http://www.taylorandfrancis.com

and the CRC Press Web site at
http://www.crcpress.com

Contents

About the Editor

Steve Rabin has been a key figure in the game AI community for more than a decade and is currently a principal software engineer at Nintendo Technology Development. After initially working as an AI engineer at several Seattle startups, he managed and edited seven game AI books in the "Game AI Pro" series and the "AI Game Programming Wisdom" series. He also edited the book *Introduction to Game Development* and has more than two dozen articles published in the "Game Programming Gems" series. He has been an invited keynote speaker at several AI conferences, founded the AI Game Programmers Guild in 2008, and founded the GDC AI Summit where he has been a summit adviser since 2009. Steve is a principal lecturer at the DigiPen Institute of Technology, Redmond, Washington, where he has taught game AI since 2006. He earned a BS in computer engineering and an MS in computer science, both at the University of Washington, Seattle, Washington.

About the Contributors

Bobby Anguelov is a South African expat currently working as a senior programmer at Ubisoft, Montreal, Canada, primarily in the field of animation. Prior to joining Ubisoft, he worked as an AI/animation programmer at IO-Interactive. Outside of the game industry, he has worked in a variety of roles ranging from computer graphics lecturer to enterprise software consultant. Bobby holds an MS in computer science from the University of Pretoria, South Africa, with a focus on computational intelligence and computer graphics.

Nicolas A. Barriga is a PhD candidate at the University of Alberta, Edmonton, Canada. He earned BSc (engineering) and MSc degrees in informatics engineering at Universidad Técnica Federico Santa María, Valparaíso, Chile. After a few years working as a software engineer for Gemini and ALMA astronomical observatories, he came back to graduate school and is currently working on state and action abstraction mechanisms for RTS games.

Doug Binks makes games at Enkisoftware Limited, having recently left his position as technical lead of Games Architecture Initiative at Intel. Prior to joining Intel in 2008 he worked in the games industry in roles ranging from lead programmer, head of studio at Strangelite, and R&D development manager at Crytek. Despite an early interest in games development, Doug careered sideways into a doctorate in physics at Oxford University, and undertook two postdoctoral posts as an academic researcher in experimental non-linear pattern formation, specializing in fluid mechanics. His earliest memories are of programming games in assembly on the ZX81.

Michael Buro is a professor in the computing science department at the University of Alberta, Edmonton, Canada. He received his PhD in 1994 for his work on *Logistello*—an Othello program that defeated the reigning human World champion 6-0. His current research interests include heuristic search, pathfinding, abstraction, state inference, and opponent modeling applied to video games and card games. In these areas, Michael and his students have made numerous contributions, culminating in developing fast geometric pathfinding algorithms and creating the World's best Skat playing program and one of the strongest *StarCraft: Brood War* bots.

Alex Champandard is the founder of AiGameDev.com, the largest online hub for artificial intelligence in games. He has worked in industry as a senior AI programmer for many years, most notably for Rockstar Games where he also worked on the animation technology of *Max Payne 3*. He regularly consults with leading studios in Europe, most notably at Guerrilla Games on the multiplayer bots for *KillZone 2 & 3*. Alex is also the event director for the Game/AI Conference, the largest independent event dedicated to AI in games.

Caroline Chopinaud received her PhD in computer science at the Pierre and Marie Curie University, Paris, France, in 2007, specializing in artificial intelligence. She joined MASA Group in 2008 as a developer of MASA LIFE, working on agent communications and the modeling of security and military behaviors. Caroline has since become head of R&D at MASA, in charge of innovation and the R&D team. She is mainly involved in research activities, in particular scientific monitoring and project building. She handles relations between MASA and academia. She published scientific papers in international conferences in the field of multiagent systems (ECAI, IAT, PAAMS, etc.).

Carle Côté has been a senior AI programmer at Eidos Montreal since 2009 and currently leads the AI development on the next *Thief* game. In 2012, he received his PhD in electrical engineering applied to AI and robotics from Sherbrooke University in Canada. His focus is mainly on decision-making systems and cognitive AI.

Michael Dawe has been solving AI and gameplay problems in games since 2007, working on games such as *Kingdoms of Amalur: Reckoning, Dance Central Spotlight*, and *Grand Theft Auto 5*. He is a frequent speaker for the AI Summit at the Game Developers Conference, is a founding member of the AI Game Programmers Guild, and has written previously for the Game Programming Gems and Game AI Pro series. Michael holds an MS in computer science from DigiPen Institute of Technology, Redmond, Washington, as well as a BSc in computer science and philosophy from Rensselaer Polytechnic Institute, Troy, New York.

Etienne de Sevin earned his PhD in artificial intelligence at École Polytechnique Fédérale de Lausanne (EPFL), Switzerland, in 2006. During his research in several renowned labs, he designed, implemented, and evaluated cognitive architectures and real-time decisionmaking processes for autonomous nonplayer characters in order to populate virtual environments such as virtual cities or video games. He published several scientific papers in international conferences (AAMAS, CGI, CASA, etc.). He joined MASA Group as a research engineer in the R&D team in 2012.

Luke Dicken is the founder of Robot Overlord Games, and a researcher with the Strathclyde Artificial Intelligence and Games group at the University of Strathclyde in the United Kingdom. He contributes to AltDevBlogADay and is a principal organizer for the AltDev Conference family. Luke has been passionate about artificial intelligence since playing *Creatures* as a teenager, and pursued it in college, first through several degrees in traditional AI before specializing in AI for games as part of a PhD he is still (occasionally) pursuing. Luke is a member of the AI Game Programmers Guild, on the board of directors for IGDA Scotland, and recently took over as chair of the IGDA's Special Interest Group on AI.

Kevin Dill is a member of the senior technical staff at Lockheed Martin Rotary & Missions Systems and the chief architect of the Game AI Architecture. He is a veteran of the game and military simulation industries with more than 15 years' experience, and has worked on AI for everything from games (including several major hits, such as *Red Dead Redemption*, *Iron Man*, and *Zoo Tycoon 2*) to military training to emotive avatars. His professional interests include improved techniques for behavior specification, tactical and strategic AI, spatial reasoning, and believable characters. He was the technical editor for *Introduction to Game AI* and *Behavioral Mathematics for Game AI*, and a section editor for "AI Game Programming Wisdom 4" and the "Game AI Pro" series. He is a prolific author and speaker, and has taught at Harvard University, Cambridge, Massachusetts, Boston University, Boston, Massachusetts, and Northeastern University, Boston, Massachusetts.

Christopher Dragert received his PhD in computer science from McGill University, Montréal, Canada. His research focused on the application of software engineering techniques to the development process of game AI, with work being published at top academic conferences, including AIIDE, FDG, FSE, and GAS. Recently, he spoke at GDC 2016 and authored a chapter in the recent book *Computer Games and Software Engineering*. Chris is currently employed at Ubisoft Toronto as an AI programmer on *Watch Dogs 2*.

Philip Dunstan, as a senior AI R&D engineer at AiGameDev.com, prototypes cutting-edge solutions to the artificial intelligence challenges found in today's games. In addition, Philip has 6 years of development experience within Electronic Arts' EATech Central Technology Group. As a specialist in physics simulation, core technology, and console performance, he worked on several of EA's biggest franchises including *FIFA*, *Need for Speed*, *Battlefield*, and *Harry Potter*.

Anthony Francis, by day, studies human and other minds to create intelligent machines and emotional robots; by night, he writes urban fantasy and draws comic books. His work explores deep learning for robotic control at Google Research. He earned his PhD at Georgia Institute of Technology, Atlanta, Georgia, studying contextual memory for information retrieval, but also worked on emotional long-term memory for robot pets, a project documented on the Google Research blog as "Maybe your computer just needs a hug." Anthony is best known for his "Skindancer" series of urban fantasy novels featuring magical tattoo artist Dakota Frost, including the award-winning *Frost Moon* and its sequels *Blood Rock* and *Liquid Fire*. Anthony lives in San Jose with his wife and cats, but his heart will always belong in Atlanta. You can follow Anthony online at http://www.dresan.com/

Steve Gargolinski has been working on games professionally since 2003, spending time at Blue Fang Games, Rockstar New England, and 38 Studios. Steve has a strong technical background, and enjoys thinking, writing, and speaking about game AI, programming, and the development process. He has presented at conferences such as the Game Developers Conference (GDC) and the AI and Interactive Digital Entertainment Conference (AIIDE), and has been interviewed by *The Independent* and *Gamasutra* for his work in gaming AI. While not programming computers Steve enjoys nonfiction, cooking, hockey, and walking in the woods.

David "Rez" Graham is a senior AI programmer currently working independently on a self-funded unannounced project. Before that, he was the director of game programming at the Academy of Art University's School of Game Development, San Francisco, California, where he built the entire game programming curriculum from scratch. He has worked in the game industry as an engineer since 2005, spending most of that time working on various kinds of AI, from platformer enemy AI to full simulation games. Most recently, he was the lead AI programmer on *The Sims 4* at Maxis. Before that, he worked at PlayFirst, Slipgate Ironworks, Planet Moon Studios, and Super-Ego Games. He is the coauthor of *Game Coding Complete* (4th edition), has two articles in *Game AI Pro*, and regularly speaks at the Game Developers Conference. Rez spends his free time acting and running tabletop RPGs.

Daniel Hilburn has been making video games since 2007. He has worked on several console games including *Kinect Star Wars*™, *Ghostbusters: The Video Game*™, and *DefJam's Rapstar*™. He currently works in Irving, Texas, at Terminal Reality, Inc.

Troy Humphreys has been involved in game mechanics and AI since 2005. Since then, he has worked on the games *The Bourne Conspiracy, Transformers: War for Cybertron*, and *Transformers: Fall of Cybertron*. He currently works as a senior programmer at High Moon Studios, where he helps lead the studio's AI development. Prior to working on games, he taught game development as an Associate Course Director at Full Sail, where he still serves as an adviser.

Matthew Jack founded Moon Collider (www.mooncollider.com) in 2010, where he consults on AI for companies in the US and Europe and builds bespoke AI systems. He specializes in *CryEngine 3* and *Recast/Detour*. He developed AI at Crytek for many years in a senior R&D role, including work on *Crysis* and *Crysis 2*. He has since worked for Microsoft and AiGameDev.com, and consulted for games and serious games companies. Clients include Xaviant LLC and Enodo, with products delivered to companies such as BMW. He has written for *Games Programming Gems* and presented at the GDC, Paris Game AI Conference, Develop and at Google.

Éric Jacopin is a professor at the French Military Academy of Saint-Cyr, Guer, France where he headed the Computer Science Research Laboratory from 1998 to 2012; this includes teaching Turing machines, war games and project management, and the management of international internships for computer science cadets. His research has been in the area of AI Planning for the past 25 years, not only from the viewpoint of artificial intelligence but also from everyday life and gaming perspectives. He received his PhD (1993) and his habilitation to direct research (1999), both from the Pierre and Marie Curie University (Paris VI), Paris, France.

Sumeet Jakatdar is the lead AI engineer at Treyarch/Activision Blizzard, Santa Monica, California, and has been working there for more than 9 years. He has been involved in developing AI for some of the Activision's most popular first-person shooter games. During his years as an AI developer, he has worked on gameplay programming, level design, behavior, animation systems, and networking. Before joining the industry in 2007, he received MS degree in computer science from University of Southern California, Los Angeles, California.

Tomoki Komatsu graduated from Tohoku University, Sendai, Japan, and completed the master's degree in computer science. Then he started his career as an AI Engineer at SQUARE ENIX in 2014. He developed the Monster AI and supported the development of the tools for *FINAL FANTASY XV*.

Mike Lewis entered the game industry as a programmer in early 2002, and has spent most of the intervening years focusing on game AI and surrounding technologies. He has lectured at the Game Developers Conference and published articles in previous volumes of *Game AI Pro*. Currently, Mike calls ArenaNet, LLC, home, where he tirelessly schemes to bring better AI to the world of massively multiplayer online gaming.

John Manslow started writing games on his Vic-20 as a teenager and gradually became more and more interested in smart AI. Having completed a degree and then a PhD in the subject, he joined Codemasters as the AI specialist in their R&D team, where he worked on several projects to bring the next generation AI to Codemasters' games. Since then, John has worked for several companies outside the industry but has remained focused on AI and statistical analytics.

Dave Mark is the president and lead designer of Intrinsic Algorithm, an independent game development studio in Omaha, Nebraska. He does consulting on AI, game design, and mathematical modeling for clients ranging from small indie game studios to AAA companies including EA, Sony Online Entertainment, and ArenaNet. Dave is the author of the book *Behavioral Mathematics for Game AI* and is a contributor to the *AI Game Programming Wisdom* and *Game Programming Gems* book series from Charles River Media and the first Game AI Pro book from CRC Press. He has also spoken at numerous game conferences and universities around the world on the subjects of AI, game theory, and psychology. He is a founding member of the AI Game Programmers Guild and has been a coadvisor of the Game Developers Conference AI Summits. Dave continues to further his education by attending the University of Life. He has no plans to graduate anytime soon.

Clodéric Mars has tried to make simulated characters behave "autonomously *and* as they are told to" for more than 6 years. At Golaem, he worked on a navigation engine used, for example, in a train passengers' simulation and a crowd simulation tool for animation and vfx. Now leading the developments of MASA LIFE, he is dedicated to make behavior authoring easy, fun, and accessible to game designers and field experts. Clodéric has a master's degree in computer science, with a specialization in AI. He spoke at the Paris Game/AI Conference 2011 and at the Game Developers Conference (GDC) 2014 AI Summit.

Bill Merrill is the AI lead at Turtle Rock Studios working hard on an unannounced project, having previously worked as AI lead and senior generalist at Double Helix Games, shipping cross-platform game projects including *Dirty Harry, Silent Hill: Homecoming, Front Mission: Evolved*, and various tools and demos. He currently splits his time between technology and toddlers.

Youichiro Miyake is the lead AI researcher at Square Enix, working as the leader of the AI unit for the next-generation game engine Luminous Studio. He is the chairman of the IGDA JAPAN SIG-AI and a board member of DiGRA JAPAN. He has been developing and researching game AI since 2004. He developed the technical design of AI for the following game titles: *Chromehounds* (2006, Xbox 360), *Demon's Souls* (2009, PlayStation 3), and *Armored Core V* (2012, Xbox 360, PlayStation 3), developed by FromSoftware. At Square Enix, he was engaged in the AI development of *FINAL FANTASY XIV: A Realm Reborn*. At present, he is developing AI in *FINAL FANTASY XV* as the lead AI technical architect. He has published papers and books about game AI technologies and has given many lectures at universities and conferences. He was a keynote speaker of GAMEON ASIA 2012 and a game AI course speaker in SIGGRAPH ASIA 2015. His paper "Current Status of Applying Artificial Intelligence in Digital Games" will be published in the *Handbook of Digital Games and Entertainment Technologies* by Springer.

Kousuke Namiki joined FROM SOFTWARE in 2009 and worked on *STEEL BATTALION* and *Monster Hunter Diary: Poka Poka Airou Village*. He has been with SQUARE ENIX since 2012 as an AI programmer developing Luminous Studio. Now he is engaged in the development of enemy character AI for *FINAL FANTASY XV*.

Sergio Ocio Barriales has been working in the game industry since 2005. He received his PhD in 2010 from the University of Oviedo, Asturias, Spain, with his thesis about hinted-execution behavior trees. He has worked on the AI for numerous major titles, such as *Driver San Francisco, Splinter Cell: Blacklist, DOOM*, and *Watch_Dogs 2*. He joined the team at Hangar 13 as a lead AI engineer in 2016, where he continues pushing character AI forward.

Prasert Prasertvithyakarn is the lead game designer for *FINAL FANTASY XV* and is responsible for the game's AI main player characters. He was the leader of the enemy team in *MAJIN AND THE FORSAKEN KINGDOM* (2010, Xbox360, PlayStations3) at GAME REPUBLIC INC. before joining SQUARE ENIX in 2010.

Andrea Schiel has more than 18 years of experience developing AAA games and has worked on most of the major EA Sports™ titles. A recognized specialist in AI, she leads the AI special interest group at EA™ and mentors other engineers in this field. Andrea has shipped over 25 titles on all major platforms and is currently working for BioWare Montreal™ on the *Mass Effect*™ franchise.

Kazuya Shimokawa researched and developed Computer Go AI in his master course at the University of Electro-Communications, Tokyo, Japan. He has been with SQUARE

ENIX since 2013. At present, he is developing AI in *FINAL FANTASY XV* and was part of the team that developed Luminous Studio Tools.

Youji Shirakami has worked as a programmer in SQUARE ENIX since 2005. Before that, he worked as an engineer for transportation systems. He was engaged in the development of *Seiken Densetsu FRIENDS of MANA* (Mobile), *KINGDOM HEARTS* (Mobile), and *FINAL FANTASY TYPE-0* (PSP). His current tasks include implementation of the AI Graph Editor and character AI development.

Marius Stanescu is a PhD candidate at the University of Alberta, Edmonton, Canada. He completed his MSc in artificial intelligence at University of Edinburgh, Edinburgh, the United Kingdom, in 2011, and became a researcher at the Center of Nanosciences for Renewable & Alternative Energy Sources of University of Bucharest, Bucharest, Romania, in 2012. Since 2013, he has been helping organize the AIIDE StarCraft Competition. Marius' main areas of research include machine learning, AI, and RTS games.

Ben Sunshine-Hill is the lead developer of Havok AI. He holds a PhD in computer science from the University of Pennsylvania, Philadelphia, Pennsylvania, for his work in perceptually driven simulation. He once saw a really cool-looking cow.

Joudan Tatsuhiro has been with SQUARE ENIX since 2011. He was engaged in the development at Luminous Studio, especially for tools. He has been developing buddy AI within the *FINAL FANTASY XV* team, especially for the meta-AI system that controls them.

William van der Sterren is an AI consultant for games and simulations at CGF-AI. He worked on the AI of Guerrilla Games' *Killzone* and *Shellshock Nam'67* games. William has spoken at the Game Developer Conference and AIGameDev conference, and has contributed chapters to both the *Game Programming Gems* and *AI Game Programming Wisdom* series. His interest is in creating tactical behaviors, from tactical path-finding and terrain analysis to squad behaviors and company level maneuver planning. William holds an MSc in computer science from University of Twente and a PDEng Software Technology from Eindhoven University of Technology.

Will Wilson recently founded Indefiant Ltd. in order to focus on developing software and consulting for improving the iteration times and reducing costs in game development and testing. His 10 years in the games industry includes being lead programmer at Firefly Studios and senior programmer at Crytek, where he worked on *Crysis 2* and the *Crysis* console conversion. At Crytek he developed the SoftCoding implementation for the CryENGINE 3 for use in *Ryse* and *Crysis 3*.

Takanori Yokoyama has worked as a game programmer in the game industry since 2004. He has been especially interested in game AI and implemented it for many game titles including *ENCHANT ARMS* (2006, Xbox360), *CHROME HOUNDS* (2006, Xbox360), and *Demon's Souls* (2009, PlayStation3) developed by FROM SOFTWARE. He is now working as an AI engineer at SQUARE ENIX.

Robert Zubek is a game developer and cofounder at SomaSim, a Chicago-based indie studio founded in 2013 to create simulation games. Previously, he built large-scale online social games at Zynga, MMO game and analytics infrastructure at Three Rings Design, and console games at Electronic Arts/Maxis. Before joining the industry, he specialized in artificial intelligence and robotics research. Robert holds a PhD in computer science from Northwestern University, Evanston, Illinois, where he also received his previous computer science degrees.

Introduction

Steve Rabin's ***Game AI Pro 360: Guide to Architecture*** gathers all the cutting-edge information from his previous three Game AI Pro volumes into a convenient single source anthology covering game AI architecture.

This volume of carefully curated content is complete with articles and real-life case studies by leading game AI programmers that further explores modern architecture such as behavior trees and share architecture used in top games such as *Final Fantasy XV*, the *Call of Duty* series and the *Guild War* series.

This book, as well as each volume in the *Game AI Pro* series, is a testament to the generous community of game AI developers as well as the larger game development community. Everyone involved in this effort believes that sharing information is the single best way to rapidly innovate, grow and develop. Right now, the game AI community is larger than ever and we invite you to discover all the wonderful resources that are available.

In addition to reading about new game AI techniques in the *Game AI Pro* series, there are annual conferences, which are academic and developer-centric, all over the globe. Organized by developers, there is the Game AI summit at GDC in San Francisco each year and the game/AI conference in Europe. Organized by academia, there is the AAAI conference on Artificial Intelligence and Interactive Digital Entertainment (AIIDE) and the IEEE Conference on Computational Intelligence and Games. Outside of events, there are two communities that have also sprung up to help developers. The game AI Programmers Guild is a free professional group with more than 500 worldwide members (www.gameai.com) and there is a wonderful community of hobbyists and professionals at www.AIgameDev.com. We warmly welcome you to come and hang out with us at any one of these conferences or participate in one of the online communities.

Web Materials

Example programs and source code to accompany some of the chapters are available at http://www.gameaipro.com.

General System Requirements

The following is required to compile and execute the example programs:

- The DirectX August 2009 SDK
- DirectX 9.0 compatible or newer graphics card
- Windows 7 or newer
- Visual C++ .NET 2008 or newer

Updates of the example programs and source code will be updated as needed.

Behavior Selection Algorithms
An Overview

Michael Dawe, Steve Gargolinski, Luke Dicken,
Troy Humphreys, and Dave Mark

1.1 Introduction

Writing artificial intelligence systems for games has become increasingly complicated as console gamers demand more from their purchases. At the same time, smaller games for mobile platforms have burst onto the scene, making it important for an AI programmer to know how to get the best behavior out of a short frame time.

Even on complicated games running on powerful machines, NPCs can range from simple animals the player might run past or hunt to full-fledged companion characters that need to stand up to hours of player interaction. While each of these example AIs may follow the Sense–Think–Act cycle, the "think" part of that cycle is ill-defined. There are a variety of algorithms to choose from, and each is appropriate for different uses. What might be the best choice to implement a human character on the latest consoles might not be suitable for creating an adversarial player for a web-based board game.

This article will present some of the most popular and proven decision-making algorithms in the industry, providing an overview of these choices and showing when each might be the best selection to use. While it is not a comprehensive resource, hopefully it will prove a good introduction to the variety of algorithmic choices available to the AI programmer.

1.2 Finite-State Machines

Finite-state machines (FSMs) are the most common behavioral modeling algorithm used in game AI programming today. FSMs are conceptually simple and quick to code, resulting in a powerful and flexible AI structure with little overhead. They are intuitive and easy to visualize, which facilitates communication with less-technical team members. Every game AI programmer should be comfortable working with FSMs and be aware of their strengths and weaknesses.

An FSM breaks down an NPC's overall AI into smaller, discrete pieces known as *states*. Each state represents a specific behavior or internal configuration, and only one state is considered "active" at a time. States are connected by *transitions*, directed links responsible for switching to a new active state whenever certain conditions are met.

One compelling feature of FSMs is that they are easy to sketch out and visualize. A rounded box represents each state, and an arrow connecting two boxes signifies a transition between states. The labels on the transition arrows are the conditions necessary for that transition to fire. The solid circle indicates the initial state, the state to be entered when the FSM is first run. As an example, suppose we are designing an FSM for an NPC to guard a castle, as in Figure 1.1.

Our guard NPC starts out in the *Patrol* state, where he follows his route and keeps an eye on his part of the castle. If he hears a noise, then he leaves *Patrol* and moves to *Investigate* the noise for a bit before returning to *Patrol*. If at any point he sees an enemy, he will move into *Attack* to confront the threat. While attacking, if his health drops too low, he'll *Flee* to hopefully live another day. If he defeats the enemy, he'll return to *Patrol*.

While there are many possible FSM implementations, it is helpful to look at an example implementation of the algorithm. First is the `FSMState` class, which each of our concrete states (*Attack*, *Patrol*, etc.) will extend:

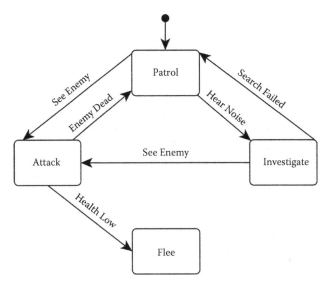

Figure 1.1

This FSM diagram represents the behavior of a guard NPC.

```
class FSMState
{
    virtual void onEnter();
    virtual void onUpdate();
    virtual void onExit();
    list<FSMTransition> transitions;
};
```

Each `FSMState` has the opportunity to execute logic at three different times: when the state is entered, when it is exited, and on each tick when the state is active and no transitions are firing. Each state is also responsible for storing a list of `FSMTransition` objects, which represent all potential transitions out of that state.

```
class FSMTransition
{
    virtual bool isValid();
    virtual FSMState* getNextState();
    virtual void onTransition();
}
```

Each transition in our graph extends from `FSMTransition`. The `isValid()` function evaluates to true when this transition's conditions are met, and `getNextState()` returns which state to transition to when valid. The `onTransition()` function is an opportunity to execute any necessary behavioral logic when a transition fires, similar to `onEnter()` in `FSMState`.

Finally, the `FiniteStateMachine` class:

```
class FiniteStateMachine
{
    void update();
    list<FSMState> states;
    FSMState* initialState;
    FSMState* activeState;
}
```

The `FiniteStateMachine` class contains a list of all states in our FSM, as well as the initial state and the current active state. It also contains the central `update()` function, which is called each tick and is responsible for running our behavioral algorithm as follows:

- Call `isValid()` on each transition in `activeState.transtitions` until `isValid()` returns true or there are no more transitions.
- If a valid transition is found, then:
  - Call `activeState.onExit()`
  - Set `activeState` to `validTransition.getNextState()`
  - Call `activeState.onEnter()`
- If a valid transition is not found, then call `activeState.onUpdate()`

With this structure in place, it's a matter of setting up transitions and filling out the `onEnter()`, `onUpdate()`, `onExit()`, and `onTransition()` functions to produce the desired AI behavior. These specific implementations are entirely design dependent. For example, say our Attack state triggers some dialogue, "There he is, get him!" in onEnter() and uses onUpdate() to periodically choose tactical positions, move to cover, fire on the enemy, and so on. The transition between *Attack* and *Patrol* can trigger some additional dialogue: "Threat eliminated!" in onTransition().

Before starting to code your FSM, it can be helpful to sketch a few diagrams like the one in Figure 1.1 to help define the logic of the behaviors and how they interconnect. Start writing the code once the different states and transitions are understood. FSMs are flexible and powerful, but they only work as well as the thought that goes into developing the underlying logic.

1.3 Hierarchical Finite-State Machines

FSMs are a useful tool, but they do have weaknesses. Adding the second, third, or fourth state to an NPC's FSM is usually structurally trivial, as all that's needed is to hook up transitions to the few existing required states. However, if you're nearing the end of development and your FSM is already complicated with 10, 20, or 30 existing states, then fitting your new state into the existing structure can be extremely difficult and error-prone.

There are also some common patterns that FSMs are not well-equipped to handle, such as situational behavior reuse. To show an example of this, Figure 1.2 shows a night watchman NPC responsible for guarding a safe in a building.

This NPC will simply patrol between the front door and the safe forever. Suppose a new state called *Conversation* is to be added that allows our night watchman to respond to a cell phone call, pause to have a brief conversation, and return to his patrol. If the watchman is in *Patrol to Door* when the call comes in, then we want him to resume patrolling to the door when the conversation is complete. Likewise, if he is in *Patrol to Safe* when the phone rings, he should return to *Patrol to Safe* when transitioning out of *Conversation*.

Since we need to know which state to transition back to after the call, we're forced to create a new *Conversation* state each time we want to reuse the behavior, as shown in Figure 1.3.

In this simple example we require two *Conversation* behaviors to achieve the desired result, and in a more complicated FSM we might require many more. Adding additional states in this manner every time we want to reuse a behavior is not ideal or elegant. It leads to an explosion of states and graph complexity, making the existing FSM harder to understand and new states ever more difficult and error-prone to add.

Thankfully, there is a technique that will alleviate some of these structural issues: the Hierarchical Finite-State Machine (HFSM). In an HFSM, each individual state can be an entire state machine itself. This technique effectively separates one state machine into multiple state machines arranged in a hierarchy.

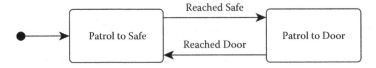

Figure 1.2

This FSM diagram represents the behavior of a night watchman NPC.

1. Behavior Selection Algorithms

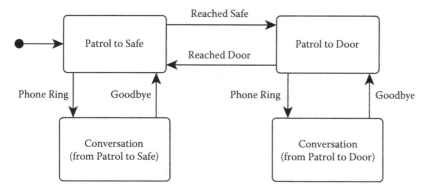

Figure 1.3

Our night watchman FSM requires multiple instances of the Conversation state.

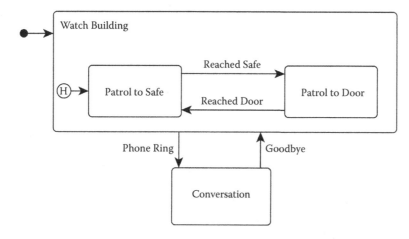

Figure 1.4

An HFSM solves the problem of duplicate Conversation states.

Returning to the night watchman example, if we nest our two *Patrol* states into a state machine called *Watch Building*, then we can get by with just one *Conversation* state, as shown in Figure 1.4.

The reason this works is that the HFSM structure adds additional hysteresis that isn't present in an FSM. With a standard FSM, we can always assume that the state machine starts off in its initial state, but this is not the case with a nested state machine in an HFSM. Note the circled "H" in Figure 1.4, which points to the "history state." The first time we enter the nested *Watch Building* state machine, the history state indicates the initial state, but from then on it indicates the most recent active state of that state machine.

Our example HFSM starts out in *Watch Building* (indicated by the solid circle and arrow as before), which chooses *Patrol to Safe* as the initial state. If our NPC reaches the safe and transitions into *Patrol to Door*, then the history state switches to *Patrol to Door*. If the NPC's phone rings at this point, then our HFSM exits *Patrol to Door* and *Watch*

Building, transitioning to the *Conversation* state. After *Conversation* ends, the HFSM will transition back to *Watch Building* which resumes in *Patrol to Door* (the history state), not *Patrol to Safe* (the initial state).

As you can see, this setup achieves our design goal without requiring duplication of any states. Generally, HFSMs provide much more structural control over the layout of states, allowing larger, complex behaviors to be broken down into smaller, simpler pieces.

The algorithm for updating an HFSM is similar to updating an FSM, with added recursive complexity due to the nested state machines. Pseudocode implementation is fairly complicated, and beyond the scope of this overview article. For a solid detailed implementation, check out Section 5.3.9 in the book *Artificial Intelligence for Games* by Ian Millington and John Funge [Millington and Funge 09].

FSMs and HFSMs are incredibly useful algorithms for solving a wide variety of problems that game AI programmers typically face. As discussed there are many pros to using an FSM, but there are also some cons. One of the major potential downsides of FSMs is that your desired behavior might not fit into the structure elegantly. HFSMs can help alleviate this pressure in some cases, but not all. For example, if an FSM suffers from "transition overload" and hooks up every state to every other state, and if an HFSM isn't helping, other algorithms may be a better choice. Review the techniques in this article, think about your problem, and choose the best tool for the job.

1.4 Behavior Trees

A *behavior tree* describes a data structure starting from some root node and made up of *behaviors*, which are individual actions an NPC can perform. Each behavior can in turn have child behaviors, which gives the algorithm its tree-like qualities.

Every behavior defines a *precondition*, which specifies the conditions where the agent will execute this behavior, and an *action*, specifying the actual things the agent should do when performing the behavior. The algorithm starts at the root of the tree and examines the preconditions of the behaviors, deciding on each behavior in turn. At each level of the tree, only one behavior can be selected, so if a behavior executes, none of its siblings will be checked, though its children will still be examined. Conversely, if a behavior's precondition does not return true, the algorithm skips checking any of that behavior's children and instead moves onto the next sibling. Once the end of the tree is reached, the algorithm has decided on the highest-priority behaviors to run, and the actions of each are executed in turn.

The algorithm to execute a behavior tree is as follows:

- Make root node the current node
- While current node exists,
    - Run current node's precondition
    - If precondition returns true,
        – Add node to execute list
        – Make node's child current node
    - Else,
        – Make node's sibling current node
- Run all behaviors on the execute list

The real strength of a behavior tree comes from its simplicity. The base algorithm can be implemented quickly due to its straightforward nature. Since trees are stateless, the algorithm doesn't need to remember what behaviors were previously running in order to determine what behaviors should execute on a given frame. Further, behaviors can (and should) be written to be completely unaware of each other, so adding or removing behaviors from a character's behavior tree do not affect the running of the rest of the tree. This alleviates the problem common with FSMs, where every state must know the transition criteria for every other state.

Extensibility is also an advantage with behavior trees. It is easy to start from the base algorithm as described and start adding extra functionality. Common additions are behavior `on_start`/`on_finish` functions that are run the first time a behavior begins and when it completes. Different behavior selectors can be implemented as well. For example, a parent behavior could specify that instead of choosing one of its children to run, each of its children should be run once in turn, or that one of its children should be chosen randomly to run. Indeed, a child behavior could be run based on a utility system-type selector (see below) if desired. Preconditions can be written to fire in response to events as well, giving the tree flexibility to respond to agent stimuli. Another popular extension is to specify individual behaviors as nonexclusive, meaning that if their precondition is run, the behavior tree should keep checking siblings at that level.

A behavior tree, though simple and powerful, is not always the best choice for a selection algorithm. Since the tree must run from the root every time behaviors are selected, the running time is generally greater than that of a finite-state machine. Additionally, the naïve implementation can have a large number of conditional statements, which can be very slow, depending on your target platform. On the other hand, evaluating every possible behavior in the tree may be slow on others where processing power is the limiting factor. Either approach can be a valid implementation of the algorithm; so the programmer would have to decide what is best.

Since behaviors themselves are stateless, care must be taken when creating behaviors that appear to apply memory. For example, imagine a citizen running away from a battle. Once well away from the area, the "run away" behavior may stop executing, and the highest-priority behavior that takes over could take the citizen back into the combat area, making the citizen continually loop between two behaviors. While steps can be taken to prevent this sort of problem, traditional planners can tend to deal with the situation more easily.

1.5 Utility Systems

Much of AI logic—and, for that matter, computer logic—is based on simple Boolean questions. For example, an agent may ask "Can I see the enemy?" or "Am I out of ammunition?" These are purely "yes or no" questions. The decisions that come out of Boolean questions are often just as polarized. As we saw in the prior architectures, the results of these questions are often mapped directly to a single action. For instance,

```
if (CanSeeEnemy())
{
    AttackEnemy();
}
```

```
if (OutOfAmmo())
{
    Reload();
}
```

Even when multiple criteria are combined, Boolean equations tend to lead to a very discrete result set.

```
if (OutOfAmmo() && CanSeeEnemy())
{
    Hide();
}
```

Many aspects of decision making aren't quite as tidy, however. There are numerous questions that can be asked where a "yes or no" answer is not appropriate. For example, we may want to consider how far away the enemy is, how many bullets I have left, how hungry I am, how wounded I am, or any number of continuous values. Correspondingly, these continuous values can be mapped over into *how much* I want to take an action rather than simply whether to take the action or not. A utility-based system measures, weighs, combines, rates, ranks, and sorts out many considerations in order to decide the *preferability* of potential actions. Using the above example as a guide, we could assess how *strongly* we want (or need!) to attack, reload, hide, etc.

While utility techniques can be used to supplement the transition logic of other architectures, it is very possible to build an entire decision engine based on utility. In fact, there are times when building a utility-based AI is far preferable to other methods. These might include games where there are many possible actions, and either there isn't a single "right" answer or the selection of a preferable action might be based on a large number of competing inputs. In these cases, we are going beyond simply using utility to measure or rate something. Instead, we are using it to drive the actual decision mechanism as well. Another way of stating it is that, rather than saying "This is the one action you will do," the utility-based system *suggests*, "Here are some possible options that you might want to do."

One well-documented example of this is the use of utility in *The Sims*. In these games, the agents (i.e., the actual "Sims") take information from their environment and combine it with their own internal state to arrive at a preferability score for each potential action. For example, the fact that I am "very hungry" combined with the availability of "poor food" would certainly be more attractive than if I was only "a little hungry." Additionally, the proximity of "spectacular" food might still make for a high priority even if I was only "a little hungry." Note that the descriptors "spectacular," "rather," "poor," and "a little" would actually be numbers between some set minimum and a maximum. (A typical method to use is a floating point number between 0 and 1.)

When it is time to select a new action (either because the current one is finished or through some sort of interrupt system), some method is used to select from among the candidates. For example, the scores for the potential actions could be sorted so that we can simply select the "most appropriate" action—that is, the one with the highest score. An alternate way is to use the scores to seed a weighted random selection. By casting a random number against these weighted probabilities, the most preferable actions have a higher chance of being selected. As an action's suitability goes up, its score goes up, as does its chance of being selected.

Another example of where utility-based architectures might be preferable to other architectures is RPGs. Often in these games, the options that an agent has are varied and possibly only subtly better or worse, given the situation. For instance, selecting what weapon, spell, item, or action should be taken given the type of enemy, the agent's status, the status of the player, etc., can be a complicated balancing act.

Another wheelhouse of utility architectures is any game system with an economic decision layer. The question of units or buildings to construct in a real-time strategy game, for example, is a juggling act of costs, times, and often many axes of priority (e.g., "offense" or "defense"). An architecture based on utility can often be more adaptable to changing game situations. As such, it can recover better from being disrupted than can more scripted models, which can suffer from either being hopelessly confused or can simply trundle along as if nothing ever happened.

The primary reason for this adaptability is that preferability scores are highly dynamic. As the game situation changes—either through a change in the environment or a change in state of the agent—the scores for most (if not all) of the actions will change. As the action scores change, so does their likelihood of being selected as a "reasonable" action. The resulting ebb and flow of action scores—especially when combined with a weighted random selection—often leads to very dynamic emergent behavior.

On the other hand, unlike the architectures that use Boolean-transitioned decision logic, utility systems are often somewhat unpredictable. Because the selections are based on how much the actions "make sense" in a given situation and context, however, the actions should tend to look *reasonable*. This unpredictability has benefits and drawbacks. It can improve believability because the variety of actions that could occur in a given situation can make for far more natural-looking agents rather than the predictably robotic if/then-based models. While this is desirable in many situations, if your design calls for specific behaviors at very certain moments, you must make a point to override the utility calculations with more scripted actions.

Another caveat to using utility-based architecture is that all the subtlety and responsiveness that you gain often comes at a price. While the core architecture is often relatively simple to set up, and new behaviors can be added simply, they can be somewhat challenging to tune. Rarely does a behavior sit in isolation in a utility-based system. Instead, it is added to the pile of all the other potential behaviors with the idea that the associated mathematical models will encourage the appropriate behaviors to "bubble to the top." The trick is to juggle all the models to encourage the most reasonable behaviors to shine when it is most appropriate. This is often more art than science. As with art, however, the results that are produced are often far more engaging than those generated by using simple science alone.

For more on utility-based systems, see the article in this book, *An Introduction to Utility Theory* [Graham 13] and the book *Behavioral Mathematics for Game AI* [Mark 09].

1.6 Goal-Oriented Action Planners

Goal-Oriented Action Planning (GOAP) is a technique pioneered by Monolith's Jeff Orkin for the game *F.E.A.R.* in 2005, and has been used in a number of games since, most recently for titles such as *Just Cause 2* and *Deus Ex: Human Revolution*. GOAP is derived from the Stanford Research Institute Problem Solver (STRIPS) approach to AI which was first developed in the early 1970s. In general terms, STRIPS (and GOAP) allows an AI system to create its own approaches to solving problems by being provided with a description of how the game world works—that is, a list of the actions that are possible, the requirements before each action can be used (called "preconditions"), and the effects of the action. The system then takes a symbolic representation of the initial state of the world and some set of objective facts that need to be achieved. In GOAP these objectives are typically chosen from a predetermined set of goals that an NPC may want to achieve, chosen by some method such as priority or state transition. The planning system can then determine a sequence of actions that will allow the agent that it is controlling to change the world from the original state into a state that contains the facts that need to be true to satisfy its current goals. In classical planning this would ideally be the critical path to the target state, and that target would be the most easily reachable state that contained all of the objective facts.

GOAP works by "*backwards chaining search,*" which is a fancy phrase which means starting with the goals you want to achieve, working out what actions are required for those to happen, then working out what needs to happen in order to achieve the preconditions of the actions you just identified and so on. You continue to work backwards in this fashion until you arrive at the state you started from. It's a fairly traditional approach, which has fallen out of favor in the scientific world, replaced by "*forwards chaining search*" which relies on heuristic search, pruning, and other tricks. Backwards search is a solid workhorse, however, and although it's less elegant, it's far easier to understand and implement than more modern techniques.

Backwards chaining search works in the following manner:

- Add the goal to the outstanding facts list
- For each outstanding fact
  - Remove this outstanding fact
  - Find the actions that have the fact as an effect
  - If the precondition of the action is satisfied,
    - Add the action to the plan,
    - Work backwards to add the now-supported action chain to the plan
  - Otherwise,
    - Add the preconditions of the action as outstanding facts

One final interesting aspect of GOAP is that it allows "context preconditions" that are ignored by the planning system, but must be satisfied at run-time in order for an action to be executed. This allows for reasoning to bypass certain aspects of the world that cannot be easily represented symbolically—such as ensuring line of sight to a target before beginning to fire—while ensuring that by accessing information not made available during planning (to ensure the search remains tractable), these constraints can be met. This allows the plan GOAP generates to be somewhat flexible, and the actions it calls for apply more at a tactical level than at the most basic level of execution. That is, the plan tells you *what* to do, but not necessarily *how* to do it. For example, detailed instructions such as how to establish a line of sight to begin shooting are omitted and can be handled more reactively.

Let's suppose we have a typical NPC soldier character, whose goal is to kill another character. We can represent this goal as `Target.Dead`. In order for the target to die, the character needs to shoot him (in a basic system). A precondition of shooting is having a weapon equipped. Assuming our character doesn't have one, we now need an action that can give the character a weapon, perhaps by drawing one from a holster. This, of course, has its own precondition—that there is a weapon available in the character's inventory. If this is the case, we have just created a simple plan of drawing the weapon and then shooting. What if the character doesn't have a weapon? Then our search would have to find a way to get one. If that isn't possible the search can backtrack and look for alternatives to the shoot action. Perhaps there is a mounted weapon nearby that could be used to provide the `Target.Dead` effect, or even a vehicle that we can use for running over the target. In either case, it's clear that by providing a comprehensive set of action choices of what *can* be done in the world, we can leave it up to the character to decide what *should* be done, letting dynamic and interesting behaviors emerge naturally, rather than having to envisage and create them during development.

Finally, consider a game in which weapons have a maximum range. As a context precondition, we can say that the target must be within that range. The planner won't spend time in its search trying to make this true—it can't, as it would involve reasoning about how the target might move and so on—but it either won't fire its weapon until the condition is true, or it will instead use an alternative tactic such as a different weapon with a longer range.

There's a lot to like about an approach to NPC control based on automated planning. It streamlines the development process by allowing designers to focus on creating simple components that will self-assemble into behaviors, and it also allows for "novel" solutions, which may never have been anticipated by the team, often making for excellent anecdotes that players will re-tell. GOAP itself remains the lowest hanging fruit of what automated planning can provide and, from a purely scientific point of view, the state of the art has progressed significantly since it was developed. With that said, it can still be a very powerful technique when used correctly, and provides a good, adaptable starting point for specific customization.

It is worth noting that these kinds of approaches that adopt a character-centric view of intelligence remove a lot of the authorial and directorial control from the development team. Characters that can "think" for themselves can become loose cannons within the game world, creating plans that, while valid for achieving the character's goals, do not achieve the broader goals of creating immersive and engaging experiences, and this can then potentially disrupt cinematic set-pieces if, for example, a soldier's plan doesn't take him past the conveniently placed Big Red Barrel.

While it's possible to avoid these kinds of issues by using knowledge engineering techniques and representational tricks, it isn't as straightforward as with architectures such as behavior trees, which would allow the desired behavior to be injected directly into the character's decision logic. At the same time, a GOAP approach is significantly easier to design than one based around hierarchical task networks, since in GOAP you just need to describe the mechanics of the objects within a world.

GOAP and similar techniques are not silver bullet solutions, but in the right circumstances they can prove to be very powerful in creating realistic behaviors and immersive-feeling characters that players can fully engage with.

1.7 Hierarchical Task Networks

Though GOAP is perhaps the best-known game planner, other types of planners have gained popularity as well. One such system, *hierarchical task networks* (HTN), has been used in titles such as Guerrilla Games' *KillZone 2* and High Moon Studios' *Transformers:*

Fall of Cybertron. Like other planners, HTN aims to find a plan for the NPC to execute. Where it differs is how it goes about finding that plan.

HTN works by starting with the initial world state and a root task representing the problem we are looking to solve. This high-level task is then decomposed into smaller and smaller tasks until we end up with a plan of tasks we can execute to solve our problem. Each high-level task can have multiple ways of being accomplished, so the current world state will be used to decide which set of smaller tasks the high-level task should be decomposed into. This allows for decision making at multiple levels of abstraction.

As opposed to *backward* planners like GOAP, which start with a desired world state and move backwards until it reaches the current state world state, HTN is a *forward* planner, meaning that it will start with the current world state and work towards a desired solution. The planner works with several types of primitives, starting with the *world state*. The world state represents the state of the problem space. An example in game terms might be an NPC's view of the world and him in it. This world state is broken up into multiple properties such as his health, his stamina, enemy's health, enemy's range, and the like. This knowledge representation would allow the planner to reason about what to do.

Next, we have two different types of tasks: *primitive tasks* and *compound tasks*. A primitive task is an actionable thing that can be done to solve a problem. In game terms, this could be *FireWeapon*, *Reload*, and *MoveToCover*. These tasks are able to affect the world state, such as how the *FireWeapon* task would use ammo and the *Reload* task would refill the weapon. *Compound tasks* are higher level tasks that can be accomplished in different ways, described as *methods*. A method is a set of tasks that can accomplish the compound task, along with preconditions determining when a method may be used. Compound tasks allow HTN to reason about the world and decide which course of action to take.

Using compound tasks, we can now build an HTN domain. The domain is a large hierarchy of tasks that represent all the ways of solving our problem, such as how to behave as an NPC of some type. The following pseudocode shows how a plan is built.

- Add the root compound task to our decomposing list
- For each task in our decomposing list
  - Remove task
  - If task is compound
    - Find method in compound task that is satisfied by the current world state
    - If a method is found, add method's tasks to the decomposing list
    - If not, restore planner to the state before the last decomposed task
  - If task is primitive
    - Apply task's effects to the current world state
    - Add task to the final plan list

As mentioned, HTN planners start with a very high-level root task and continuously decompose it into smaller and smaller tasks. This decomposition is steered with each compound task's set of methods by comparing each method's conditions with the current world state. When we finally come across a primitive task, we add it to our final plan. Since each primitive task is an actionable step, we can apply its effects to the world state, essentially moving forward in time. Once the decomposing list is empty we will either have a valid plan or have backed out entirely leaving us with no plan.

To demonstrate how an HTN works, suppose a game has a Soldier NPC that needs its AI written. The root compound task might be named *BeSoldierTask*. Next, the soldier should behave differently if he had an enemy to attack or not. Therefore, two methods are needed to describe what to do in these cases. In the case where an enemy is present, the *BeSoldierTask* would decompose using the method that required that condition. The method's task in this case would be *AttackEnemyTask*. This task's methods define the different ways that the soldier could attack. For example, the soldier could shoot from a cover position if he has ammunition for his rifle. If he didn't have ammo for his firearm, he could charge the enemy and attack him with his combat knife. Writing these give *AttackEnemyTask* two methods to complete the task.

The more we drill down on a soldier's behavior, the more the hierarchy forms and refines. The structure of the domain fits naturally in how one might describe the behavior to another person.

Since HTNs describe behavior using a hierarchical structure, building and reasoning about characters is done in a natural way, allowing designers to more easily read through HTN domains, assisting with collaboration between programming and design. Like other planners, the work that is actually done by the AI is kept in nice modular primitive tasks, allowing a lot of reuse across different AI characters.

Since HTN is a search through a graph, the size of your graph will affect search times, but there are two ways to control search size. First, the method's conditions can be used to cull entire branches of the hierarchy. This happens naturally as behaviors are built. Second, having partial plans can defer complex calculations until plan execution. For example, consider the compound task *AttackEnemy*. One method might have the subtasks *NavigateToEnemy* followed by *MeleeEnemy*. *NavigateToEnemy* requires pathing calculations, which can not only be costly, but could be affected by the state of the world, which might change between planning and execution. To utilize partial plans, split these two tasks into two methods, rather than one method with subtasks: *NavigateToEnemy*, if the enemy is out of range, and *MeleeEnemy* when in range. This allows us to only form a partial plan of *NavigateToEnemy* when the enemy is out of range, shortening our search time.

One other note is that the user needs to build the network for HTN to work. This is a double-edged sword when comparing it to GOAP-style planners. While this allows the designer to be very expressive in the behavior they are trying to achieve, it removes the NPC's ability to build plans that the designer might not have thought of. Depending on the game you are building, this can be considered either a strength or a weakness.

1.8 Conclusion

With such a wide variety of behavior selection algorithms available, it is imperative that the AI programmer have knowledge of each tool in the toolbox in order to best apply each to a given situation. Which algorithm is best for a given NPC can depend on the game, the knowledge state of the NPC, the target platform, or more. While this is not a comprehensive treatment on every available option, knowing a bit about where to start with the options can be invaluable. By taking time to think carefully about the needs of the game, an AI system can be crafted to give the best player experience while maintaining the balance between development time and ease of creation.

References

[Graham 13] R. Graham. "An Introduction to Utility Systems." In *Game AI Pro*, edited by Steve Rabin. Boca Raton, FL: CRC Press, 2013.

[Mark 09] D. Mark. *Behavioral Mathematics for Game AI*. Boston, MA: Cengage Learning, 2009.

[Millington and Funge 09] I. Millington and J. Funge. *Artificial Intelligence for Games*. Burlington, MA: Morgan Kaufmann, 2009, pp. 318–331.

2

Structural Architecture— Common Tricks of the Trade

Kevin Dill

2.1 Introduction

When discussing game AI, developers often get hyper-focused on advocating for a particular approach or a particular architecture, but many of the problems that make AI programming so hard appear regardless of the architecture you use, and many of the most common solutions have been reinvented time after time in architecture after architecture. For example, we can use *hierarchy* to divide up the AI logic, simplifying both configuration and execution. We can use *option stacks* to allow one option to temporarily suspend another, without changing the overall plan of attack. We can use a *blackboard* to share information and ideas between AI components or between characters. We can *move the intelligence* into the objects, the terrain, the abilities, or the events in order to more logically divide the code and data, and to improve our ability to extend the game. (Some games, such as *The Sims* franchise, have used this approach to ship downloadable content or even entire expansion packs without a change to the executable.) Finally, we can use modularity to extract reusable pieces of AI logic, thus simultaneously eliminating duplicate code and enabling the AI's author to think at a coarser level of granularity.

In the remainder of this chapter we describe each of these ideas. The intent is to provide enough information to paint the big picture, to spark new ideas and solutions to problems that you, the reader, might face, but not to dig deeply into the technical details of any given solution. For that, we refer you to the bibliography and the references contained therein.

2.2 Definitions

The ideas that we will address in this paper are fairly universal, but there aren't necessarily universal terms to describe them—and in some cases, terms mean one thing to one person and something different to another. As a result, this section will define terms that might not be clear, so that we can have a common vocabulary to work with as we forge ahead.

The *AI architecture* is the underlying code—typically in C++—that controls the process by which the AI evaluates the situation and makes a decision. Several examples of architectures will be given below, and the other articles in this section describe many of them in detail.

A *configuration* is the behavioral specification that maps from specific sensory data (i.e., specific inputs) to specific decisions or actions (i.e., specific outputs). For example, the configuration for a First-Person Shooter (FPS) character would contain all of the logic necessary to decide what that character should do at each point in the game—e.g., should it attack, should it run away, should it reload its weapon, and so on. The configuration is built on top of the architecture and usually specified in data (i.e., XML or similar).

We will often refer to the thing that an AI controls as the *character*. Not all AIs control single characters—for example, you might be working on the AI for an opposing player in a strategy game (which controls many characters), or the AI for a missile in a flying game, or even an AI that controls some aspect of the user interface. You will also hear AI-controlled entities referred to as *agents*, *enemies*, or simply as *AIs*. The generic term *character*, however, is a convenient term, and most AI does apply to characters, so we will stick with it in this chapter.

It is often the case that a character will contain more than one decision-maker. For example, a character might have one algorithm that selects which weapon to use, another that selects the target to shoot at, and a third that decides what emotion he should display. We refer to these decision makers as *reasoners*. Reasoners may have clear cut responsibilities (such as those described above), or they may be organized in a more ad hoc fashion (such as the selectors in a behavior tree [Isla 05]).

Similarly, we will refer to the things that reasoners choose as *options*. A reasoner functions by first evaluating the situation, and then selecting one or more options to execute. When a reasoner picks a new option and starts executing it, we say that it has *selected* the option, and when it stops executing an option we say that the option is *deselected*. These options might be *actions* (that is, physical things that the AI does), but they might also be more abstract. For example, a character's emotional reasoner might simply change the AI's internal state (perhaps by setting an enumerated value to the appropriate state—eHappy, eSad, eAngry, etc.—or by assigning an intensity value to each emotion) so that other reasoners can then select appropriate actions (smiling, frowning, attacking the player, etc.) based on that state.

2.3 Common Architectures

Although the techniques described here are intended to be architecture-agnostic, it is often useful to discuss a specific architecture when describing them. All of these architectures are described in detail elsewhere, so we give just a very high level definition of each one.

2. Structural Architecture—Common Tricks of the Trade

Scripting is perhaps the most basic architecture possible. In it, the designer or AI programmer specifies the sequence of options that the AI will select and when they will be selected (e.g., wait 48 seconds, and then spawn three units and attack the player). Scripts may include very simple sensory input, such as trigger zones, but in general the idea is that every decision is fully specified by the AI's author [Berger et al. 02].

Finite-state machines (FSMs) were once the most popular game AI architecture, but have been largely replaced by behavior trees in recent years. An FSM is a collection of states and transitions. The states represent the options that the reasoner can select, whereas the transitions represent the conditions under which the AI will change from one state to another. For example, a very simple first-person shooter (FPS) character might have four states: *Attack*, *Flee*, *Reload*, and *Search for Enemy*. The *Attack* state would contain transitions to *Flee* (which fires if the character is nearly dead), *Reload* (which fires when the character is out of ammo), and *Search for Enemy* (which fires when the character loses sight of the enemy) [Buckland 05, Rabin 00].

A *rule-based AI* is one that consists of a sequence of predicate-option pairs. The AI evaluates the predicate for each rule in order. When it gets to a rule whose predicate is true, it executes the option for that rule and stops evaluating additional rules. Thus, a rule-based AI for our simple FPS character would have four rules. The first would make it flee if its health is low. The second would make it reload if it is out of ammo. The third would make it attack the player if the player is in sight. Finally, the fourth would search for the player [Millington et al. 09a, Nilson 94].

A *utility-based AI* uses a *heuristic function* to assign a floating-point value (typically called a *weight*, *priority*, or *utility*) to each option. It then selects the option to execute based on those values—for example, by taking the option with the highest utility, or by assigning a weight to each option and using that to guide the probability of random selection. Our simple FPS character would still have the same four possible options, but now it would decide which one to do by evaluating the heuristic function for each option and using the resulting values to guide its final selection [Mark 09, Dill 06, Dill et al. 12a, Dill 12c].

Planners such as *goal-oriented action planners (GOAP)* or *hierarchical task-network (HTN) planners* build a sequence of options that will get them to some goal state. For example, our FPS character might have the goal *Enemy Dead*. It would search through its possible options and the ways in which they can change the state of the world in order to find a sequence of options which will get it into the goal state. That plan might be something like *Search for Enemy–Attack–Reload–Attack* (if it expects two magazines of ammo to be enough to get the job done). Planners typically have the ability to replan if the situation changes. So if our character finds itself nearly dead then it might replan with a new goal, such as *Don't Die*. This new plan might have only a single option: *Flee* [Orkin 04, Gorniak et al. 07].

The *behavior tree (BT)* architecture is a bit of a special case, because it is an architecture that can contain other architectures. A BT is a tree of *selectors*, each of which makes a single piece of the overall decision. In their original formulation [Isla 05], the selectors were all exceedingly simple and not really architectures in their own right. However, more recent work has discussed the ability to use nearly any architecture in a selector [Dill 11a], making the behavior tree more of a framework (or meta-architecture) than an architecture in its own right.

2.4 Hierarchical Reasoning

The difficulty of building an AI configuration generally scales worse than linearly with the size of the configuration. In other words, the more situations your AI can handle, the more things it takes into account, the more options it contains, etc., the more complex it is to add yet another of one of those things. The reason for this should be fairly intuitive. Whenever you add something new to your AI you need to put at least some effort into considering how that new thing interacts with each thing already in existence. Thus, the cost of adding a new thing increases the more things you have.

The severity of that increase depends in large part on the architecture you are using. FSMs, for example, scale exponentially because the number of transitions that is exponential on the number of states. This becomes unmanageable very quickly. This is one of the principal reasons that FSMs have largely passed out of use for complex problems. Utility-based AI, on the other hand, only requires you to balance the heuristic functions appropriately, while rule-based AI typically just requires you to place your new rule at the proper place in the list. With that said, even a rule-based AI will become brittle when it contains hundreds or thousands of rules (which is not an unreasonable size for many games).

One common way to address this challenge—an approach that has been applied to nearly every architecture, both in games and in academia—is to break the decision making up hierarchically. That is, have a high-level reasoner that makes the big, overarching decisions, and then one or more lower-level reasoners that handle implementation of the higher-level reasoners' decisions. For example, a high-level reasoner might decide whether to execute a daily schedule of ambient tasks (e.g., get up, get breakfast, go to work, etc.), start a conversation with the player, go into combat, and so forth. Each of those options would contain another reasoner, which decides how to go about accomplishing the goal.

The advantage here is that the complexity of AI configuration scales worse than linearly on the number of options *in a particular reasoner*. To give a sense of the relevance, imagine that the cost of configuring the AI is $O(n^2)$ on the number of options (as it is for FSMs). If we have 25 options, then the cost of configuring the AI is on the order of $25^2 = 625$. On the other hand, if we have five reasoners, each with five options, then the cost of configuring the AI is only $5 \times (5^2) = 125$. Conceptually, this makes sense. When we add a new option, we only need to consider how it relates to other options within the same reasoner—which is much simpler than comparing it to every other option anywhere in the AI.

Examples of this approach abound, from hierarchical FSMs [Millington et al. 09b] to HTN planners [Gorniak et al. 07] and GOAP implementations [Cerpa et al. 08] to strategy game AIs that break the opposing player AI into command hierarchies [Pittman 08]. Behavior trees are perhaps the archetypical example—a BT is really nothing more than a hierarchical infrastructure in which you can place whatever sorts of reasoning architectures best encapsulate the decisions to be made.

2.5 Option Stacks

Most reactive AIs function by evaluating the situation very frequently (often every frame), and deciding what is the best thing to do right at that particular moment. They may have a history of past decisions that guides their choices, they may even have some greater plan that they're following, but decisions are made moment-to-moment. This is what allows the AI to respond if the situation changes.

Of course, we do want options to be persistent. That is, we don't want the AI to be constantly flip-flopping between different decisions—attacking on one frame, fleeing on the next, and then attacking again on the frame after. Or, for another example, attacking with a shotgun, and then a flamethrower, and then right back to the shotgun after only a frame or two, switching weapons too fast to even get a shot off. That sort of indecisiveness makes the AI look stupid, even if there is a good reason *at that moment* for the decision being made. As we discussed in an earlier chapter [Dill 13], looking stupid is the single worst thing that an AI can do. It breaks the player's suspension of disbelief—that is, their immersion in the experience. As a result, most architectures have some form of *inertia* built in, which keeps the AI doing the same thing unless there is a good reason for the change.

When the AI does change options, one of two possible situations pertains. In most cases, the AI's decision is lasting—that is, it has decided to stop the old option and start a new one, and it's not expecting to go back to what it was doing before. For example, if the AI is in a fight and it kills one enemy, now it can pick a new enemy to attack (or pick something else to do if the fight is over). The decision can be lasting even if the AI wasn't done with the previous option. For example, when an AI decides to flee, that's a lasting decision, even though it typically happens *before* the AI finishes its attack. Regardless, the AI has made a deliberate decision to stop doing what it was doing and do something else instead. In this case, we should stop applying inertia to the deselected option, and in fact may even want to apply a *cooldown* which will prevent us from returning to it for a short period of time.

There are situations, however, when the AI needs to react to an immediate need or opportunity, but once that reaction is complete it should return to its previous option. For example, if an AI needs to reload, it should return to the same action (presumably firing a particular weapon) when it finishes reloading. It wouldn't make sense to reload your shotgun, only to then immediately switch weapons to a flamethrower (or decide to flee). That's not to say that the AI can't change its mind, but it should have to overcome the option's inertia to do so, just as if that option were still executing. Thus, we might switch to the flamethrower immediately after reloading the shotgun—but only if we suddenly spotted some new enemy who is highly vulnerable to fire.

One common trick which has been applied to a great many architectures is to have a stack of currently executing options. This stack is sometimes referred to as a *state stack* [Tozour 04], or a *goal stack* [Cerpa 08], or *subsumption* [Heckel et al. 09], depending on the underlying architecture, but we will simply call it an *option stack*, since that is an architecture-agnostic term. Option stacks allow us to push a new, high priority option on top of the stack, *suspending* the currently executing option but retaining its internal state. When the high priority option completes execution, it will pop itself back off of the stack, and the previously executing option will *resume* as if nothing had ever happened.

There are a myriad of uses for option stacks, and they can often be several levels deep. For example, a high-level strategic reasoner might have decided to send a unit to attack a distant enemy outpost. Along the way, that unit could be ambushed—in which case, it might push a *React to Ambush* option on top of its option stack. While responding to the ambush, one of the characters in the unit might notice that a live grenade has just been thrown at its feet. That character might then push an *Avoid Grenade* option on top of

React to Ambush. Once the grenade has gone off (assuming the character lives) it can pop *Avoid Grenade* off the stack, and *React to Ambush* will resume. Once the enemy ambush is over, it will be popped as well, and the original *Attack* option will resume.

One handy trick is to use option stacks to handle your hit reaction. If a character is hit by an enemy attack (e.g., a bullet), we typically want them to play a visible reaction. We also want the character to stop whatever it was doing while it reacts. For instance, if an enemy is firing their weapon when we hit them, they should not fire any shots while the hit reaction plays. It just looks wrong if they do. Thus, we push an *Is Hit* option onto the option stack, which suspends all previously running options while the reaction plays, and then pop it back off when the reaction is done.

We mentioned this above, but it's worth reemphasizing that the option stack is not meant to *prevent* the AI from changing what it's doing, but simply to preserve its previous state so that can be figured into the decision appropriately. To extend the previous example, imagine that the character was hit in the arm and as a result lost the use of that arm—and therefore could no longer fire its weapon. In that case, it should certainly pick a different option. The option stack simply ensures that the AI has the context of the previous actions available to it so that it can make an informed decision.

Option stacks are surprisingly simple to implement for most architectures. In the AI configuration, each option can specify whether it should suspend the previous option (i.e., push the new option on the stack) or deselect it (i.e., this is a lasting decision). When an option that suspended its predecessor finishes execution, it automatically pops the stack and resumes the previous option. There are a few edge cases to handle (e.g., What to do if another option is selected while there are options on the stack?), but they're not difficult to manage. An example of the interfaces to support this can be found in our GAIA architecture [Dill 12c].

2.6 Knowledge Management

Knowledge is the key to good decision making. This is true in the real world, and it is doubly true in the realm of game AI, where most decisions boil down to relatively simple checks against the current situation. Of course, there are two different kinds of knowledge implied in that statement—knowledge of the situation itself, and knowledge of how to evaluate the situation in order to make a decision. Looked at that way, there isn't much to an AI beyond knowledge.

Given knowledge's central role in game AI, it's worth putting effort into thinking about how to best store and access our knowledge.

2.6.1 Blackboards

In the academic AI community, blackboard architectures typically refer to a specific approach in which multiple reasoners propose potential solutions (or partial solutions) to a problem, and then share that information on a *blackboard* [Wikipedia 12, Isla et al. 02]. Within the game community, however, the term is often used simply to refer to a shared memory space which various AI components can use to store knowledge that may be of use to more than one of them, or may be needed multiple times. In our architecture, for example, every character has access to two blackboards. The *character blackboard* stores information specific to the character, and is only accessible by that character's AI. The *global blackboard* is accessible by all characters, and is used to store general information.

There are many types of information that can be stored on a blackboard. One common use is to store expensive checks on the blackboard, so as to avoid the cost of running them more than once. Line of sight (LOS) checks are a common example. Quite often, more than one component in the AI (or more than one character's AI) will want to check for visibility between the same two objects. These checks can be extremely expensive. To lessen the impact of this problem, we can run the check once and then cache it on the blackboard. Path-planning checks are similar.

Another common use is to store information used to coordinate AI components. This could include partial solutions such as those found in classic blackboard systems, but it could also simply be information used to coordinate between multiple characters or between different AI components within a character. For example, if you want your characters to focus their attacks on a single enemy or to ensure that every enemy is attacked, you can store target assignments on the blackboard. If you want to coordinate spatial motion—perhaps flanking, or placing the tanks in front and the DPS and healers in back, then you can store movement plans on the blackboard. If you want to ensure that two characters don't try to use the same cover spot, then you can have them reserve it on the blackboard. If you have one reasoner whose output is the input for another—for example, the emotional reasoner that we discussed earlier in this paper—then that output can be placed on the blackboard.

There is an interview with Damián Isla on AIGameDev.com, which gives an excellent introduction to blackboard architectures as they are commonly used in games [Isla 10].

2.6.2 Intelligent Everything

When we think about the AI for a character, it seems intuitive to put all of the knowledge needed in the character. This can result in a monolithic, difficult to extend AI, however. It can also result in considerable duplication between similar (but not identical) characters.

One trick is to put the intelligence in the world, rather than in the character. This technique was popularized by *The Sims*, though earlier examples exist. In *The Sims* (and its sequels), objects in the world not only advertise the benefits that they offer (for example, a TV might advertise that it's entertaining, or a bed might advertise that you can rest there), they also contain information about how to go about performing the associated actions [Forbus et al. 01].

Another advantage of this approach is that it greatly decreases the cost of expansion packs. In the *Zoo Tycoon 2* franchise, for example, every other expansion pack was "content only." Because much of the intelligence was built into the objects, we could create new objects that would be used by existing animals, and even entirely new animals, without having to make any changes to the source code. This greatly reduced the cost of developing those expansions, allowing us to focus our efforts on the larger expansions and put out two expansions a year instead of just one.

Intelligence can also be placed in the world itself. For example, in *Red Dead Redemption* the people who populate the towns have very little intelligence of their own—but the town has hundreds of hotspots. Each hotspot has information about who can use it, what time of day the hotspots is valid, and the behavior tree for characters who are on that hotspot. Some hotspots can even require multiple characters. So, for example, a chair in a tavern might have a hotspot for sitting and drinking and another hotspot for playing poker—but the latter is only valid if there are four people at the table (and includes a mechanism for coordinating their actions). The piano bench has a hotspot that only the piano player can use, and the bar has multiple hotspots for the bartender (some that require other characters to join him, some not). Even the conversation AI works by creating a dynamic hotspot for the two characters that are going to have a conversation.

Of course, intelligence can go anywhere, not just in physical objects or locations. For example, games that have a wide range of special abilities can put the intelligence into those abilities. *Darkspore*, a game that had hundreds of abilities—many of them quite unique—took this approach [McHugh et al. 11]. Similarly, events can carry information about appropriate responses. For example, a fire in a school could carry information about how different categories of people (e.g., teachers, children, firemen, parents, etc.) should react [Stocker et al. 10].

2.7 Modularity

Component systems for characters have become commonplace in the games community. For example, a character might have a *Movement* component, an *Animation* component, an *AI* component, a *Weapon* component, and so forth. Each component encapsulates one aspect of the character's functionality behind a shared interface. This sort of modularity—breaking a large piece of code into small, reusable pieces with a consistent interface—can be tremendously powerful [Dill et al. 12b]. It can allow us to greatly reduce code duplication and to reuse more of our code both within a project and across projects. In addition, we can more rapidly implement our characters, because we simply have to plug in the appropriate module, rather than reimplement the functionality in code. It is tremendously liberating to be able to think at the level of broad concepts (i.e., entire modules), rather than having to concentrate on individual lines of code.

One extremely powerful use of modules is to create *considerations*, which are modules that can be combined to evaluate the validity of an option [Dill 11b, Dill 12c]. Hearkening back to our simple FPS character, the *Reload* option would have only a single consideration, which checks how much ammo is left in the current weapon. The *Flee* option, on the other hand, might have considerations to evaluate the current health, the number of allies left, how much health the enemy has left, what weapons are available, and so forth. The AI would combine the output of these considerations into a final evaluation of how important it is to flee, given the current situation. The output of these considerations sets might be Boolean (for example, to drive a rule-based reasoner or the transition in an FSM), or it might be continuous (for example, to drive a utility-based AI). The big advantage of considerations is that those exact same considerations can be used for other decisions—such as whether to attack aggressively, whether to use a health pack, etc. What's more, the considerations themselves can be reused across projects. Even a very different game (say, a real-time strategy game or a role-playing game) might require health checks, counts of surviving allies, distance checks, and so forth. Furthermore, many meta-concepts such as option inertia and cooldowns (described in a previous section) can be expressed easily as considerations.

Once you embrace modularity, you will find that it can be applied throughout your code base. For example, we often have an action that needs a target. The target could be a particular character (perhaps the player), or the camera, or a specific (*x*, *y*, *z*) position. It could even be the output of another reasoner—perhaps one which evaluates all enemies and selects the best one to attack. By having a modular *target* class, we can decouple the logic for specifying and updating the target from the actions that use it [Dill 12c]. Furthermore, targets can also be used elsewhere, such as in considerations—for example, a distance consideration might measure the distance between two targets without knowing or caring what types of targets they are. Targets can even be stored on the blackboard, allowing characters to communicate about them (as described in a previous section).

Another example of modularity is a weight function. When we are using considerations to drive utility-based AI, we have found that there are a great many considerations that need to map from a floating-point value (such as a distance, the amount of health remaining, the amount of ammo remaining, the number of enemies remaining, the time since some action was taken, the character's current hunger, bathroom need, opinion of the player, etc.) to a utility value. Although there might be dozens or even hundreds of considerations like that, there are actually only a few ways to handle the mapping from input value (i.e., the value the consideration computes) to return value (i.e., the consideration's output). For example, we might simply return the input value directly, apply a mathematical function to the input value and return the result, or divide the input value into ranges and return a specific output value for each range. *Weight functions* are modular components that use one of those three techniques to do the mapping for us [Dill et al. 12b]. They allow us to decouple the mapping from the consideration, ensure that we have a consistent data specification for each type of mapping, and enable us to move massive amounts of duplicate code, some of it quite complex, into a few relatively simple classes. In addition, they allow us to add advanced features, such as hysteresis, in a consistent, well-tested way.

These are just a few of the many ways in which AI concepts can be abstracted into reusable modules. Other ideas for the widespread use of modularity can be found in our previous papers [Dill 11b, Dill et al. 12b, Dill 12c]. Our experience has been that finding ways to think about our AI in terms of reusable, pluggable modules (rather than in terms of C++ code) provides a tremendous boost in productivity, even on extremely fast-paced projects.

2.8 Conclusion

In this paper we have discussed a number of common techniques that have been used across many AI architectures, which can facilitate the creation of your game. Hierarchy can be used to divide up the decision making into reasonably-sized pieces, greatly easing the process of configuration. Option stacks can enable the AI to respond to a temporary situation or opportunity, and then return to what it was previously doing. Knowledge can be shared on a blackboard, or placed in an object, in the terrain, in an action, or in an event. Finally, modularity can be used when implementing your AI to eliminate massive amounts of duplicate code, and to allow you to think in terms of broad concepts, rather than individual lines of code, when performing configuration.

References

[Berger et al. 02] L. Berger, F. Poiker, J. Barnes, J. Hutchens, P. Tozour, M. Brockington, and M. Darrah. "Section 10: Scripting." In *AI Game Programming Wisdom*, edited by Steve Rabin. Hingham, MA: Charles River Media, 2002, pp. 503–554.

[Buckland 05] M. Buckland. *Programming Game AI by Example*. Plano, TX: Wordware Publishing 2005, pp. 43–84.

[Cerpa 08] D. H. Cerpa. "A goal stack-based architecture for RTS AI." In *AI Game Programming Wisdom 4*, edited by Steve Rabin. Boston, MA: Course Technology, 2008, pp. 457–466.

[Cerpa et al. 08] D. H. Cerpa and J. Obelleiro. "An advanced motivation-driven planning architecture." In *AI Game Programming Wisdom 4*, edited by Steve Rabin. Boston, MA: Course Technology, 2008, pp. 373–382.

[Dill 06] K. Dill. "Prioritizing actions in a goal-based RTS AI." In *AI Game Programming Wisdom 3*, edited by Steve Rabin. Boston, MA: Charles River Media, 2006, pp. 321–330.

[Dill 11a] K. Dill. "A game AI approach to autonomous control of virtual characters." In *Proceedings of the 2011 Intraservice/Industry Training, Simulation, and Education Conference*. Available online (http://www.iitsec.org/about/PublicationsProceedings/Documents/11136_Paper.pdf).

[Dill 11b] K. Dill. "A pattern-based approach to modular AI for Games." In *Game Programming Gems 8*, edited by Adam Lake. Boston, MA: Course Technology, 2011, pp. 232–243.

[Dill et al. 12a] K. Dill, E. R. Pursel, P. Garrity, and G. Fragomeni. "Design patterns for the configuration of utility-based AI." In *Proceedings of the 2012 Intraservice/Industry Training, Simulation, and Education Conference*, 2012.

[Dill et al. 12b] K. Dill, E. R. Pursel, P. Garrity, and G. Fragomeni. "Achieving modular AI through conceptual abstractions." In *Proceedings of the 2012 Intraservice/Industry Training, Simulation, and Education Conference*, 2012.

[Dill 12c] K. Dill. "Introducing GAIA: A Reusable, Extensible architecture for AI behavior." In *Proceedings of the 2012 Spring Simulation Interoperability Workshop*. Available online (http://www.sisostds.org/conference/download.cfm?Phase_ID=2&FileName=12S-SIW-046.docx).

[Dill 13] K. Dill. "What is game AI?" In *Game AI Pro*, edited by Steve Rabin. Boca Raton, FL: CRC Press, 2013.

[Forbus et al. 01] K. Forbus and W. Wright. "Some Notes on Programming Objects in the Sims." Available online (http://www.qrg.northwestern.edu/papers/files/programming_objects_in_the_sims.pdf).

[Gorniak et al. 07] P. Gorniak and I. Davis. "SquadSmart: Hierarchical planning and coordinated plan execution for squads of characters." In *Proceedings, The Third Artificial Intelligence and Interactive Digital Entertainment Conference*, pp 14–19. Available online (http://petergorniak.org/papers/gorniak_aiide07.pdf).

[Heckel et al. 09] F. W. P. Heckel, G. M. Youngblood, and D. H. Hale. "BehaviorShop: An intuitive interface for interactive character design." In *Proceedings, The Fifth AAAI Artificial Intelligence and Interactive Digital Entertainment Conference*, pp. 46–51. Available online (http://www.aaai.org/ocs/index.php/AIIDE/AIIDE09/paper/viewFile/811/1074).

[Isla 05] D. Isla. "Handling complexity in the *Halo 2* AI." *2005 Game Developer's Conference*, 2005. Available online (http://www.gamasutra.com/view/feature/130663/gdc_2005_proceeding_handling_.php).

[Isla 10] D. Isla. "HALO Inspired Blackboard Architectures and Knowledge Representation." On AIGameDev.com, interview with Alex Champandard, 2002. Available online (http://aigamedev.com/premium/masterclass/blackboard-architecture/).

[Isla et al. 02] D. Isla and B. Blumberg. "Blackboard architectures." In *AI Game Programming Wisdom*, edited by Steve Rabin, pp. 333–342. Hingham, MA: Charles River Media, 2002.

[Mark 09] D. Mark. *Behavioral Mathematics for Game AI*. Boston, MA: Course Technology, 2009.

[McHugh et al. 11] L. McHugh, D. Kline, and R. Graham. "AI Development Postmortems: Inside Darkspore and The Sims: Medieval." Lecture, *Game Developer's Conference 2011 AI Summit*, 2011. Available online (http://twvideo01.ubm-us.net/o1/vault/gdc2011/slides/Lauren_McHugh_AI_Development_Postmortems.ppt).

[Millington et al. 09a] I. Millington and J. Funge. *Artificial Intelligence for Games*, Second Edition. Burlington, MA: Morgan Kaufmann, 2009, pp. 427–457.

[Millington et al. 09b] I. Millington and J. Funge. *Artificial Intelligence for Games*, Second Edition. Burlington, MA: Morgan Kaufmann, 2009, pp. 318–330.

[Nilson 94] N. Nilson. "Teleo-reactive programs for agent control." In *Journal of Artificial Intelligence Research* 1: 139–158, 1994. Available online (http://www.jair.org/media/30/live-30-1374-jair.pdf).

[Orkin 04] J. Orkin. "Applying goal oriented action planning to games." In *AI Game Programming Wisdom 2*, edited by Steve Rabin. Hingham, MA: Charles River Media, 2004, pp. 217–228.

[Pittman 08] D. Pittman. "Command hierarchies using goal-oriented action planning." In *AI Game Programming Wisdom 4*, edited by Steve Rabin. Boston, MA: Course Technology, 2008, pp. 383–392.

[Rabin 00] S. Rabin. "Designing a general robust AI engine." In *Game Programming Gems* 8, edited by Mark DeLoura. Rockland, MA: Charles River Media, 2000, pp. 221–236.

[Stocker et al. 10] C. Stocker, L. Sun, P. Huang, W. Qin, J. Allbeck, and N. Badler. "Smart events and primed agents." In *Proceedings of the 10th International Conference on Intelligent Virtual Agents*, pp. 15–27, 2010.

[Tozour 04] P. Tozour. "Stack-based finite-state machines." In *AI Game Programming Wisdom 2*, edited by Steve Rabin. Hingham, MA: Charles River Media, 2004, pp. 303–306.

[Wikipedia 12] Wikipedia. "Blackboard System." http://en.wikipedia.org/wiki/Blackboard_system, 2012.

3

The Behavior Tree Starter Kit

Alex J. Champandard and Philip Dunstan

3.1 Introduction

You've done your homework and found that behavior trees (BTs) are a proven and established technique that game developers regularly use to build their AI [Isla 05, Champandard 07]. Not only does a BT give you a solid foundation to build upon, but it also gives you a lot of flexibility to include other techniques in a way that gives you full control over behavior and performance. Now you're ready to start coding!

This article introduces the simplest piece of code that you can call a behavior tree, and builds it up incrementally. The associated source code is called the Behavior Tree Starter Kit [BTSK 12], and is intended to serve as an example of a working BT for you to learn from. Since it's under an open-source license, you can use this as a starting point for your own projects. This is not a reusable middleware library, however, and it's important that you understand the core concepts and take ownership of the code.

The first section of this article paints the big picture for behavior trees, introducing a simple example tree, and explaining how to build BTs and how to use them for making AI decisions. The second section dives into the implementation of a first-generation BT, along with all its building blocks (e.g., sequences and selectors) and a discussion of the API. Finally, the third section explains the principles of second-generation BTs, and the improvements they offer. You'll learn about memory optimizations and event-driven implementations that scale up significantly better on modern hardware.

Throughout this article, source code examples are provided to demonstrate the concepts. Note, that the code listings in this article are edited for print, in particular using C++11 syntax, and some shortcuts have been taken for the sake of brevity. For the original implementations see the source code at http://github.com/aigamedev.

3.2 The Big Picture

To assist in the demonstration of the components that comprise a behavior tree it is first useful to see how such a tree might be structured. Following is an example of how a simple behavior tree might be designed for a robot guard that is hunting the Player.

3.2.1 A Simple Example

This AI is split into three main behaviors. First, if the robot guard can see the Player then it will either shoot three times at the Player if it is close enough, or move closer to the Player. Second, if the robot has recently seen the Player but can no longer see them then it will move to the Player's last known position and look around. Third, in case the robot has not seen the Player for some time, the fallback behavior is to move to some random location and look around.

```
BehaviorTree* bt = BehaviorTreeBuilder()
    .activeSelector()
    .sequence()     //Attack the player if seen!
        .condition(IsPlayerVisible)
        .activeSelector()
            .sequence()
                .condition(IsPlayerInRange)
                .filter(Repeat, 3)
                    .action(FireAtPlayer)
            .action(MoveTowardsPlayer)
    .sequence()     //Search near last known position.
        .condition(HaveWeGotASuspectedLocation)
        .action(MoveToPlayersLastKnownPosition)
        .action(LookAround)
    .sequence()     //Randomly scanning nearby.
        .action(MoveToRandomPosition)
        .action(LookAround)
    .end();
```

The example above demonstrates the use of the Tree Builder Pattern to separate the construction of the behavior tree from the behavior tree nodes. (This example has been edited for print.) The full source code for the tree builder and its examples can be found with the rest of the Behavior Tree Starter Kit source code as described in Section 3.1.

3.2.2 Updating the Behavior Tree

Given a behavior tree, how does the game logic update it? How often is this done and does it involve traversing the tree from the root every time? These are common questions about BTs.

To assist in the updating of a behavior tree it is useful to introduce a `BehaviorTree` object, which will serve as the central point for storing and updating the tree. The BehaviorTree object is most often created by a `BehaviorTreeBuilder` as shown in the example in Section 3.2.1, or using another builder that loads a tree from a file.

```
class BehaviorTree {
protected:
    Behavior* m_pRoot;
public:
    void tick();
};
```

This is a first-generation BT, and as such, the `BehaviorTree` class remains simple. It contains a single pointer to the root of the behavior tree, and a `tick()` function which performs the traversal of the tree. This is the entry point of the BT, and is called anytime an update is needed. It is often not necessary to update the behavior tree every game frame, with many games deciding to update each behavior tree every other frame or at 5Hz so that the load for updating the behavior trees of all characters can be spread across multiple game frames.

While this example seems straightforward and the implementation simply delegates the `tick()` to the root node, Section 3.4 of this article shows the advantages of such a centralized `BehaviorTree` class. It enables several advanced features such as improving runtime performance by controlling the memory allocation of BT nodes (Section 3.4.3), and an event-driven traversal that modifies the functionality of the `tick()` function to reduce node accesses.

3.3 Building Blocks

Moving on from the big picture, this section jumps to the lowest level of the implementation, progressing bottom-up and building up complexity incrementally with new features.

3.3.1 Behaviors

The concept of a *behavior* is the most essential part of a BT. The easiest way to think of a behavior from a programming perspective is an abstract interface that can be activated, run, and deactivated. At the leaf nodes of the tree, *actions* (e.g., "open door," "move to cover," "reload weapon") and *conditions* (e.g., "do I have ammunition?" "am I under attack?") provide specific implementations of this interface. Branches in the tree can be thought of as high-level behaviors, hierarchically combining smaller behaviors to provide more complex and interesting behaviors.

Here is how such an interface is implemented in the BTSK:

```
class Behavior {
public:
    virtual void onInitialize()        {}
    virtual Status update()            = 0;
    virtual void onTerminate(Status)   {}
    /*... */
};
```

This API is the core of any BT, and it's critical that you establish a clear specification for these operations. For example, the code expects the following contracts to be respected:

- The `onInitialize()` method is called once, immediately before the first call to the behavior's update method.
- The `update()` method is called exactly once each time the behavior tree is updated, until it signals it has terminated thanks to its return status.
- The `onTerminate()` method is called once, immediately after the previous update signals it's no longer running.

When building behaviors that rely on other behaviors (such as the sequence and selector behaviors described later in this section), it's important to keep these API contracts in mind. To help make sure you don't break these assumptions, it can help to wrap these functions into a single entry point.

```
class Behavior {
protected:
    /* API identical to previous code listing. */
private:
    Status m_eStatus;
public:
    Behavior() : m_eStatus(BH_INVALID) {}
    virtual ~Behavior() {}
    Status tick() {
        if (m_eStatus != BH_RUNNING) onInitialize();
        m_eStatus = update();
        if (m_eStatus != BH_RUNNING) onTerminate(m_eStatus);
        return m_eStatus;
    }
};
```

This approach is a bit slower, since you must use conditional branches every `tick()`. Most composite behaviors could handle this more efficiently since they process the return statuses anyway. However, having such a wrapper function avoids many beginner mistakes.

3.3.2 Return Statuses

Each behavior, when executed, passes back a return status. The return status is a critical part of any behavior tree, without which it simply wouldn't work. In practice, return statuses plays two roles:

- **Completion Status**—If the behavior has terminated, the return status indicates whether it achieved its purpose. There are two completion statuses most commonly used: SUCCESS (indicates that everything went as expected) and FAILURE (specifies that something apparently went wrong).
- **Execution Hints**—While the behavior is running, each update of the behavior also returns a status code. Most of the time, this is RUNNING, but modern BTs can leverage this status code to provide much more efficient implementations. For example, the SUSPENDED status code is an essential part of an event-driven BT, as you will see in Section 3.4.4.

In certain special cases, you might be tempted to add additional return statuses to the list. For example, there are some implementations that distinguish between expected issues (FAILURE) and unforeseen problems (ERROR). However, this quickly makes the code in the rest of the tree much more complex, and does not make the BT any more powerful. A more convenient approach to deal with failures is to let behaviors check for specific types of failure they expect, and deal with those cases outside of the tree's return statuses.

3.3.3 Actions

In a behavior tree, the leaf nodes have the responsibility of accessing information from the world and making changes to the world. Leaf behaviors that make such changes are called `Actions`.

When an action succeeds in making a change in the world it returns `SUCCESS`; otherwise it's simply a `FAILURE`. A status code of `RUNNING` indicates processing is underway. Actions are little more than a `Behavior`, except for initialization and shutdown that require extra care.

- **Initialization**—All but the simplest of actions will need to interface with other systems and objects to do the work. For example, a particular action may need to fetch data from a blackboard, or make a request of the animation systems. In a well-defined modular architecture getting access to these other games systems can be problematic. Extra work is required during the setup of behavior tree actions to provide the systems that those actions will use. This is often solved by passing extra parameters during node instantiation or through the use of the Visitor software design pattern.

- **Shutdown**—Like initialization, the shutdown of actions can be problematic due to the dependencies on external systems. Special care must be taken when shutting down an action to ensure that freeing resources does not interfere with other behaviors. For example, you cannot simply reset the animation system once an action shuts down as another instance of that action may have recently been activated elsewhere.

Helper functions can be set up to facilitate initialization and shutdown of actions if needed. In most cases, actions will simply inherit the functionality from the base `Behavior` class.

An example action used in the robot guard example of Section 3.2.1 is the action to move to the Player's last known location if the robot can no longer see the Player. This action will likely instruct the navigation system to move the robot to that location and return a `SUCCESS` status code. If for some reason the navigation system is unable to perform the request—for instance, a door has closed and the navigation system is unable to find a path to the target location—the action will return a `FAILURE` status code.

3.3.4 Conditions

Conditions are also leaf nodes in the tree and are the tree's primary way of checking for information in the world. For example, conditions would be used to check if there's cover nearby, if an enemy is in range, or if an object is visible. All conditions are effectively Boolean, since they rely on the return statuses of behaviors (success and failure) to express True and False.

In practice, conditions are used in two particular cases:

- **Instant Check Mode**—See if the condition is true given the current state of the world at this point in time. The check is run once immediately and the condition terminates.

- **Monitoring Mode**—Keep checking a condition over time, and keep running every frame as long as it is True. If it becomes False, then exit with a `FAILURE` code.

As well as being able to specify the mode of execution of a Condition, it's also useful to provide a negation parameter that effectively tells the code to do the exact opposite. This allows for the simpler reuse of existing code, such as checking to see if an enemy is in range, to create a condition to test for the opposite, i.e., that the enemy is not within range. In *Check* mode, this is Boolean negation, but in *Monitoring* mode the condition would keep running as long as it is False.

3.3.5 Decorators

The next step to building up an interesting BT is to wrap behaviors with other behaviors, adding detail, subtlety, and nuance to its logic. Decorator behaviors, named after the object-oriented design pattern, allow you to do this. Think of them as a branch in the tree with only a single child, for example, a behavior that repeats its child behavior n times, a behavior that hides the failure of its child node, or a behavior that keeps going forever even if its child behavior exits. All of these are decorators, and are very useful for technically minded developers using BTs.

```
class Decorator : public Behavior {
protected:
    Behavior* m_pChild;
public:
    Decorator(Behavior* child) : m_pChild(child) {}
};
```

The base `Decorator` class provides all the common functionality for implementing a decorator efficiently, only storing a single child for instance. Specific types of decorators are implemented as derived classes; for instance the update method on the `Repeat` decorator might be implemented as follows.

```
Status Repeat::update() {
    while (true) {
        m_pChild->tick();
        if (m_pChild->getStatus() == BH_RUNNING) break;
        if (m_pChild->getStatus() == BH_FAILURE) return BH_FAILURE;
        if (++m_iCounter == m_iLimit) return BH_SUCCESS;
    }
}
```

In this example, the repeating behavior keeps executing its child behavior until a limit is reached. If the child fails, the decorator also fails. When the child behavior succeeds, its next execution happens immediately in the same update once it has been reset.

The robot guard example introduced in Section 3.2.1 uses a *Repeat* condition to fire three times if the player is within firing range. Decorators like this provide a simple way to introduce subtle behavior patterns to the behavior tree without duplicating nodes in the tree.

3.3.6 Composites

Branches with multiple children in a behavior tree are called *composite behaviors*. This follows the composite pattern in software engineering, which specifies how objects can be assembled together into collections to build complexity. In this case, we're making more interesting, intelligent behaviors by combining simpler behaviors together.

It's often a good idea to have a base class for composite behaviors to avoid redundant code in the subclasses. The helper functions to add, remove, and clear children can be implemented just once in this base class.

```
class Composite : public Behavior {
public:
    void addChild(Behavior*);
    void removeChild(Behavior*);
    void clearChildren();
protected:
    typedef vector<Behavior*> Behaviors;
    Behaviors m_Children;
};
```

Common composite behaviors, like sequences and selectors, derive from this base class.

3.3.7 Sequences

Sequences are one of the two most common branch types. Sequences allow the BT to purposefully follow "plans" that are hand-specified by the designers. Sequences execute each of their child behaviors in sequence until all of the children have executed successfully or until one of the child behaviors fail.

The example behavior tree introduced in Section 3.2.1 for the robot guard uses sequences at several points to group together behaviors into larger behaviors. An example is the branch that the guard uses to search near the player's last known position when the player is not visible. In this branch the first behavior node is a condition node to check whether the robot has a suspected location for the player. If this condition succeeds the action to move to the suspected location and search around that location will be run. Otherwise, if the condition fails the sequence node will fail and the behavior tree will continue on to the next branch outside the sequence—searching a random location.

In the code shown below, a sequence is a composite behavior, which just happens to chain together its child behaviors one by one.

```
class Sequence : public Composite {
protected:
    Behaviors::iterator m_CurrentChild;
    virtual void onInitialize() override {
        m_CurrentChild = m_Children.begin();
    }
    virtual Status update() override {
        //Keep going until a child behavior says it's running.
        while (true) {
            Status s = (*m_CurrentChild)->tick();
            //If child fails or keeps running, do the same.
            if (s != BH_SUCCESS) return s;
            //Move on until we hit the end of the array!
            if (++m_CurrentChild == m_Children.end())
                return BH_SUCCESS;
        }
        return BH_INVALID;//Unexpected loop exit.
    }
};
```

The initialization code for the sequence starts at the beginning of the array of children. The update processes each child behavior in the list one by one, bailing out if any of them fail. The sequence returns a SUCCESS status if all of the children execute successfully.

There's one important thing to note about this implementation; the next child behavior is processed immediately after the previous one succeeds. This is critical to make sure the BT does not miss an entire frame before having found a low-level action to run.

3.3.8 Filters and Preconditions

A filter is a branch in the tree that will not execute its child behavior under specific conditions. For instance, if an attack has a cooldown timer to prevent it from executing too often, or a behavior that is only valid at a specific distance away from a target, etc. Designers can easily use filters to customize the execution of common behaviors—for instance, customizing them for a specific character or situation.

Using the modular approach of the BTSK, it's trivial to implement a filter as a type of sequence. Assuming the filter has a single condition, you can attach it to the start of the sequence—ensuring that it gets executed (and therefore, checked) first. If the filter has a single branch (or action), it comes next in the sequence. Of course, it's equally easy to set up a sequence with multiple preconditions and multiple action branches afterwards.

```
class Filter : public Sequence {
public:
    void addCondition(Behavior* condition) {
        //Use insert() if you store children in std::vector
        m_Children.push_front(condition);
    }
    void addAction(Behavior* action) {
        m_Children.push_back(action);
    }
};
```

You can also easily create Boolean combinations of conditions to add to the filter, as a testimony to the power of core BT nodes like sequences (AND) and selectors (OR).

3.3.9 Selectors

Selectors are the other most common branch type. Selectors let the BT react to impediments in the world, and effectively trigger transitions between different fallback behaviors. A selector executes each of its child behaviors in order until it finds a child that either succeeds or that returns a RUNNING status.

In the robot guard behavior tree example described in Section 3.2.1 a selector is used to decide which of the three main behavior branches should be picked. The first branch—attacking the player—is first executed. If this branch fails—if the player is not visible, for instance—the sequence node will execute the second branch, searching near the player's last known position. If that behavior also fails the sequence will execute the final behavior—searching a random location.

From the code perspective, a selector is the counterpart of a sequence; the code not only derives from a composite, but looks very similar as well. Only the two lines dealing with the specific return statuses are different.

```
virtual Status update() {
    //Keep going until a child behavior says it's running.
    while (true) {
        Status s = (*m_Current)->tick();
        //If child succeeds or keeps running, do the same.
        if (s != BH_FAILURE) return s;
        //Continue search for fallback until the last child.
        if (++m_Current == m_Children.end())
            return BH_FAILURE;
    }
    return BH_INVALID;//"Unexpected loop exit."
}
```

The rest of the selector is identical to the sequence implementation. Similarly, note that the selector keeps searching for fallback behaviors in the same `update()` until a suitable behavior is found or the selector fails. This allows the whole BT to deal with failures within a single frame without pausing.

3.3.10 Parallels

A parallel node is another type of composite branch in the tree that allows you to do more advanced control structures, such as monitoring if assumptions have been invalidated while you are executing a behavior. Like other composites, it's made up of multiple behaviors; however, these are all executed at the same time! This allows multiple behaviors (including conditions) to be executed in parallel and for those behaviors to be aborted if some or all of them fail.

A parallel node is not about multithreading or optimizations, though. Logically speaking, all child behaviors are run at the same time. If you trace the code, their update functions would be called sequentially one after another in the same frame.

```
class Parallel : public Composite {
public:
    enum Policy {
        RequireOne,
        RequireAll,
    };
    Parallel(Policy success, Policy failure);
protected:
    Policy m_eSuccessPolicy;
    Policy m_eFailurePolicy;
    virtual Status update() override;
};
```

It's important for the parallel to be extremely precisely specified, so that it can be understood intuitively and relied upon without trying to second-guess the implementation. In this case, there are two parameters; one specifies the conditions under which the parallel succeeds and the other for failure. Does it require all child nodes to fail/succeed or just one before failing/succeeding? Instead of enumerations, you could also add counters to allow a specific number of behaviors to terminate the parallel, but that complicates the everyday use of the parallel without any additional power. Most useful BT structures can be expressed with these parameters, using decorators on child nodes if necessary to modify their return statuses.

```
virtual Status update() {
    size_t iSuccessCount = 0, iFailureCount = 0;
    for (auto it: m_Children) {
        Behavior& b = **it;
        if (!b.isTerminated()) b.tick();
        if (b.getStatus() == BH_SUCCESS) {
            ++iSuccessCount;
            if (m_eSuccessPolicy == RequireOne)
                return BH_SUCCESS;
        }
        if (b.getStatus() == BH_FAILURE) {
            ++iFailureCount;
            if (m_eFailurePolicy == RequireOne)
                return BH_FAILURE;
        }
    }
    if (m_eFailurePolicy == RequireAll && iFailureCount == size)
        return BH_FAILURE;
    if (m_eSuccessPolicy == RequireAll && iSuccessCount == size)
        return BH_SUCCESS;
    return BH_RUNNING;
}
```

The implementation of the parallel iterates through each child behavior, and updates it. Counters are kept for all terminated behaviors, so the failure policy and success policy can be checked afterwards. Note that failure takes priority over success since the BT itself should assume the worst case and deal with it rather than proceed regardless. Also, in this implementation the parallel terminates as soon as any policy is satisfied, even if there are behaviors not yet run.

When a parallel terminates early because its termination criteria are fulfilled, all other running behaviors must be terminated. This is done during the onTerminate() function that iterates through all the child nodes and handles their termination.

```
void Parallel::onTerminate(Status) {
    for (auto it: m_Children) {
        Behavior& b = **it;
        if (b.isRunning()) b.abort();
    }
}
```

Parallels are the foundation of more advanced BT control structures and therefore tend to uncover a wide variety of little issues, like how to cleanly shutdown (see Section 3.3.3) and how to handle interrupting behaviors. There are two schools of thought on how to handle behaviors that need to be interrupted before they terminate on their own, for example, when they are run together in a parallel node.

- All behaviors should have the option to keep running if they want to, effectively having a noninterruptible flag that will cause the parent behavior to wait for termination. In this case, the abort() function becomes a request that is taken into account during the next update() if appropriate. Low-level BTs, in particular those dealing with animation control directly, tend to benefit from this option.

- All behaviors should support immediate termination, though they are given the option to clean-up after themselves using `onTerminate()`, which can optionally be given a special ABORTED status code. High-level BTs work best this way, since they don't want to micro-manage low-level states; the noninterruptible animation can be handled elsewhere in supporting systems.

The BTSK takes this second approach. When the behavior tree switches from a branch to another, this is done instantly, and any transitions (e.g., audio, animation) must be set up during the switch and managed by external systems. Then, in the next branch, if the same system is requested, it will simply delay the BTs request until the transition is over (e.g., play sound, play animation).

3.3.11 Monitors

Arguably, continuously checking if assumptions are valid (i.e., monitoring conditions) is the most useful pattern that involves running behaviors in parallel. Many behaviors tend to have assumptions that should be maintained while a behavior is active, and if those assumptions are found invalid the whole sub-tree should exit. Some examples of this include using an object (assumes the object exists) or melee attacks (assumes the enemy is in range), and many others.

The easiest way to set this up is to reuse the parallel node implementation, as a Monitor node can be thought of as a parallel behavior with two sub-trees; one containing conditions which express the assumptions to be monitored (read-only), and the other tree of behaviors (read–write). Separating the conditions in one branch from the behaviors in the other prevents synchronization and contention problems, since only one sub-tree will be running actions that make changes in the world.

```
struct Monitor : public Parallel {
    //Implementation is identical to the Filter sequence.
    void addCondition(Behavior* condition);
    void addAction(Behavior* action);
};
```

In the exact same way as a `Filter`, the monitor provides simple helper functions to ensure the conditions are set up first in the parallel. These conditions will be checked first before the actions are executed, bailing out early if there are any problems. This API is useful only if you create your BTs in C++, but most likely you'll impose these orderings in your BT editing tool.

3.3.12 Active Selectors

One final building block you'll most likely need in a production BT is an "active" selector, which actively rechecks its decisions on a regular basis after having made them. This differs from the traditional "passive" selectors by using another form of parallelism to retry higher-priority behaviors than the one that was previously chosen. You can use this feature to dynamically check for risks or opportunities in select parts of the tree, for example, interrupting a patrol with a search behavior if a disturbance is reported.

Active selectors appear twice during the short behavior tree example in Section 3.2.1. At the top level of the behavior tree an active selector is used to allow the high priority behavior of attacking a visible enemy to interrupt lower-priority behaviors such as searching for the player or randomly patrolling. A second instance of an active selector is during the evaluation of behaviors when the player is visible to the guard robot. Here, an active selector is used so that the higher-priority behavior of shooting at the player if the player is within range preempts the lower-priority behavior of moving towards the player if they are not in range.

One simple way to implement this is to reuse a Monitoring node within a passive selector from Section 3.3.9 that terminates the low-priority node if the higher-priority behavior's preconditions are met. This type of implementation can be easier for straightforward cases with one condition, and works efficiently for event-driven implementations discussed in Section 3.4.4. However, you'll most likely require a specialized implementation to deal with more complex situations.

```
Status ActiveSelector::update() {
    Behaviors::iterator prev = m_Current;
    Selector::onInitialize();
    Status result = Selector::update();
    if (prev != m_Children.end() && m_Current != prev)
        (*previous)->abort();
    return result;
}
```

This active selector implementation reuses the bulk of the underlying `Selector` code, and forces it to run every tick by calling `onInitialize()`. Then, if a different child node is selected the previous one is shutdown afterwards. Separately, the `m_Current` iterator is initialized to the end of the children vector. Keep in mind that forcefully aborting lower-priority behaviors can have unwanted side effects if you're not careful; see Section 3.3.3.

3.4 Advanced Behavior Tree Implementations

As BTs have grown in popularity in the games industry the forms of implementation have become increasingly diverse, from the original implementation in *Halo 2* [Isla 05] to *Bulletstorm*'s event-driven version [PSS 11]. Despite the diversity there have been some common changes over the past couple of years in the ways that behavior trees have been implemented. These changes led to our coining of the terms first- and second-generation behavior trees at the Paris Shooter Symposium 2011 [PSS 11].

3.4.1 First- versus Second-Generation Trees

While there are no hard rules for classifying a behavior tree implementation, there are some common patterns behind original implementations and more modern ones. In general, first-generation BTs have the following characteristics:

- Small and shallow trees with relatively few nodes in them.
- Large behaviors written in C++ with "complex" responsibilities.
- No (or little) sharing of data between multiple behavior tree instances.
- Simple implementations with no worry about performance.
- Often written in one .h and .cpp file, not necessarily reusable outside of AI.
- The behavior tree concept is mostly used as a pattern for writing C++.

In contrast, second-generation trees have had to deal with a console hardware transition and designs with additional complexity and scale. They are defined as follows:

- Larger and deeper trees with many more nodes.
- Smaller powerful nodes that better combine together.
- BT data that is shared between multiple instances wherever possible.
- A heavily optimized implementation to improve scalability.
- Written as a reusable library that can be applied to any game logic.
- The behavior tree becomes a DSL with efficient interpreter.

It's important to point out that first-generation implementations are not necessarily worse than their successor, they just fulfill different requirements. If you can use a simpler implementation that avoids the complexity of the second-generation, then don't hesitate to do so!

3.4.2 Sharing Behavior Trees Between Entities

A powerful extension to first-generation behavior trees is the ability to share data between multiple instances, in particular, the structure of the tree or common parameters. This can significantly reduce the memory requirements for BT-based systems, especially in scenes with large numbers of complex characters.

The most important requirement for sharing data is the separation of two concepts:

- **Nodes**—Express the static data of the BT nodes, for instance the pointers to children of a composite node, or common parameters.
- **Tasks**—The transient node data required to execute each BT node. For example, sequences need a current behavior pointer and actions often require context.

In practice, the Task is a base class for runtime instance data and managing execution.

```
class Task {
protected:
    Node* m_pNode;
public:
    Task(Node& node);
    //onInitialize(), update() and onTerminate() as 3.3.1
};
```

The Task refers to a tree node which stores the shared data, including tree structure and parameters. Then, the Node implementation effectively becomes a factory for creating these tasks at runtime, when the node is executed by the tree.

```
class Node {
public:
    virtual Task* create() = 0;
    virtual void destroy(Task*) = 0;
};
```

To make these two classes compatible with the Behavior of Section 3.3.1, all that's required is to keep a Node and a Task together as member variables, and track their

Status. The node's factory functions create() must be called before the behavior's tick() function can be run the first time, and destroy() after the task has terminated.

While separating these two forms of BT data is relatively simple mechanically, it has a profound impact on the rest of the code. All composite nodes, for instance, must be able to "convert" nodes into tasks before execution. This can be done locally in all composites, or the Task instances can be managed centrally in a BehaviorTree class similar to Section 3.2.2. Then, the decision remains whether to allocate these instances on-the-fly or pre-allocate them—which will often depend on the size and complexity of the tree. The next section discusses similar memory issues relating to the allocation of Node objects forming the tree structure.

3.4.3 Improving Memory Access Performance

One of the significant drawbacks of first-generation behavior trees on modern hardware is the memory access patterns exhibited when executing the BTs. This is especially an issue on current generation console hardware with small cache sizes and limited hardware memory prefetching.

The primary cause of the poor memory access patterns is the dynamic memory allocation of the behavior tree nodes. Without careful management, the BT node storage may be scattered throughout memory, resulting in frequent cache misses as the BT execution moves from one node to the next. By changing the layout of the BT nodes in memory, it is possible to significantly improve the memory performance of behavior trees.

3.4.3.1 Node Allocation

The core mechanism for changing the memory layout of the behavior tree nodes is the introduction of centralized memory allocation API to the central BehaviorTree object that was introduced in Section 3.2.2. These additional allocate functions will be responsible for all node allocations.

When this object is constructed it allocates a block of memory into which all of the BT nodes will be allocated. To instantiate a BT node, the templated allocate function is used rather than the normal allocation functions. This function uses in-place new to allocate the new node within the block of memory owned by the BehaviorTree object.

```
class BehaviorTree {
public:
    BehaviorTree()
    : m_pBuffer(new uint8_t[k_MaxBehaviorTreeMemory])
    , m_iOffset(0)
    {}
    ~BehaviorTree() {
        delete [] m_pBuffer;
    }
    void tick();
    template <typename T>
    T& allocate() {
        T* node = new ((void*)((uintptr_t)m_pBuffer+m_iOffset)) T;
        m_iOffset += sizeof(T);
        return *node;
    }
```

```
protected:
    uint8_t* m_pBuffer;
    size_t m_iOffset;
};
```

By allocating all of the BT nodes via the custom allocate function it is possible to ensure that all of the nodes for a tree are allocated in the same localized area of memory. Furthermore, by controlling the order in which nodes are allocated (depth- or breadth-first), it is possible to optimize the layout so that it reduces cache misses during traversal. Improving the memory usage patterns as a BT is traversed can have significant impacts on the runtime performance.

3.4.3.2 Composite Node Implementations

As this change only affects the node memory allocations, the internal implementations of many of the behavior tree nodes described in Section 3.3 are completely unaffected. There are, however, additional optimizations that can be made to some of these implementations to further improve the resultant memory layout.

The primary candidates for further optimizations are the Composite nodes: Sequences, Selectors, and Parallels. In the simple implementation described in Section 3.3.6 each of these node types stored their children in a vector<Behavior*> in the Composite base class, resulting in additional heap allocations by the vector class for the data storage. This can be prevented by replacing the vector storage by an internal static array as shown in the code below.

```
class Composite : public Behavior
{
public:
    Composite() : m_ChildCount(0) {}
    void addChild(Behavior& child) {
        ptrdiff_t p = (uintptr_t)&child - (uintptr_t)this;
        m_Children[m_ChildCount++] = static_cast<uint32_t>(p);
    }
protected:
    uint32_t m_Children[k_MaxChildrenPerComposite];
    uint32_t m_ChildCount;
};
```

In this example, the child nodes store the child node address information as part of the primary node data. Each composite node contains static storage for n child nodes. In most trees, a limit of 7 on the maximum number of child nodes is more than sufficient. In cases where there are more children than this, then it is typically possible to use additional composite nodes to split apart the larger composite nodes (e.g., multiple nested sequences or selectors).

Rather than storing pointers to each of the child nodes, it is also possible to take advantage of the spatial locality of the nodes in memory and store only the offset of each child node from the composite node. As compiling software with support for 64-bit pointers becomes more common, this can result in significant memory savings. The Composite node example shown here requires 32 bytes of memory, whereas a naïve implementation storing pointers would require 64 bytes, occupying half of a cache line on current generation consoles.

3.4.3.3 Transient Data Allocation

The same transformations that were applied to the memory layout of the BT nodes in Section 3.4.3.2 can equally by applied to the transient data that is stored when each node is executed.

It is useful to think of this transient data as a stack. As a node is executed, its transient data is pushed onto the top of the stack. When a node execution is terminated, the transient data is popped back off the stack. This stack-like data structure is perfect for the depth-first iteration used in behavior trees. It allows for very simple management of transient data and results in very cache-friendly memory access patterns.

3.4.4 Event-Driven Behavior Trees

A final approach for optimizing BT traversal involves event-driven techniques. Instead of traversing the tree from the root every frame, simply to find previously active behaviors, why not maintain them in a list (of size one or more) for fast access? You can think of this list as a *scheduler* that keeps active behaviors and ticks the ones that need updating.

This is the essence of an event-based approach, and there are two ways to maintain it:

- Traverse the whole tree from scratch if the currently executing behaviors terminate, or there are changes in the world (or its blackboard). This effectively repopulates the task list from scratch when necessary, in a similar way than a planner would.
- Update the list of active behaviors incrementally as they succeed or fail. The parent of behaviors that terminate can be requested to decide what to do next, rather than traversing the whole tree for the root.

The first approach is a simple optimization to a traditional first-generation BT, but the second requires a much more careful implementation of the scheduler, which we'll dig into in the following sections.

3.4.4.1 Behavior Observers

The most important part of an event-driven BT is the concept of an observer. When a behavior terminates, the scheduler that was updating it also fires a notification to the parent, which can deal with the information as appropriate.

```
typedef Delegate<void (Status)> BehaviorObserver;
```

In the BTSK, the observer is implemented using a template-based fast delegate implementation, but this could be replaced with any functor implementation.

3.4.4.2 Behavior Scheduler

The central piece of code responsible for managing the execution of an event-driven BT is called a *scheduler*. This can be a stand-alone class, or left for the BehaviorTree class to implement such as in the BTSK. Essentially, the class is responsible for updating behaviors in one central place rather than letting each composite manage and run its own children. The example object below expands on the BehaviorTree class API that was first introduced in Section 3.2.2 to provide the management of BT tasks.

```
class BehaviorTree {
protected:
    deque<Behavior*> m_Behaviors;
public:
    void tick();
    bool step();
    void start(Behavior& bh, BehaviorObserver* observer);
    void stop(Behavior& bh, Status result);
};
```

The scheduler stores a list of active behaviors, in this case in a deque that has behaviors taken from the front and pushed to the back as they are updated. The main entry point is the tick() function, which processes all behaviors until an end-of-update marker is found.

```
void tick() {
    //Insert an end-of-update marker into the list of tasks.
    m_Behaviors.push_back(NULL);
    //Keep going updating tasks until we encounter the marker.
    while (step()) {}
}
```

One of the many benefits of this type of implementation is support for single-stepping of behaviors. This can be done directly via the step() function if necessary.

```
bool step() {
    Behavior* current = m_Behaviors.front();
    m_Behaviors.pop_front();
    //If this is the end-of-update marker, stop processing.
    if (current == NULL) return false;
    //Perform the update on this individual behavior.
    current->tick();
    //Process the observer if the task terminated.
    if (current->isTerminated() && current->m_Observer)
        current->m_Observer(current->m_eStatus);
    else//Otherwise drop it into the queue for the next tick()
        m_Behaviors.push_back(current);
    return true;
}
```

As for managing the execution of behaviors, the implementations of start() simply pushes a behavior on the front of the queue, and stop() sets its status and fires the observer manually.

3.4.4.3 Event-Driven Composites

The event-driven paradigm is most obvious in the composite nodes in the tree. Every composite has to make a request to the scheduler to update its child nodes rather than execute them directly.

For example, let's take a look at how a Sequence would be implemented.

```
class Sequence : public Composite {
protected:
    BehaviorTree* m_pBehaviorTree;
    Behaviors::iterator m_Current;
```

```
public:
    Sequence(BehaviorTree& bt);
    virtual void onInitialize() override;
    void onChildComplete(Status);
}
```

Since the composites rely on the scheduler to update the child nodes, there's no need for an `update()` function. The setup of the first child in the sequence is done by the `onInitialize()` function.

```
void Sequence::onInitialize() {
    m_Current = m_Children.begin();
    auto observer = BehaviorObserver::                        \
        FROM_METHOD(Sequence, onChildComplete, this);
    m_pBehaviorTree->insert(**m_Current, &observer);
}
```

Every subsequent child in the sequence is set up in the `onChildComplete()` callback.

```
void onChildComplete() {
    Behavior& child = **m_Current;
    //The current child behavior failed, sequence must fail.
    if (child.m_eStatus == BH_FAILURE) {
        m_pBehaviorTree->terminate(*this, BH_FAILURE);
        return;
    }
    //The current child succeeded, is this the end of array?
    if (++m_Current == m_Children.end()) {
        m_pBehaviorTree->terminate(*this, BH_SUCCESS);
    }
    //Move on and schedule the next child behavior in array.
    else {
        BehaviorObserver observer = BehaviorObserver::         \
            FROM_METHOD(Sequence, onChildComplete, this);
        m_pBehaviorTree->insert(**m_Current, &observer);
    }
}
```

Event-driven code has a reputation for being more complex, but this composite code remains very easy to understand at a glance. However, it is a little harder to trace the tree of behaviors by simply looking at a callstack, unlike first-generation BT implementations.

3.4.4.4 Event-Driven Leaf Behaviors

Many actions and conditions remain unaffected by an event-driven implementation, though some could be optimized to use an event-driven approach rather than polling. For instance, a monitoring condition that's waiting for a callback from the navigation system to terminate does not need to be updated every frame. Instead, this condition can be rewritten to return the SUSPENDED status, in which case the scheduler would ignore the behavior during its tick.

Upon receiving an external notification (e.g., from the navigation system), an event-driven condition could then tell the scheduler to reactivate it and process it during the next step of the update. This kind of logic requires special care and ordering of behaviors during the update, but can save a lot of unnecessary function calls.

3.5 Conclusion

In this article, you saw multiple variations of BTs, including a simple first-generation implementation to learn from, as well as a second-generation version that you can use as a starting point in your own project. A few principles recur throughout the code:

- Modular behaviors with simple (unique) responsibilities, to be combined together to form more complex ones.
- Behaviors that are very well specified (even unit tested) and easy to understand, even by nontechnical designers.

While there are always exceptions to these rules in practice, this approach works reliably for creating in-game behaviors. If you're having trouble with code duplication, explaining a bug to a designer, or not being able to understand interactions between your behaviors, then it's best to break down the code into simpler behaviors.

The original un-edited source code for this article can be found online under an open-source license [BTSK 12]. If you'd like to see the details, especially the stuff that couldn't be covered in this article, you're highly encouraged to check out the code!

References

[BTSK 12] A. Champandard and P. Dunstan. The Behavior Tree Starter Kit. http://github.com/aigamedev, 2012.

[Champandard 07] A. Champandard. "Behavior trees for Next-Gen AI." *Game Developers Conference Europe*, 2007.

[Isla 05] D. Isla. "Handling complexity in the Halo 2 AI." *Game Developers Conference*, 2005.

[PSS 11] M. Martins, G. Robert, M. Vehkala, M. Zielinski, and A. Champandard (editor). "Part 3 on Behavior Trees." Paris Shooter Symposium, 2011. http://gameaiconf.com/.

4

Real-World Behavior Trees in Script

Michael Dawe

4.1 Introduction

While there are many different architectures for an AI programmer to pick from, behavior trees are one of the most popular algorithms for implementing NPC action selection in games due to their simplicity to code and use. They are quick to implement from scratch and can be extended to add additional features or provide game-specific functionality as needed. While not as simple as a finite-state machine, they are still simple enough to be easily debugged and designed by other team members as well, making them appropriate to use on games with a large team implementing the behaviors.

On *Kingdoms of Amalur: Reckoning*, we wrote a behavior tree system that used behaviors written in script, while the algorithm itself was processed within the C++ engine. This allowed the design team to have rapid iteration on the behaviors while the programming team retained control over the algorithm features and how the engine processed the behavior tree. Here, we present a functional implementation of a simplified version of the algorithm (available on the book's website http://www.gameaipro.com). It can be used "as is" or extended for a more demanding application. Additionally, we discuss some of the pros and cons we found using such a system in the development of *Reckoning*.

4.2 Architecture Overview

The behavior tree algorithm implemented in the sample code is straightforward and assumes only the knowledge of a tree data structure. Each node in the tree is a *behavior*,

Listing 4.1. Pseudocode for running the behavior tree. Called with the root node to start, this recursively determines the correct branch behaviors to run.

```
process_behavior_node(node)
    if (node.precondition returns true) {
        node.action()
        if (node.child exists)
            process_behavior_node(node.child)
    } else {
        if (node.sibling exists)
            process_behavior_node(node.sibling)
    }
```

with some *precondition* defining when that behavior should run and an *action* defining what the agent should do to perform that behavior. A root behavior is defined to start at, with child behaviors listed in order. Starting from the root, the precondition of the behavior is examined, and if it determines that the behavior should run, the action is performed. The algorithm would continue with any children of that behavior. If a precondition determines that a behavior should not be run, the next sibling at that behavior is examined in turn. In this manner, the algorithm recurses down the tree until the last leaf behavior is run. The pseudocode for the algorithm is shown in Listing 4.1. This process on the behavior tree can be run as often as needed to provide behavior fidelity, either every frame or considerably less often for lower level-of-detail.

In the code sample, we define classes for each `Behavior`, as well as a `BehaviorMgr` to keep track of each `Behavior` loaded. The `BehaviorTree` is its own class as well, so that we can define multiple trees that use the same behaviors and process them separately. Since each `BehaviorTree` is made up of a list of `Behaviors`, multiple characters running the same behavior tree can run separate instances of the `BehaviorTree` class.

4.3 Defining Script Behaviors

There are several compelling reasons to define behaviors in script. First, when developing intelligent agents, quick iteration is often a key factor in determining final behavior quality. Having an environment where behaviors can be written, changed, and reloaded without restarting the game is highly desirable. Another reason to use a scripting language might be to take advantage of your team. On *Reckoning*, a large percentage of the design team had a programming background, making it feasible for them to implement behaviors in script without much programming input or oversight. While some programming time was needed to support the creation of new ways to pass information back and forth between the C++ engine and script, overall the time spent by engineers on the behavior creation process was much less than it would have been otherwise.

In order to write our behavior tree to take advantage of behaviors written in script, we first need to integrate a scripting language to a C++ engine. For *Reckoning*, we chose Lua, a popular scripting language within the games industry. Since Lua is written in C, it can easily be plugged into an existing engine, and since its source is distributed for free, it can even be modified as necessary and compiled into the game.

Lua defines a native data structure—a *table*—which is analogous to a *dictionary* or *map* in other languages. For each behavior, we defined a table with that behavior's name (to avoid name collisions). The members of the table were functions named "precondition" and "behavior." With known names, the C++ algorithm could look for and call the appropriate functions at the correct times.

4.4 Code Example

Besides the behavior classes, the code sample used in this article also defines a `LuaWrapper` class to manage the Lua integration, and an `NTreeNode` class as a generic tree class. In `main()`, a `LuaWrapper` is created and used to load all *.lua files in the Scripts directory, where every *.lua file is a well-defined behavior. While the `LuaWrapper::load_all_scripts()` function is written for Windows systems, all operating-system specific calls are in that function, so porting to a different system should be confined to that function.

From there, a test behavior tree is created based on the script files loaded. Using the `add_behavior_as_child_of()` function, an entire behavior tree can be created from scratch. Finally, the tree is run using `process()`, which simply starts the recursive function at the root of the behavior tree and tests each behavior in turn.

4.5 Integration into a Game Engine

While functional, the sample provided holds more power if plugged into a full game engine. The `Behavior` and `BehaviorTree` classes can be taken "as is" and extended as needed. The `LuaWrapper` could also be taken as written, but ideally an engine would include functionality for reloading the Lua state at runtime, in order to take advantage of being able to rewrite behaviors and test them without restarting or recompiling the game.

Each agent can define its own `BehaviorTree`, either in code or as some sort of data file. For *Reckoning*, behavior trees were assets just as behaviors were, so trees had their own manager and data definition for ease of sharing among multiple different types of NPCs. If the behaviors are written generically enough, many different agents could share not only the behaviors, but even whole trees.

4.6 Script Concerns

While the benefits of having script-defined behaviors are manifest, there are particular concerns that should be kept in mind if using the approach.

Perhaps the first thing to come to mind for game programmers is performance. While written in C, Lua is still a garbage-collected language, and has a floating-point representation for all numbers within the Lua environment. With this in mind, *Reckoning* took a few precautions to safeguard the framerate of the game from poor script performance.

First, since Lua can be compiled directly into the game engine, all Lua allocations can be routed through whatever allocation scheme the engine implements, which means it's possible to take advantage of small-block allocators to avoid general fragmentation issues. By preemptively garbage collecting at known times, it's possible to prevent the Lua garbage collector from running anytime it would be disadvantageous. In particular, *Reckoning* ran the garbage collector every frame at a predetermined time to avoid mid-frame collection that can occur when left up to Lua.

To further increase performance when in Lua, the source was changed to make Lua's internal number system use traditional integers instead of floating-point numbers. This had a few consequences for scripters, the most obvious of which was dealing with integers for percentages, i.e., the number "56" instead of "0.56" for 56%. Once this was well communicated, it was merely a matter of scripting style.

Trigonometry and geometry became impossible to complete within Lua, though, and while this is precisely the outcome planned for, it was a larger workflow change. Since the point was to avoid any complex math in script, it was planned that anytime a behavior or other script needed a trigonometric or geometric problem solved, it would ask the C++ engine for an answer. This meant that while most of the mathematical calculation was kept out of script, more programmer time was required to write and test the necessary functions for script any time a new result was needed.

In general, though it was still a positive time gain to have designers writing more script behaviors, programmers could not be entirely hands-off during behavior development. After *Reckoning* completed, both the designers and programmers agreed that more formal engineering oversight was needed in the scripting process; so while a majority of behaviors in the game were written by designers, the team thought more collaboration would be warranted. A suggested workflow was to have members of the engineering team code review script check-ins, though periodic reviews would also work.

4.7 Enhancements

While the sample can be used "as is," part of the appeal of a behavior tree is implementing extensions as needed for your own project. There are a wide variety of additional features that can be added to this base tree. Here are some examples used on *Reckoning*.

4.7.1 Behavior Asset Management

Although this example just loads files in a given directory, if the behavior tree system needs to interact with a large number of behaviors, it will become easier to have some sort of behavior asset manager to load and track each behavior. While initially this simply shifts the responsibility of loading the behaviors to the new asset manager, the manager can add new functionality by creating a unique ID for each behavior. Trees can reference behaviors by this ID, while the manager can enforce uniqueness of names among behaviors. By having a centralized place to do error-checking on the scripts, finding and recovering from data errors can be handled more easily.

Having an asset manager for your behaviors has other advantages, as well. While this sample creates the trees as part of the program, ideally trees are defined by some data file that's read in when the game starts. This allows the development of external tools to create trees or even define trees containing other trees.

4.7.2 Behavior Definition Extras

As noted, our behavior definitions are simply tables in Lua, which are analogous to dictionaries or maps. Tables can hold arbitrary data, a fact this implementation takes advantage of by storing functions within our behavior table. Since there's no limit on the data, though, we can also store any data with the behavior we want besides just the precondition and behavior functions themselves. For example, a behavior could store a separate table of parameterized data for use within the behavior, or data for use by the behavior tree. In *Reckoning*, behaviors specified a hint to the behavior-level-of-detail system based on how important it was that they run again soon. For example, creatures running combat behaviors had a higher probability of getting to process their tree than creatures merely walking to a destination.

4.7.3 Behavior Class Improvements

The `Behavior` class itself can be improved to allow for faster processing of the tree. In this example, behaviors must define a precondition function and a behavior function, or else the tree will fail to process correctly. It is possible to use the `lua_isfunction()` family of functions to determine if the behavior or precondition functions exist before calling them. While the behavior tree could push the known function location onto the Lua stack to determine its existence every frame, a better solution is one where the behavior itself checks and tracks what functions are defined when it first loads. Then the behavior tree can call or skip a behavior function call based on a flag within the behavior itself without incurring a significant performance cost while processing the tree.

4.7.4 Previously Running Behaviors

Often it is useful when debugging a behavior tree to know which behaviors were running on a given frame. The behavior tree can keep track of which behaviors were running on the last frame or on an arbitrary number of frames prior. The smallest way to do this is by using a bit field. By taking advantage of the fact that a behavior tree is laid out in the same way every run, we can assign the first position in the bit field to the root, then the next its first child, followed by any children that child behavior has before moving on similarly. Algorithmically, we can then simply mark the behaviors to be run while checking behavior preconditions, then save that bit field off when we are finished processing.

In fact, a behavior tree can be compressed considerably using this technique. For example, instead of storing the behaviors in a tree, once the behaviors are loaded by an asset system and given a unique id, the `BehaviorTree` class can store an array of pointers to the behaviors, and the tree can store indices into that array, which simplifies the bit field approach.

4.7.5 on_enter/on_exit Behavior

Once a list of previously running behaviors is established, a behavior can define a function for the first-time setup or a cleanup function for when it ceases running. As a part of *Reckoning*, we defined on_enter and on_exit functions for each behavior. To implement these, the behavior tree class needs to track over subsequent process() calls which behaviors were running the previous time, as above. If a list of behaviors run the previous tick is kept, then any behavior in the previous list but not in the current one can call its on_exit function before new behaviors are started. On_enter and behavior functions are then called in order.

4.7.6 Additional Selectors

The algorithm can also be extended by changing the way behaviors are selected. Some different selectors used on *Reckoning* included *nonexclusive, sequential,* and *stimulus* behaviors. Each of these slightly changed how behaviors could be selected to run or altered the logic of how the tree progressed after running a behavior.

Nonexclusive behaviors run as normal behaviors do, but the tree continues checking siblings at that tree level after doing so. For example, a nonexclusive behavior might play a sound or set up some knowledge tracking while leaving it to other sibling behaviors to determine an actual action.

Sequential behaviors run each of their children in order so long as their precondition returned true. An example might be a behavior to perform a melee attack, with children to approach the target, launch the attack, and then back away. So long as the parent melee behavior returns true, the tree will execute the child behaviors in order.

Stimulus behaviors are a way of hooking the behavior tree up to an in-game event system so that agents can define reaction behaviors to events happening around them. Each stimulus behavior defines a particular stimulus, such as spotting the player or hearing a sound, which it can react to. Stimulus behaviors are a way of specializing a commonly used precondition. In *Reckoning*'s implementation, stimulus behaviors were treated exactly as normal behaviors with a separate precondition function that would check for a defined stimulus on the character running the tree. This specialized precondition also handled cleanup of the stimulus when finished.

Any kind of selection algorithm can work with a behavior tree, which is one of the major strengths of the system. For example, a utility-based selector could pick among its children based on their utility scores, or a goal system could be implemented that picks children based on their postconditions. While any selection algorithm can be made to work, often they will change how the behaviors must be defined, either through additional functions or data needed by the selector. The flexibility of using any kind of selector must be weighed carefully against the time and cost of implementing each different algorithm.

4.8 Conclusion

Behavior trees are a flexible, powerful structure to base an agent's decision-making process around, and utilizing script is one method to drive faster iteration and greater ease of behavior authoring. Being able to edit and reload behaviors at runtime is a huge advantage when refining and debugging behaviors, and having a data-driven approach to behavior creation opens up the process to a much wider group of people on the team, helping production speeds. Additionally, with the behavior tree algorithm being as flexible as it is, improvements and game-specific features can be implemented quickly, and with behaviors implemented in script, each can be updated to take advantage of the new features quickly. Changing their parameters can be done without recompiling or restarting the game, so rapid testing of these features can be accomplished.

If a behavior tree is a fit for a game, having script support for implementing the behaviors provides tremendous flexibility. Though careful analysis of the performance costs is necessary any time a scripting language is used, strategies can be employed to minimize the impact while maintaining the advantages of having a rapid iteration environment for behavior development.

5

Simulating Behavior Trees
A Behavior Tree/Planner Hybrid Approach

Daniel Hilburn

5.1 Introduction

Game AI must handle a high degree of complexity. Designers often represent AI with complex state diagrams that must be implemented and thoroughly tested. AI agents exist in a complex game world and must efficiently query this world and construct models of what is known about it. Animation states must be managed correctly for the AI to interact with the world properly. AI must simultaneously provide a range of control from fully autonomous to fully designer-driven.

At the same time, game AI must be flexible. Designers change AI structure quickly and often. AI implementations depend heavily on other AI and game system implementations, which change often as well. Any assumptions made about these external systems can easily become invalid—often with little warning. Game AI must also interact appropriately with a range of player styles, allowing many players to have fun playing your game.

There are many techniques available to the AI programmer to help solve these issues. As with any technique, all have their strengths and weaknesses. In the next couple of sections, we'll give a brief overview of two of these techniques: behavior trees and planners. We'll briefly outline which problems they attempt to solve and the ones with which they struggle. Then, we'll discuss a hybrid implementation which draws on the strengths of both approaches.

5.1.1 Behavior Trees

A behavior tree in game AI is used to model the behaviors that an agent can perform. The tree structure allows elemental actions (e.g., jump, kick) to be combined to create

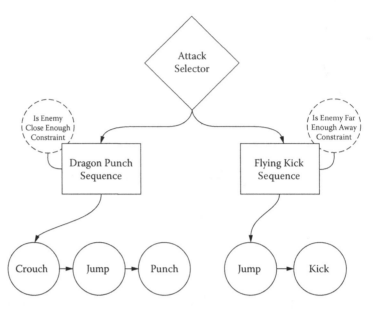

Figure 5.1

Example of a behavior tree.

a higher level behavior (e.g., flying kick). This higher level behavior can then be treated as an elemental behavior and used to compose even higher level behaviors (e.g., attack). Behavior trees also include the concept of *constraints*, which can be attached to behaviors at any level in the tree to keep that behavior from being selected when the state of the world does not match the state required by the constraint (Figure 5.1).

Behavior trees are great at modeling what an AI *can* do. They allow designers to take very low-level actions and combine them to create exactly the set of high-level actions that the designer wants available to the AI. The tree structure easily models any complex design that is thrown at it. Conveniently, this structure also closely resembles the diagrams that designers often use to describe the AI, which allows designers and programmers to speak the same language when discussing AI implementation. The tree structure is also easily configurable, especially if a graphical design tool is available. This allows the designer to rapidly iterate and refine the AI design.

Unfortunately, behavior trees are not so great at specifying what an AI *should* do. In order for the tree to know which action it should perform, it must have intimate knowledge about the world state, including how other AI or game systems are implemented. It must also know how each of its behaviors affects—and is affected by—changes in the world state. This results in a web of dependencies on other systems which are likely to change. If any of these systems change, you'll have to update your behavior tree accordingly. This sort of design is far more brittle than we would like. It is much more preferable that the behavior tree works properly with no modifications even when other systems or its own internal structure changes. Later, we'll discuss ways to solve these issues by taking some cues from AI planners.

5.1.2 Planners

A planner in game AI is used to create a sequence of elemental actions to achieve some goal, given the current world state. This sequence of actions is called a *plan*. The planner maintains a model of the world state, a collection of all elemental actions available to an AI, and a goal heuristic. The world state model contains any information about the world that the heuristic needs. For example, a world state might include a list of available enemies and their health values. The planner understands how each action affects the world state, and since a plan is simply a sequence of these actions, the planner also understands how any plan affects the world state. For example, a kick action deals some damage to an enemy if it is close by, while a jump action moves the AI closer to an enemy.

The goal heuristic scores a given plan by how much it achieves the heuristic's goal. In our example, a combat heuristic would give a high score to a plan that results in enemies being damaged. So, if the AI is close to an enemy, a high scoring plan might consist of just a kick action. However, if the AI is too far from an enemy for the kick to deal damage, the plan will receive a low score. But if we insert a jump action before the kick, now the AI can move in and attack an enemy, a plan which would receive a high score. With all of these pieces available, the planner can create plans that achieve high-level goals dynamically, regardless of the current world state (Figure 5.2).

As you can see, planners are great at managing what an AI *should* do. They allow designers to specify high-level goals for the AI by evaluating world states in the planner's heuristic, rather than trying design specific behaviors for specific situations. Planners are able to do this by keeping a very strict separation between what an AI *does* (actions) and what the AI *should do* (heuristics). This also makes the AI more flexible and durable in the face of design changes. If the jump action gets cut because the team didn't have time to

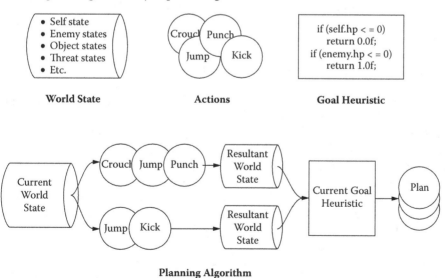

World State   **Actions**   **Goal Heuristic**

Planning Algorithm

Figure 5.2

Example of a planner.

polish the animations, just remove it. The AI will still create the best possible plan for its current world state. If the kick action suddenly also sends out a shockwave, you only need to add that to the kick action's result description. You don't need to change what the AI *should do* just because you changed what it *does*.

While the flexibility of planners is a great strength, it can also be a great weakness. Often, designers will want to have more control over the sequences of actions that an AI can perform. While it is cool that your AI can create a jump kick plan on its own, it could also create a sequence of 27 consecutive jumps. This breaks the illusion of intelligence our AI should produce, which is obviously not what we want to happen. There are techniques to prevent such undesirable plans, but it is difficult to predict all of the situations where a planner can break down. This, understandably, causes distaste for planners among many designers, as they often prefer more control over how their characters behave.

This is the classic tradeoff that AI designers and programmers have to deal with constantly: the choice between the fully designed (brittle) AI that behavior trees provide and the fully autonomous (unpredictable) AI that planners provide. While this battle has been raging for a while now, it is happily not a binary choice. The space between these two approaches is where the best solutions lie. There are numerous implementations of behavior trees and planners and many other techniques that attempt to solve this problem, one of which is our next topic. I'll quickly describe how this approach works, and then we'll dive into how I implemented it on a recent project.

5.1.3 A Behavior Tree/Planner Hybrid

The basic premise of the hybrid approach is simple: combine the strengths of behavior trees and planners to produce an AI system that is flexible and durable in the face of design changes while allowing the designers full control over the structure of the actions available to the AI. It uses a world state model and heuristic, just like the planner. However, where a planner builds sequences of elemental actions dynamically and uses its heuristic to choose the best one, the hybrid approach uses its heuristic to choose between branches of a premade behavior tree.

Using the behavior tree allows the designers to have full control over what actions are available and to easily redesign the structure of these actions while iterating. However, as we mentioned previously, the behavior tree is usually pretty resistant to design changes, as changing the internal structure of an action must be reflected in parent selector nodes back up the tree. This is where our planner half swoops in to save the day.

Remember that our approach also includes a planner's world state model and a heuristic. We incorporate these into the behavior tree by implementing a simulation step for each node type. For *leaf* nodes, this simulation step simply returns a resultant world state just like elemental actions in the planner system. However, the recursive structure of the behavior tree allows us to recursively simulate composite behaviors as well. *Sequence* nodes simulate each of their child behaviors in sequence and then return the accumulated result. *Selector* nodes simulate each of their child behaviors to determine what the resultant world state would be if that node was selected. These results are then fed through the heuristic function to generate a score for each child behavior. The *selector* node then uses these scores to determine which node to select and returns that node's result as its own.

This design allows us to construct behavior trees that know nothing of their internal structure. We can make an *Attack Selector* node that is composed of any number of attack behaviors, and it will choose the one most appropriate to the current world state without knowing about *Dragon Punch* or *Flying Kick* or when they are most appropriate. Any selector node just needs to simulate each of its children and select the one with the highest heuristic score. This allows us to change the internal structure of the tree without changing any code further up the hierarchy. It also allows us to change how a leaf action affects the world without worrying about updating the entire tree to compensate for the changed design. This is what we are looking for. The behavior tree structure allows designers to have full control over what the AI *can* do, while the planner mechanism handles determining what the AI *should* do.

5.2 The Jedi AI in *Kinect Star Wars*™

We developed this behavior tree/planner hybrid approach while working on the Jedi AI for *Kinect Star Wars*™ at Terminal Reality Inc.™, which has been gracious enough to provide the source code for this article as example material. We only have space to go over a subset of the system in this article, but the entire system with sample code is provided on the book's website (http://www.gameaipro.com). The proprietary engine stuff is stubbed out, but all of the Jedi AI bits are there if you are interested in looking them over. Without further ado, let's make a Jedi!

5.2.1 Jedi Memory

The first thing our Jedi needs is an internal knowledge of the world. This is the world state model from our previous discussion, which we called the Jedi AI Memory (see Listing 5.1). It encapsulates everything that our actions can manipulate in the world, including the Jedi, the Jedi's current victim, any nearby enemies, and any incoming threats. It also provides a `simulate()` method, which allows any action to update the parts of memory that change over time (e.g., position), and a `simulateDamage()` method, which allows any behavior to easily simulate damage dealt to a given enemy.

5.2.2 Jedi Behavior Tree

Now that we have our world state representation, let's look at the Jedi's behavior tree implementation. All of our behavior tree nodes, which we called *Actions*, provide the standard begin/update/end behavior tree node interfaces. These nodes return an `EJediAiActionResult` value to their parent from their begin and update operations to let the parent know the Action's current status (see Listing 5.2).

The *Actions* also provide a `checkConstraints()` method, which iterates over a list of attached *Constraint* objects (see Listing 5.3). This method may also be overridden to allow *Action* subclasses to check *Constraints* which are specific to those subclasses. The *Constraint* objects provide options to skip the constraint while the action is in progress or while the action is being simulated, which allow the constraint subclasses a bit of stability. For example, let's consider the *Distance Constraint* attached to the *Dragon Punch* sequence to prevent our AI from executing it when the enemy is too far away. If we start the sequence and the enemy moves far enough away to cause the constraint to fail, the AI will immediately bail out of the sequence, which may not be desirable. It may be more desirable for the AI to continue executing the sequence and simply miss the enemy. If we set up the constraint to be skipped while the action is in progress, this is exactly what will happen.

```cpp
class CJediAiMemory {
public:
    //simulate this AI memory over a given timestep
    void simulate(float dt);
    //simulate damage to an actor
    void simulateDamage(float dmg, SJediAiActorState &actor);
    //data about my self's current state
    struct SSelfState {
        float skillLevel, hitPoints;
        CVector pos, frontDir, rightDir;
    } selfState;
    //knowledge container for world entities
    struct SJediAiEntityState {
        CVector pos, velocity;
        CVector frontDir, rightDir, toSelfDir;
        float distanceToSelf, selfFacePct, faceSelfPct;
    };
    //knowledge container for other actors
    struct SJediAiActorState : SJediAiEntityState {
        EJediEnemyType type;
        float hitpoints;
    };
    //victim state
    SJediAiEntityState *victimState;
    //enemy state list
    enum {kEnemyStateListSize = 8};
    int enemyStateCount;
    SJediAiActorState enemyStates[kEnemyStateListSize];
    //knowledge container for threats
    struct SJediAiThreatState : SJediAiEntityState {
        EJediThreatType type;
        float damage;
    };
    //threat state list
    enum {kThreatStateListSize = 8};
    int threatStateCount;
    SJediAiThreatState threatStates[kThreatStateListSize];
};
```

Finally, the *Actions* provide our simulation interface. Each *Action* contains a simulation summary object which encapsulates everything that our heuristic function cares about. This summary also contains an EJediAiActionSimResult value, which is computed by the heuristic and specifies the desirability of the action. Originally, we used a floating-point number between 0 and 1 to specify this value, but it was very difficult to get stable, predictable results from the heuristic that way. We simplified the result to the values in Listing 5.4.

Now that we have specified all of the pieces of an *Action*, we can bring them all together in the CJediAiAction class in Listing 5.5. It provides the standard begin/update/end interface, the simulation interface, and the Constraint interface.

Listing 5.2. The returned results of an Action's begin and update operations:

```
//jedi ai action results
enum EJediAiActionResult {
    eJediAiActionResult_Success = 0,
    eJediAiActionResult_InProgress,
    eJediAiActionResult_Failure,
    eJediAiActionResult_Count
};
```

Listing 5.3. The behavior tree's Constraint implementation.

```
//base class for all jedi ai constraints
class CJediAiActionConstraint {
public:
    //next constraint in the list
    CJediAiActionConstraint *nextConstraint;
    //don't check this constraint while in progress
    bool skipWhileInProgress;
    //don't check this constraint while simulating
    bool skipWhileSimulating;
    //check our constraint
    virtual EJediAiActionResult checkConstraint(
        const CJediAiMemory &memory,
        const CJediAiAction &action,
        bool simulating) const = 0;
};
```

Listing 5.4. The behavior tree's simulation summary, which the heuristic uses to score an Action's desirability.

```
//jedi ai action simulation result
enum EJediAiActionSimResult {
    eJediAiActionSimResult_Impossible,
    eJediAiActionSimResult_Hurtful,
    eJediAiActionSimResult_Irrelevant,
    eJediAiActionSimResult_Cosmetic,
    eJediAiActionSimResult_Beneficial,
    eJediAiActionSimResult_Urgent,
    eJediAiActionSimResult_Count
};
//jedi ai action simulation summary data
struct SJediAiActionSimSummary {
    EJediAiActionSimResult result;
    float selfHitPoints, victimHitPoints, threatLevel;
};
```

Listing 5.5. The behavior tree's abstract base Action class.

```
class CJediAiAction {
public:
    //standard begin/update/end interface
    virtual EJediAiActionResult onBegin();
    virtual EJediAiActionResult update(float dt) = 0;
    virtual void onEnd();
    //simulate this action on the specified memory object
    virtual void simulate(
        CJediAiMemory &simMemory,
        SJediAiActionSimSummary &simSummary) = 0;
    //check my constraints
    virtual EJediAiActionResult checkConstraints(
        const CJediAiMemory &memory, bool simulating) const;
};
```

Listing 5.6. The behavior tree's abstract base Composite Action class.

```
class CJediAiActionComposite : public CJediAiAction {
public:
    //child actions accessors
    CJediAiAction *getAction(int index);
    virtual CJediAiAction **getActionTable(int *count) = 0;
};
```

Next, we define a *Composite Action*, the base class of all nodes which are composed of subnodes (e.g., *Sequence* or *Selector*). It is pretty simple, providing a common interface for accessing the list of child nodes (see Listing 5.6).

Next, let's look at the *Sequence Action* (see Listing 5.7). It simply runs all of its child *Actions* in sequence, using the method `beginNextAction()`. If any of the actions fail, the *Sequence Action* fails as well. Also, simulating a sequence simulates each of its children, starting with the currently running child if the *Sequence* is currently executing. Each child is simulated using the resultant world state of the previous child's simulation. After all children have been simulated, the *Sequence* computes its own simulation result from the resultant world state.

The *Sequence* class provides a few parameters to let you customize how it operates. One thing that you'll notice is that we encapsulate the parameters into their own object. Encapsulating the parameters this way allows a simple `memset()` to initialize all of the parameter variables, preventing you from forgetting to initialize a new parameter.

Next up is the most important part of the behavior tree: the *Selector* (see Listing 5.8). This class is what decides what the AI will or won't do. The *Selector* does this by calling `selectAction(CJediAiMemory *memory)`, which simulates each of its child behaviors using the provided memory to generate simulation summaries for each. It then calls `compareAndSelectAction()`, which compares these *Action* summaries and selects the *Action* whose summary has the highest result.

Listing 5.7. The behavior tree Sequence class.

```
class CJediAiActionSequence : public CJediAiActionComposite {
public:
    //parameters
    struct {
        //specify a delay between each action in the Sequence
        float timeBetweenActions;
        //allows the Sequence to loop on completion
        bool loop;
        //allows the Sequence to skip over failed actions
        bool allowActionFailure;
        //specify what action result is considered a failure
        EJediAiActionSimResult minFailureResult;
    } sequenceParams;
    //get the next available action in the sequence,
    //starting with the specified index
    virtual CJediAiAction *getNextAction(int &nextActionIndex);
    //begin the next available action in the sequence
    virtual EJediAiActionResult beginNextAction();
};
```

Listing 5.8. The behavior tree Selector class.

```
class CJediAiActionSelector : public CJediAiActionComposite {
public:
    //parameters
    struct SSelectorParams {
        //specify how often we reselect an action
        float selectFrequency;
        //prevents the selected action from being reselected
        bool debounceActions;
        //allow hurtful actions to be selected
        bool allowNegativeActions;
        //if results are equal, reselect the selected action
        bool ifEqualUseCurrentAction;//default is true
    } selectorParams;
    //simulate each action and select which one is best
    virtual CJediAiAction *selectAction(CJediAiMemory *memory);
    //compare action simulation summaries and select one
    virtual int compareAndSelectAction(
        int actionCount, CJediAiAction *const actionTable[]);
};
```

5.2.3 Jedi Simulation

Now that we've defined our behavior tree components, let's have a look at the planner side of things: the simulation. When we begin simulating an *Action*, we create a summary of the current world state. Then, we modify the world state in the same way that the simulating *Action* actually would if it were executed. For example, when simulating the

Listing 5.9. This shows how we condense a Jedi Memory object into a Simulation Summary.

```
//condense the specified memory into a summary
void setSimSummaryMemoryData(
    SJediAiActionSimSummary &summary,
    const CJediAiMemory &memory);
//initialize a summary from the specified memory
void initSimSummary(
    SJediAiActionSimSummary &summary,
    const CJediAiMemory &memory)
{
    summary.result = eJediAiActionSimResult_Impossible;
    setSimSummaryMemoryData(summary, memory);
}
//compute the resultant world state summary
void setSimSummary(
    SJediAiActionSimSummary &summary,
    const CJediAiMemory &memory)
{
    summary.result = computeSimResult(summary, memory);
    setSimSummaryMemoryData(summary, memory);
}
```

SwingSaber Action, we apply damage to the victim and run the world state simulation forward by the same amount of time that it takes to swing our lightsaber. After the simulation is complete, we create a summary of the resultant world state and compute the desirability of this new state compared to the summary of the initial state (see Listing 5.9). This final summary is passed back to the parent *Action* and will be used by the behavior tree when selecting this *Action* from a set of other *Actions*.

The real meat of this system is the planner heuristic, where we compute the simulation result (see Listing 5.10). This function represents our AI's current goal. In this case, the Jedi's only goal was to avoid damage and threats while causing damage to his victim. The heuristic does this by classifying an *Action*'s post-simulation world state as one of the `EJediAiActionSimResult` values (impossible, hurtful, irrelevant, beneficial, etc.).

Now that we've defined how our AI's simulation result is computed, let's have a look at how it fits into an actual simulation step: the *SwingSaber Action* (see Listing 5.11).

5.3 Now Let's Throw in a Few Monkey Wrenches …

Game development is an iterative process, and your system will change many times between conception and final product. Even when your system isn't being redesigned, design changes in other systems can change how your implementation behaves. So, it is imperative that our system handles these changes well. As we discussed earlier, the whole point of our hybrid system is to provide flexibility to handle these changes with as few changes as possible. So let's see how well it does by looking at some design changes from *Kinect Star Wars*™.

Listing 5.10. The planner heuristic, which computes the simulation result.

```
//determine the result of a simulation by comparing a summary
//of the initial state to the post-simulation state
EJediAiActionSimResult computeSimResult(
    SJediAiActionSimSummary &summary,
    const CJediAiMemory &memory)
{
    //if we are more hurt than before, the action is hurtful
    //if we are dead, the action is deadly
    if (memory.selfState.hitPoints < summary.selfHitPoints) {
        if (memory.selfState.hitPoints <= 0.0f) {
            return eJediAiActionSimResult_Deadly;
        } else {
            return eJediAiActionSimResult_Hurtful;
        }
    //if our threat level increased, the action is hurtful
    } else if (memory.threatLevel > summary.threatLevel) {
        return eJediAiActionSimResult_Hurtful;
    //if our threat level decreased, the action is helpful
    //if it decreased by a lot, the action is urgent
    } else if (memory.threatLevel < summary.threatLevel) {
        float d = (summary.threatLevel - memory.threatLevel);
        if (d < 0.05f) {
            return eJediAiActionSimResult_Safe;
        } else {
            return eJediAiActionSimResult_Urgent;
        }
    //if victim was hurt, the action is helpful
    } else if (memory.victimState->hitPoints < summary.victimHitPoints) {
        return eJediAiActionSimResult_Beneficial;
    }
    //otherwise, the sim was irrelevant
    return eJediAiActionSimResult_Irrelevant;
}
```

5.3.1 Jedi Skill Level

Kinect Star Wars™ featured three different types of Jedi: Master Jedi, low-level Padawan Jedi, and the second player Jedi. Originally, these were all implemented using the same design. Later, the design team added the caveat that each Jedi should have a skill level to specify how competent he was at combat. This would allow us to make a Master Jedi, like Mavra Zane, more capable in a fight than your Jedi buddy or the other Padawan Jedi in the game.

We implemented this by having the skill level specify how quickly the Jedi could defeat each enemy type. This allowed Mavra to dispatch enemies quickly, while the Padawan Jedi took much longer. To make this work, we added a `victimTimer` member to our world state to track how much time had elapsed since we acquired our current victim. Then, we added a statement to the heuristic to discourage killing the victim before timer specified by the current skill level had expired (see Listing 5.10).

That was it. We didn't have to change any behavior tree *Actions* or simulation code. The heuristic was already aware if a given action would kill the victim, because we were

Listing 5.11. The SwingSaber Action's simulation method.

```
void CJediAiActionSwingSaber::simulate(
    CJediAiMemory &simMemory,
    SJediAiActionSimSummary &simSummary)
{
    initSimSummary(simSummary, simMemory);
    EJediAiActionResult result;
    for (int i = data.swingCount; i < params.numSwings; ++i)
    {
        //simulate a single swing's duration
        CJediAiMemory::SSimulateParams simParams;
        simMemory.simulate(
            kJediSwingSaberDuration, simParams);
        //apply damage to my target
        simMemory.simulateDamage(
            simMemory.selfState.saberDamage,
            *simMemory.victimState);
        //if my target is dead, I'm done
        if (simMemory.victimState->hitPoints <= 0.0f)
            break;
    }
    setSimSummary(simSummary, simMemory);
}
```

simulating each action instead of hard-coding the selection logic into the selectors. So the planner held up its end of the bargain, allowing us to change goals without modifying any *Actions*.

5.3.2 Jedi Mistakes

Another wrinkle that arose was the idea of mistakes. It isn't realistic for the Jedi to always defeat their enemies; they should sometimes fail. Also, the designers wanted the Jedi AI to demonstrate what not to do against various enemy types. However, our entire system is built on the idea that the Jedi will choose the **best** option. We could make a custom selector that chooses the worst option instead of the best option, but it would still return a negative simulation result to its parent, which would then not select it to run.

At first this seemed like a flaw in the system, until we thought about what defines a "mistake." Obviously, the Jedi will always *try* to choose the best Action available. But what if they made a miscalculation and chose an Action which actually was hurtful? This would pass correctly back up the behavior tree and the hurtful Action would then be chosen. In order to create this miscalculation, we needed to insert incorrect information into the simulation step for any *Action*. Rather than add these special cases to each *Action*, we added a special *Action* called a *FakeSim*. The *FakeSim Action* is a special type of *Composite Action* called a *decorator*, which wraps another *Action* to add extra functionality to it. The *FakeSim* was responsible for adding incorrect information to the wrapped *Action*'s simulation step by modifying the world state directly. For example, there are some enemies that have a shield which makes them invulnerable to lightsaber attacks. If we want a Jedi to attack the enemy to demonstrate that the enemy is invulnerable while the shield is up, we can wrap the *SwingSaber Action* with a *FakeSim Decorator* which lowers the victim's shield during the simulation step. Then, the *SwingSaber* simulation will think that the Jedi can damage the enemy and give it a good simulation result. This would allow *SwingSaber* to be chosen, even though it won't actually be beneficial.

This ended up being a great way to handle this design requirement. It allows us to insert specific mistakes anywhere in the system without modifying any of the *Action* classes. And it allows us to avoid writing special case code to handle inserting these mistakes. We simply insert a bit of incorrect domain knowledge into the system, which reflects how people make mistakes in real life. So the behavior tree held up its end of the bargain, allowing us to easily design very specific *Action* sequences that the planner couldn't handle on its own.

5.4 Conclusion

We've discussed some of the strengths and weakness with both behavior trees and planners. Behavior trees are great at allowing designers to define exactly what an AI *can* do, and planners are great at allowing designers to easily specify what an AI *should* do. And we've discussed how we can utilize a hybrid approach to realize the strengths of both approaches. Finally, we looked at how this system was used in *Kinect Star Wars*™ to create the Jedi AI. This approach provides designers with all of the control of a behavior tree and all of the durability and flexibility of a planner, allowing it to handle design changes smoothly and with few changes to the code. And that is really the whole point.

6

An Introduction to Utility Theory

David "Rez" Graham

6.1 Introduction

Decision making forms the core of any AI system. There are many different approaches to decision making, several of which are discussed in other chapters in this book. One of the most robust and powerful systems we've encountered is a utility-based system. The general concept of a utility-based system is that every possible action is scored at once and one of the top scoring actions is chosen. By itself, this is a very simple and straightforward approach. In this article, we'll talk about common techniques, best practices, pitfalls to avoid, and how you can best apply utility theory to your AI.

6.2 Utility

Utility theory is a concept that's been around long before games or even computers. It has been used in game theory, economics, and numerous other fields. The core idea behind utility theory is that every possible action or state within a given model can be described with a single, uniform value. This value, usually referred to as *utility*, describes the usefulness of that action within the given context. For example, let's say you need a new toy for your cat; so you go online and find the perfect one. One website has it for $4.99 while another website sells the exact same toy for $2.99. Assuming delivery times are the same, you will likely choose the toy for $2.99. That option typically has a higher utility than the toy for $4.99 because, in the end, you are left with more money.

This process gets more difficult when you need to compare the value of two things that aren't directly comparable. For instance, in the previous example let's assume that the two websites have different delivery times. The toy for $4.99 will arrive at your house in two days while the toy for $2.99 will arrive in five days. In this case, the choice is no longer a simple matter of comparing the two price values. Some conversion between time and money has to be made in order to measure the overall worth of an action. We could say that each day is worth $1, which means that the total cost of the $4.99 toy is $6.99 while the total cost of the $2.99 toy is $7.99. The $4.99 toy is the winner in this case (because it costs you less in combined money + time). You can also weigh things such as website loyalty, recommendations from friends, history, customer reviews, and anything else that you might consider a relevant factor. All of these factors have utility scores of their own, which you can then combine to create the total *expected utility* of for the decision.

It's important to note that *utility* is not the same as *value*. Value is a measurable quantity (such as the prices above). Utility measures how much we desire something. This can change based on personality or the context of the situation. If you were a billionaire, you would likely choose the cat toy for $4.99 because you might value time more than money. The $2.00 you save is a negligible amount. On the other hand, if you were very poor, you would likely choose the cheaper toy and wait the extra time because that extra $2 is really important to you. That money has the exactly the same *value*, but the *utility* of the money is variable, based on the context in which it is being considered. This can change from moment to moment. Right now, the utility of having a bandage with you might be pretty small. If you were to accidentally cut yourself, the utility of having a bandage would climb.

6.2.1 Consistent Utility Scores

When calculating utility scores, it's important to be consistent. Because utility scores are compared to each other to come up with a final decision, they must all be on the same scale across the entire system. As you'll see later in this article, scores are often combined in meaningful ways to produce other scores. Therefore, using *normalized scores* (values that go from 0–1) provide a reasonable starting point. Normalized scores combine very easily through averaging, can be easily calculated given any value within a set range of numbers, and are easily comparable since they are on the same scale. It's important to note that any value range will work, as long as there is consistency across the different variables. If an AI agent scores an action with a value of 15, you should know immediately what that means in the context of the whole system. For instance, does that 15 mean 15 out of 25 or 15%?

6.3 Principle of Maximum Expected Utility

The key to decision making using utility-based AI is to calculate a utility score (sometimes called a weight) for every action the AI agent can take and then choose the action with the highest score. Of course, most game worlds are nondeterministic so calculating the exact utility is not usually possible. It's hard to know if an action will be preferable if you can't determine the results of performing that action. This is the heart of utility theory and where it is most useful. For example, if we had the processing power to compute the entire game tree for a chess game, scoring of moves wouldn't be necessary—we would simply determine if sequences of moves resulted in a win, loss, or tie. We currently don't have that ability, so we score each move based on how strong we think the move is. Provided a reasonable scoring system, utility-based AI is very good at making a "best guess" based on incomplete information.

The most common technique is to multiply the utility score by the probability of each possible outcome and sum up these weighted scores. This will give you the *expected utility* of the action. This can be expressed mathematically with Equation 6.1.

$$EU = \sum_{i=1}^{n} D_i P_i \qquad (6.1)$$

In this case, D is the desire for that outcome (i.e., the utility), and P is the probability that the outcome will occur. This probability is normalized so that the sum of all the probabilities is 1. This is applied to every possible action that can be chosen, and the action with the highest expected utility is chosen. This is called the principle of *maximum expected utility* [Russell et al. 09].

For example, an enemy AI in an RPG attacking the player has two possible outcomes— either the AI hits the player or it misses. If the AI has an 85% chance to hit the player, and successfully hitting the player has a calculated utility score of 0.6, the adjusted utility would be $0.85 \times 0.6 = 0.51$. (Note that, in this case, missing the player has a utility of zero, so there's no need to factor it in.) Taking this further, if this attack were to be compared to attacking with a different weapon, for example, with a 60% chance of hitting but a utility score of 0.9 if successful, the adjusted utility would be $0.60 \times 0.9 = 0.54$. Despite having a lesser chance of hitting, the second option provides a greater overall *expected utility*.

6.4 Decision Factors

It is rare that any given decision will only rely on a single piece of data. A decision factor can be thought of as a single point of consideration for a decision. For example, when deciding which website to purchase the cat toy from, we don't usually just consider price, but also consider brand loyalty, shipping times, customer reviews, etc. Each of these data points are factors that we weigh into the calculation of the final utility score for whether or not to buy from that website. Factors can also be further modified by weights that determine how much the AI cares about that particular factor, which emulates personality.

One way to achieve this result is to apply the expected utility calculation in Equation 6.1 to each decision factor to come up with the utility of that factor. Assuming those scores are all normalized, you can average them together to come up with a final utility score for that decision. This lets us define a decision as nothing more than some combination of decision factors.

This principle is best illustrated with an example. Let's say we have an ant simulation game where the AI must determine whether to expand the colony or whether to breed. There are three different factors we want to consider for these decisions. The first is the overall crowdedness of the colony. If there are too many ants, we need to expand to make room for more. The second is the health of the colony, which we'll say is based on how full the food stores are. Ant eggs need to be kept at a specific temperature; so there are specially built nurseries that house the eggs where they are taken care of. The amount of room in these nurseries is the third decision factor. These decision factors are based on game statistics that determine the score for each factor. The population and max population determine how many ants are in the colony and how many can exist based on the current

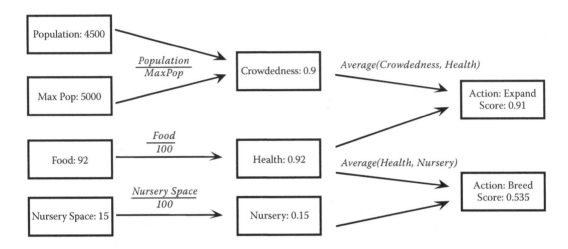

Figure 6.1

An example of combining utility scores from different decision factors to arrive at a final score.

colony size. The food stat represents how full the food stores are and is measured as a number from 0 to 100. The nursery space stat is also measured from 0 to 100 and represents how much space there is in the nursery. You can think of the last stats as percentages.

The scores for the decision factors are then combined to form the final score for the two actions. In this case, crowdedness and health are averaged together to form the score for the expand action while nursery space and health are averaged together to get the score for the breed action. Figure 6.1 shows this combination.

By averaging the normalized scores together, we can build an endless chain of combinations. This is a really powerful concept. Each decision factor is effectively isolated from every other decision factor. The only thing we know or care about is that the output will be a normalized score. We can easily add more game stat inputs, like the distance to an enemy ant colony. This could feed into a decision factor for deciding what kind of ants to breed. You can easily move decision factors around as well, combining them in different ways. If you wanted crowdedness to factor negatively into the decision for breeding, you could subtract crowdedness from 1.0 and average that into the score for breeding.

One of the most powerful uses of this technique is to build a tool that allows you to manipulate decision factors and game state data directly. This tool would allow designers to drag and drop boxes around and connect them with arrows, much like the layout of Figure 6.1. Each arrow would combine the decision factors in different ways. For example, you might average some decision factors together, multiply others, choose the *max* or *min* of another set, etc. Certain decision factors can also be given a weight, making those factors more or less important. There are almost endless possibilities.

6.5 Calculating Utility

So far, we've seen how to calculate the utility given a set of outcomes, and how to combine the utility of multiple decision factors to arrive at the final utility for a decision. The next

6. An Introduction to Utility Theory

step is taking an arbitrary game value and converting it to a utility score. Calculating the initial utility for a decision factor is highly subjective; two different programmers will write two different utility functions that produce different outputs, even given the same inputs. In the ant example above, we chose to represent health as a linear ratio by dividing the current amount of food with the maximum amount of food. This probably isn't a very realistic calculation since the colony shouldn't care about food when the stores are mostly full. Some kind of quadratic curve is more of what we want.

The key to utility theory is to understand the relationship between the input and the output, and being able to describe that resulting curve [Mark 09]. This can be thought of as a conversion process, where you are converting one or more values from the game to utility. Coming up with the proper function is really more art than science and is usually where you'll spend most of your time. There are a huge number of different formulas you could use to generate reasonable utility curves, but a few of them crop up often enough that they warrant some discussion.

6.5.1 Linear

A linear curve forms a straight line with a constant slope. The utility value is simply a multiplier of the input. Equation 6.2 shows the formula for calculating a normalized utility score for a given value and Figure 6.2 shows the resulting curve.

$$U = \frac{x}{m} \tag{6.2}$$

In Equation 6.2, x is the input value and m is the maximum value for that input. This is really just a normalization function, which is all we need for a linear output.

6.5.2 Quadratic

A quadratic function is one that forms a parabolic curve, causing it to start slow and then curve upwards very quickly. The simplest way to achieve this is to add an exponent to Equation 6.2. Equation 6.3 shows an example of this.

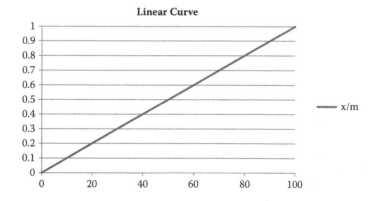

Figure 6.2

A linear curve.

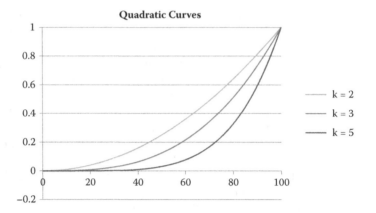

Figure 6.3

Several quadratic curves for various values of k.

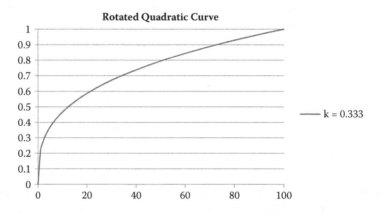

Figure 6.4

A rotated quadratic curve.

$$U = \left(\frac{x}{m} \right)^k \tag{6.3}$$

As the value of k rises, the steepness of the curve will also rise. Since the equation normalizes the output, it will always converge on 0 and 1, so a large value of k will have very little impact for low values of x. Figure 6.3 shows curves for three different values of k.

It's also possible to rotate the curve so that the effect is more urgent for low values of x rather than high values. If you use an exponent between 0 and 1, the curve is effectively rotated, as shown in Figure 6.4.

6.5.3 The Logistic Function

The logistic function is another common formula for creating utility curves. It's one of several sigmoid functions that place the largest rate of change in the center of the input

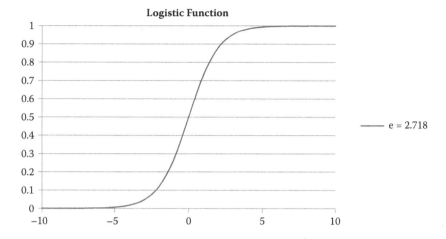

Logistic Function

Figure 6.5

The output of a logistic function.

range, trailing off at both ends as they approach 0 and 1. The input range for the logistic function can be just about anything, but it is effectively limited to [–10 … 10]. There really isn't much point generating a curve larger than that and the range is often clamped down even further. For example, when x is 6, *EU* will be 0.9975.

Equation 6.4 shows the formula for the logistic function and Figure 6.5 shows the resulting curve. Note the use of the constant *e*. This is Euler's number—the base of the natural logarithm—which is approximately 2.718281828. This value can be adjusted to affect the shape of the curve. As the number goes up, the curve will sharpen and begin to resemble a square wave. As the number goes down, it will soften.

$$U = \frac{1}{1 + e^{-x}} \tag{6.4}$$

6.5.4 Piecewise Linear Curves

The curves we've listed so far are by no means a complete list. There are many, many different ways you can transform the input into something else. Sometimes, having a mathematical formula isn't good enough. Designers often need to fine-tune the specific outputs for various given inputs.

For example, consider a problem faced by all Sims games, which is making a Sim eat when they are hungry. All Sims have a *Hunger* stat which measures how full they are. The lower this *Hunger* stat, the more hungry a Sim is. A naïve scoring implementation might be to model hunger with a rotated quadratic curve like the one in Figure 6.4, or perhaps one with a smaller value for *k*. That would make Sims get really hungry when their *Hunger* stat got low. The problem is that there would still be a chance they would choose to eat, even when their hunger stat was mostly filled up. The chance would be small, but it would eventually get chosen. Designers want a finer degree of control. They want the ability to have a Sim completely ignore hunger until it reaches a threshold, then get a little hungry, then

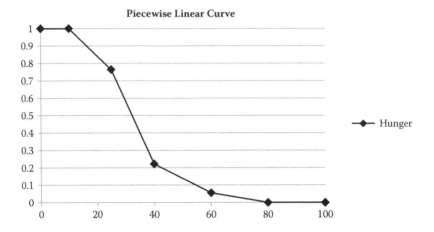

Figure 6.6

A reasonable piecewise linear curve for Hunger.

suddenly get *very* hungry. There's no way to build and tune that specific curve with a simple mathematical formula, so the solution is to create a custom curve. One example of a custom curve is a piecewise linear curve.

A piecewise linear curve is just a custom-built curve. The idea is that you hand-tune a bunch of 2D points that represent the thresholds you want. When the curve is asked for the *y* value given an *x* value, it finds the two closest points to that *x* value and linearly interpolates between them to arrive at the answer. This allows you to create any shaped curve you want and is exactly what *The Sims* uses. Figure 6.6 shows a simple response curve that might be used for hunger.

There are many other types of custom curves. For example, the curve in Figure 6.6 could be changed so that the values from 15 to 60 are calculated with a quadratic curve, while the rest are linear. There's no limit to the number of combinations you can have.

6.6 Picking an Action

Once the utility has been calculated for each action, the next step is to choose one of those actions. There are a number of ways you can do this. The simplest is to just choose the highest scoring option. For some games, this may be exactly what you want. A chess AI should definitely choose the highest scoring move. A strategy game might do the same.

For some games (like *The Sims*), choosing the absolute best action can feel very robotic due to the likelihood that the action will *always* be selected in that situation. Another solution is to use the utility scores as weight, and randomly choose one of the actions based on the weights. This can be accomplished by dividing each score with the sum of all scores to get the percentage chance that the action will be chosen. Then you generate a random number and select the action that number corresponds to. This tends to have the opposite problem, however. Your AI agents will behave reasonably well most of the time, but every now and then, they'll choose something utterly stupid.

6. An Introduction to Utility Theory

You can get the best of both worlds by taking a subset of the highest scoring actions and choosing one of those with a weighted random. This can either be a tuned value, such as choosing from among the top five scoring actions, or it can be percentile based where you take the highest score and also consider things that scored within, say, 10% of it.

This will generally solve the problem at hand, but there could also be times when some set of actions are just completely inappropriate. You may not even want to score them. For example, say you're making an FPS and have a guard AI. You might have some set of actions for him to consider, like getting some coffee, chatting with his fellow guard, checking for lint, etc. If the player shoots at him, he shouldn't even consider any of those actions and only try to score actions that involve combat. In a similar example from *The Sims*, if a Sim is starving to death, she shouldn't bother scoring actions that result in her satisfying her *Fun* motive.

The most straightforward way to solve this is with *bucketing*, also known as *dual utility AI* [Dill 11]. All actions are categorized into buckets and each bucket is given a weight. The higher priority buckets are always processed first. If there are any valid actions in those higher priority buckets, they are always selected before actions in lower priority buckets. In the FPS example above, all combat actions would be in a higher priority bucket than the idle actions. If there are any valid combat actions to take (i.e., they score higher than 0), the guard will always choose one of them and won't consider any of the idle actions. Only when none of the combat actions are valid will the guard choose an idle action.

Buckets can also change priority based on the situation. On *The Sims*, motives are bucketed based on their utility value. The highest scoring motives are grouped into a bucket, and none of the motives below are considered. Once the bucketing is complete, the Sim will score the individual actions on each object, but only the ones that solve for those bucketed motives. Thus, a starving Sim will never even consider watching TV unless they fail to find anything that can solve their hunger. This concept is illustrated in Figure 6.7.

In Figure 6.7, you can see that there are two buckets, one for *Hunger* and one for *Fun*. *Hunger* has scored 0.8 while *Fun* has scored 0.4. The Sim will walk through all possible actions in the *Hunger* bucket and, assuming any of those actions are valid, will choose one. The Sim will not consider anything in the *Fun* bucket, even though some of those actions

Hunger Bucket	0.8
Eat at Table	20
Drink Juice	5
Make Sushi	0

Fun Bucket	0.4
Watch TV	30
Play Video Games	28
Dance	15

Figure 6.7

The Hunger and Fun buckets, each with three actions.

are scoring higher. This is because hunger is more urgent than fun. Of course, if none of the actions in the *Hunger* bucket were valid, the Sim would move on to the next highest scoring bucket. The buckets themselves are scored based on a response curve created by designers. This causes Sims to always attempt to solve the most urgent desire and to choose one of the best actions to solve for that desire.

6.7 Inertia

One issue that's worth bringing up in any AI system is the concept of inertia. If your AI agent is attempting to decide something every frame, it's possible to run into oscillation issues, especially if you have two things that are scored similarly. For example, say you have FPS where the AI realizes it's in a bad spot. The enemy soldier starts scoring both "attack the player" and "run away" at 0.5. If the AI was making a new decision every frame, it is possible that they would start appearing very frantic. The AI might shoot the player a couple times, start to run away, then shoot again, then repeat. Oscillations in behavior such as this look very bad.

One solution is to add a weight to any action that you are already currently engaged in. This will cause the AI to tend to remain committed until something truly better comes along. Another solution is to use *cooldowns*. Once an AI agent makes a decision, they enter a cooldown stage where the weighting for remaining in that action is extremely high. This weight can revert at the end of the cooldown period, or it can gradually drop as well.

Another solution is to stall making another decision—either for a period of time or until such time as the current action is finished. This really depends on the type of game you're making and how your decision/action process works, however. On *The Sims Medieval*, a Sim would only attempt to make a decision when their interaction queue was empty. Once they chose an action, they would commit to performing that action. Once the Sim completed (or failed to complete) their action, they would choose a new action.

6.8 Demo

The demo on the book website (gameaipro.com) demonstrates many of the concepts from this article. It's a simple text-based combat program similar to the menu-based combat RPG's from the '80s, like *Dragon Warrior* (aka *Dragon Quest*) and *Final Fantasy*. You fight a single monster and each of you has the ability to attack the other, heal with a healing potion, or run away. Attacking will do a random amount of damage, healing will use up one of three healing potions to heal a random amount of hit points, and running away has a 50% chance of successfully running away. The relevant code is in AiActor.cpp, which has all of the scoring functions and is responsible for choosing the action when it's the AI actor's turn. The key function is ChooseNextAction(), which takes in the opponent actor and returns an action to perform. This function calls each of the scoring functions to calculate their scores and chooses one using a weighted random.

6.8.1 Decision Factors

When making decisions, the AI considers four basic factors. The first is a desire to attack, which is based on a tuned value that scales linearly as it becomes possible to kill the player

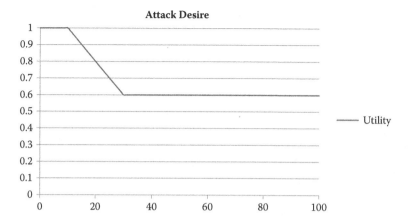

Figure 6.8

The Attack Desire curve.

in a single hit. This causes the actor to get more aggressive during the end-game and take more risks, as shown in Equation 6.5. This is a good example of a range-bound linear curve. The value of a in the equation is the tuned aggression of the actor, which is the default score.

$$U = \max\left(\min\left(\left(1 - \frac{hp - minDmg}{maxDmg - minDmg}\right) \times (1-a) + a, 1\right), 0\right) \quad (6.5)$$

Figure 6.8 shows the resulting curve from Equation 6.5 where a is set to 0.6.

The second decision factor is the threat. This is a curve that measures what percentage of the actor's current hit points will be taken away if the player hits for maximum damage. It has a shape similar to a quadratic curve and is generated with Equation 6.6.

$$U = \min\left(\frac{maxDmg}{hp}, 1\right) \quad (6.6)$$

Figure 6.9 shows the resulting curve for Threat.

The third decision factor is the actor's desire for health. This uses a variation of the logistics function in Equation 6.4. As the actor's hit points are reduced, its desire to heal will rise. Equation 6.7 shows the formula for this decision factor.

$$U = 1 - \frac{1}{1 + (e \times 0.68)^{-\left(\frac{hp}{maxHp} \times 12\right) + 6}} \quad (6.7)$$

The resulting curve is a nice, smooth, sigmoid curve, which is shown in Figure 6.10. Note the addition of +6 to the exponent. This is what pushes the curve over to the positive x-axis rather than centering around 0.

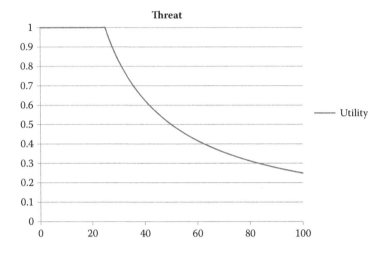

Figure 6.9

The Threat curve.

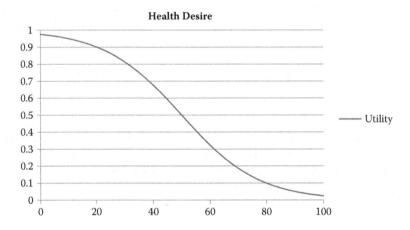

Figure 6.10

The Health Desire curve.

The final decision factor is the desire to run away. This is a quadratic curve with a steepness based on the number of potions the agent has. If the agent has several potions, the likelihood of running away is extremely small. If the agent has none, this desire grows much faster. Equation 6.8 shows the formula for the run desire.

$$U = 1 - \left(\frac{hp}{maxHp} \right)^{\frac{1}{(p+1)^4} \times 0.25}$$

(6.8)

The curve itself is dependent on the value of p, which is the number of potions the actor has left. Figure 6.11 shows various curves for various values of p.

6. An Introduction to Utility Theory

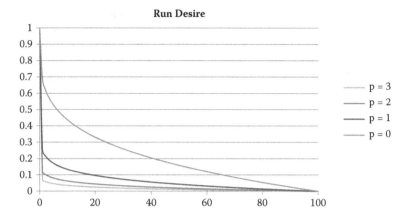

Figure 6.11

The Run Desire curve for several values of *p*.

These curves all represent the various decision factors the AI will use to choose one of the three options. The decision to attack is based entirely on the Attack Desire curve. The decision to heal is based on the Health Desire curve multiplied with the Threat curve. This mitigates the case where the actor may want to heal prematurely and changes behavior based on the maximum damage of the player. It's worth noting that we originally had this set to the average damage the player can do since that's more in the spirit of *expected* utility, but this didn't yield strict enough results. This is a good example of how tuning utility curves and formulas is more art than science. The decision to run away works the same way as the decision to heal; it multiplies in the desire to run with the threat.

6.8.2 Decision Making and Gameplay

The demo is a turn-based duel between you and a ferocious utility curve. You start first by choosing one of the available actions, and then your opponent decides how to respond. This continues until one of you is dead or has run away. The AI opponent starts by calculating the score for each decision factor by running through the utility formulas above. The score for each action is calculated by combining the decision factors. The Attack action is just the outcome of the Attack Desire decision factor. The Run action is scored by multiplying the Run Desire decision factor with the Threat. The Heal action is scored by multiplying the Heal Desire decision factor with the Threat. The final decision is chosen with a weighted random.

6.9 Conclusion

Utility theory is a very powerful way to get rich, life-like behavior out of your AI and has been used in countless games of nearly every genre. It can be extremely fast, especially if you choose simple utility functions, and it scales very well. One of the great appeals of this system is the amount of emergent behavior you can get with just a few simple values and a handful of weights to add some personality. By combining decision factors in meaningful ways, you can build up decisions from these atomic components to provide very deep AI.

In this article, we had a whirlwind tour of utility theory and how it can be applied to games. We showed you some basic principles of decision making and dug into the math behind it. With the tools in this article and a bit of work, you can build a powerful, emergent AI system.

References

[Dill 11] K. Dill. "A game AI approach to autonomous control of virtual characters." *Interservice/ Industry Training, Simulation, and Education Conference, 2011*, pp. 4–5. Available online (http://www.iitsec.org/about/PublicationsProceedings/Documents/11136_Paper.pdf).

[Mark 09] D. Mark. *Behavioral Mathematics for Game AI*. Reading, MA: Charles River Media, 2009, pp. 229–240.

[Russell et al. 09] S. Russell and P. Norvig. *Artificial Intelligence: A Modern Approach.* Reading, MA: Prentice Hall, 2009, pp. 480–509.

Building Utility Decisions into Your Existing Behavior Tree

Bill Merrill

7.1 Introduction

While there is no "silver bullet" approach to authoring AI behavior, behavior trees tend to strike a strong overall balance across ease of implementation, ease of visualization, and adoptability for new team members. Building supporting tools is straightforward, and a rapid workflow can be established in relatively short order. On the other hand, behavior trees have a fundamental limitation. They are poor at modeling analog concepts such as uncertainty over multiple valid options. Game characters are simply fun and engaging machines for players to interact with and even exploit, but requirements still often demand more than strictly Boolean selection logic. Because hand-coding analog selection logic everywhere that it is required gets messy quickly, a better solution is needed.

Utility-based decision-making addresses this problem head-on. Rather than creating variation through randomness or forcing agents to arbitrarily take one valid option over another, we can apply existing, well-documented techniques to deal with "gray area" decisions in an elegant manner. Most satisfyingly, we can do all of this without uprooting an existing implementation by imposing structural changes and we don't have to give up any of the most desirable traits of behavior trees.

This article proposes a few simple components that enable the integration of utility considerations into a behavior tree's normal selection process. The express goal of this integration is to overcome much of the behavior tree architecture's biggest weaknesses without sacrificing its strengths.

7.2 Why Behavior Trees?

Behavior trees have been growing steadily in popularity, and for good reason. Put simply, they offer a very pragmatic approach to making decisions. It is their simplicity I find most valuable, and in a world of increasingly complex software, simplicity should not go undervalued. The aggregation of systems comprising AI in modern games is becoming vast, and isn't shrinking anytime soon. It's important to find what works for the team and try not to force new learning curves unnecessarily.

Behavior trees have become somewhat of a standard in the industry. Many AAA studios make use of behavior tree technology, including Bungie with the Halo series [Bungie 07], and Crytek with Crysis 2 [Crytek 11]. A wealth of information on behavior trees is available online and existing toolkits are available for developers looking to get started quickly [Champandard 08, Brainiac 09]. This implementation included with this chapter is basic, but also relatively complete and free for any use. To see more on how developers are constantly improving on the traditional behavior tree, Alex Champandard's behavior tree toolkit provides tips on how to implement your behavior tree to optimize performance and memory access patterns on systems such as consoles that demand the extra attention [Champandard 12].

For my team in particular, the accessibility and scalability of behavior trees has us using them as our primary mechanism for decision making. Productivity depends largely on designers, scripters, and animators gaining a clear understanding of how a given character intends to behave and react to change. We never fully attained this when using a STRIPS-based planner or our finite state machine (FSM) prior to that. In both cases, so much of what was occurring "under the hood" was largely opaque to anyone other than the AI programmer(s). In the case of the planner, it was too organic and mysterious for the designers' comfort. Additionally, emergent behavior is still not a desirable feature most of the time. Planners also make it difficult to string together specific sequences of actions in a defined order when needed. As for FSMs, the lack of true modularity, complex state logic, and a tendency to get messy negatively affected both the designers and programmers alike. This was especially true as NPC characters developed over time, requiring more complex transition logic. Special cases seemed to become the norm, generating many uninvited surprises along the way as we attempted to share functionality with past projects and other game teams.

With behavior trees, our designers can effectively visualize what's happening, in real-time, and can intuitively apply changes or additions with a clear picture of what to expect. Programmers can also easily oversee the changes. Tree structures are a familiar and relatively easy concept to digest, with many designers industry-wide already using them in some form for major aspects of their workflow. This enables us to provide the designers with easily-adoptable debugging and authoring tools. This is invaluable during development when creating complex tools and chasing bugs can steal precious resources from iteration and content creation.

7.3 It's Not All Candy Canes and Gum Drops

The features required by a game change constantly, putting strain on nearly every system in your codebase. AI is particularly susceptible to this problem because it's driven directly by design, and changes more rapidly over the course of a project than other systems of similar breadth and complexity. It's our responsibility as programmers to question the fitness of our solutions in addressing the problems at hand. In terms of decision making, I found myself regularly questioning the fitness of behavior trees while implementing behaviors that didn't have easily quantifiable static priority, or didn't intuitively distill down to simple yes/no criteria.

In a standard behavior tree, priority is static. It is baked right into the tree. The simplicity is welcome, but in practice it can be frustratingly limiting. The same behavior may require different relative priorities, depending on the context. Ensuring our Monster Hunter's primary weapon has a full clip should always be a consideration, even if we're casually patrolling the jungle. But if we're engaged with a savage monster, it's absolutely necessary that we continue to deal damage. Behavior tree authors often deal with this conundrum by duplicating sections of the tree at different branches, with different conditions and/or priorities. Even with slick sub-tree instancing or referencing, this still becomes inefficient, verbose, and potentially fragile.

Even more troublesome cases surface when a simple yes versus no determination isn't easily established. If our *Combat* selector is evaluating its options, should it choose to have us seek a rendezvous with our medic and his space-age healing tech, or should we put everything we have into quickly dropping the giant alien beast threatening to eat us all? This sort of decision is best made only after considering a potentially broad combination of inputs.

Decisions are rarely binary, and many behaviors simply do not have priorities we can comfortably establish offline. Let's start with a simple example behavior tree (Figure 7.1). Having no ability to shoot is a precondition for the *Seek Medic* behavior, forcing us to duplicate the behavior, as seen in Figure 7.2. We could start by giving *Seek Medic* stricter conditions and prioritizing it over *Shoot*, but this will likely create the opposite problem where the Monster Hunter immediately takes the *Seek Medic* action the instant conditions pass. This is the sort of fundamental problem we want to address with the integration of utility.

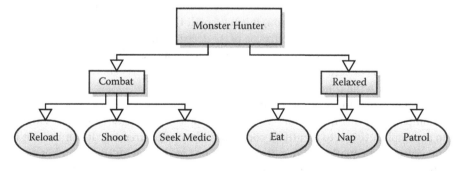

Figure 7.1

Here is a simple, minimal behavior tree for the Monster Hunter.

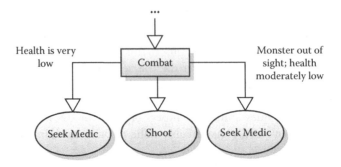

Figure 7.2

In order to implement *Seek Medic* with two different priorities depending on runtime conditions, we're limited to duplication within the tree.

7.4 What Is Utility Theory?

As it applies to game AI behavior, utility theory is simply the process of measuring the relative suitability of a particular action [Mark 09]. To make good decisions, we need to quantify how *worthwhile* an option is, given all the relevant facts, rather than make a determination on validity alone. Industry veterans who advocate the use of utility theory like to remind us that there is rarely just one correct decision to make. So the question is: why do we still favor decision-making architectures that fail to address this problem elegantly?

In reality, an agent of moderate complexity may have dozens of potential options on the table at once. There may even be several perfectly sensible options. Utility theory recognizes that decisions are seldom black and white, and attempts to formally address the complexities of combining various pieces of analog information together to make a final determination. Figuring out how to identify and compare the information in a logical manner is much of the challenge. The most important goal is to ensure that the overall computation is reliable given any combination of inputs, and always results in a reasonable choice.

7.5 Applying Utility in Decision Making

Game agents are *approximations* of autonomous entities within the limited scope of a game's specific design. For this reason, it's not worth the effort in most games to deeply analyze mountains of data for the purpose of AI decision making. Going too broad with the inputs effectively dilutes their meaning, resulting in muddy, or even illogical, formulas. All that should concern us is building an experience that feels believable and engaging to the player within the context of the game.

It's worth first making an effort to represent the input values in a manner that enables direct comparison. This helps avoid a confusing apples-to-oranges quagmire. One easy way to accomplish this is to identify a common unit of measurement. It can be a lot like solving a system of equations. We can substitute one variable with some combination of other, better understood variables. If we're combining two inputs, it makes sense to represent them both in terms of time, health, ammo, a rate of growth/consumption, or something even more abstract. For example, if our Monster Hunter is low on health and wishes to consider rendezvousing with the squad's medic for a health boost, we can measure the benefits of receiving treatment in health points gained. However, running frantically to a safe position is likely to gain the attention of the alien beast, putting us at a risk. If we can measure the risk by predicting the health we're likely to lose in transit, both inputs are now in terms of health points and can be combined and/or compared directly, as in Equation (7.1). We could simply take their sum, and if the net value is positive, taking this action has some benefit we can weigh against other actions.

$$RawUtility = HealthGained - HealthLost \qquad (7.1)$$

More desirably, by attaching more weight to the amount of health we'll lose in transit, we can ensure that we only take this action if we expect to net a significant amount of health, as seen in Equation (7.2). After all, breaking even would be a waste of the time we could've otherwise spent slaying the creature. We also want a high degree of confidence that, even if our predictions were overly optimistic, we're unlikely to end up with a net loss in health and looking rather boneheaded as a result. Naturally there's more we could do, such as apply an exponential scale to *HealthLost*, which causes the utility to fall off more rapidly as the risk grows, as in Equation (7.3).

$$Value = HealthGained - (HealthLost \times 2.0) \qquad (7.2)$$

$$Value = HealthGained - (pow(HealthLost, 1.2)) \qquad (7.3)$$

What happens if we're unable to represent our input values in such easily relatable units, and we wish to consider much more than just a net change in health? One way to combat this scenario is to combine the various influences into higher-level, more abstract values such as "Morale," "Threat," etc. The utility of running to visit our medic could also take into consideration the lost time we could've otherwise spent damaging the monster. Specifically, we could take our formula above, normalize the result, and classify it as a "Heal" factor. Next, we could generate a second formula representing this time lost, normalize it, and classify it as "Delay." We now have two normalized quantities representing higher-level valuations, which we can combine into a final utility value.

$$Utility = \frac{\left(Heal * HealPower - Delay * DelayPower \right)}{HealPower + DelayPower} \qquad (7.4)$$

I have glossed over the concept of normalization in our example above. However, in order to logically compare apples to oranges, the normalization process is fundamentally important, as it essentially "bakes" more complex underlying computations into a single usable value. Typically this involves running a raw value (health, time, ammunition, damage, etc.) through a normalization function to generate a real number from 0 and 1. Normalization functions are most commonly linear, exponential, or sigmoidal, but can be of any form. Response curves are an elegant solution in cases where a single formula is not sufficient for representing the desired normalization, allowing the curve to be broken up into segments that can be further fine-tuned [Mark 10]. The curve you choose can dramatically impact the result, and thus are often the target of on-the-fly tuning. For this reason, I'd recommend building these formulas into components you can represent as reloadable data that you and your designers can tweak. Normalization is a deep subject, and much wisdom can be discovered in available material. Papers available on GameAI.com, the GDC Vault, and the reading material referenced herein all provide excellent background on utility-based AI and behavioral modeling.

7.6 The Utility Selector

The behavior tree structure lends itself well to extensibility. After all, it's nothing more than a tree traversal where the nodes themselves are responsible for and are able to customize the expansion of the tree. The tree already features a component for selecting which branches are taken during execution, namely the *selector*. To introduce utility-based selection, we'll simply create a new specialized type of selector that considers not just the binary validity of its children, but their relative utility as well. We'll cleverly dub the new node type the *utility selector*.

For simplicity's sake, let's consider a vanilla behavior tree implementation. Each execution pass will traverse the tree until a busy node is encountered, at which point execution will yield until the next update. When a utility selector executes, it first queries each child sub-tree for a utility value. If we gather these results first, we can apply any one of several selection methods. For one, we could simply take the child with the highest utility. Alternatively, we could sort the children into buckets and conduct a weighted random selection. Depending on the scenario, we could even apply an unweighted random selection among the children with utility values over some threshold beyond which options are considered desirable. All we're essentially doing is adding utility-gathering to a standard selector, and using the data to determine priority dynamically. With minimal effort, we've busted wide open what is arguably the biggest drawback of behavior tree-based architectures—static priorities. In fact, we can address our problem with *Seek Medic* by switching *Combat* to a utility selector, as we've done in Figure 7.3.

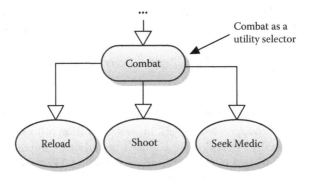

Figure 7.3

The *Shoot* vs. *Seek Medic* conundrum has been solved by converting *Combat* to a utility selector in the original tree.

7. Building Utility Decisions into Your Existing Behavior Tree

Listing 7.1. Pseudocode for a basic selector.

```
Status Execute()
{
    if(CurrChild == null) then CurrChild = FirstChild;
    //Execute all children until we encounter a valid one.
    while(CurrChild != null)
    {
        Status s = CurrChild.Execute();
        if(s == Busy || s == Done) return s;
        CurrChild = CurrChild.Next;
    }
    return Failed;
}
```

Listing 7.2. Pseudocode for a basic utility selector.

```
Status Execute()
{
    if(Utility.Size() == 0) then
    {
        //Query for child utility values.
        for(CurrChild = FirstChild; CurrChild != NULL; CurrChild =
CurrChild.Next)
        {
            Utility[CurrChild] = CurrChild.CalculateUtility();
        }
        //Sort from highest utility to lowest.
        SortChildrenByUtility();
        CurrChild = FirstChild;
    }
    //Evaluate in utility order and select the first valid child.
    while(CurrChild != null)
    {
        Status s = CurrChild.Execute();
        if(s == Busy) then return Busy;
        else if(s == Done) then
        {
            Utility.Clear();
            return Done;
        }
        CurrChild = CurrChild.Next;
    }
    Utility.Clear();
    return Failed;
}
```

7.7 Propagating Utility

The utility selector simply queries its children for their utility values. Typically only leaf behaviors will conduct utility calculations, but the utility selector's children may be of any node type, including composite nodes or even another utility selector. For utility information to intuitively propagate up the tree, we need to override `CalculateUtility()` for all composite node types.

For both selectors and sequencers, the simplest method is to return the highest utility value gathered from its own children. Consequently, in order to gather necessary utility data, a utility selector must expand all nodes in its child sub-trees, potentially conducting large quantities of utility calculations in a single pass. This may or may not be a problem depending on the scale you're working with, but with complex utility calculations in large behavior trees on platforms sensitive to random memory access patterns, it's certainly not ideal.

Thankfully, there are ways to mitigate this problem. For one, we could limit utility calculations to some interval within our leaf behaviors' implementations, and return cached values. Alternatively, we could compute utility values for all of our tree's leaf nodes within a completely separate pass, with its own load balancing, leaving only cached values to be used during calls to `CalculateUtility()`.

7.7.1. Transforming Utility During Propagation

For additional flexibility, nodes can choose to modify utility as it works its way up the tree. *Decorators* are a fundamental concept in behavior trees, referring to single-child nodes that can be used to introduce various useful behavior features. Some common examples include repeating the child node *n* times, monitoring a runtime condition, or limiting the child's execution time, but they're a general-purpose tool with infinite potential uses. In fact, there's nothing stopping us from creating a utility decorator that applies some transformation to the utility value of its child. Perhaps it could multiply its child's utility by some factor for weighting purposes, or it could run the value through a custom function.

To provide a simple example, let's say our *Reload* behavior is a black box that internally computes a normalized utility value. Under most circumstances, we may choose to compare *Reload*'s utility directly to that of its siblings. However, we may encounter a case in our game where we wish to limit *Reload*'s utility until we're desperate for ammunition. We can accomplish this goal by adding a utility decorator above *Reload* that runs the utility value through a simple `square()` or `cube()` function, as illustrated in Figures 7.4 and 7.5.

7.8 A Twist on Behavior Trees: Evaluation versus Execution

The behavior tree coupled with this chapter differs from some traditional implementations in that it separates the idea of tree evaluation from actual execution, which I've also done in the version I use for professional work. Doing so provides opportunity for a few improvements over a typical behavior tree implementation. One of those opportunities is to more optimally integrate utility-based decisions. Most notably, the utility selector is able to evaluate its children prior to calculating utility, meaning it must update utility only for valid children. This can be seen in the accompanying source code's `UtilitySelector` implementation. Furthermore, leaf nodes with costly utility calculations can do the work while verifying its conditions in `Evaluate()`, and return a cached value in `CalculateUtility()`.

7. Building Utility Decisions into Your Existing Behavior Tree

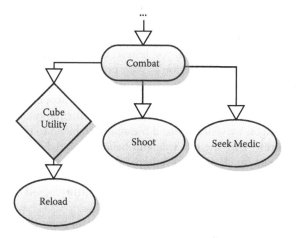

Figure 7.4

We've added a decorator to modify *Reload*'s standard utility value at execution time.

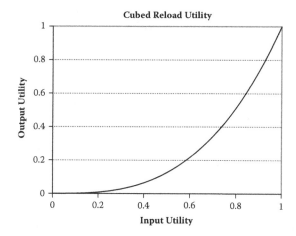

Figure 7.5

Reload's utility is now being cubed as it propagates up the tree, delaying the urgency to reload.

Another useful benefit is the ability to evaluate the tree independently of an agent's behavior execution. While an agent is actively executing behaviors, we can freely evaluate the tree in parallel without interfering with the executing nodes, and only interject if the results vary from the presently executing plan.

Evaluating the tree in its entirety also means we can optionally perform a limited version of look-ahead planning, since we can ensure that an entire plan is valid to the end, at least at the time of evaluation, before committing any of it to the agent. In cases where this is not desirable, nodes can still defer validation until they are executed, enabling them to behave as they would in a typical behavior tree flow.

7.9 Conclusion

Behavior trees and utility are both powerful concepts, made practical by their ease of implementation and experimentation. If you haven't done so already, I highly recommend tinkering with them as a potential solution in your professional endeavors. When combining utility behavior trees, these two otherwise disjoint techniques can help tackle the wide variety of behavioral problems found across genres and scopes.

We started with a straightforward behavior tree implementation, and without making any fundamental changes, we've introduced the ability to blend in utility-based decisions *only where desired*, preserving the tree's default behavior elsewhere. While the examples here are limited in scope for clarity, you've hopefully identified cases where this will help you solve real-world problems you've already encountered while applying behavior trees in practice. Beyond that, hopefully you can make use of utility-based decisions to improve your characters' behaviors further.

I am continuing to develop the coexistence of behavior trees and utility for my own needs in a very demanding commercial project, featuring dozens of unique NPC characters spanning a wide range of classifications. I wanted to share my discoveries thus far, as the results have been pleasantly surprising in practice. We've been able to represent characters ranging from simple wildlife to autonomous beasts with a vast repertoire of special abilities to soldiers with unique and obscure capabilities that must effectively emulate human players, all with the same behavioral foundation and toolset. For example, giant beasts can weigh different types of attacks against multiple targets dynamically, and human soldiers can evaluate and use their deep inventories to cooperatively take down targets, heal and revive teammates, and combine strategies. The integration of utility helped tremendously in mitigating complexity since characters can weigh multiple factors during decision making in a manner that's intuitive and "just makes sense." Rather than fight against the limitations of a single textbook architecture, a simple-to-implement hybrid has provided a great deal of power without sacrificing usability.

If you have questions, suggestions, or simply want to discuss something nerdy, don't hesitate to email bill.merrill at outlook.com.

References

[Brainiac 09] "Brainiac Designer." http://brainiac.codeplex.com/, 2009.

[Bungie 07] M. Dyckhoff. "Evolving Halo's Behavior Tree AI." http://www.bungie.net/images/Inside/publications/presentations/publicationsdes/engineering/gdc07.pdf, 2007.

[Champandard 08] A. Champandard. "Behavior Trees for Next-Gen Game AI." http://aigamedev.com/insider/article/behavior-trees/, 2008.

[Champandard 12] A. Champandard. "Behavior Tree Starter Kit." http://aigamedev.com/ultimate/release/behavior-tree-starter-kit-source-release/, 2012.

[Crytek 11] R. Pillosu. "Coordinating Agents with Behavior Trees." http://staff.science.uva.nl/~aldersho/GameProgramming/Papers/Coordinating_Agents_with_Behaviour_Trees.pdf, 2011.

[Mark 09] D. Mark. *Behavioral Mathematics for Game AI*. Boston, MA: Charles River Media, 2009.

[Mark 10] D. Mark and K. Dill. "Improving AI Decision Modeling Through Utility Theory." http://www.intrinsicalgorithm.com/media/2010GDC-DaveMark-KevinDill-Utility-Theory.pdf, 2010.

8
Reactivity and Deliberation in Decision-Making Systems

Carle Côté

8.1 Introduction

Designing decision-making systems for video games can be quite complex and is typically based on experience, intuition, and continuous refactoring. Over the years, successful games shipped using two main types of decision models: *graphical modeling language-based* decision models such as finite-state machines (FSMs), hierarchical finite-state machines (HFSMs), and behavior trees (BTs), and *symbolic planning language-based* decision models such as goal-oriented action planners (GOAP) and hierarchical task networks (HTNs). Unfortunately, little literature exists that explains how and when each approach should be used and for which family of architectural problems they are best suited.

This chapter will present a collection of considerations and thoughts about **Reactivity** and **Deliberation**, two key decision-making system mechanisms. *Reactivity* is about the ability of an agent to be responsive when stimuli are perceived in its environment, while *deliberation* is about the ability of an agent to make decisions and engage consequent actions. Typically, both are required to some extent in the design of every video game agent. By showing how to integrate these key concepts as core design principles, we'll explain how to avoid common pitfalls and create more scalable and flexible decision-making systems.

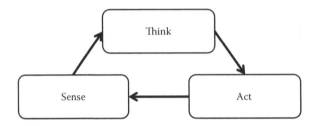

Figure 8.1

Sense-Think-Act paradigm.

8.2 Let's Begin at the Beginning

At its simplest expression, a typical decision-making system revolves around the Sense–Think–Act model, as shown in Figure 8.1. It describes that an agent needs to gather information from its environment (Sense), use the collected information in some decision process to decide what to do next (Think), engage new actions accordingly (Act), and repeat these steps over and over to create autonomy.

While this model shows a very intuitive relationship between an agent's "inner self" and its environment, it doesn't describe anything about the nature of the decision-making mechanisms involved in creating adapted behaviors. In fact, most games require at least two main decision-making mechanisms: reactivity and deliberation. The next sections describe in more detail what they are and their specific roles in a decision-making system.

8.2.1 What Is Reactivity?

Reactivity is the ability of an agent to be responsive to stimuli perceived in its environment. Most of the fun in video games comes from the fact that agents will react to the player's presence—either from direct perceptions (e.g., seeing the player) or indirect perceptions (e.g., hearing broken objects crashing on the ground). In order to be responsive, an agent must engage certain actions in a very short time, otherwise it would create behavioral artifacts that could be perceived by the player as either not believable or not challenging enough compared to their own abilities. These specific actions are called "reactions" and are, as we will see later, crucial when designing decision-making systems. Figure 8.2 illustrates a behavioral timeline with typical examples of reactions.

Reactions can be classified in two categories: *involuntary reactions* and *cognitive reactions*. Involuntary reactions refer to a body's uncontrolled reactions to some events

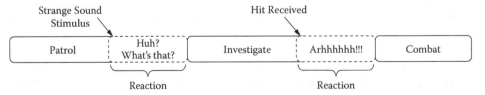

Figure 8.2

Behavioral timeline with reactions.

8. Reactivity and Deliberation in Decision-Making Systems

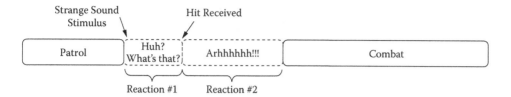

Figure 8.3

Behavioral timeline showing a reaction within a reaction pattern.

like pain, suffocation, or sneezing. Cognitive reactions are reactions that require a minimum of contextual interpretations to be triggered. For example, a loud sound will probably attract attention in a library but would probably be expected on a construction field.

According to our definition, a reaction can have a very short duration (e.g., split second necessary to reorient an agent toward the player) or it can last for a while (e.g., an agent in pain for 10 seconds). This means that during a reaction, other stimuli can be perceived which can potentially create other reactions as illustrated in the timeline in Figure 8.3.

8.2.2 What Is Deliberation?

Deliberation is the ability of an agent to take into consideration many elements of knowledge to decide what to do next. In video games, it's mostly what defines agent behavior in every situation, from high-paced action situations (e.g., combat) to more strategic situations (e.g., investigating an area). In fact, deliberation includes all the rational and irrational introspection mechanisms necessary to execute any tasks. For example, it includes information analysis process, intuition, past experiences, emotions, thinking process, random evaluation, logic, etc. In this article, we'll use the term "decision model" to refer to all these types of introspection mechanisms.

A decision model can take split second, seconds, minutes, days, or even years. For video games, most of the decisions are generally done in seconds or less.

8.3 Common Pitfall #1 : One Decision Model to Rule Them All!

A typical approach to support reactivity in decision-making systems is to use a decision model that can fulfill both reactivity and deliberation requirements. Although this approach seems tempting, it has many drawbacks that are discussed in the following sections.

8.3.1 Different by Nature

Based on reactivity and deliberation definitions, it is effectively possible to conclude that reactivity and deliberation can be merged together as long as the deliberation implementation allows for taking decisions and engaging actions in a very short time. However, this conclusion only considers the responsiveness aspect of the decision model itself; it doesn't consider what triggered the need for a decision and the dynamics of the engaged actions itself. So, let's analyze this a bit.

The first distinction about deliberation and reactivity is the difference between what triggers the need for new actions in both mechanisms. For reactivity, triggering reactions is caused by interruptions that have a higher priority than what is currently ongoing.

8.3 Common Pitfall #1 : One Decision Model to Rule Them All!

93

For deliberation, the need for a decision comes from two different sources: (1) the current deliberate action (or reaction) is completed and a new action must be engaged, and (2) the current context is changed in a way that it is invalidating or canceling the current action or plan of actions. While some deliberation decisions must be taken rapidly, others can take awhile without causing any problems. This means that deliberation isn't *only* about responsiveness. On the other hand, it is the *main* aspect of reactivity. In video games in general, deliberation tends to be fast because it isn't fun to see inactive agents in a thinking position for a long period of time before taking any action. It is mainly accepted that agents know instantly what to do and how to do it, without hesitation. Still, the very nature of what triggered the need for a decision in both cases is fundamentally different.

The second observation about reactivity and deliberation's nature is related to the nature of their respective undertaken actions. While it is accepted that an agent knows instantly what to do and how to do it, it is also expected that agents will engage in deliberate actions without changing their minds every second for unapparent reasons. Based on this, we can see a second important distinction between reactivity and deliberation: the goal of reactivity mechanisms is to create instantaneous changes in action to reflect body/environmental awareness, while the goal of deliberation mechanisms is to engage the best action possible that can be sustained for the longest time possible according to the context. While this difference seems pretty subtle, it has a big impact on the reactivity and deliberation decision models.

The example illustrated in Figure 8.4 represents a very simple FSM describing the deliberation decision models of an agent in a typical action game.

This FSM can evaluate and execute transitions instantly, that is, it can be used to support reactivity decision models. The states are describing very high-level behaviors like chasing a threat, patrolling the environment, engaging combat, and fleeing a threat. These behaviors can be decomposed in many sub-actions, but they aren't part of the deliberation

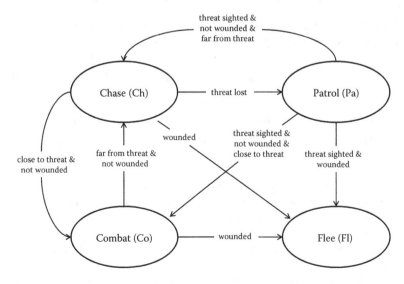

Figure 8.4

Example of a simple FSM describing the deliberation decision model of an agent.

8. Reactivity and Deliberation in Decision-Making Systems

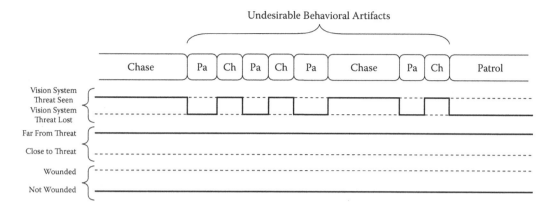

Figure 8.5

Behavioral timeline showing undesirable behavioral artifacts.

decision model expressed into that FSM. The transitions are described using symbols that are also representing high-level concepts such as seeing a threat, being wounded, or being close or far from a threat. It's important to note that no reactivity decision model is shown in this example.

To understand the proper dynamic of this FSM, we need to understand how the agent perceives and analyzes information from its sensors and what it means for this agent to be wounded. For this example, we'll focus on the perception system and presume that the transitions' *threat sight* symbol is directly hooked to the vision system. Figure 8.5 shows a timeline of a situation where the agent can momentarily lose sight of the threat during a chase because of objects preventing the agent to see the threat at all time.

By looking at the timeline, we can observe a lot of transitions in the behavior track. They represent the agent changing its stance from running at the threat to a slow-paced patrol stance multiple times within a couple of seconds because of the vision system losing direct line of sight with the threat. From the player's perspective, the behavior transitions would seem off, and they would most likely be judged as undesirable behavioral artifacts caused for no apparent reason. This is without mentioning that the animation system might not even be responsive enough to execute these fast stance transitions without creating animation popping artifacts. This is a good example to show where responsiveness isn't the only criterion that needs to be considered by deliberation decision models; sustaining actions for the proper amount of time is also crucial to delivering believable behaviors.

In this case, we can solve this issue by hooking the transition's *threat-sighted* symbol to a logical representation of seeing/losing a threat in a chase that would include some form of filtering (using hysteresis algorithms or other similar methods) to avoid creating undesirable oscillations. Figure 8.6 shows an ideal version of the timeline resulting from that logical representation.

8.3.2 Hard to Unify

Considering the different natures of the reactivity and deliberation mechanisms, trying to unify them is very challenging: reactivity is mostly about interruptions while deliberation

8.3 Common Pitfall #1 : One Decision Model to Rule Them All!

95

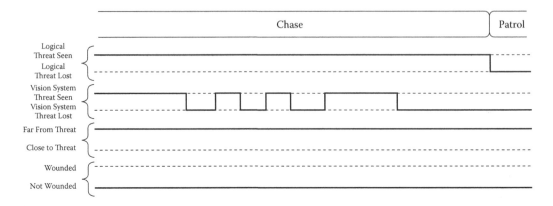

Figure 8.6

Behavior timeline showing the usage of a logical data representation to avoid behavioral artifacts.

is mostly about sustaining states. Any attempt to conciliate them using a unique model is trying to represent conceptual antipodes.

Figure 8.7 represents the same FSM example presented in Section 8.3.1 but including two reaction states: *Hurt* and *Suffocate*.

Because *Chase, Patrol, Combat,* and *Flee* are deliberation states that are designed to be active as long as possible, they are susceptible to be interrupted at any time. This explains why, in Figure 8.7, we can see that every deliberation state has transitions to every reaction state. Consequently, adding new reaction states to the model would require new transitions from all of the existing deliberation states. The same applies when adding new deliberation states to the model. With increased complexity, it's easy to see that the model will be hard to understand and maintain mostly because it tries to mix two very different kinds of transition dynamics within the same model. To solve this issue, it would be interesting to consider using multiple decision models that can interact together.

8.3.3 Using Multiple Decision Models

It is possible to avoid the limitation of using only one decision model. Figure 8.8 shows an architectural solution allowing multiple decision models. The design principle is pretty simple: create a module (Action Selector) responsible to act as a selector switch between Deliberation and Reactivity modules.

With this architectural solution, Deliberation and Reactivity modules can use their own decision models as long as they can both receive the same stimuli and output their respective set of actions. For example, the Deliberation module could use the FSM presented in Figure 8.4, while the Reactivity module could use a very simple set of rules or a decision tree to evaluate which reaction should be requested according to perceived stimuli. As for the implementation of the Action Selector itself, it can also be done with its own decision model as long as it's able to signal the Deliberation module when a new decision must be taken or to cancel the current deliberate action in order to execute a reaction. Figure 8.9 shows the resulting timeline.

8. Reactivity and Deliberation in Decision-Making Systems

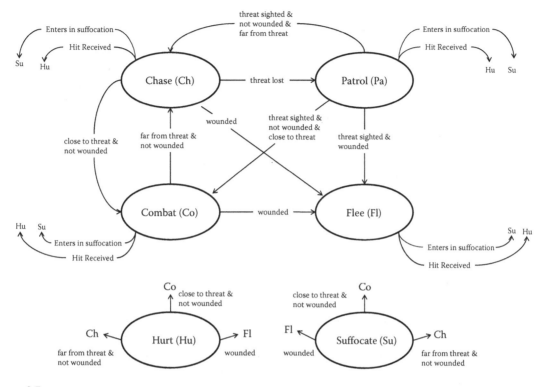

Figure 8.7

Example of an FSM including reaction states.

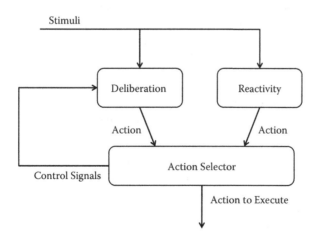

Figure 8.8

Using a selector switch between Deliberation and Reactivity modules.

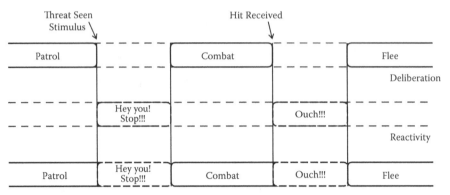

Figure 8.9

Behavioral timeline showing the results of the Action Selector.

8.4 Common Pitfall #2 : One Conceptual Model to Rule Them All!

Another common pitfall is that reactivity and deliberation mechanisms are implemented using the same conceptual model to describe how an agent must behave in every situation. A conceptual model comprises all of the required concepts' definitions and their static/dynamic relationships to create a decision-making system. In fact, when looking closely at each mechanism, we can see many important distinctions that are discussed in the following sections.

8.4.1 Awareness versus Procedural Knowledge

Reactivity is concerned with "danger awareness," whereas deliberation deals with procedural knowledge. Reactions play an important role in a decision-making system that is trying to mimic the physiology associated with the body's inner mechanisms towards self-protection. Two main categories of reaction are presented in Section 8.2.1: involuntary reactions and cognitive reactions. Involuntary reactions are typically created by the body to motivate the individual to withdraw from a dangerous situation. Cognitive reaction is the proactive counterpart where an individual will react preemptively before something can threaten its physical integrity.

By looking closely at these physiological phenomena, we can extract interesting design requirements:

- *Involuntary reactions have a higher priority level than cognitive reactions.* Reactions due to taking physical damages like pain, suffocation, or burning have precedence over any preemptive reactions.
- *Simultaneous involuntary reactions can be combined.* Different physical damages can be received at the same time resulting in simultaneous involuntary reactions. For example, an individual suffocating can simultaneously be hurt by a ranged weapon.
- *Some involuntary reactions have higher priority than others.* Some critical physical damages like being blown away by an explosion or being in heavy pain have precedence over less critical ones.

8. Reactivity and Deliberation in Decision-Making Systems

- *Cognitive reactions depend on the level of danger awareness.* Depending on whether an individual expects danger or not, it might or might not be reacting to some stimuli. For example, hearing a loud broken object sound in the middle of a brawl won't surprise anyone, while it might create a huge surprise reaction in a quiet classroom.

Deliberation isn't tied the same way to the notion of danger awareness. In fact, deliberation is taking this danger awareness notion into account along with many other notions to execute tasks that are important but not necessarily endangering an agent. This means that deliberation's main focus is knowledge and, more precisely, procedural knowledge. Procedural knowledge is the knowledge required to perform any task. When programming an agent to do tasks in its environment, a programmer is actually encoding all of its required procedural knowledge using various decision mechanisms. Depending on what the agent is trying to achieve, different conceptual models can be used. For example, an agent will not use the same decision rules when he's involved in a close-combat situation as when he's involved in a ranged-combat situation. Typically, both situations use different concepts to represent what's important in the environment and the best strategies to use.

8.4.2 Using Multiple Conceptual Models

Using different conceptual models generally allows breaking the complexity in simpler models. This means that, by using the right level of abstraction, it should be easier to write simpler rules and less complex code to maintain. The Action Selector presented in Section 8.3.3 is a good example of this approach. In addition to allowing Reactivity and Deliberation modules to use their own decision models, it also allows them to use their own conceptual models independently. Using the Action Selector as a sequencer between Reactivity and Deliberation modules also simplified the Reactivity module implementation by removing most of the dependencies on Deliberation's conceptual model to select which deliberate action should follow every reaction (as illustrated in Figure 8.7).

The same reasoning applies to the implementation of the Action Selector. It can be implemented with a few simple rules because it uses the right level of abstraction. In this case, the Action Selector only needs to share a minimum set of concepts with the Reactivity and Deliberation modules, that is, knowing if a specific action is a reaction or deliberate action. Figure 8.10 shows the expected timeline from the Action Selector according to its conceptual model.

8.4.3 Separating Decision from Execution

As described in Section 8.4.2, procedural knowledge is a key concept when programming an agent to perform some tasks (or actions). In fact, procedural knowledge generally describes two aspects of what is required to perform a task: the decision model to execute the task (e.g., sequence of actions, various options, how to manage events, etc.) and the decision

Figure 8.10

Action Selector's timeline.

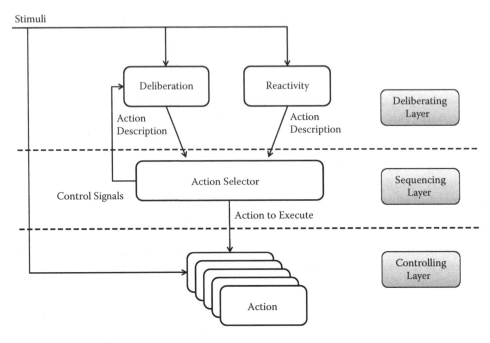

Figure 8.11

An example of a three-layer architecture.

model to manage the task (e.g., starting conditions, canceling conditions, completing conditions, etc). Splitting these decision models can be very useful to reduce the complexity.

In the FSM in Figure 8.4, each state describes a task that an agent should perform if the conditions are met. In fact, it doesn't describe what the agent will do precisely during the execution of this task; it only describes the decision model to manage the task. This means that details of the execution model can somehow be abstracted from the decision model itself without impacting the deliberation mechanisms. This idea has been used many times to create what is called "hybrid architecture" [Murphy 01]. Figure 8.11 illustrates an example of hybrid architecture based on the example presented in Section 8.3.3.

There are only three differences with the example presented in Section 8.3.3. The first one is that the Deliberating Layer explicitly uses decision models to manage actions, instead of the action itself. The second difference is that the role of the Action Selector must not only sequence actions but must also select which actions to execute from the Controlling Layer's action pool. The last difference is the addition of the Controlling Layer, which contains a pool of actions containing the necessary implementations to be executed. Each of these actions can use different decision models and/or conceptual models. They must also be designed to be reactive if required by their respective execution model.

This kind of architecture can be very powerful to use as it offers many ways to break the complexity of a big decision-making system into simpler modules. For example, it can be really easy to change a specific algorithm used to implement an action without impacting other actions or any component from the other layers. Adding a new concept into the conceptual model of an existing action to enhance its implementation could also represent a very isolated modification to the system.

8.5 Conclusion

This article presented deliberation and reactivity mechanisms as two primary elements to consider when designing decision-making systems. And by understanding their fundamental distinctions, it was discussed that it can be possible to reduce inherent complexity of decision-making systems. Consequently, choosing when to use an FSM, a BT, a Planner, or any other decision models can be a lot easier and based on more solid grounds than pure empirical methods.

Reference

[Murphy 01] R. R. Murphy, *Introduction to AI Robotics*. MIT Press, Cambridge, MA, 2001, pp. 257–274.

9
Exploring HTN Planners through Example

Troy Humphreys

9.1 Introduction

As programmers we may find ourselves perpetually looking for that "better solution" to whatever problems we've encountered—better performance, maintainability, or usability. It's only after we implement those solutions that we understand some of the nuances that come with them. Often, these nuances might be the deciding factor in what solution we go with.

In AI development, a common problem to solve is behavior selection. There are many solutions to this problem, such as finite-state machines, behavior trees, utility-based selection, neural networks, and planners. This article aims to explore the nuances of a type of planner called *hierarchical task networks* (HTN) by using real world examples that one can run into during development.

Planning architectures such as HTN take a problem as input and supply a series of steps that solves it. In HTN terms, the series of steps is called a *plan*. What makes hierarchical task networks unique to other planners is that it allows us to represent the problem as a very high level task, and through its planning process, recursively breaks this task into smaller tasks. When this process is completed, we are left with a series of atomic tasks that represent a plan. Breaking up high level tasks into smaller ones is a very natural way of solving many sorts of problems. In our case, the problem is simply "figuring out what to do." With a high degree of modularity and fast run time execution, HTNs make an attractive choice as a solution. For those of you that are familiar with behavior trees, these benefits might also seem familiar. Unlike behavior trees, however, HTN planners can reason about the *effects* of possible actions. This ability to reason about the future allows HTN planners to be incredibly expressive in how they describe behavior.

There have been many different systems used for HTN planning [Erol 95]. The system we will be exploring is the system that we used on *Transformers: Fall of Cybertron* [HighMoon 12], which is based on a *total-order forward decomposition* planner. The following example will walk through some of the challenges we faced and the benefits we received during development by using a simplified, fictional example.

For our example, we will use a troll NPC called a "Trunk Thumper." The designer's initial description is that he's a big, nasty, lumbering troll that patrols its numerous bridges and attacks passing enemies with a large tree trunk. And just like development in the real world, this design is bound to change.

9.2 Building Blocks of HTN

Before building the behavior for our Trunk Thumper, it's important to go over the basic building blocks of hierarchical task networks so you can get an idea of how it all works. An NPC, in our case the Trunk Thumper, has a *planner* that uses a *domain* and *world state* to build a sequence of tasks called a *plan*. This plan will be run by the Trunk Thumper's *plan runner*. The world state is updated by the NPC's sensors and by the successfully completed tasks executed by the plan runner. A diagram of the system is Figure 9.1.

9.2.1 The World State

Like any type of behavior algorithm, hierarchical task networks need some type of knowledge representation that describes the current problem space. In the case of our Trunk Thumper, this would be a representation that describes what our troll knows about the world and himself in it. Other types of behavior algorithms might query the actual state of different objects in the world. For example, query an object's location or their health. But with HTN, this information needs to be encoded into something it can understand, called the *world state*. The world state is essentially a vector of properties that describe what our HTN is going to reason about. Here is some simple pseudocode.

```
enum EHtnWorldStateProperties
{
    WsEnemyRange,
    WsHealth,
    WsIsTired,
    …
}
```

```
enum EEnemyRange
{
    MeleeRange,
    ViewRange,
    OutOfRange,
    …
}
vector<byte> CurrentWorldState;
EEnemyRange currentRange = CurrentWorldState[WsEnemyRange];
CurrentWorldState[WsEnemyRange] = MeleeRange;
```

As you can see from the pseudocode, world state can simply be an array or vector indexed by an enum such as `EhtnWorldStateProperties`. Each entry in the world state can have its own set of values. In the case of `WsIsTired`, the byte can represent the Boolean values zero and one. With `WsEnemyRange`, the values in the enum `EEnemyRange` are used. It's important to note that the world state only needs to represent what is needed for the HTN to make decisions. That's why `WsEnemyRange` is represented by abstract values, instead of the actual range. The goal of the world state isn't to represent every possible state of every possible object in the game. It only needs to represent the problem space that our planner needs to make decisions. What this means for our example, of course, is that it only needs to represent what the Trunk Thumper needs to make decisions.

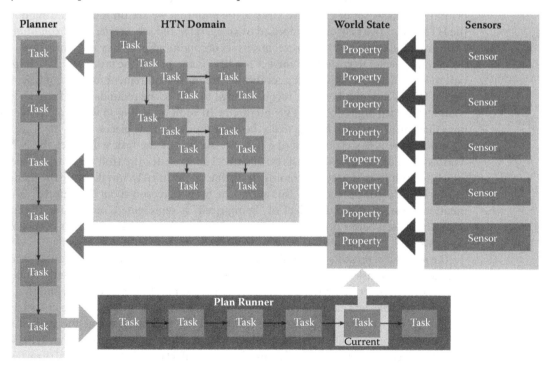

Figure 9.1

Overview of the HTN system.

9.2.2 Sensors

If you recall, an HTN outputs a plan or sequence of tasks. These tasks will have an effect on the world state as it is executed. There are outside influences such as the player or other NPCs, however, that will affect the world state as well. For example, both the enemy and the troll can affect the world state property, WsEnemyRange. The tasks executed by the troll could update this property if they were to move the troll. There is nothing in the HTN planner to handle changes produced by the enemy moving, however.

There are many different ways these changes can be translated into the world state. One preferable way is a simple sensor system that manages a set of time-sliced sensors. Each sensor can manage different world state properties. Examples of some different sensors include vision, hearing, range, and health sensors. These sensors would work the same as in any other AI system, with an added step of encoding their information into the world state that our HTN can understand.

9.2.3 Primitive Tasks

As we mentioned already, a hierarchical task network is made up of tasks. There are two types of tasks that are used to build a HTN, called *compound tasks* and *primitive tasks*. Primitive tasks represent a single step that can be performed by our NPC. In our Trunk Thumper example, uprooting a tree or attacking with a trunk slam would be examples of primitive tasks. A set of primitive tasks is the *plan* that we are ultimately getting out of the HTN. Primitive tasks are comprised of an *operator* and sets of *effects* and *conditions*.

In order for a primitive task to execute, its set of conditions must be valid. This allows the task's implementer to ensure the correct conditions are met for the task to run. It's important to note that a primitive task's conditions are not a requirement for the implementation of HTN. They are, however, recommended to reduce the redundancy of checks that would be needed higher in the HTN hierarchy. In addition, doing so will avoid potential bugs that can arrive from having to do these checks in multiple places.

A primitive task's effects describe how the success of the task will affect the NPC's world state. For example, the task DoTrunkSlam executes the troll's tree trunk melee attack and results in the troll becoming tired. The DoTrunkSlam's *effects* are the manner in which we describe this result. This allows the HTN to reason about the "future" as was mentioned earlier. Since the effect of "being tired" is represented, our Trunk Thumper is able to make a better decision of what to do after DoTrunkSlam or if it's even worth doing so at all.

The *operator* represents an atomic action that a NPC can do. This might sound exactly like the primitive task itself. The difference being that the primitive task along with its effects and conditions describe what the operator means in terms of the HTN we are building.

As an example, let's take the two tasks SprintToEnemy and WalkToNextBridge. Both of these tasks use the MoveTo operator, but the two tasks change the state of our NPC in different ways. On the successful completion of SprintToEnemy, our NPC will be at the enemy and tired, specified by the task's effects. WalkToNextBridge task's effects would set the NPC's location to the bridge and he'd be a little more bored. As you can see, we are able to use the same *operator* but describe two different uses for it in terms of our network. Here is the notation we will use to describe a primitive task going forward along with the SprintToEnemy and WalkToNextBridge tasks as an example.

Primitive Task [*TaskName(term1, term2,...)*]
 Preconditions [*Condition1, Condition2, ...*]//optional
 Operator [*OperatorName(term1, term2,...)*]
  Effects [*WorldState op value, WorldState = value, WorldState += value*]//optional
Primitive Task [SprintToEnemy]
 Preconditions [WsHasEnemy == true]
 Operator [NavigateTo(EnemyLoc, Speed_Fast)]
  Effects [WsLocation = EnemyLoc, WsIsTired = true]
Primitive Task [WalkToNextBridge]
 Operator [NavigateTo(BridgeLoc, Speed_Slow)]
  Effects [WsLocation = BridgeLoc, WsBored += 1]

9.2.4 Compound Tasks

Compound tasks are where HTN get their "hierarchical" nature. You can think of compound task as a high level task that has multiple ways of being accomplished. Using the Trunk Thumper as an example, he may have the task AttackEnemy. Our Thumper may have different ways of accomplishing this task. If he has access to a tree trunk, he may run to his target and use it as a melee weapon to "thump" his enemy. If no tree trunks are available, he can pull large boulders from the ground and toss them at our enemy. He may have a multitude of other approaches if the conditions are right.

In order to determine which approach we take to accomplish a compound task, we need to select the right *method*. Methods are comprised of a set of conditions and tasks. In order for the method to be the selected approach, the conditions are validated against the world state. The set of tasks, or *subtasks*, represent the method's approach. This subtask set can be comprised of primitive tasks as well as compound. The ability to put compound tasks into the methods of other compound tasks is where hierarchical task networks get their hierarchical nature. Here is an example of the notation we will use to describe a compound task going forward.

Compound Task [*TaskName(term1, term2,...)*]
 Method 0 [*Condition1, Condition2,...*]
  Subtasks [*task1(term1, term2,...). task2(term1, term2,...),...*]
 Method 1 [*Condition1, Condition2,...*]
  Subtasks [*task1(term1, term2,...). task2(term1, term2,...),...*]

In our previous example, using the tree trunk as a melee weapon and throwing boulders are both methods to the AttackEnemy compound task. The conditions in which we decide which method to use depend on whether the troll has a tree trunk or not. Here is an example of the AttackEnemy task using the notation above.

Compound Task [AttackEnemy]
 Method 0 [WsHasTreeTrunk == true]
  Subtasks [NavigateTo(EnemyLoc). DoTrunkSlam()]
 Method 1 [WsHasTreeTrunk == false]
  Subtasks [LiftBoulderFromGround(). ThrowBoulderAt(EnemyLoc)]

By understanding how compound tasks work, it's easy to imagine how we could have a large hierarchy that may start with a `BeTrunkThumper` compound task that is broken down into sets of smaller tasks—each of which are then broken into smaller tasks, and so on. This is how HTN forms a hierarchy that describes how our troll NPC is going to behave.

It's important to understand that compound tasks are really just containers for a set of methods that represent different ways to accomplish some high level task. There is no compound task code running during plan execution.

9.3 Putting Together an HTN Domain

Now that we have an overview of the main building blocks of HTN, we can build a simple *domain* for our Trunk Thumper to illustrate how it works. A *domain* is the term used to describe the entire task hierarchy. As we mentioned before, our troll has numerous bridges that he actively patrols and attacks enemies with a large tree trunk. We start with a compound task called `BeTrunkThumper`. This root task encapsulates the "main idea" of what it means to be a Trunk Thumper.

```
Compound Task [BeTrunkThumper]
    Method [WsCanSeeEnemy == true]
        Subtasks [NavigateToEnemy(), DoTrunkSlam()]
    Method [true]
        Subtasks [ChooseBridgeToCheck(), NavigateToBridge(), CheckBridge()]
```

As you can see with this root compound task, the first method defines the troll's highest priority. If he can see the enemy, he will navigate using `NavigateToEnemy` task and attack his enemy with the `DoTrunkSlam` task. If not, he will fall to the next method. This next method will run three tasks; choose the next bridge to check, navigate to that bridge, and check the bridge for enemies. Let's take a look at the primitive tasks that make up these methods and the rest of the domain.

```
Primitive Task [DoTrunkSlam]
    Operator [AnimatedAttackOperator(TrunkSlamAnimName)]
Primitive Task [NavigateToEnemy]
    Operator [NavigateToOperator(EnemyLocRef)]
        Effects [WsLocation = EnemyLocRef]
Primitive Task [ChooseBridgeToCheck]
    Operator [ChooseBridgeToCheckOperator]
Primitive Task [NavigateToBridge]
    Operator [NavigateToOperator(NextBridgeLocRef)]
        Effects [WsLocation = NextBridgeLocRef]
Primitive Task [CheckBridge]
    Operator [CheckBridgeOperator(SearchAnimName)]
```

The first task `DoTrunkSlam` is an example of how a primitive task can describe an operator in terms of the HTN domain. Here, the task is really executing an animated attack operator and the animation name is being passed in as a term. The next task

NavigateToEnemy is also an example of this, but on the successful completion of this task, the world state WsLocation is set to EnemyLocRef via the primitive task's effect.

9.4 Finding a Plan

With a domain made up of compound and primitive tasks, we are starting to form an image of how these are put together to represent an NPC. Combine that with the world state and we can talk about the work horse of our HTN, the *planner*. There are three conditions that will force the planner to find a new plan: the NPC finishes or fails the current plan, the NPC does not have a plan, or the NPC's world state changes via a sensor. If any of these cases occur, the planner will attempt to generate a plan. To do this, the planner starts with a root compound task that represents the problem domain in which we are trying to plan for. Using our earlier example, this root task would be the BeTrunkThumper task. This root task is pushed onto the TasksToProcess stack. Next, the planner creates a copy of the world state. The planner will be modifying this *working world state* to "simulate" what will happen as tasks are executed.

After these initialization steps are taken, the planner begins to iterate on the tasks to process. On each iteration, the planner pops the next task off the TasksToProcess stack. If it is a compound task, the planner tries to decompose it—first, by searching through its methods looking for the first set of conditions that are valid. If a method is found, that method's subtasks are added on to the TaskToProcess stack. If a valid method is not found, the planner's state is rolled back to the last compound task that was decomposed. We will go into more detail about restoring the planner's state later.

If the next task is primitive, we need to check its preconditions against the working world state. If the conditions are met, the task is added to the final plan and its effects are applied to the working world state. The effects are applied because the planner assumes that task is going to succeed. This allows future methods to consider that new state. If the primitive task's conditions are not met, the planner's state is rolled back such as was done for the compound task. This iteration process is continued until the TasksToProcess stack is empty. Upon completion, the planner will either end up with a list of primitive tasks or the planner will have rolled back far enough that the result was no plan. Below is the example pseudocode that shows this process.

```
WorkingWS = CurrentWorldState
TasksToProcess.Push(RootTask)
while TasksToProcess.NotEmpty
{
    CurrentTask = TasksToProcess.Pop()
    if CurrentTask.Type == CompoundTask
    {
        SatisfiedMethod = CurrentTask.FindSatisfiedMethod(WorkingWS)
        if SatisfiedMethod != null
        {
            RecordDecompositionOfTask(CurrentTask, FinalPlan, DecompHistory)
            TasksToProcess.InsertTop(SatisfiedMethod.SubTasks)
        }
        else
        {
            RestoreToLastDecomposedTask()
        }
    }
```

```
    else//Primitive Task
    {
        if PrimitiveConditionMet(CurrentTask)
        {
            WorkingWS.ApplyEffects(CurrentTask.Effects)
            FinalPlan.PushBack(CurrentTask)
        }
        else
        {
            RestoreToLastDecomposedTask()
        }
    }
}
```

There is a bit of magic going on in the RecordDepositionOfTask and RestoreTo-LastDecomposedTask functions that should be explained in more detail. The record function records the planner's state onto the DecompHistory stack. This includes the TasksToProcess and FinalPlan containers as well as the method chosen for the decomposition and its owning compound task. By popping off this recorded state to the planner via the restore function, the planner can backtrack either when a compound task cannot be decomposed or when a primitive's conditions aren't satisfied.

As you might have realized, the planner uses a depth-first search to find a valid plan. This does mean that you may have to explore the whole domain to find a valid plan. However, it's important to remember that you are traversing a *hierarchy* of tasks. This hierarchy allows the planner to cull large sections of the network via the compound task's methods. Because we aren't using a heuristic or cost—such as with A* and Dijkstra searches—we can skip any kind of sorting. These features allowed the HTN planner in *Transformers: Fall of Cybertron* to be considerably faster than our GOAP system used in *Transformers: War for Cybertron* [HighMoon 10].

Now that the planner has been explained, we can expand our example and see how a modified version of the Trunk Thumper domain might decompose (Figure 9.2). This domain's root task is still BeTrunkThumper, but the DoTrunkSlam is now a compound task. DoTrunkSlam has two methods—each doing a different version of the trunk slam. The method's conditions for both compound tasks have been omitted for simplicity. Underneath the domain you can see the planner's iterations going from top to the bottom. For each iteration, you can see the left-most task in the TasksToProcess stack being processed.

9.5 Running the Plan

Running an HTN plan is pretty straightforward. The NPC's *plan runner* will attempt to execute each primitive task's operator in sequence. As it successfully completes each task, the planner applies the task's effects to the world state. If the task fails for some reason that is specific to the operator it's running, the plan also fails and forces a re-plan.

The plan can also fail if the current or any of the remaining task's conditions become invalid. The plan runner monitors these tasks' preconditions against a "working world state" much like the planner. As it confirms each task's preconditions, its effects are applied

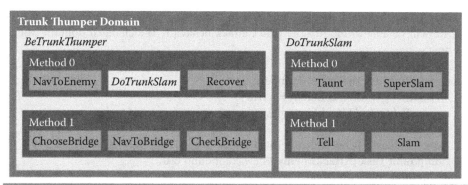

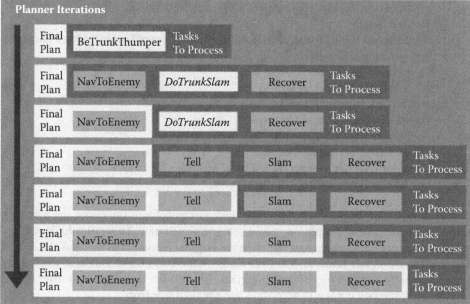

Figure 9.2

Decomposition of the Trunk Thumper domain, showing the resulting plan if BeTrunkThumper. Method0 and DoTrunkSlam.Method.1 were chosen.

to the working world state. It's important that it applies the effects because following task's preconditions might rely on these effects being applied in order to be valid. This plan validation allows the HTN domain to be a bit more expressive and reactive to the changes of the world state.

9.6 Using Recursion for Greater Expressiveness

After seeing our troll in game, the designers think that the tree trunk attack is a little overpowered. They suggest that the trunk breaks after three attacks, forcing the troll to search for another one. First we can add the property WsTrunkHealth to the world state.

By wrapping up the attack method into its own compound task and adding a little recursion, we will be able to modify the troll's attack behavior. The changed domain would now be:

Compound Task [BeTrunkThumper]
    Method [WsCanSeeEnemy == true]
        Subtasks [AttackEnemy()]// *using the new compound task*
    Method [true]
        Subtasks [ChooseBridgeToCheck(), NavigateToBridge(), CheckBridge()]
Compound Task [AttackEnemy]//new compound task
    Method [WsTrunkHealth > 0]
        Subtasks [NavigateToEnemy(), DoTrunkSlam()]
    Method [true]
        Subtasks [FindTrunk(), NavigateToTrunk(), UprootTrunk(), AttackEnemy()]
Primitive Task [DoTrunkSlam]
    Operator [DoTrunkSlamOperator]
        Effects [WsTrunkHealth += -1]
Primitive Task [UprootTrunk]
    Operator [UprootTrunkOperator]
        Effects [WsTrunkHealth = 3]
Primitive Task [NavigateToTrunk]
    Operator [NavigateToOperator(FoundTrunk)]
        Effects [WsLocation = FoundTrunk]

When our troll can see the enemy, he will attack just as before—only now, the behavior is wrapped up in a new compound task called AttackEnemy. This task's high priority method performs the navigate and slam like the original domain, but now has the condition that the trunk has some health. The change to the DoTrunkSlam task will decrement the trunk's health every successful attack. This allows the planner to drop to the lower priority method if it has to accommodate a broken tree trunk.

The second method of AttackEnemy handles getting a new tree trunk. It first chooses a new tree to use, navigates to that tree, and uproots it, after which it is able to AttackEnemy. Here is where the recursion comes in. When the planner goes to decompose the AttackEnemy task again it can now consider the methods again. If the tree trunk's health was still zero, this would cause the planner to infinite loop. But the new task UprootTrunk's effect sets WsTrunkHealth back to three, allowing us to have the plan FindTrunk → NavigateToTrunk → UprootTrunk → NavigateToEnemy → DoTrunkSlam. This new domain allows us to reuse methods already in the domain to get the troll back to thumping.

9.7 Planning for World State Changes not Controlled by Tasks

So far all of the plans we have been building depend on the primitive task's effects changing the world state. What happens when the world state is changed *outside* the control of primitive tasks, however? To explore this, let's modify our example once again. Let us assume that a designer notices that when the troll can't see the enemy, he simply goes back to patrolling the bridges. The designer asks you to implement a behavior that will chase after the enemy and react once he sees the enemy again. Let's look at the changes we could make to the domain to handle this issue.

> Compound Task [BeTrunkThumper]
>   Method [WsCanSeeEnemy == true]
>   Subtasks [AttackEnemy()]
>   **Method [WsHasSeenEnemyRecently == true]//New method**
>   Subtasks [NavToLastEnemyLoc(), RegainLOSRoar()]
>   Method [true]
>   Subtasks [ChooseBridgeToCheck(), NavigateToBridge(), CheckBridge()]
> **Primitive Task [NavToLastEnemyLoc]**
>   **Operator [NavigateToOperator(LastEnemyLocation)]**
>   **Effects [WsLocation = LastEnemyLocation]**
> **Primitive Task [RegainLOSRoar]**
>   **Preconditions[WsCanSeeEnemy == true]**
>   **Operator [RegainLOSRoar()]**

With this rework, if the Trunk Thumper can't see the enemy, the planner will drop down to the new method that relies on WsHasSeenEnemyRecently world state property. This method's tasks will navigate to the last place the enemy was seen and do a big animated "roar" if he once again sees the enemy. The problem here is that the RegainLOSRoar task has a precondition of WsCanSeeEnemy being true. That world state is handled by the troll's vision sensor. When the planner goes to put the RegainLOSRoar task on the final task list it will fail its precondition check, because there is nothing in the domain that represents what the expected world state will be when the navigation completes.

To solve this, we are going to introduce the concept of *expected effects*. Expected effects are effects that get applied to the world state only during planning and plan validation. The idea here is that you can express changes in the world state that *should* happen based on tasks being executed. This allows the planner to keep planning farther into the future based on what it believes will be accomplished along the way. Remember that a key advantage planners have at decision making is that they can reason about the future, helping them make better decisions on what to do next. To accommodate this, we can change NavToLastEnemyLoc in the domain to:

> Primitive Task [NavToLastEnemyLoc]
>   Operator [NavigateToOperator(LastEnemyLocation)]
>   Effects [WsLocation = LastEnemyLocation]
>   **ExpectedEffects [WsCanSeeEnemy = true]**

Now when this task gets popped off the decomposition list, the working world state will get updated with the expected effect and the RegainLOSRoar task will be allowed to proceed with adding tasks to the chain. This simple behavior could have been implemented a couple of different ways, but expected effects came in handy more than a few times during the development of *Transformers: Fall of Cybertron*. They are a simple way to be just a little more expressive in a HTN domain.

9.8 How to Handle Higher Priority Plans

To this point, we have been decomposing compound tasks based on the order of the task's methods. This tends to be a natural way of going about our search, but consider these attack changes to our Trunk Thumper domain.

```
Compound Task [AttackEnemy]
    Method [WsTrunkHealth > 0, AttackedRecently == false,
CanNavigateToEnemy == true]
        Subtasks [NavigateToEnemy(), DoTrunkSlam(), RecoveryRoar()]
    Method [WsTrunkHealth == 0]
        Subtasks [FindTrunk(), NavigateToTrunk(), UprootTrunk(), AttackEnemy()]
    Method [true]
        Subtasks [PickupBoulder(), ThrowBoulder()]
Primitive Task [DoTrunkSlam]
    Operator [DoTrunkSlamOperator]
        Effects [WsTrunkHealth += -1, AttackedRecently = true]
Primitive Task [RecoveryRoar]
    Operator [PlayAnimation(TrunkSlamRecoverAnim)]
Primitive Task [PickupBoulder]
    Operator [PickupBoulder()]
Primitive Task [ThrowBoulder]
    Operator [ThrowBoulder()]
```

After some play testing, our designer commented that our troll is pretty punishing. It only lets up on its attack against the player when it goes to grab another tree trunk. The designer suggests putting in a recovery animation after the trunk slam and a new condition not allowing the slam attack if the troll has attacked recently. Our designer has also noticed that our troll behaves strangely if he could not navigate to his enemy (due to an obstacle, for example). He decided to put in a low priority attack to throw a boulder if this happened.

Everything about these behavior changes seems fairly straightforward, but we need to take a closer look at what could happen while running the trunk slam plan. After the actual slam action, we start running the `RecoveryRoar` task. If, while executing this roar, the world state were to change and cause a re-plan, the `RecoveryRoar` task will be aborted. The reason for this is that, when the planner gets to the method that handles the slam, the `AttackedRecently` world state will be set to true because the `DoTrunkSlam` completed successfully. This will cause the planner to skip the "slam" method tasks and fall through to the new "throw boulder" method, resulting in a new plan. This will cause the `RecoveryRoar` task to be aborted mid-execution, even though the currently running plan is still valid.

In this case, we need a way to identify the "priority" of a running plan. There are a couple ways of solving this. Since HTN is a graph, we can use some form of a cost-based search such as A* or Dijkstra, for example. This would involve binding some sort of cost to our tasks or even methods. Unfortunately, tuning these costs can be pretty tricky in practice. Not only that, we would now have to add sorting to our planner, which will slow its execution.

Instead we would like to keep the simplicity and readability of "in-order priority" for our methods. The problem is a plan does not know the decomposition order of compound tasks that the planner took to arrive at the plan—it just executes primitive tasks' operators.

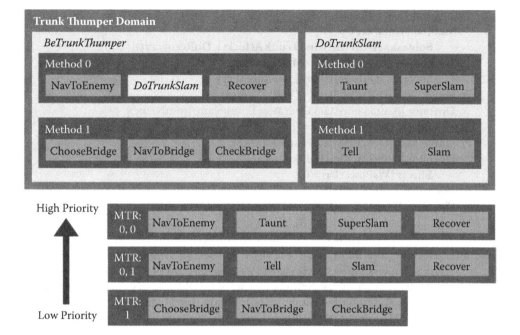

Figure 9.3

All possible plans with the Trunk Thumper domain and the Method Traversal Record for each plan, sorted by priority.

The order of a compound task's methods are what we want to use to define priority—yet the plan isn't aware of what a compound task is. To get around this, we can encode our traversal through the HTN domain as we search for a plan. This *method traversal record* (MTR) simply stores the method index chosen for each compound task that was decomposed to create the plan. Now that we have the MTR we can use it in two different ways to help us find the better plan. The simplest method would be to plan normally and compare the newly found plan's MTR with the currently running plan's MTR. If all of the method indexes chosen in the new plan are equal or higher priority, we found our new plan. An example is shown in Figure 9.3.

We can also choose to use the current plan's MTR during the planning process, as we decompose compound tasks in the new search. We can use the MTR as we search for a valid method only allowing methods that are equal to or higher priority. This allows us to cull whole branches of our HTN based on the current plan's MTR. Our first method is the easier of the two, but if you find you're spending a lot of your processing time in your planner, the second method could help speed that up.

Now that we have the ability to abort currently running plans for higher priority plans, there is a subtle implementation detail that can cause unexpected behaviors in your NPCs. If you set up your planner to re-plan on world state changes, the planner will try to re-plan when tasks apply their effects on successful execution. Consider this altered subsection of the Trunk Thumper's domain below.

Compound Task [AttackEnemy]
   Method [WsPowerUp = 3]
      Subtasks [DoWhirlwindTrunkAttack(), DoRecovery()]
   Method [WsEnemyRange > MeleeRange,]
      Subtasks [DoTrunkSlam(), **DoRecovery()**]
Primitive Task [DoTrunkSlam]
   Operator [AnimatedAttackOperator(TrunkSlamAnimName)]
      Effects [**WsPowerUp += 1**]
Primitive Task [DoWhirlwindTrunkAttack]
   Operator [DoWhirlwindTrunkAttack()]
      Effects [**WsPowerUp = 0**]
Primitive Task [DoRecover]
   Operator [PlayAnimation(TrunkSlamRecoveryAnim)]

This new behavior is designed to have the troll do the DoWhirlwindTrunkAttack task, after executing the DoTrunkSlam three times. This is accomplished by having the DoTrunkSlam task's effect increase the WsPowerUp property by one each time it executes. This might seem fine at first glance, but you will have designers at your desk informing you that the troll now combos a trunk slam directly into a whirlwind attack every time. The problem arises on the third execution of DoTrunkSlam. The task's effects are applied and the planner forces a re-plan. With WsPowerUp equal to three, the planner will pick the higher priority Whirlwind attack method. This cancels the DoRecovery task that is designed to break the attacks up, allowing the player some time to react.

Normally, the whirlwind method should be able to cancel plans of lower priority. But the currently running plan is still valid, and the only reason this bug is occurring is that the planner is replanning on all world state changes, including changes by successfully completed primitive task's effects. Simply not replanning when the world state changes via effects being applied from a primitive tasks will solve this problem—which is fine, because the plan was found with those world state changes in mind anyway. While this is a good change to make, it won't be the full solution. Any world state changes *outside* of the tasks the plan runner is executing will force a replan and cause the bug to resurface.

The real problem here is the domain and how it's currently setup. There are a couple of different ways we can solve this, and it really matters how you view it. One could say that the recovery animation is part of the attack, so it might be worth incorporating that animation into the attack animation. That way the recovery *always* plays after the slam attack. This hurts the modularity of the domain. What if the designers want to chain three slams then do a recovery?

A better way would be to use world state to describe the reason that DoRecovery is needed. Consider the change below:

Compound Task [AttackEnemy]
   Method [WsPowerUp = 3]
      Subtasks [DoWhirlwindTrunkAttack(), DoRecovery()]
   Method [WsEnemyRange > MeleeRange,]
      Subtasks [DoTrunkSlam(), DoRecovery()]

Primitive Task [DoTrunkSlam]
    Operator [AnimatedAttackOperator(TrunkSlamAnimName)]
        Effects [WsPowerUp += 1, **WsIsTired = true**]
Primitive Task [DoWhirlwindTrunkAttack]
    Preconditions [WsIsTired == false]
    Operator [DoWhirlwindTrunkAttack()]
        Effects [WsPowerUp = 0]
Primitive Task [DoRecover]
    Operator [PlayAnimation(TrunkSlamRecoveryAnim)]
        Effects [WsIsTired = false]

Using the `WsIsTired` world state, we can properly describe the reason we need the `DoRecovery` task. The `DoTrunkSlam` task now makes the Trunk Thumper tired, and he can't execute `DoWhirlwindTrunkAttack` until he gets a chance to recover. Now, when the world state changes, the `DoRecovery` task won't be interrupted and yet we save the modularity of `DoTrunkSlam` and `DoRecovery`. When implementing priority plan picking, these subtle details can really throw a wrench in your HTN behaviors. It's important to ask yourself if you are properly representing the world when you run into these types of behavior issues. As we saw in this case, a simple world state is all that was needed.

9.9 Managing Simultaneous Behaviors

A lot of different behavior selection algorithms are very good at doing one thing at a time, but complications arise when it comes time to do two things at once. Luckily, there are a couple ways you can handle this problem with HTN.

One's first reaction might be to roll multiple operators into one. This will work, but this has a couple pitfalls: it removes the ability to reuse operators we have already developed, the combining of multiple operators brings an added complexity that hurts maintainability, and any variation to this combined operator can force us to duplicate code if not handled correctly. Chances are you are going to run into behavior that will need to do multiple things at once, often enough that you are going to want to avoid this method.

A more intuitive way to handle this is to build a separate HTN domain to handle different components of your NPC. Using our troll example, we might have a behavior where we need him to navigate towards his enemy but guard himself from incoming range attacks. We can break this up into multiple operators that control different parts of the body—a navigation operator that would handle the lower body and a guard operator to handle the upper body. Knowing that, we can build two domains and use two planners to deal with the upper and lower bodies.

You may find early on that this can be tricky to implement. The issue that arises is that you need to sync up the tasks in each planner. You can accomplish this by making sure you have world state that describes what's going on in each planner. In our troll example, we can have a world state called *Navigating* that will be set to true when any lower body navigation task is running. This will allow the upper body planner to make decisions based on this information. Below is an example of how these two domains might be set up.

```
Compound Task [BeTrunkThumperUpper]//Upper domain
    Method [WsHasEnemy == true, WsEnemyRange <= MeleeRange]
        Subtasks [DoTrunkSlam()]
    Method [Navigating == true, HitByRangedAttack == true]
        Subtasks [GuardFaceWithArm()]
    Method [true]
        Subtasks [Idle()]
Compound Task [BeTrunkThumperLower]//Lower domain
    Method [WsHasEnemy == true, WsEnemyRange > MeleeRange]
        Subtasks [NavigateToEnemy(), BeTrunkThumperLower()]
    Method [true]
        Subtasks [Idle()]
Primitive Task [DoTrunkSlam]
    Operator [DoTrunkSlamOperator]
Primitive Task [GuardFaceWithArm]
    Operator [GuardFaceWithArmOperator]
Primitive Task [NavigateToEnemy]
    Operator [NavigateToOperator(Enemy)]
        Effects [WsLocation = Enemy]
Primitive Task [Idle]
    Operator [IdleOperator]
```

Now this works great, but there are a couple minor problems with it. A second planner will add a bit of performance hit. Keeping these domains synchronized will hurt their maintainability. Lastly, you will not gain any friends when other programmers run into the debugging headache you just created with your multiple planners—trust me.

There is another alternative for our troll shielding example that does not involve two planners. Currently, navigation tasks complete after successfully *arriving* at the destination. Instead, we can have the navigation task start the path following and complete *immediately*, since the path following is happening in the background and not as a task in the plan runner. This frees us to plan during navigation, which allows us to put an arm up to shield the troll from incoming fire. This works as long as we have a world state that describes that we are navigating and the current distance to the destination. With this we can detect when we arrive and plan accordingly. Below is an example of how the domain would look.

```
Compound Task [BeTrunkThumper]
    Method [WsHasEnemy == true, WsEnemyRange <= MeleeRange]
        Subtasks [DoTrunkSlam()]
    Method [WsHasEnemy == true, WsEnemyRange > MeleeRange]
        Subtasks [NavigateToEnemy()]
    Method [Navigating == true, HitByRangedAttack == true]
        Subtasks [GuardFaceWithArm()]
    Method [true]
        Subtasks [Idle()]
Primitive Task [DoTrunkSlam]
    Operator [DoTrunkSlamOperator]
```

```
Primitive Task [GuardFaceWithArm]
    Operator [GuardFaceWithArmOperator]
Primitive Task [NavigateToEnemy]
    Operator [NavigateToOperator(Enemy)]
        Effects [Navigating = true]
Primitive Task [Idle]
    Operator [IdleOperator]
```

As you can see, this domain is similar to our dual domain approach. Both approaches rely on world state to work correctly. With the dual domain, the *Navigating* world state was used to keep the planners in sync. In the later approach, world state was used to represent the path following happening in the background, but without the need of two domains and two planners running.

9.10 Speeding up Planning with Partial Plans

Let us assume that we have built the Trunk Thumper's domain into a pretty large network. After optimizing the planner itself, you have found the need to knock a couple milliseconds off your planning time. There are a couple of ways we can still eek more performance out of it. As we explained, HTN naturally culls out large portions of the search space via the methods in compound tasks. There may be instances, however, where we can add a few more methods to cull more search space. In order to do this, we need to have the right world state representation.

If those techniques don't get you the speed you need, *partial planning* should. Partial planning is one of the most powerful features of HTN. In simplest terms, it allows the planner the ability to not fully decompose a complete plan. HTN is able to do this because it uses forward decomposition or forward search to find plans. That is, the planner starts with the *current* world state and plans *forward* in time from that. This allows the planner to only plan ahead a few steps.

GOAP and STRIPS planner variants, on the other hand, use a *backward* search [Jorkin 04]. This means the search makes its way from a desired goal state toward the current world state. Searching this way means the planner has to complete the entire search in order to know what *first* step to take. We will go back to a simple version of our Trunk Thumper domain to demonstrate how to break it up into a partial plan domain.

```
Compound Task [BeTrunkThumper]
    Method [WsCanSeeEnemy == true]
        Subtasks [NavigateToEnemy(), DoTrunkSlam()]
Primitive Task [DoTrunkSlam]
    Operator [DoTrunkSlamOperator]
Compound Task [NavigateToEnemy]
    Method […]
        Subtasks […]
```

Here, we have a method that will expand both the `NavigateToEnemy` and `DoTrunkSlam` tasks if `WsCanSeeEnemy` is true. Since whatever tasks that make up

NavigateToEnemy might take a long time, it would make this a good option to split into a partial plan. There isn't much point to planning too far into the future since there is a good chance the world state could change, forcing our troll to make a different decision. We can convert this particular plan into a partial plan:

Compound Task [BeTrunkThumper]
    Method [WsCanSeeEnemy == true, WsEnemyRange > MeleeRange]
        Subtasks [NavigateToEnemy()]
    Method [WsCanSeeEnemy == true]
        Subtasks [DoTrunkSlam()]
Primitive Task [DoTrunkSlam]
    Operator [DoTrunkSlamOperator]
Compound Task [NavigateToEnemy]
    Method [...]
        Subtasks [...]

Here, we have broken the previous method into two methods. The new high priority method will navigate to the enemy only if the troll is currently out of range. If the troll is not outside of melee range, he will perform the trunk slam attack. Navigation tasks are also prime targets for partial plans, since they often take a long time to complete. It's important to point out that splitting this plan is only doable if there is a world state available to differentiate the split.

This method of partial planning requires the author of the domain to create the split themselves. But there is a way to automate this process. By assigning the concept of "time" to primitive tasks, the planner can keep track of how far into the future it has already planned. There are a couple issues with this approach, however. Consider the domain.

Compound Task [BeTrunkThumper]
    Method [WsCanSeeEnemy == true]
        Subtasks [NavigateToEnemy(), DoTrunkSlam()]
Primitive Task [DoTrunkSlam]
    Preconditions[WsStamina > 0]
    Operator [DoTrunkSlamOperator]
Compound Task [NavigateToEnemy]
    Method [...]
        Subtasks [...]

With this domain, assume the primitive tasks that make up the navigation cross the time threshold that is set in the planner. This would cause the troll to start navigating to the enemy. But if the world state property WsStamina is zero, the troll can't execute the DoTrunkSlam anyway because of its precondition. The automated partial plan split removed the ability to validate the plan properly. Of course the method can be written to include the stamina check to avoid this problem. But since both ways are valid, it is better to insure both will produce the same results. Not doing so will cause subtle bugs in your game.

Even if you feel that this isn't a real concern, there is also the question of how to continue where the partial plan left off. We could just replan from the root, but that would require us to change the domain in some way to understand that it's completed the first part of the full plan. In the case of our example, we would have to add a higher priority method that checks to see if we are in range to do the melee attack. But if we have to do this, what's the point of the automated partial planning?

A better solution would be to record the state of the unprocessed list. With that we can modify the planner to start with a list of tasks, instead of the one root task. This would allow us to continue the search where we left off. Of course, we would not be able to roll back to *before* the start of the second part of the plan. Running into this case would mean that you've already run tasks that you should not have. So if the user runs into this case, they can't use partial planning because there are tasks later in the plan that need to be validated in order to get the correct behavior.

With *Transformers: Fall of Cybertron*, we simply built the partial plans into the domains. For us, the chance of putting subtle bugs into the game was high and we found that we were naturally putting partial plans in our NPC domains anyway when full plan validation wasn't necessary. A lot of our NPCs were using the last example from Section 9.9 for navigation, which is also an example of partial planning.

9.11 Conclusion

Going through the process of creating a simple NPC can be a real eye-opener to the details involved with implementation of any behavior selection system. Hopefully we have explored enough of hierarchical task networks to show its natural approach to describing behaviors, the re-usability and modularity of its primitive tasks. HTN's ability to reason about the future allows an expressiveness only found with planners. We have also attempted to point out potential problems a developer may come across when implementing it. Hierarchical task networks were a real benefit to the AI programmers on *Transformers: Fall of Cybertron* and we're sure it will be the same for you.

References

[Erol et al. 94] K. Erol, D. Nau, and J. Henler, "HTN planning: Complexity and expressivity." *AAAI-94 Proceedings*, 1994.

[Erol et al. 95] K. Erol, J. Henler, and D. Nau. "Semantics for Hierarchical Task-Network Planning." Technical report TR 95-9. The Institute for Systems Research, 1995.

[Ghallab et al. 04] M. Ghallab, D. Nau, and P. Traverso, *Automated Planning*. San Francisco, CA: Elsevier, 2004, pp. 229–259.

[HighMoon 10] *Transformers: War for Cybertron*, High Moon Studios/Activision Publishing, 2010.

[HighMoon 12] *Transformers: Fall of Cybertron*, High Moon Studios/Activision Publishing, 2012.

[Jorkin 04] Jeff Orkin. "Applying goal-oriented action planning to games." In *AI Game Programming Wisdom 2*, edited by Steve Rabin. Hingham, MA: Charles River Media, 2004, pp. 217–227.

Hierarchical Plan-Space Planning for Multi-unit Combat Maneuvers

William van der Sterren

10.1 Introduction

In combat simulators and war games, coming up with a good plan is half the battle. Good plans make the AI a more convincing opponent and a more reliable assistant commander. Good plans are essential for clear and effective coordination between combat units toward a joint objective.

This chapter describes the design of an AI planner capable of producing plans that coordinate multiple units into a joint maneuver on the battlefield. First, it looks at how planning for multiple units is different from planning for a single unit. Then it introduces the basic ideas of hierarchical plan-space planning. These ideas are made more concrete for the case of combat maneuvers. The article wraps up with an evaluation of the design and ideas for further application of hierarchical plan-space planning.

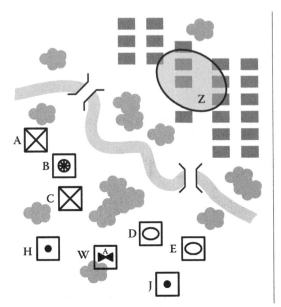

"Our plan:
We'll clear objective Z, with A, B, C, D and E platoons forming up and launching a two pronged simultaneous attack. Afterwards, we'll regroup at objective Z.

B platoon will transport A and C to their form up areas. A and C platoons will attack across the northern bridge, D and E platoons will attack across the southern bridge.

Fire support is provided by batteries H and J and gunships W. Batteries H and J will fire smoke screens to cover the bridge crossings. W flight will be on call."

Figure 10.1

A multi-unit planning problem (left) and the result (right) as briefed to the player.

10.2 Planning for Multiple Units

Creating a plan for multiple units is different from planning for a single unit. Obviously, the plan needs to cater to all the units instead of a single unit, and will involve more actions. In many cases, these units will perform their actions concurrently.

But there is more to it: in most cases, these units will have to interact with each other to accomplish the goal. To coordinate this interaction, the plan needs to tell who needs to interact with whom, where, and at what time.

Another difference is in communication of the plan: the actions making up a single unit's plan typically require no additional explanation. However, when multiple units work together towards an objective, additional explanation is often expected (for example, as part of the briefing in Figure 10.1). How is the work split across subgroups? Who is assisting whom? What is each group's role? And for combat plans, what is the overall concept?

Given these differences, can we take a single-unit planner such as GOAP [Orkin 06] or an HTN planner [Ghallab et al. 04, Humphreys 13] and create plans for multiple units? For all practical purposes, we cannot. Both these kinds of planners construct their plan action for action, and traverse a search space consisting of world states (the state-space [StateSpaceSearch]). Our problem is the enormous state-space resulting from multiple units acting concurrently. For example, assume a single unit has four alternative actions to move about or manipulate its environment, and we are in need of a five-step plan. For this "single unit" case, the total state-space consists of $4^5 = 1024$ states, and can easily be searched. If we attempt to tackle a similar problem involving six units acting concurrently, the state-space size explodes to $(4^6)^5 \sim 1.15 \ 10^{18}$ combinations. GOAP and, to a lesser extent, standard HTN planners struggle to search efficiently in such a large state-space.

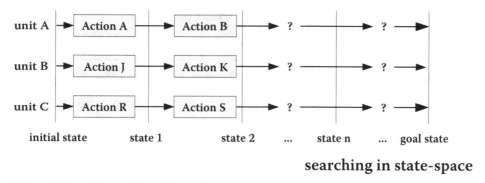

initial state   state 1   state 2   ...   state n   ...   goal state

searching in state-space

searching in plan-space

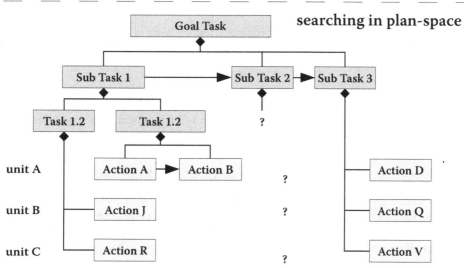

Figure 10.2

State-space search (top) compared with plan-space search (bottom).

Instead of searching in state-space, we can attempt to search in plan-space (see Figure 10.2). Plan-space represents all incomplete and complete plans. This may sound vague, but it actually is quite similar to how human project planners tackle planning problems. Project planners break down the overall problem into smaller tasks that together accomplish the goal. They then repeatedly break down these smaller tasks until the resulting activities are small enough to be accomplished by a single unit's action. See Figure 10.3 for an example of a fully detailed plan.

Working in plan-space offers three key advantages when tackling multiunit planning problems. First, we can make planning decisions at a higher level than individual actions by reasoning about tasks and subtasks. Second, we have the freedom to detail the plan in any order we like, which allows us to start focusing on the most critical tasks first. And, third, we can explicitly represent coordination (as tasks involving multiple units), and synchronization (as tasks not able to start before all actions of a preceding subtask have completed) in our plan. With these advantages, we are able to generate plans describing coordinated actions for multiple units even for a large search space.

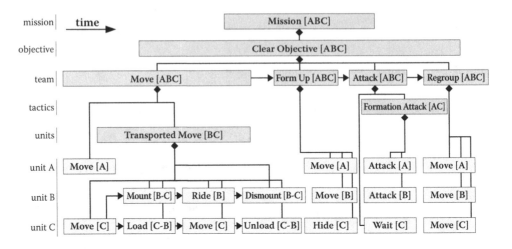

Figure 10.3

A complete plan with higher level tasks (top) and resulting unit actions (bottom).

This article continues by detailing this approach of hierarchical plan-space planning for a combat maneuver problem as illustrated in Figure 10.1.

10.3 Hierarchical Planning in Plan-Space: The Ingredients

We need four ingredients to implement hierarchical planning in plan-space: a planner main loop, the tasks and actions to represent the plan, a set of planner methods which can refine a partial plan by detailing one task in that plan, and finally the plan-space that holds and ranks all partial plans. We will look into these ingredients in this order.

10.4 Planner Main Loop: An A* Search through Plan-Space

The planner main loop executes the search through plan-space. The search starts with a single plan consisting of a single top-level task (the "mission"). Next, the main loop repeatedly picks the most promising plan from the open plans in plan-space and attempts to expand that plan by refining the plan's tasks. The main loop exits successfully when a plan is found that is complete. The main loop exits with a failure when there is no open plan left to be expanded. Figure 10.4 shows the pseudocode for the planner main loop.

The main loop expands a selected plan as follows. It first picks a single task requiring refinement from the plan. It then selects from the catalog of planner methods the methods that can refine this selected task. Each of these methods is applied separately, resulting in zero or more alternative expanded plans (we will discuss this in more detail later). Every expanded alternative plan is assigned a cost and added to the open list.

The main loop is quite generic and similar to an A* path search. Here, we are expanding plans into one or more neighboring plans which are closer to a fully detailed plan, instead of expanding paths into one or more neighboring locations which are closer to the destination. We are expanding plans in a best-first approach, something that is explained in more detail when looking into the plan-space.

10. Hierarchical Plan-Space Planning for Multi-unit Combat Maneuvers

```
loop
  current = get most promising plan from open list
  break if current.complete? or current.null?
  add current to closed list
  pick t = current.task_to_detail
  for every method m that applies to task t
      alternatives = m.generate(current, t)
      for every a in alternatives
          plan = clone current
          // refine using method m and alternative a
          m.plan(plan, t, a)
          compute plan's cost
          add plan to open list
```

Figure 10.4

Pseudocode for the planner main loop.

10.5 A Plan of Tasks

A plan consists of interdependent tasks. A task represents an activity for one or more units and consumes time. For our combat maneuver domain, we need tasks to represent basic unit actions, and we need tasks to represent higher level activity. Table 10.1 lists examples of both types of tasks, with unit level tasks in the bottom row. The scope reflects the various levels at which decisions are made and problems are broken down in the military: mission, objective, team, tactics, units, unit.

The basic unit tasks simply follow from the activity that a unit—such as an infantry squad, a tank platoon, or a gunship section—is capable of. We call these tasks "primitive" since we cannot decompose them. The higher level tasks are intended to help us make higher level planning decisions and break down the plan (as shown in Figure 10.3). In general, these tasks are about assigning resources to subgoals and coordinating subtasks. Concrete examples for our combat maneuver domain include a complete team moving to a form-up position, preparatory strikes by artillery and aircraft, or a para drop. These tasks are called "compound" since we can break them down into smaller tasks.

Tasks have a start time and duration. A task's duration is computed as the activity duration for primitive tasks, as the latest subtask's end-time minus earliest subtask's start-time for tasks already refined into subtasks, and as an estimated duration for a compound tasks not yet refined. We'll look into these estimates later.

In the plan, the tasks are organized as a graph. Every task has a parent except for the root task. Compound tasks have children (subtasks implementing their parent). Tasks

Table 10.1 Examples of tasks for combat maneuver domain, arranged by scope

Scope	Task examples
Mission	Mission
Objective	Clear, occupy, defend
Team	Move, form up, attack, air land, defend, counter-attack, para drop
Tactic	Formation ground attack, planned fire support, smoke screen
Units	Transported move, defend sector
Unit	Defend, guard, attack, hide, move, wait, air ingress, air egress, mount, dismount, load, unload, ride, para jump, fire artillery mission, close air support

```
# A LoadTask expects:
# - a start_state, indicating the unit's initial state
# - a target state, indicating the unit's loaded state
# - the passenger
class LoadTask < Task
  is_primitive
  has_scope :unit
  has_input :start_state,    :type => :unit
  has_input :target_state,   :type => :unit
  has_input :passenger,      :type => :unit

  def compute_expected_costs(context)
    15.0
  end
end
```

```
# An AttackAfterFormUpTeamTask expects:
# - an objective
# - a start state (as unit states preceding the form-up & attack)
# - an avenue of approach to use for this attack
# It outputs:
# - the objective area indicating what terrain to attack & from where
# - the assembly area for pre-attack form-up
# - per unit assembly positions in the form-up area
# - an end-state, as unit states after the attack in the objective area
class AttackAfterFormUpTeamTask < Task
  has_scope   :team
  has_input   :start_state,       :type => :units
  has_input   :objective,         :type => :objective
  has_input   :avenue_of_approach, :type => :avenue_of_approach
  has_output  :objective_area,    :type => :area
  has_output  :assembly_area,     :type => :area
  has_output  :assembled_state,   :type => :units
  has_output  :end_state,         :type => :units

  def compute_expected_costs(context)
    ...
  end
end
```

Figure 10.5

Two examples of tasks, with inputs and outputs.

may have preceding tasks which require completion before the task can start. For example, a team formation attack won't be able to start until all the form-up tasks of all involved units have been completed. These precedence relations between two tasks also imply all of the first task's subtasks precede the second task. Tasks may have successor tasks in the same way.

Tasks are parameterized with inputs and may provide outputs. In our combat maneuver domain all tasks take the units involved as input, typically with the units in the planned state (position, ammo level) at the start of the task. Primitive tasks deal with one single unit; compound tasks typically take an array of units. Many tasks take additional inputs—for example, to denote cooperating units, assigned targets or zones, or target states (in unit positions at the end of the task).

Figure 10.5 shows an example of two kinds of tasks, each taking inputs. The *LoadTask* represents the loading activity by a transporter unit such as an APC platoon. The *LoadTask* takes three inputs. The start-state input identifies the transporter unit and its initial state consisting of its position, and identifiers for any passenger units already being mounted. The target-state input is similar to the start-state but with the indicated passenger unit mounted. The passenger input identifies the passenger unit.

The *AttackAfterFormUpTeamTask* represents a multi-unit ground attack from a form-up position. It takes three inputs. The start-state input takes an array of units that will execute the attack. The objective input and avenue-of-approach inputs provide additional guidance from "higher up" on how to refine this team level task.

The *AttackAfterFormUpTeamTask* also provides outputs, as do many other tasks. The purpose of an output is to provide values to other tasks' inputs, enabling them to work from a resulting unit state, or from a tactical decision such as an avenue of approach.

A task input need not be set on task creation. It may be left open until the task is being refined. Or it can be connected to the input or output of another task and receive a value when the other side of the connection is set. Figure 10.6 illustrates this.

10. Hierarchical Plan-Space Planning for Multi-unit Combat Maneuvers

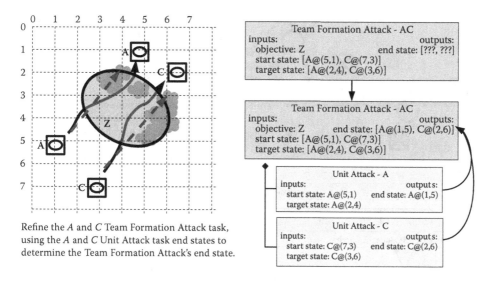

Refine the A and C Team Formation Attack task, using the A and C Unit Attack task end states to determine the Team Formation Attack's end state.

Figure 10.6

A parent's task output being determined by child tasks.

In Figure 10.6, a *TeamFormationAttack* task has been created involving tank platoons A and C. The task is given a start-state consisting of the A and C units with their start positions. The task's target-state indicates the tank platoons should move into positions at the far end of objective Z. The *TeamFormationAttack's* end-state output is left open intentionally, leaving detailed positioning of the tank platoons to more specialized subtasks. When the planner refines the *TeamFormationAttack*—for example, by adding two *UnitAttack* tasks, it connects the *UnitAttack's* end-state outputs to the *TeamFormationAttack* end-state output. When the planner refines the *UnitAttacks*, it will set the end-states with values representing positions close to the desired target-state but outside the woods. As soon as these *UnitAttack's* end-states are set, they will propagate to the *TeamFormationAttack's* end-state (and propagate further, if other inputs have been connected to that end-state).

Task outputs thus serve to pass on planning decisions and states along and up the chain of tasks. Connections between outputs and inputs determine how tasks share values. Connections can link inputs and outputs as a whole, but also (for arrays) on a per-element basis. In Figure 10.6, each of the *UnitAttack* tasks sets an element in the *TeamFormationAttack's* end-state.

We call *task* inputs that have all their values set "grounded" tasks. "Ungrounded" tasks lack one or more values in their inputs. We will revisit this distinction when discussing the order in which tasks are being refined.

10.6 Planner Methods

When the planner wants to refine a task in a partial plan, it selects the planner methods that apply to this task. It then applies each of these planner methods separately on a clone of the partial plan, and has the planner method generating alternative and more refined versions of the partial plan.

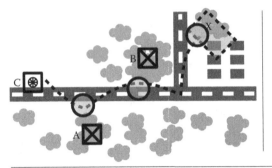

The task is for truck platoon C to pick up infantry squads A and B, and transport them to form-up area X. There A and B are to dismount, and all are to move to their target positions.

This requires decisions on:
– where to pick up A, and where B
– whether to pick up A before B
– where to drop off A and B
– exact final positions for A, B and C

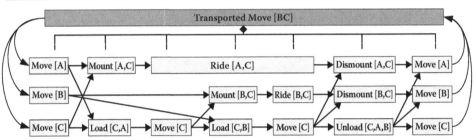

Figure 10.7

Decisions and subtasks when refining a TransportedMove task.

The role of the planner methods (we'll refer to them simply as "methods" from now on) is to refine a specific task in the plan. Methods themselves indicate which task or tasks they are able to refine. If the task to be refined is a primitive task, the method should compute and set this task's outputs. Figure 10.6 shows how the tank platoon's *UnitAttack* is given an output (a destination position outside the woods at the far end of the objective) that matches the tank unit's movement capabilities.

If the task to be refined is a compound task, then the method's responsibility is to decide how to implement that task, create the necessary subtasks, and connect the inputs and outputs of the task and subtasks. The method should ensure the outputs of the task being refined are set or have connections into them. Figure 10.7 illustrates an example of the decisions to be made, and the tasks, relations, and input/output connections to be created by a *TransportedMove* method in order to refine a nontrivial *TransportedMove* task.

To break down a *TransportedMove* task for a truck platoon C and two infantry squads A and B (in Figure 10.7), the *TransportedMove* method first makes a number of decisions. The method selects positions for the truck platoon to pick up squads A and B. Such a pick-up position needs to be accessible for the truck platoon and preferably close to the infantry squad. If the infantry squad had been in the open, the truck platoon might have picked it up at the squads' initial position. In this example, however, the infantry is positioned in the woods and needs to move into the open in order to be picked up. The drop-off point near form-up area X is picked in a similar way. The third decision is about picking up A before B or the other way around. Based on a few path-finding queries, picking up A before B is chosen. The final decision involves picking final positions for A, B, and C if not already given.

Table 10.2 Examples of planner methods and their responsibilities, arranged by scope

Scope	Planner method responsibility
Mission	Arrange objectives, allocate units to objectives
Objective	Define team activities, assign combat units and support units to teams
Team	Execute tasks as a team, distributing the work according to roles
Tactic	Synchronize tactical activity between multiple units
Units	Arrange cooperation between complementary units
Unit	Define end-state

Based on these decisions, the *TransportedMove* method can create the tasks for the two infantry squads and truck platoon. By making one task a predecessor of the other task, the method creates a sequence of tasks for each of the units. In addition, it synchronizes the load/mount actions and the unload/dismount actions by also making specific actions from other units a predecessor of these tasks. For example, the action for C to load A cannot start before both C and A have completed their moves to the pick-up position. Similarly, the infantry squads cannot disembark before the truck platoon has arrived at the drop-off position.

Since the *TransportedMove* method in this example already makes most of the decisions for all units and tasks involved, it can simply set output values and input values for most of the tasks.

To fully cover our combat maneuver domain, we need methods to set end-states for each of the primitive unit tasks, and we need methods to break down each of the compound tasks. For breaking down compound tasks into smaller tasks, we mirror the hierarchy chosen for tasks, from mission level methods down to unit level methods. As a rule of thumb, methods break down tasks into tasks of the next level, sometimes one level more. At each level, the methods have slightly different responsibility, as is illustrated in Table 10.2.

For most tasks, there will be a single corresponding method that is able to break the task down. For a few tasks it makes sense to have multiple methods for refining the task, each specialized in one type of tactical approach. To defend an objective, one method would create subtasks that make the available platoons each occupy a static position around the objective. Another method could create subtasks that have infantry platoons defending from static positions and keeping armor platoons in the rear for a counter-attack.

One benefit of using separate methods implementing different tactics is the ability to configure the planner's tactical approach (doctrine) by enabling or disabling certain methods for planning.

In the example of Figure 10.7, the *TransportedMove* method was able to consider two combinations (picking up A before B, and B before A) and pick the optimal one, because it understood how the task would be implemented in terms of primitive tasks. Methods working with higher level tasks often lack the understanding of how the plan will work out in detail, and have troubles make an optimal (or even "good enough") choice by themselves when facing multiple combinations. In these cases, the method will indicate to the planner main loop that it sees more than one alternative to refine the plan. The planner main loop then will iterate over these alternatives and create new plans by cloning the parent plan and asking the method to refine the plan for the given alternative (see Figure 10.4). Although this adds a little complexity to the planner main loop, the benefit is for us developers having to write and maintain just a single method to break down a specific compound task.

A method may fail to set a task output or break down a compound task and not generate a more refined plan. For example, if an artillery unit has already spent all its rounds in two artillery missions early in the plan, it should not be planned to perform a third artillery mission. If a team of three mechanized platoons is tasked to attack in formation but has to cross a narrow bridge doing so, it won't be an attack in formation and the method should not refine the task.

When one method fails to refine a task, this is only a local dead end in planning if no other method is capable of refining the same task in the same plan. Remember that we're searching through alternative plans with A*: a dead end here doesn't mean there isn't another, perhaps very different, variant of a plan that is feasible.

10.7 Plan-Space

The plan-space is the collection of all generated (partial) plans. We keep track of all plans that can be further refined in an open list. The open list is sorted for the lowest cost (Figure 10.8).

We can choose what to use for costs: plan duration works in most cases and is particularly suited for combat maneuvers, where time plays a considerable role in the plan's quality. The quicker we launch an attack, or the quicker our defending units occupy their positions, the better.

We compute a plan's duration the way project planners do, using accurate data from primitive tasks when available and using estimates for compound tasks that have not been detailed yet. Starting at the root task, we repeatedly pick a child task that has no preceding tasks without a start-time and end-time. For this child task we set as the start-time the maximum end-time of its predecessors, and recursively compute its duration and end-time (start-time plus duration). After doing so for all children, we can set the task's end-time. The root task's end-time minus start-time gives us the plan's duration.

We need to recompute a plan's duration every time we update the plan. Newly added primitive tasks may have a duration different from what their compound parent task estimated. We can, however, cache a compound task's estimate once computed for its specific inputs.

We leave the estimation of a compound task's duration to the task itself. Each compound task should implement an "estimate duration" function. These functions use heuristics to come up with a decent estimate. Since we are using A* to search through plan-space, the estimate should be a close estimate without overestimating the duration. Figure 10.9 illustrates how to come up with a good estimate.

Figure 10.9 shows the same situation and *TransportedMove* task as Figure 10.7. Now we are interested in estimating the duration without going into all the decisions and details that we considered when refining the task. A good estimate would be for C to move to A, then to B and finally to X at its top speed, with time for loading and unloading A and B added. In the estimate, we can decide to move to A before B based on a simple geometric comparison: A is closer to C than is B. Alternatively, we can evaluate path durations for both cases, and pick the lowest estimate. We are underestimating the real costs in most situations, since actual movement will be slower than C due to the terrain.

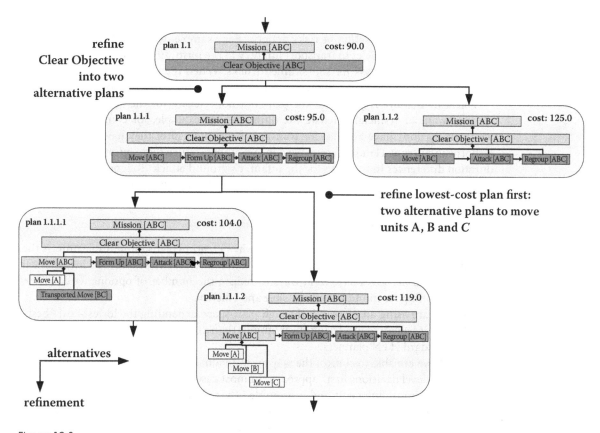

refine
Clear Objective
into two
alternative plans

refine lowest-cost plan first:
two alternative plans to move
units A, B and C

alternatives

refinement

Figure 10.8

Plan-space, with incomplete plans as nodes and links representing refinement.

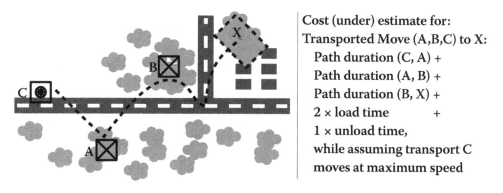

Cost (under) estimate for:
Transported Move (A,B,C) to X:
    Path duration (C, A) +
    Path duration (A, B) +
    Path duration (B, X) +
    2 × load time   +
    1 × unload time,
    while assuming transport C
    moves at maximum speed

Figure 10.9

Estimating the duration of a compound TransportedMove task.

As with A* pathfinding, we make the planner avoid certain tasks and plans by artificially inflating the duration of risky actions. For example, to make the attacker avoid using soft-skinned vehicles to transport infantry to the form-up location, we can raise the duration of the move task for soft-skinned trucks. When the planner also has available armored personnel carriers, he will be more likely to use these to transport infantry.

For tasks that are required for the plan, but not relevant for the quality of the plan, we may want to artificially deflate the duration. For example, for combat maneuvers, we typically don't have any use for transport helicopters after they have inserted their airborne infantry at a landing zone. We don't want their return flight duration to mask any duration differences in the tasks for the infantry's ground attack. To ignore the irrelevant return flight, we can use a small and fixed duration for the return flight tasks.

10.8 Making Planning More Efficient

As mentioned earlier, the biggest risk we run when creating plans for multiple units is the combinatorics problem (better known as the *combinatorial explosion*). Our hierarchical plan-space planner gives us several ways to reduce the number of options we consider, making planning for multiple units feasible and efficient.

First, we are using an A* search through plan-space expanding the lowest-cost "best" plan first. This helps us considering fewer options than a depth-first backtracking approach used by standard HTN planners.

Second, we are able to control the way an individual plan is expanded, and turn this into a "high-level decisions first" approach. In most cases, a plan will have more than one task that requires refinements and is grounded (has all its inputs set). The planner main loop in Figure 10.3 needs to pick a single task to refine. For the combat maneuver domain, where each task is associated with a command scope, we can have the planner main loop always pick the task with the highest scope as the task to refine first.

In Figure 10.10, this highest scope first task selection is illustrated. The partial plan consists of many compound tasks requiring refinement. Some of these, such as the *Attack* and *Regroup* tasks, cannot be refined yet, since they need inputs from preceding tasks.

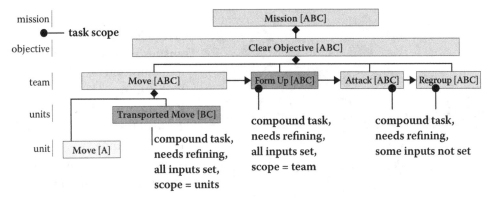

Figure 10.10

Selecting the highest scope task with all inputs set: FormUp.

10. Hierarchical Plan-Space Planning for Multi-unit Combat Maneuvers

Two tasks are grounded and ready to be refined: the *TransportedMove*, with "units" scope, and the *FormUp*, with "team" scope. Since "team" scope is higher, the planner will pick the *FormUp* task as the task to be refined first. Refining the *FormUp* task will set the inputs for the *Regroup* task, allowing that task to be refined next.

The benefit of refining higher level tasks first is that these tasks have larger impact on plan feasibility (do we have the maneuvering space for a combined attack by all our mechanized platoons?) and the cost of the plan. The planner should not busy himself detailing seating arrangements for the move to the form-up position before the attack is fleshed out. By making high-level decisions first, the planner needs far fewer steps to find a good plan.

A third way to consider fewer plans is the hierarchical plan-space planner's ability to plan from the "middle-out." In the military, planning specialists mix forward planning and reverse planning, sometimes starting with the critical step in the middle. When starting in the middle (for example, with the air landing or a complex attack), they subsequently plan forward to mission completion and backward to mission start. The military do so because starting with the critical step drastically reduces the number of planning options to consider.

We can mimic this by changing the input/output relations between tasks, and shifting some decisions from one method to another. Keep in mind that the only tasks that can be refined are the grounded tasks. Figure 10.11 shows an example of tasks connected to enable middle-out planning.

In Figure 10.11, a *ClearObjective* task is shown that has been broken down into a *Move*, a *FormUp*, an *AttackAfterFormUp*, and a *Regroup*. These tasks are to be executed in that order. However, refinement of these tasks should start with the *AttackAfterFormUp*. The input/output connections between the tasks are made in such a way that the *AttackAfterFormUp* is the first task having all its inputs set. The *FormUp* and *Regroup* task inputs depend on outputs from the *AttackAfterFormUp* task. The *Move* task depends on outputs from the *FormUp* task. The method refining the *AttackAfterFormUp* task has been

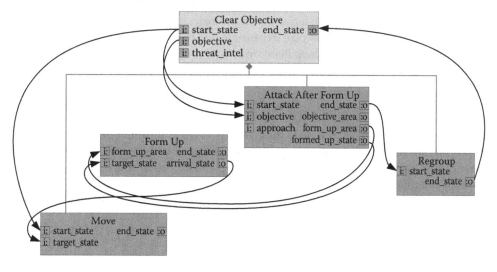

Figure 10.11

Middle-out planning from the AttackAfterFormUp by linking inputs.

modified to work with initial unit positions and the objective, and defines the attack move from the form-up locations through the objective. The *AttackAfterFormUp* task outputs the chosen form-up location and the positions of the involved units after form-up. It also outputs the positions of the units after attacking through the objective. These outputs enable the *FormUp* and *Regroup* tasks to be refined. The method refining the *FormUp* task defines where the units should enter the form-up area and with that output enables the *Move* task to be refined.

Middle-out planning requires changes to tasks and methods but it can greatly reduce the number of plans to consider by making critical decisions first. For combat maneuvers, middle-out planning also resembles a military practice, which makes it easier to translate military doctrine into tasks and planner methods.

10.9 Conclusion

We are able to successfully plan combat maneuvers involving over a dozen mechanized platoons, armor troops, gunship sections, and artillery batteries, taking into account tactical preferences and time. By working in plan-space instead of state-space, by breaking down the problem into high-level and low-level tasks and decisions, and by using a cost-based best-first search that expands high-level tasks first, we can avoid combinatorial explosion and deliver a good plan on short notice. The resulting plan includes not only the actions for each individual unit, but also the relations between these actions for coordination, and all higher level decisions. Turning such a plan into human understandable explanation or briefing is trivial.

The planner's design described here has been in action since mid-2009, generating tens of thousands of combat maneuvers from user input as downloadable missions [PlannedAssault 09]. The current implementation is in Ruby, running single-threaded on a Java VM (through JRuby) on an Intel Core2Quad Q8400, taking some 10s to 30s to generate a maneuver for 4×3 km terrain, with the majority of CPU time spent on terrain analysis and path-finding, not on plan expansion. The majority of plans are constructed in fewer than 200 planner main loop iterations.

10.10 Future Work

One nice side effect of planning in plan-space is the availability of all higher level tasks and decisions in the resulting plan, next to the actions for each of the units. Not only does this availability make it easier to turn the plan into a human readable briefing, it also makes the resulting plan great for use in monitoring the plan's execution. The original plan contains all the information to decide who is impacted by a task running late, which part of the plan needs repairs, and what the maximum allowed duration is for an alternative implementation of a plan part.

References

[Ghallab et al. 04] M. Ghallab, D. Nau, and P. Traverso. *Automated Planning, Theory and Practice*, pp. 229–259. San Francisco, CA: Morgan Kaufmann, 2004.

[Humphreys 13] T. Humphreys. "Exploring HTN planners through example." In *Game AI Pro*, edited by Steve Rabin. Boca Raton, FL: CRC Press, 2013.

[Orkin 06] J. Orkin. "Three states and a plan: The A.I. of F.E.A.R." *Game Developers Conference, 2006*. Available online (http://web.media.mit.edu/~jorkin/goap.html).

[PlannedAssault 09] PlannedAssault on-line mission generator for ARMA/ARMA2 games, http://www.plannedassault.com, 2009.

[StateSpaceSearch] Wikipedia. http://en.wikipedia.org/wiki/State_space_search.

11

Phenomenal AI Level-of-Detail Control with the LOD Trader

Ben Sunshine-Hill

11.1 Introduction

Of all the techniques which make modern video game graphics possible, level-of-detail (LOD) management may very well be the most important, the most groundbreaking, and the most game-changing. While LOD seems like a rather boring thing to think of as "groundbreaking," in order to get the graphical quality we want in the world sizes we want, it's crucial to *not* render everything as though the player was two centimeters away from it. With conservatively chosen LOD transition distances, immense speedups are possible without compromising the realism of the scene in any way. Viewed broadly, even things like visibility culling can be considered part of LOD—after all, the lowest detail possible for an object is to not render it at all. Graphics programmers rely on LOD. It is, in a sense, "how graphics works."

AI programmers use some form of LOD, too, of course, but we don't really *rely* on it. We'll use lower quality locomotion and collision avoidance systems for characters more than ten meters away, or simulate out-of-view characters at a lower update rate, or (similar to visibility culling above) delete characters entirely when they're too far away. But while graphics programmers can use LOD without compromising realism, whenever *we* employ LOD, in the back of our mind, our conscience whispers, "That's just a hack ... someone's going to *notice*." We use LOD only when we absolutely must, because we know that it's bringing down the quality of our AI.

There's another sense in which we don't rely on AI LOD. In graphics, LOD acts as a natural limit on scene complexity. The player can only be next to so many objects at once, and everything that's not near the player is cheaper to render, so framerate tends to even out. It's far from a guarantee, of course, but LOD is the first line of defense for maintaining the framerate. For AI, however, the techniques we'd really like to use often aren't feasible to run on more than a small handful of NPCs at once, and a cluster of them can easily blow our CPU time budget. There's no "LOD threshold distance" we could pick which would respect our budget *and* give most visible characters the detail we want.

So we use LOD. But it's not "how AI works."

What if LOD was smarter? What if it didn't even use distances, but instead could determine, with uncanny precision, how "important" each character was? What if it could read the player's mind, and tell the game exactly when to start using high-quality collision avoidance for a character, and when to stop? What if it knew which characters the players remembered, and which characters they had forgotten? And what if its LOD selections *always* respected the CPU time budget when NPCs decided to cluster around the player, but always made good use of the time available when they didn't?

Well, then, we could *trust* LOD. We could use techniques as expensive as we wanted, because we could rely on LOD to keep them from blowing our budget. We could move away from the endless task of tuning LOD thresholds, and hardcoding hack after hack to compensate for the endless special cases where our LOD thresholds weren't enough. LOD could become "how AI works."

That, in a nutshell, is the LOD Trader. It can't read the player's mind, but its simple heuristics are light-years beyond distance thresholds in determining how important a character is to the player. Rather than relying on fixed transition rules, it treats the entire space of detail levels—for all the AI features we'd like to control—as a puzzle to be solved each frame. It attempts to maximize the realism of the game simulation without going over the computation budget, and does it in a remarkably short period of time (tens of microseconds).

It's not magical. Its heuristics are far from infallible, and the optimality of its LOD solutions is approximate. But it is worlds beyond distance-based LOD, and the first time it outsmarts you—its LOD reductions becoming subtle and then invisible—you'll wonder a bit.

11.2 Defining the Problem

The first thing to do when attacking a problem like "optimal LOD selection" is to figure out what we mean by *optimal*. The graphics guys don't need to do this, because their LOD selections can be made *perfectly*—they can transition far enough away that they're not giving up any realism. But every detail reduction we make is going to potentially reduce realism, so we need to define, in a numeric sense, what we're trying to maximize, and what our constraints are. We need to come up with a metric, a system of units for measurement of realism. Yikes.

Well, let's grab the bull by the horns. I claim that what we're trying to do is pick a detail level for each AI feature, for each character, to minimize the *probability* that the player will notice an issue, an unrealistic reduction in detail. This helps nail things down, because we all know all about probabilities and how to compare and do arithmetic with them. In this model, Choice A won't be "a little less realistic" than Choice B, but will rather be "a little less likely to be noticed." We'll refer to the event of the player actually noticing an issue as a

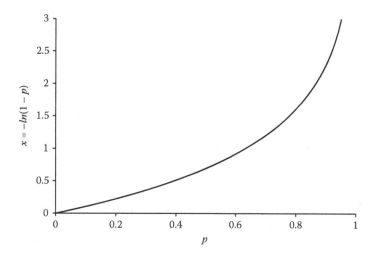

Figure 11.1

Logarithmic probability compared to linear probability.

Break in Realism (BIR). A BIR only occurs when the player notices the issue; just reducing the detail of an entity isn't a BIR if she doesn't notice it as unrealistic.

11.2.1 Diving Into X-Space

Let's make things a little cleverer, though. Suppose that the probability of the user noticing that some entity is unrealistic is p. Rather than work with that number directly, we'll work with the number $x = -\log(1 - p)$. That's the negative logarithm (base whatever, let's use the traditional e) of the *complement* of the probability—the probability of getting away with it, of the user *not* noticing. A plot of p versus x is shown in Figure 11.1. As p goes up, x goes up. If p is zero, x is zero; as p approaches 1, x approaches infinity. (The inverse equation is $p = 1 - e^{-x}$.)

Why this complication? Well, actually, it's a simplification; x turns out to be much better-behaved than p. First, if we have two potential sources of unrealistic events, with (independent) probabilities of being noticed p_1 and p_2, and we want to know the total probability p_{tot} of the user noticing either one, that's $p_{tot} = p_1 + p_2 - p_1 p_2$, not especially nice. For three sources it gets even uglier: $p_{tot} = p_1 + p_2 + p_3 - p_1 p_2 - p_1 p_3 - p_2 p_3 + p_1 p_2 p_3$. In contrast, $x_{tot} = x_1 + x_2 + x_3$. Second, this transformation gives us a better interpretation of phrases like "twice as unrealistic." If some event has probability $p_1 = 0.6$ of being noticed, and some other event is "twice as unrealistic" as p_1, what is its probability? Clearly it can't be 1.2—that's not a valid probability. But in x-space things work out fine: $x_2 = 2x_1$, which leads to $x_1 = 0.91$, $x_2 = 1.82$, $p_2 = 0.84$. What is 0.84? It's the probability of noticing it either time, if the first event happened twice. It's extremely useful to be able to describe probabilities relative to each other in that sort of an intuitive way, because it's a lot easier to do that than to determine absolute probabilities. x-space gives us well-behaved addition and multiplication, which (as we'll see later) are crucial to the LOD Trader. In practice, there's actually very little reason to work with p at all.

11.3 Criticality and Probability

The next thing we have to look at is what we'll call the *criticality* of a character. That represents how "critical" the character's realism is to the realism of the scene as a whole—or, if you like, how critical the player is likely to be about the character's detail level. In a sense, that's what distance stood for when we were using distance-based LOD: All else being equal, a closer character is more critical to the scene than a farther character.

But all else is *not* equal. There are other things to use in sussing out criticality. It would be great if we could hook up eye trackers and EEGs and Ouija boards to the player, but even without that, there's plenty of metrics we can pull from the game to help estimate the criticality of a given entity to the player at a given time.

Before we go further, though, there's a really key thing about BIRs, and about criticality, to realize: not all unrealism is alike. Consider two characters. One is a suspected assassin who the player has been following at a distance for some time. The other is a random villager crossing the road a few feet ahead of the player. Both characters are *important*, in a sense. The first character is clearly the object of the player's conscious attention; if we can only afford high-quality path planning for one character, it had better be that one, because the player is more likely to notice if he's wandering randomly. But the second one occupies more screen space, and possibly more of the player's visual attention—if we can only afford high-quality locomotion IK for one, it should probably be that one.

11.3.1 A Field Guide to BIR's

It's tempting to throw in the towel at this point, concluding that there are as many kinds of unrealism as there are AI features whose detail level we'd like to move up and down. But I think there's a small set of categories that nearly all BIR's fall into. Any given reduced detail level will create the potential for a BIR in at least one of these categories, and sometimes more. The reason to categorize things like this is because each category of BIR can have its own criticality model.

11.3.1.1 Unrealistic State

An *unrealistic state (US)* BIR is the most immediate and obvious type of BIR, where a character's immediately observable simulation is wrong. A character eating from an empty plate, or running in place against a wall, or wearing a bucket on his head creates the potential for an unrealistic state BIR. (Not a *certainty*, mind you—the player might not be looking.) US's don't require any long period of observation, only momentary attention, and the attention need not be voluntary—the eye tends to be drawn to such things.

11.3.1.2 Fundamental Discontinuity

A *fundamental discontinuity (FD)* BIR is a little more subtle, but not by much: it occurs when a character's current state is incompatible with the player's memory of his past state. A character disappearing while momentarily around a corner, or having been frozen in place for hours while the player was away, or regaining the use of a limb that had been broken creates the potential for a fundamental discontinuity BIR. These situations can cause US BIR's too, of course. But even if the character is not observed while they happen, as long as the player remembers the old state and later returns, the potential for an FD BIR remains.

11.3.1.3 Unrealistic Long-Term Behavior

An *unrealistic long-term behavior (ULTB)* BIR is the subtlest: It occurs only when an extended period of observation reveals problems with a character's behavior. A character wandering randomly instead of having goal-driven behaviors is the most common example of an unrealistic long-term behavior BIR, but so is a car that never runs out of gas. At any given time, only a small handful of characters are likely to be prone to ULTB BIR's.

11.4 Modeling Criticality

Let's see about coming up with criticality models for these different categories. Each model calculates a *criticality score* as the product of several factors, some of which are shared between multiple models.

For unrealistic state, the factors are observability and attention. *Observability* comes closest to graphical LOD: it measures how feasible it is for the player to see the character in question. *Attention* is self-evident: it estimates how much attention the player is paying to a particular character. As you might guess, it's the most difficult factor to estimate.

For fundamental discontinuity, the two related factors are memory and return time. *Memory* estimates how effectively the player has memorized facts about a character, and how likely they are to notice changes to the character. *Return time* acts as a modifier to the memory factor: It estimates how attenuated the player's memory for the character will be when she returns to the character, or even if she will ever return at all.

For unrealistic long-term behavior, the three factors are attention, memory, and duration. Attention and memory have already been introduced (note that the return time factor is not acting on memory here); the last one, *duration*, simply refers to how much time and attention the player has devoted to that character.

There's the cast of characters. Now let's come up with actual equations for each one. Note that later factors will often use earlier factors in their input; the order we've listed them in is a good order to calculate them in.

Before we go into these, though, we need to introduce a tool which will be used in a lot of them: the *exponential moving average (EMA)*. The EMA is a method for smoothing and averaging an ongoing sequence of measurements. Given an input function $F(t)$ we produce the output function $G(t)$. We initialize $(0) = F(0)$, and then at each time t we update $G(t)$ as $G(t) = (1-\alpha)F(t) + \alpha G(t-\Delta t)$, where Δt is the timestep since the last measurement. The α in that equation is calculated as $\alpha = e^{-k \cdot \Delta t}$, where k is the *convergence rate* (higher values lead to faster changes in the average). You can tune k to change the smoothness of the EMA, and how closely it tracks the input function. We're going to use the EMA a *lot* in these models, so it's a good idea to familiarize yourself with it (Figure 11.2).

11.4.1 Observability

This is a straightforward one—an out-of-view character will have an observability of 0, a nearby and fully visible character will have an observability of 1, and visible but faraway characters will have an observability somewhere in the middle. For character i, you can calculate this factor as proportional to the amount of screen space (or number of pixels) p_i taken up by the character, divided by some "saturation size" p_{sat} referring to how big a character needs to get before there's no difficulty observing them, and limited to 1: $O_i = min(p_i / p_{sat}, 1)$.

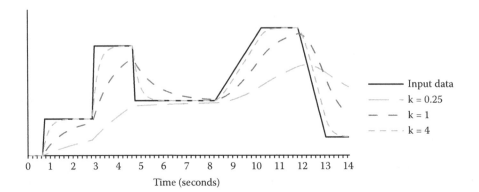

Figure 11.2

The exponential moving average of a data set, with various convergence rates.

We used the amount of screen space taken up by a fully visible character 4 meters away from the camera as p_{sat}. A smaller saturation value may be more appropriate for games intended for high-definition displays.

11.4.2 Attention

As mentioned earlier, attention is the most difficult factor to estimate. There are two steps in determining attention: estimating attempted attention, and applying the effect of interference.

As a first pass, attempted attention $\hat{A}_i$ can be calculated as the EMA of observability: $\hat{A}_i(t) = \alpha \hat{A}_i(t - \Delta t) + (1 - \alpha) O_i(t)$. For observability, you should tune k to have a rapid falloff; we used $k = 2$, which provides a 95% falloff in 1.5 seconds.

You can mix other things into the attempted attention model to improve its accuracy, though. One player behavior strongly associated with attention is *focusing*, where the player attempts to keep the character centered in the camera view. This can be calculated as the EMA of the dot product between the camera's forward vector and the vector to the character, then multiplied by observability. The convergence rate k should be much lower for this term. Other, more game-specific sources can be drawn on for attempted attention as well, such as how much of a threat the character is, or how rapid his motions are. The weighted sum is then used as the attempted attention estimate. For the simple observability-and-focusing model, we found weights of 0.7 and 0.3, respectively, predicted attention well.

The player's attention is not an unlimited resource; the more things they need to concentrate on, the less well they concentrate on each one. Once attempted attention has been calculated for all characters, you should sum the factors up, producing the *total attentional load L*. To compensate for the nonlinearity of this interference effect (as well as interference from sources outside the game), you should also add a constant *ambient attentional load* to L. The actual attention estimate for each character is then the ratio of their attempted attention to the total attentional load: $A_i = \dfrac{\hat{A}_i}{L}$, where $L = \hat{A}_{amb} + \sum_{j=1}^{n} A_j$. The value $\hat{A}_{amb}$ is a difficult factor to tune; I would suggest setting it such that it represents about 1/3 of L during the most attention-intensive situations in your game. Increasing it will tend to bias resources towards background characters; decreasing it will bias resources towards foreground characters.

11.4.3 Memory

Our model of memory is a simple one based on cognitive models for an experimental memory task known as *associative recognition*, and on a phenomenon known as *retroactive interference*. In general, a player's memory M_i of a character will tend toward their current attention A_i for that character over time. While memorizing (that is, while memory is increasing), the convergence rate will be a fixed $k = k_m$. While forgetting (that is, while memory is decreasing), we'll use a different convergence rate $k = k_f L$, where L is the total attentional load. So it's an EMA again, but with $k = k_m$ if $M_i < A_i$, and $k = k_f L$ if $M_i > A_i$. We used $k_m = 0.6$ and $k_f = 0.001$, which (for our highest observed attentional load) resulted in a 95% memorization rate in about 5 seconds, and a 50% forgetting rate in 10 seconds under a high attentional load. The latter tended to overestimate long-term retention of memory for characters; this wasn't a problem for us, but you may need to tune that factor upward.

11.4.4 Return Time

Return time is much more objective, because it estimates a player's actions rather than her thoughts. It's somewhat misnamed: the output is not an expected number of seconds until the player's return, but rather an expected attenuation factor to current memory at the moment the player does return, as well as to the probability of the player ever returning at all. It's based on something known as the *Weibull hazard function*. The derivation is rather involved, but the resultant equation is $R_i = k(L)^{-k} e^{Lt_0} \Gamma(k, Lt_0)$. L is the expected future attentional load (you can either use the current attentional load, or smooth it with an EMA), and t_0 is the time since the character was last visible (that is, had an observability greater than 0). k is a tweakable parameter which you can experimentally determine by fitting observed return times to a Weibull distribution; the value we determined was approximately 0.8, and we think that's unlikely to differ much in other games. $\Gamma(s, x)$ is the *upper incomplete gamma function*. Implementations of this function are included in many popular math libraries, including Boost.Math.

11.4.5 Duration

To finish the criticality model factors on a nice, easy note, duration is the total amount of attentive observation: the integral of $O_i A_i$ over time. That is, $D_i(t) = D_i(t - \Delta t) + O_i A_i \Delta t$.

11.4.6 Modeling Costs

Compared to criticality scores, costs are much more straightforward and objective to model. Simply set up your game so that a hundred or so characters are simulating using a particular detail level, then compare the profiler output with a run using a different detail level.

11.5 LOD's and BIR's

Again, the reason to categorize BIR's at all is because each category can have its own criticality score. Having a bit of foot skate is probably less noticeable than running in place against a wall: The latter behavior is more obvious. We will refer to it as having higher *audacity*—that is, a lower LOD will be more *audaciously* unrealistic. But given two characters, if one is twice as likely to be noticed foot skating as the other, it is also twice as likely to be noticed running in place as the other. We don't need to have separate criticality models for the two behaviors, because the same factors affect both. So for a particular category of BIR (in this case, unrealistic state) each character has a criticality score, and each detail level (in this case, a type of local steering which can lead to running into walls) will have an audacity score. To sum up, we have three categories of BIRs, three criticality scores per character, and three audacity scores per detail level. (Note that we're only looking at one AI feature for now—in this example, local steering. We'll move to multiple features later.)

By the way, that "twice as likely" mentioned above should remind you of Section 11.2.1, and not by accident. For a single BIR category, we can think of a detail level's audacity score in that category as a base probability in x-space (for some "standard-ly critical character"), and a character's criticality score in that category as a multiplier to it, the product being the probability of *that* character using *that* detail level causing a BIR in *that* category.

But it gets better! Or, at least, more elegantly mathy! Since we're assuming independence, the probability of that character/detail level combination causing a BIR in *any* category is the sum of the products over all three categories. If we stick the detail level's audacity scores for all categories into a vector, call it the *audacity vector A*, and the character's criticality scores for all categories into another vector, call it the *criticality vector C*, the total BIR probability for the combination is given by the dot product $A \cdot C$. Linear algebra—it's not just for geometry anymore!

11.6 The LOD Trader

Now that we have our model, it's time to introduce the LOD Trader algorithm itself. We'll be adding more capabilities to it through the rest of the article; this initial version controls a single LOD feature (say, how pathfinding is performed) with multiple available detail levels, and limits a single resource (say, CPU time).

As you might guess from the name, the LOD Trader is based on a stock trader metaphor. Its "portfolio" consists of all the *current* detail levels for all characters. The LOD Trader's goal is to pick a portfolio that minimizes the total probability of a BIR. Of course, the best possible portfolio would be one where all characters had the highest detail level; but it must additionally limit the total cost of the portfolio to its available resources, so that's (usually) not an option.

Each time the LOD Trader runs, it evaluates its current portfolio and decides on a set of trades, switching some characters to a higher detail level and other characters to a lower detail level, as their relative criticalities and the available resources change. Remember, the total BIR probability for a character being simulated at a particular detail level is the dot product of the character's criticality vector and the detail level's audacity vector. So the LOD Trader will try to pick detail levels that have low audacity scores corresponding to a character's high criticality scores.

Note that for a given trade, we can find a *relative* cost, but also a *relative audacity* which is the difference in the two detail levels' audacity vectors. Just as the absolute BIR probability for a particular detail level is the dot product of the character's criticality vector and the detail level's audacity vector, the relative BIR probability for a particular trade is the dot product of the criticality vector with the change in audacity. We'll refer to increases in BIR probabilities as *upgrades*, and to decreases in BIR probabilities as *downgrades*.

The heuristic the LOD Trader uses to guide its decisions is a simple *value*-based one: units of realism improvement divided by units of resource cost. If a character is simulated at a low detail level, the value of upgrading it to a high detail level is the relative reduction in the total probability of a BIR divided by the relative increase in resource cost. Valuable upgrades will have a large reduction in BIR probability and a low increase in cost. Likewise, if a character is at a high detail level, the value of downgrading it to a lower detail level is the relative increase in the total probability of a BIR divided by the relative reduction in cost; valuable downgrades will increase BIR probability only slightly and decrease the cost by a lot. To keep the math simple, we'll toss in a negative sign, so that upgrade values are positive, and more valuable upgrades have larger magnitude values. For downgrades, values are positive as well, but the most valuable downgrades will have *smaller* magnitudes. (The exception, which should be handled specially. Under some circumstances, a detail upgrade will result in a reduction in cost, or a detail downgrade may result in an increase in cost. The former should always be chosen; the latter never should.)

During a single run, the LOD Trader runs one or more iterations. In each iteration, it hypothesizes making a set of trades (both upgrades and downgrades) that would respect the resource limits and that might result in an overall reduction in BIR probability. If the hypothetical set of trades does, in fact, reduce BIR probability, the trades are actually performed, and the trader continues to iterate, to try to find additional trades to make. Once it finds a hypothetical set of trades which does *not* reduce BIR probability, it stops (and does not make those trades).

The algorithm for choosing the hypothetical set of trades is simple. First it considers upgrades. It repeatedly picks the most valuable available upgrade to add to its set of trades until it has *over*spent its resource budget. Then, it repeatedly picks the most valuable available downgrade to add to its set of trades until it has not overspent its resource budget. Upgrades and downgrades are stored in priority queues to reduce the search cost. Pseudocode for the LOD Trader is in Listing 11.1; remember that this is the initial version, and we'll add more features and improve performance later.

11.6.1 Multiple Features

One of the most useful effects of the multicategory criticality modeling is the ability to control different *kinds* of LOD at the same time. For instance, we can control pathfinding quality (the quality of which primarily affects the probability of a ULTB BIR) and hand IK (which affects the probability of a US BIR). Put differently, we'd like to control multiple *features* (AI systems whose detail is set on a per-character basis). Of course, we could do that by running multiple LOD Traders, one for each feature. But then we'd have to give each one a separate budget; there'd be no way to automatically shift resources between pathfinding and IK as one or the other became important, or to trade a downgrade in the pathfinding quality of one character for an upgrade in the IK quality of another.

Another problem with the multi-Trader approach is that certain features might depend on each other. For instance, we might control both a character's basic behavior (goal-driven or just standing around) and his pathfinding (high quality, low quality, or disabled). Goal-driven behavior and disabled pathfinding, of course, aren't compatible

Listing 11.1. Initial code for the LOD Trader, supporting only one LOD feature and one resource type.

```
def runLODTrader(characters, lodLevels, availableResource):
    acceptedTrades = []
    while True:
        upgrades, downgrades = calcAvailableTrades(characters,
lodLevels) # returns p-queues, sorted by value
        hypTrades = []
        charactersWithTrades = []
        hypBenefit = 0
        hypAvailableResource = availableResource
        while not upgrades.empty() and availableResource > 0:
            upgrade = upgrades.pop()
            hypTrades.append(upgrade)
            charactersWithTrades.append(upgrade.character)
            hypAvailableResource -= upgrade.costIncrease
            hypBenefit += upgrade.probDecrease
        while not downgrades.empty() and availableResource < 0:
            downgrade = downgrades.pop()
            if downgrade.character in charactersWithTrades: continue
            hypTrades.append(downgrade)
            charactersWithTrades.append(downgrade.character)
            hypAvailableResource += downgrade.costDecrease
            hypBenefit -= downgrade.probIncrease
        if hypAvailableResource >= 0 and hypBenefit > 0:
            acceptedTrades += hypothesizedTrades
            availableResource = hypAvailableResource
        else
            return acceptedTrades
```

as detail levels, but there would be no effective way to coordinate the two traders to avoid that result.

Instead, we let a single LOD Trader balance detail levels of all the features at the same time. A character's current "state" as seen by the LOD Trader will not be a single detail level, but will be the combination of their current detail levels for *all* the features. We refer to a set of levels for all features, which respects all the inter-feature constraints, as a *feature solution*. Rather than picking individual feature transitions, we will pick *feature solution transitions* from one feature solution to another, each of which may result in several feature transitions. For each feature solution, we'll precompute and store a list of possible upgrade transitions and possible downgrade transitions, so that we know which ones to look at for a character currently at any particular feature solution.

If the set of features is small, this has little impact on the algorithm; the only major change is the need to check that we don't pick multiple upgrade or downgrade transitions for a single character. However, the number of feature solutions increases exponentially with the number of features. Since we would have to evaluate every character/feature solution combination and insert it into our priority queues, this could result in a lot of computation, and a *lot* of memory usage. Most of this work would be wasted, because it would be spent on evaluating lots of expensive upgrades for lots of faraway, unimportant characters—ones we should know we won't upgrade in *any* way, given their teeny criticality vectors.

Listing 11.2. Expanding a character.

```
def expandCharacter(char, transType):
    bestRatio = None; bestTrans = None
    for trans in char.featureSolution.availableTransitions[transType]:
        ratio = dotProduct(char.C, trans.A)/trans.cost
        if isBetterRatio(ratio, bestRatio):
            bestRatio = ratio; bestTrans = trans
    return bestRatio, bestTrans
```

11.6.2 The Expansion Queue

Instead, we'll use a new, lazier strategy. Instead of a priority queue of upgrade transitions, we'll start with a priority queue of *characters*; we'll refer to this as the *expansion queue*. The sort key we'll use for the expansion queue will be the *expansion heuristic*, which estimates the *best possible* value that could *possibly* be attainable by *any* transition for that character. This value represents an upper limit on transition value for each character, and may be over-optimistic, but it will never be pessimistic; in this sense it is similar to an admissible heuristic for A* search. We'll select upgrade transitions by "expanding" the character at the front of the queue (the one with the highest expansion heuristic) into all of its possible upgrade transitions, and selecting the most valuable one. The pseudocode for expanding a character is shown in Listing 11.2.

Because the heuristic may be over-optimistic, we can't guarantee that the character at the front of the expansion queue actually has the most valuable upgrade transition among all characters. To compensate for this, we will continue expanding characters from the expansion queue, even after we've overspent our resource budget. Once we're overspent, each time we expand a character and choose a new upgrade for our set of hypothetical trades, we'll then repeatedly remove and discard the lowest-valued trade from the upgrades, until we're only overspending by one trade (that is, removing another lowest-valued trade would make us underspend). To make this efficient, we'll store the set of chosen hypothesized upgrades itself as a priority queue, ordered so that the front element has the *lowest* value. Often, the just-expanded, just-inserted upgrade will itself be the lowest-value trade, and will be removed immediately after being added.

When can we stop doing this? When the worst-value transition already picked—the one at the front of the hypothesized upgrades queue—has a higher value than the heuristically predicted value at the front of the expansion queue. Because of the admissibility of the heuristic, we know at this point that we'll never find a better upgrade than we've already picked, so we can stop without expanding any more characters, and the chosen set of upgrades is the ones remaining in the hypothesized upgrades queue. In practice, this happens quite quickly.

The downgrade phase works analogously: we keep an expansion queue sorted by smallest possible value, and pick the lowest value downgrade for each expanded character, inserting it into our hypothesized downgrade queue. Once our resource constraint is no longer violated, after each pick, we continue to pop largest-value downgrades off the hypothesized downgrades queue until popping the next one would violate the resource constraint. Once the character at the front of the expansion queue has a larger heuristic value than the downgrade at the front of the hypothesized downgrades queue, we stop expanding characters.

11.6.3 Pruning Transitions

Before we get to the best-possible-value heuristic, let's look at a certain class of feature solution transitions. These transitions are what one might call "penny-wise and pound-careless." Or perhaps one might technically refer to them as *stupid*. For instance, a feature transition that upgraded animation IK to the highest possible quality, but kept collision avoidance turned off, would be stupid. It's *allowed*, yes, but it should never be chosen; well before you decide to spend CPU time on high-quality IK, you should first decide to keep the character from walking through walls. The possibility of stupid transitions isn't a problem for the LOD Trader, because it won't ever choose them, but it does spend time evaluating them. As it turns out, a lot of solution transitions—well over half of them, in our experience—are stupid.

What typifies a stupid transition? In a mathematical sense, it's being "strictly dominated" by other transitions; that is, regardless of circumstances, there's always a more valuable transition. Let's examine how we go about identifying those, so we can ignore them.

Remember, the value (for upgrades) is probability benefit—the dot product of criticality and audacity—divided by relative cost increase. To put this in equation form, for switching character i from feature solution α to feature solution β, we'll refer to the change in resource cost as $r_{\alpha,\beta} = r_\beta - r_\alpha$, the change in audacity as $A_{\alpha,\beta} = A_\beta - A_\alpha$, and the resultant value as $V_{i,\alpha,\beta} = -(A_{\alpha,\beta} \cdot C_i)/r_{\alpha,\beta}$. (Remember the negative sign—we want positive values for upgrades, even though higher quality is lower audacity.) That depends on the criticality vector C_i. The transition from α to β is "stupid" if, for *any possible* criticality vector, there's some *other*, better feature solution χ such that $V_{i,\alpha,\beta} < V_{i,\alpha,\chi}$.

For a given feature transition, figuring out whether it is strictly dominated can be formulated as a linear programming problem. Alternatively, you can just generate a large number of random criticality vectors, and find the best transition for each. Any transition which isn't chosen at least once is assumed to be strictly dominated, and removed from the list of upgrades to evaluate at that starting feature solution. For stupid downgrades the same thing is done but the "best" transitions are the ones with the smallest-magnitude value.

11.6.4 The Expansion Heuristic

Returning to the heuristic, we'll use it for the expansion queue—that is, estimating the best possible value for any transition for each character. Let's look at that value formula again: $V_{i,\alpha,\beta} = (A_{\alpha,\beta} \cdot C_i)/r_{\alpha,\beta}$. Rearranged, it's $V_{i,\alpha,\beta} = C_i \cdot W_{\alpha,\beta}$, where $W_{\alpha,\beta} = A_{\alpha,\beta}/r_{\alpha,\beta}$. For a particular starting feature solution α, we can gather the W-vectors for all upgrade transitions into a matrix $\mathbf{W}_\alpha = [W_{\alpha,\beta}, W_{\alpha,\gamma}, \cdots]$. Then we can prune it, removing any column that does not have at least one entry greater than the corresponding entry in a different column. Once we have the W-matrix stored for each starting feature solution, we can calculate the heuristic value quite quickly, as the maximum entry in the vector $C_i \mathbf{W}_\alpha$. We do the same thing for downgrade transitions, using a separate matrix for those. (Remember, for downgrades we want smaller values, so we prune columns that do not have at least one *lower* entry.) This value heuristic calculation is shown in the pseudocode of Listing 11.3.

Listing 11.3. Calculating the value heuristic for a character.

```
def calcValueHeuristic(char, transType):
    elems = matrixMul(char.C, char.featureSolution.W)
    if transType == 'upgrade': return max(elems)
    else: return min(elems)
```

11.6.5 Multiple Resources

CPU time may not be our only resource constraint. For instance, suppose one of the features we'd like to control is whether a character remembers other characters who have been friendly or hostile towards him. That could easily become a large RAM sink, so we'd like to keep our memory usage under a particular budget as well. This is a situation where we might be able to use multiple LOD Traders, one for each resource type, but it's possible that a single feature might have ramifications for more than one resource. As before, we'd like a single trader to do all the work of balancing things. The cost of a detail level will now be vector-valued, as will the total cost of a feature solution and the relative cost of a feature solution transition.

The first thing we have to do is adapt our value heuristic. "Dividing by cost" doesn't work anymore because cost is a vector. We'll use a *resource multiplier vector M* to generate a scalar metric for cost. During the upgrade phase, the resource multiplier for each resource type is the reciprocal of the amount of that resource, which is currently unused. If CPU time is at a premium but there's plenty of free memory, the resource multiplier vector will have a larger entry for CPU than RAM. In case a resource is neither over- nor underspent, it should have a large but not infinite resource multiplier. During the downgrade phase, the resource multiplier is directly proportional to the amount of overspending; resources that are not overspent have a resource multiplier of 0. The resource multiplier vector is recalculated before each upgrade and each downgrade phase, but not during an upgrade or downgrade phase.

Next, we need to adapt our stopping criteria. Rather than picking upgrades such that the only resource is overspent by a single upgrade, we will pick upgrades until *any* resource is overspent. We will then pick downgrades until *no* resources are overspent.

We also need to adapt our definition of stupid feature solutions, and our expansion heuristic. When determining whether a feature solution will ever be chosen, we need to check it against not only a large number of random criticality vectors, but also resource multiplier vectors. And when generating $W_{\alpha,\beta}$, we need to maximize it over all possible resource multiplier vectors: $W_{\alpha,\beta} = A_{\alpha,\beta} / \left(\min_M M \cdot r_{\alpha,\beta} \right)$. (For both of these, you should consider only *normalized* resource multipliers.) In order to get the best performance results out of both feature solution pruning and the expansion heuristic, you should come up with expected limits on the ratios between resource multipliers, and clip actual resource multipliers to these limits.

Finally, note that some feature solution transitions will have both positive and negative resource costs: these should be allowed as upgrades, but not allowed as downgrades.

Listing 11.4. Making the expansion queue over all characters.

```
def makeExpansionQueue(characters, M, transType):
    if transType == 'upgrade': expansionQueue = maxQueue()
    else: expansionQueue = minQueue()
    for char in characters:
        valueHeuristic = calcValueHeuristic(char, M, transType)
        expansionQueue.insert(char, valueHeuristic)
```

Listing 11.5. Final pseudocode for the LOD trader, supporting multiple features and resource types.

```
def runLODTrader(characters, availableResources):
    acceptedTrades = []
    while True:
        M = calcResourceMultiplier(availableResources)
        hypUpgrades, hypAvailableResources =
selectTransitions(characters, M, 'upgrade', availableResources)
        M = calcResourceMultiplier(availableResources)
        hypDowngrades, hypAvailableResources =
selectTransitions(characters, M, 'downgrade', hypAvailableResources)
        hypTrades = hypUpgrades + hypDowngrades
        if calcTotalBenefit(hypTrades) > 0:
            acceptedTrades += hypTrades
            availableResources = hypAvailableResources
        else:
            return acceptedTrades
def selectTransitions(characters, M, transType, availableResources):
    expansionQueue = makeExpansionQueue(characters, M, transType)
    if transType == 'upgrade': transitionHeap = minQueue()
    else: transitionHeap = maxQueue()
    while availableResources.allGreaterEqual(0) or
isBetterRatio(expansionQueue.peekKey(), transitionHeap.peekKey()):
        char = expansionQueue.popValue()
        bestRatio, bestTrans = expandCharacter(char, M, transType)
        transitionHeap.insert(bestTrans, bestRatio)
        availableResources -= bestTrans.costs
        while (availableResources + transitionHeap.peekValue().costs).
anyLess(0):
            discardedTrans = transitionHeap.popValue()
            availableResources += discardedTrans.costs
    return transitionHeap.values(), availableResources
```

11.6.6 Putting it All Together

Listing 11.5. shows the updated pseudocode for multiple features and resources.

11.6.7 Other Extensions to the LOD Trader

In addition to constraining which levels for different features can be used together, it's possible to constrain which levels of a single feature can transition to which other features. For instance, you might transition a character from prerecorded animation to fully dynamic motion, but not be able to transition back from dynamic motion to prerecorded animation. This can be done simply by discarding feature solution transitions that include such a transition.

It's also possible to attach costs and audacities to a feature transition itself, instead of just to feature levels. Attaching costs to transitions can be useful if the transitioning process itself requires nontrivial computation; attaching audacity can be useful if the transition is liable to produce a visible "pop" or if it involves a loss of character information which could later lead to a FD or ULTB BIR.

In some situations it's useful to introduce the concept of a "null" detail level for a particular LOD feature. For instance, the "standing around" behavior detail level would only be compatible with the "null" locomotion detail level, and the "doing stuff" behavior detail level would be compatible with all locomotion detail levels *except* the null level.

An unusual but useful application of the LOD Trader is as an alternative to the "simulation bubble" often used to delete faraway characters. This is done by means of an "existence" LOD feature, with "yes" and "no" levels, where the "no" level is compatible with all other LOD features being "null" and has zero audacity and zero cost, but where the transition from "yes" to "no" itself has US and FD audacity. When a character transitions to the "no" existence level, it is removed.

Another unusual but useful application is to consider "save space" as an additional resource. This can be constrained only when the game is about to be saved, and ensures that the most useful and memorable bits of game state are kept around when saving to a device with limited space.

The LOD Trader can also be leveraged in multiplayer games, simply by adding up the criticality for a given character based on all players currently observing that character. Because of the additive nature of the x-space probabilities, this will result in correct estimation and minimization of BIR probability. Additionally, the LOD Trader can be used to ration network bandwidth by controlling update rates and update detail for different characters; in this situation, a separate LOD Trader instance is run for each player.

Finally, not all characters controlled by the LOD Trader need to have the same LOD features; you need only maintain different transition sets for each "kind" of character, and then have the LOD Trader control, say, both pedestrians and stationary shopkeepers. In fact, not all "characters" controlled by the LOD Trader need be characters at all: it can heterogeneously manage humans, vehicles, destructible objects, and anything and everything which can benefit from criticality-driven LOD control.

11.7 The LOD Trader in Practice

We've had great results with the LOD Trader. We implemented it in a free-roaming game involving hundreds of characters, having it control eight separate features with hundreds of potential feature solutions. We also implemented conventional distance-based LOD picking, so that we could compare the two. The trickiest part of the LOD Trader implementation process was tuning the criticality metrics and audacity vectors, due to their subjectivity. This is an area where playtester feedback could be extremely helpful.

As expected, distance-based LOD picking was only marginally acceptable. In order to guarantee a reasonable framerate, it was necessary to set the threshold distances so close that things like low-quality locomotion could be clearly seen, particularly in sparsely populated areas of the game world and where there were long, unobstructed lines of sight. The LOD Trader, in contrast, was very effective at maintaining framerate in the most crowded situations, and in sparse areas it simulated most characters at the highest LOD.

A controlled, blinded experimental study verified out this impression: Viewers shown videos of the game running with distance-based LOD picking were consistently more likely to experience BIRs, and to experience them more often, than viewers shown videos of the game running with the LOD Trader [Sunshine-Hill 11].

The LOD Trader itself had very good performance: its average execution time was 57 microseconds per frame, or 0.17% of the target frame time. Its memory usage was 500 kB for the transition data and 48 bytes per entity, both of which could easily be halved by picking narrower datatypes, with no reduction in functionality.

11.8 Conclusions

As mentioned in the introduction, the LOD Trader isn't magical. It can't read the player's mind. Its criticality models are approximate, and often very inaccurate.

But that's okay. The goal of the LOD Trader is not to make wildly audacious detail reductions and get away with them. Rather, the goal is to be clever enough to do detail reduction in the *right places* in those moments when detail reduction has to happen *somewhere*. In those moments, the question is not *whether* to reduce LOD but *how* to reduce LOD without causing glaring problems, and we just can't depend on distance-based LOD picking to do that.

And we *need* to be able to depend on our LOD picker. Because detail reduction is always, *always* going to be needed. We'll never have enough computational resources to do all the things we want to do. And when we're not doing detail reduction at runtime, that just means we're doing it at development time, throwing away good techniques because we don't know if we'll always be able to afford them. That's the real benefit of the LOD Trader: the power to implement AI techniques as lavishly detailed as we can imagine, and others as massively scalable as we can devise, with the confidence that our game will be able to leverage each one when it counts the most.

Reference

[Sunshine-Hill 11] B. Sunshine-Hill. *Perceptually Driven Simulation* (Doctoral dissertation). Available online (http://repository.upenn.edu/edissertations/435), 2011.

12

Runtime Compiled C++ for Rapid AI Development

Doug Binks, Matthew Jack, and Will Wilson

12.1 Introduction

Scripting languages have always been a foundation of rapid AI development but with the increasing demands of AI, their performance drawbacks are becoming ever more problematic. On the other hand, traditional C++ development approaches generally lead to lengthy compile and link times, which limit the amount of iteration and testing that programmers can undertake. Though development tools are progressing in this area, developers still need to run the build and load content to see the end result, and edit-and-continue style approaches do not work for all codebases or changes.

In this article we demonstrate how the same fast iteration times and error-handling can be achieved using pure C++ through a novel approach, which we call Runtime

Compiled C++ (RCC++). RCC++ allows developers to change code while the game is running, and have the code compiled and linked into the game rapidly with state preserved. Programmers can thus get feedback on their changes in seconds rather than minutes or more. The technique has been used in the development of AAA games at Crytek, and gives similar results to Hot Reload as seen in *Epic's Unreal Engine 4*. The RCC++ code is available as a permissively licensed open source project on GitHub and the accompanying disk [Jack, Binks, Rutkowski 11].

12.2 Alternative Approaches

A variety of alternative approaches can be used to achieve fast iteration times in games, each with their own pros and cons. Overall we believe that none offer the main benefits of Runtime Compiled C++, and many techniques can be enhanced by using RCC++ alongside them.

12.2.1 Scripting Languages

Scripting languages provide perhaps the most common solution to achieving fast iteration. A recent games engine survey showed Lua to be the foremost scripting language in game development [DeLoura 09], though UnrealScript [Epic 12a] likely represents a substantial proportion of the market, given the size of the Unreal Engine community. Despite the popularity of scripting languages, we feel that they have a number of issues when used for core features, namely integration overheads, performance, tools and debugging, and low level support such as vector operations and multithreading. In fact, many of the game engine implementations we have encountered do not permit runtime editing of game scripts, which reduces the benefit of using them considerably.

Games written in C++ need an interface to the scripting language in order to allow features to be implemented. A variety of techniques and methods are available to make this relatively simple, but a recompile and game reload will be forced when an interface change is required.

While script performance is improving, it is still well below that of compiled code such as C++ [Fulgham 12]. Indeed, Facebook moved their PHP script code to pre-compiled C++ using the open source cross compiler HipHop, which they developed to address performance issues. They found significant benefits in terms of reduced CPU overhead and thus expenditure and maintenance of systems [Zao 10]. Garbage collection can also be an issue, with optimized systems even spending several milliseconds per frame [Shaw 10]. On consoles, Data Execution Protection (DEP) prevents VMs from Just-In-Time (JIT) compiling, limiting an opportunity for performance optimizations offered by cutting-edge VMs running on PC.

Debugging a C++ application that enters a script VM can prove difficult to impossible, and many of the tools developers use on a day-to-day basis, such as performance and memory profilers, also may not have visibility of the internals of a VM in a way that can be traced back to the original source code.

C++ provides easy integration with native instruction sets via assembly language, as well as direct access to memory. This low level support permits developers to target enhanced, yet common, feature sets such as SIMD vector units, multithreading, and coprocessor units such as the Sony PS3's SPUs.

Havok Script (originally Kore Script) was developed out of the motivation of solving some of these issues [Havok 12], providing an optimized VM along with performance improvements, debugger support, and profiling tools.

12.2.2 Visual Studio Edit and Continue

Edit and Continue is a standard feature of Visual Studio for C++ introduced in Visual C++ 6.0, allowing small changes to code to be made while debugging through a technique known as "code patching" [Staheli 98]. However, there are some major limitations, the most critical of which are that you can't make changes to a data type that affect the layout of an object (such as data members of a class), and you can't make changes to optimized code [Microsoft 10].

12.2.3 Multiple Processes

Multiple processes can be used to separate code and state so as to speed compile and load times, with either shared memory, pipes, or more commonly TCP/IP used to communicate between them. This is the fundamental approach used by many console developers with the game running on a console and the editor on a PC, and as used by client/server style multiplayer games. Support for recompiling and reloading of one of the processes can be implemented reasonably simply if the majority of the state lies in the other process, and since there is a clean separation between processes, this can be a convenient approach to take. However, the communication overhead usually limits this to certain applications such as being able to modify the editor, while having the game and its game state still running while the editor process is recompiled and reloaded. Turnaround times can still be relatively long since the executable needs to be compiled, linked, and run.

12.2.4 Data-Driven Approaches

Many game engines provide data-driven systems to enhance the flexibility of their engine, for example the *CryENGINE 3* uses XML files to specify AI behavior selection trees [Crytek 2012]. Since the underlying functionality can be written in C++, this methodology can overcome many of the issues with scripting languages, while providing designers not fluent in programming languages a safe and relatively easy to use environment for developing gameplay. While frameworks such as data-driven behavior trees can allow a good balance to be struck, this approach can descend into implementing a scripting language in XML, with all the associated problems.

12.2.5 Visual Scripting

Visual Scripting systems such as Epic Games' *Unreal Kismet* and Crytek's *CryENGINE* Flow-Graph provide a graphical user interface to game logic [Epic 12b, Crytek 12]. Functionality blocks are typically written in C++ with inputs, outputs, and data members that can be graphically edited and linked to other functional blocks, thus providing the potential for complex systems to be created. This is fundamentally a data-driven system with an enhanced user interface.

12.2.6 Library Reloading

Dynamic link libraries (DLLs, called "shared objects" on Unix variants) can be loaded during runtime, providing an obvious means to allow fast iteration by recompiling and reloading the DLL. A key feature for game developers is that both the Xbox 360 and PS3 consoles support dynamically loaded libraries, as do iOS (for development purposes only—not in released code) and Android. Function and object pointers need to be patched up, and the interfaces to the DLL can't be changed. If the code for the DLL project is large, compile times can be significant limiting the iteration turnaround. Despite the attraction of this approach, in practice the difficulty of splitting up and maintaining a game with many small-sized DLLs, along with the infrastructure required for delay load linking and state preservation, means this approach is rarely used.

12.3 Runtime Compiled C++

Runtime Compiled C++ permits the alteration of compiled C++ code while your game is running. RCC++ uses DLLs, but rather than building an entire project, the runtime compiler only rebuilds and links the minimal source files required. By using loose coupling techniques, dependencies are kept to a minimum. The resulting dynamic library is loaded, and game state is saved and then restored with the new code now being used. Changes to C++ code are thus possible during a gameplay or editor session with a turnaround time of several seconds. Developers do not need to manage multiple project configurations, as the DLLs are constructed automatically on the fly as required. Indeed, the codebase can be built as a single executable. RCC++ can be seen in action in Figure 12.1.

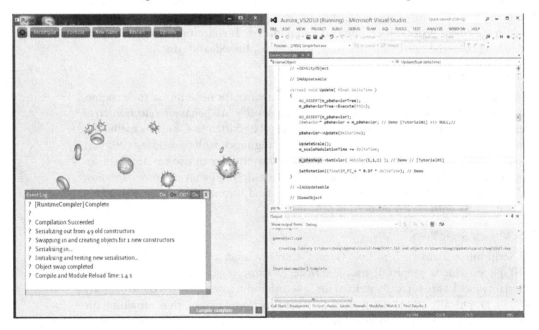

Figure 12.1

The demo game *Pulse* compiling files at runtime after a change, with Visual Studio on the right being used to make the changes. Compiler output goes to both demo event log and Visual Studio Output window to enable navigation to errors with double clicking. Time taken to compile and load changed code is 1.4s as shown by event log in this instance.

Unlike Edit and Continue, RCC++ permits changes to object layout including the addition of entirely new classes, and it works with optimized code as well as debug. Since we're dealing with compiled C++, we enjoy the full feature set this gives along with the ability to use intrinsic functions which access instruction set features like SIMD and atomics, along with OS level functionality such as multithreading. By using one language for development we can use all the tools we have at our disposal, from seamless debugging to performance profilers. Intriguingly, both fixing bugs and optimizing code can now be done on the fly.

We believe that this approach is well suited to replacing scripting as used by programmers for fast iteration, and that designer tools such as data-driven systems and visual scripting languages can be easily enhanced through the use of RCC++. Other developers appear to agree; for example, Epic has dropped UnrealScript entirely in *Unreal Engine 4* by switching to an approach similar in results to RCC++ called Hot Reload. Flexibility for designers is preserved through improvements to the Kismet Visual Scripting system [EPIC 12c].

12.4 Runtime Compiled C++ Implementation

The Runtime Compiled C++ implementation consists of two main components: the Runtime Compiler and the Runtime Object System. The Runtime Compiler handles file change notification and compilation. The Runtime Object System handles tracking of source files and their dependencies. It also provides the `IObject` base class interface and `IObjectFactorySystem` for creating objects and swapping them when new code is loaded. This separation is intended to allow developers to create their own dynamic reloading code while keeping the compiler functionality. Additionally, for console and mobile games, the Runtime Compiler can more easily be moved to a separate process running on the host system.

12.4.1 The Runtime Compiler

The Runtime Compiler provides a simple C++ interface to a compiler. Currently Visual Studio 8.0, 9.0, and 10.0 compilers are supported (Visual Studio 2005, 2008, and 2010) in both the free Express and full versions, and both x86 and x64 targets can be built.

A primary goal of the compiler is to provide rapid turnaround. Compiles are run from a command line process which is instantiated on initialization of the compiler and preserved between compiles. We found that setting up the environment variables for compiles took a substantial amount of time, so by setting these only once and keeping the process active we cut down the time of small compiles significantly. A simple compiler logging interface is provided that can be implemented and passed to the compiler to get compilation output. A handy trick on Windows is to output this using the `OutputDebugString()` function in addition to any other logging; with Visual Studio any errors or warnings can then be doubled clicked to navigate to the offending source.

The Runtime Compiler monitors files that have been registered with the system by the Runtime Object System, and when changes are detected it compiles these files and any dependencies into a DLL module, which is then loaded by the Runtime Object System.

12.4.2 The Runtime Object System

The Runtime Object System provides the functionality needed to have code changes detected, compiled with the correct dependencies, and for the resulting module to be loaded and objects switched over to using the new code. To make compilation as fast as possible, the minimal number of dependencies is compiled.

The runtime object system relies on the C++ virtual function feature to be able to swap objects by simply swapping pointers from the old object to the new object. If the functions were non-virtual, the function pointer would be embedded in any code that calls the function, so the old code would always be run. A simple runtime-modifiable class could be comprised of a header declaring the class as follows:

Listing 12.1. An example runtime object, deriving from IObject.

```
class MyRuntimeModifiableObject : public IObject
{
public:
    virtual void DoSomething();
};
```

In order to be able to make changes at runtime we need to expose this class via a factory style constructor. This is done by applying the macro REGISTERCLASS(MyRuntime ModifiableObject) in the.cpp file, which adds the path of the source file to a list that the Runtime Compiler monitors. When this source file is changed, we compile the source file along with the common Runtime Object System interface code into a DLL and then load the resulting module. Even if the project contains many source files only two need to be compiled and linked into the module in the minimum case. After module load we now have two or more classes called MyRuntimeModifiableObject along with their respective constructors, which is possible as each is in a different module (for example, one is in the executable and another in a DLL). The Runtime Object System can be used to create a new set of objects to replace old ones using the new constructor, and their pointers swapped so that code now references the new class.

We considered several techniques for achieving the runtime swapping of pointers. The two main candidates were a smart pointer, which added one further level of indirection through a pointer table, allowing object pointer swapping to occur at extremely low cost, and serialization of all objects with pointer replacement occurring using an object ID that offered low runtime overhead but a higher cost to swap pointers. In order to preserve object state when changing code we need to have serialization in place anyway, and the reduced runtime overhead seemed a win for serialization. Since the state only needs to be written and read from memory, this serialization can be extremely fast. For non runtime modifiable code, an event system permits developers to use the Object ID to swap object pointers when new code is loaded.

Using virtual functions introduces one level of indirection, so developers of performance-critical areas of code should look at the Section 12.8 on Code Optimizations for

Listing 12.2. Accessing functionality via a system table.

```
//Interface to Runtime Object System
struct IRuntimeObjectSystem
{
public:
    ...
    virtual void CompileAll(bool bForceRecompile) = 0;
    ...
}
//System table to access engine functionality
struct SystemTable
{
    IRuntimeObjectSystem * pRuntimeObjectSystem;
    //other interface pointers can be added here
};
//Example usuage in a GUI button event:
class OnClickCompile : public IGUIEventListener
{
public:
    virtual void OnEvent(int event_id, const IGUIEvent& event_info)
    {
        SystemTable* pSystemTable = PerModuleInterface::GetInstance()->
GetSystemTable();
        pSystemTable->pRuntimeObjectSystem->CompileAll(true);
    }
};
```

suggestions. Note that the use of virtual functions does not imply that the developer needs to implement a complex polymorphic class system with deep inheritance trees.

In order for runtime code to access features of nonruntime modifiable code, we provide a mechanism for passing a System Table object pointer to runtime modifiable code. This System Table can then be used to store pointers to interfaces of the game engine's subsystems, such as rendering, audio, physics, etc. In Listing 12.2, we make accessible the Runtime Object System subsystem itself to allow the user to force a full recompile. This example is taken from the Pulse demo in the code sample included with this book (called SimpleTest in the code base).

The overall architecture of the Runtime Object System is best illustrated by looking at a full example of its application, which we'll do in the next section.

12.5 Runtime Compilation in Practice—a Step-by-Step Example

In this example we'll look at implementing a simple Win32 console application which runs a main loop every second, calling an update function on a runtime object. In the following listings we've removed some of the implementation so as to focus on the main elements. Once again see the included source code for full details, in the ConsoleExample project.

The main entry point of the project simply constructs a ConsoleGame object, calls its Init() function, and then calls the MainLoop() function in a loop until this returns

Listing 12.3. The `ConsoleGame` class declaration in ConsoleGame.h.

```
class ConsoleGame : public IObjectFactoryListener
{
public:
    ConsoleGame();
    virtual ~ConsoleGame();
    bool Init();
    bool MainLoop();
    virtual void OnConstructorsAdded();
private:
    //Runtime Systems
    ICompilerLogger*       m_pCompilerLogger;
    IRuntimeObjectSystem*  m_pRuntimeObjectSystem;
    //Runtime object
    IUpdateable*  m_pUpdateable;
    ObjectId      m_ObjectId;
};
```

Listing 12.4. ConsoleGame initialization. The string "`RuntimeObject01`" refers to the class name of the object we wish to construct.

```
bool ConsoleGame::Init()
{
    //Initialize the RuntimeObjectSystem
    m_pRuntimeObjectSystem = new RuntimeObjectSystem;
    m_pCompilerLogger = new StudioLogSystem();
    m_pRuntimeObjectSystem->Initialize(m_pCompilerLogger, 0);
m_pRuntimeObjectSystem->GetObjectFactorySystem()->AddListener(this);
    //construct first object
    IObjectConstructor* pCtor =
m_pRuntimeObjectSystem->GetObjectFactorySystem()->
GetConstructor("RuntimeObject01");
    if(pCtor)
    {
        IObject* pObj = pCtor->Construct();
        pObj->GetInterface(&m_pUpdateable);
        if(0 == m_pUpdateable)
        {
            delete pObj;
            return false;
        }
        m_ObjectId = pObj->GetObjectId();
    }
    return true;
}
```

false. The `ConsoleGame` class, which derives from `IObjectFactoryListener`, receives an event call when a new constructor has been added after a code change, allowing us to swap the runtime object pointers using an ID lookup. The data member `m_pUpdateable` is where we store the native pointer, while `m_ObjectId` stores the id of the runtime object.

ConsoleGame.cpp contains the fundamental aspects required for a RCC++ implementation. The initialization requires creating a logging system (which simply writes the log output to `stdout`), and the Runtime Object System, followed by adding the `ConsoleGame` as a listener for events and then creating our runtime object—in this case, a class called simply `RuntimeObject01`.

When new code is loaded, the `IObjectFactoryListener::OnConstructors Added()` method is called, and we use this to swap our object pointer to the new code as in the listing below.

Listing 12.5. Swapping runtime object pointers after new code is loaded.

```
void ConsoleGame::OnConstructorsAdded()
{
    if(m_pUpdateable)
    {
        IObject* pObj =
m_pRuntimeObjectSystem->GetObjectFactorySystem()->GetObject(m_ObjectId);
        pObj->GetInterface(&m_pUpdateable);
    }
}
```

The main loop first checks for compilation completion, and loads a new module if a compile has just completed. We then update the file change notification system and our runtime object through the `IUpdateable` interface.

If we want to change the class declaration at runtime, a separate virtual interface is needed for nonruntime modifiable code. This interface shouldn't be modified at runtime, though header tracking allows the interfaces between different runtime source files to be changed. In practice, the more code that is moved to being runtime compiled, the less restrictive this becomes. Our console example has a simple interface as in Listing 12.6; this defines the `Update()` function and also derives from `IObject`.

Listing 12.6. The update function is declared as an abstract interface.

```
struct IUpdateable : public IObject
{
    virtual void Update(float deltaTime) = 0;
};
```

Listing 12.7. The runtime object. This code can be modified while the console example is running, with saving the file out causing compilation and reloading of the code.

```cpp
class RuntimeObject01 : public TInterface<IID_IUPDATEABLE,IUpdateable>
{
public:
    virtual void Update(float deltaTime)
    {
        std::cout << "Runtime Object 01 update called!\n";
    }
};
REGISTERCLASS(RuntimeObject01);
```

The runtime object code is correspondingly simple. The class, defined in Listing 12.7, derives from a template which implements the `GetInterface()` member function, which in this case allows us to get hold of a pointer to an `IUpdateable*` using the interface ID, `IID_IUPDATEABLE`.

Putting this together, and running the sample, we're able to change the `Update()` function and save out, seeing our changes in action in the console. Listing 12.8 shows example output from a session where we've added "NEW!" to the output.

12.6 Runtime Error Recovery

We felt that for RCC++ to be really practical, it had to have a form of crash protection. After all, it would be a frustrating experience if you could avoid quitting, recompiling, reloading only until your first simple mistake, when a null pointer forces you to close it all down and start over. We looked at two main approaches to achieving this: using a separate process, and structured exception handling.

Google Chrome uses the process approach for each of its tabs, allowing one to crash without affecting any of the others. This is a very robust approach, but unless your engine's architecture has this in mind, it may result in a very large number of interprocess function calls, which would have severe performance impact. We wanted an approach that would be easy to drop into existing projects.

Structured exception handling (SEH) is a Win32 API feature that allows handling of runtime errors such as access violations. It behaves much like standard exceptions but is in fact quite separate; there are various reasons why standard exceptions are not used on games consoles, but these don't affect SEH. When a runtime error such as a null pointer dereference occurs, the OS checks a stack of possible handlers registered by the application to see how to proceed. The crash dialogs you see in Windows are, in fact, the default handler; when Visual Studio's debugger is attached, that adds another.

Using SEH it is quite easy to catch an error and carry straight on. In our case, the key place for this is around the update calls on our game objects. When an update fails, we disable it until the code has been runtime-recompiled, then we try again. During this process the rest of the application—rendering, GUI, logging—all keep running.

But actually, you don't want to handle a crash silently—you'd really like to find out what caused it first! You could add code to produce a stack trace. However, debuggers like

Listing 12.8. The console example compiling files at runtime after a change. Note the added 'NEW!' to the output of the update function.

```
Main Loop - press q to quit. Updates every second.
Runtime Object 01 update called!

Main Loop - press q to quit. Updates every second.
Runtime Object 01 update called!

Main Loop - press q to quit. Updates every second.
FileChangeNotifier triggered recompile of files:
Compiling...
Created intermediate folder "Runtime"
cl /nologo /O2 /LD /Zi /MP /Fo"Runtime\\" /D WIN32 /EHa /FeC:\Temp\
BFCB.tmp "e:\aurora\examples\consoleexample\runtimeobject01.cpp"
"e:\aurora\runtimeobjectsystem\objectinterfacepermodulesource.cpp"
echo _COMPLETION_TOKEN_
Runtime Object 01 update called!
Microsoft Windows [Version 6.1.7601]
Copyright (c) 2009 Microsoft Corporation.  All rights reserved.

E:\Aurora\Examples\ConsoleExample>
Setting environment for using Microsoft Visual Studio 2010 x64 tools.

runtimeobject01.cpp
objectinterfacepermodulesource.cpp
    Creating library C:\Temp\BFCB.lib and object C:\Temp\BFCB.exp

[RuntimeCompiler] Complete
'ConsoleExample.exe' (Win32): Loaded 'C:\Temp\BFCB.tmp'. Symbols loaded.
Compilation Succeeded
Serializing out from 1 old constructors
Swapping in and creating objects for 1 new constructors
Serialising in...
Initialising and testing new serialisation...
Object swap completed

Main Loop - press q to quit. Updates every second.
NEW! Runtime Object 01 update called!

Main Loop - press q to quit. Updates every second.
NEW! Runtime Object 01 update called!
```

that in Visual Studio already provide a really ideal interface when crashes occur, allowing you to inspect state easily. So really, we would like to crash, but then continue.

In fact, this is exactly what we do; we first allow the crash to proceed as normal so we can use Visual Studio to debug it, after which the user can hit the "continue" button in the IDE. Usually the "continue" option is quite useless but in our case we catch the crash on the second attempt—and proceed with execution. We get the best of both.

As an aid to productivity, we include a runtime assert macro that is compatible with the runtime exception handling process.

12.6.1 Handling Errors on Loading New Code

When new code is loaded (see the `ObjectFactorySystem::AddConstructors` function in the prototype), we need to construct the new objects, serialize state into them, and initialize them (if required). Since the process is reliant on working serialization, we also test serializing out from the newly constructed objects. Structured exceptions (crashes) could occur during this process, so we use the runtime exception filter to handle them, and revert to running the old code and state. This gives the developer an opportunity to fix the problem and reload the new code without restarting the application.

Should an error be caught, the new objects that were constructed are deleted. This introduces a new failure path in the destructor, so this also uses runtime exception handling and simply leaks the objects when an error occurs.

Another issue which can commonly occur is that the new code pollutes the data during this process in such a way as to not crash, but to render the application instance unusable. A trivial solution, which has not yet been implemented in our codebase, would be to maintain an undo list of code and data to allow developers to revert back to a previously working state and make further changes from there.

Further stability could be added by unit testing new code prior to loading, and/or creating a save point on disk. If developers intend to use the Runtime Compiled C++ approach in an editing tool we would recommend adding these features, but for a programming productivity tool we believe these steps would be counterproductive due to the extra delay in turnaround.

12.7 More Complex Code-State Preservation and Header File Handling

When swapping new code for old, it is desirable to ensure that the state of the old object is propagated to the new one. The Runtime Object System includes a simple serialization system designed for the needs of runtime modification of code.

The SERIALIZE macro can be used for any type that implements the operator = method, which also permits types to be changed to compatible types, such as float to double or int etc. Non runtime pointers can be serialized by their value since the address doesn't change, but runtime pointers are serialized through their ObjectId.

Listing 12.9. An example serialization function.

```
virtual void Serialize(ISimpleSerializer *pSerializer)
{
    IBaseClass::Serialize(pSerializer);
    //any type which implements operator = including pointers
    SERIALIZE(m_SomeType);
    //serialize a runtime object pointer
    SERIALIZEIOBJPTR(m_pIObjectPointer);
    if (pSerializer->IsLoading()) {
        //do something only when loading values
    }
    //serialize something whose name has changed
    pSerializer->Serialize("m_Color", m_Colour);
}
```

12. Runtime Compiled C++ for Rapid AI Development

To save developer time, the same serialization function is called on both load and save of state. For situations where different behavior is needed, the `IsLoading()` function can be used.

Values are serialized by name, so if the name of the object changes the developer should use the `Serialize` function directly rather than the macro, and replace with the macro once it's been loaded.

A simple header file dependency tracking method has been implemented. To use this, add the `RUNTIME_MODIFIABLE_INCLUDE` to the header file (defined in `RuntimeInclude.h`), and when this file changes any code which includes it and has a runtime modifiable class will be recompiled. This macro expands to a recursive template specialization that, when such headers are included from a.cpp file, uses the _COUNTER_ macro to assign successive numbers to the filenames of each. This enables the system to iterate through all of the include files for a given class.

12.8 Code Optimizations for Performance-Critical Code

We use virtual functions to give runtime redirection of function calls when new code is loaded. This adds a small performance penalty to the function call. For many AI and scripting style use cases, this is still equal or better performance than alternatives such as running a script VM or using a data-driven approach. However, some simple approaches can reduce or eliminate this penalty.

For developers who only use the virtual functions for runtime compiling of code, it is possible to write a macro for final release builds which declares the appropriate functions to be nonvirtual, so long as polymorphic behavior is not required. This introduces a potentially substantial difference between builds, so a strong test regime is required.

Listing 12.10. Optimization for final release builds by removing virtual from performance-critical functions. Note that we don't declare an abstract interface, so the developer must take care to ensure they only use virtual or RUNTIME_VIRTUAL functions in nonruntime code.

```
#ifdef RUNTIME_COMPILED
#define RUNTIME_VIRTUAL virtual
#else
#define RUNTIME_VIRTUAL
#endif
class SomeClass : public Tinterface<IID_ISOMECLASS,IObject>
{
public:
    virtual void SomeVirtualFunction();
    RUNTIME_VIRTUAL void OnlyVirtualForRuntimeCompile();
private:
    //members which are not virtual or RUNTIME_VIRTUAL
};
```

A simpler alternative is to base the high performance areas of the code around aggregated calls, similar to the approaches taken in data oriented programming. For example, if we consider the following function performing operations on a game object:

Listing 12.11. Simple virtual function example declaration and definition.

```
virtual void Execute(IGameObject* pObject)
{
    //perform actions on one game object
}
```

If we have many calls to execute in our game the virtual call overhead may become significant. So we could replace this by aggregating all calls as follows:

Listing 12.12. Redesigned function to reduce virtual function call overhead and improve cache coherency by processing multiple objects per call.

```
virtual void Execute(IGameObject* pObjects, size_t numObjects)
{
    //perform actions on many game objects
}
```

Here, we've defined this based on a new interface that requires the developer to pass in an array of game objects to process, and so have reduced the cost of the virtual function call to 1/numObjects times the original cost. Additionally there are potential benefits from cache coherency, which could give even further performance benefits.

12.9 Use Case: A Behavior Tree and Blackboard Architecture

The ability to change code freely at runtime doesn't just speed up iteration on existing workflow. It can also allow us to approach problems in an entirely different manner. Some of the first techniques we reevaluated this way were behavior trees and blackboards.

Bastions of modern game AI, behavior trees provide a framework for breaking down complex AI into modular pieces with structured reactive decision making, and have been described widely, including in this very book. Blackboards are a simple approach to sharing data between aspects of an AI while remaining loosely coupled. Often the two are used together, with conditionals within the behavior tree reading primarily from the blackboard, while that data is updated regularly from sensory systems and written to by the operations of the behaviors themselves.

12.9.1 A "Soft-Coded" Behavior Tree

Here, we take as an example a "first-generation" behavior tree—essentially a decision tree with behavior states as its leaves, a very common design in modern games including *Crysis 2*.

Implementations have included the use of snippets of Lua to form flexible conditions at each node, or in *Crysis 2* a simple virtual machine executing a tree specified by XML [Martins 11]. However, in essence, the structure is a simple tree of if-else statements—the rest of the behavior tree architecture deriving from the requirement for rapid iteration, as a set of hardcoded C++ if-else clauses would bring AI development to a near halt.

We can now reevaluate that assumption. Under RCC++ such decision code can be thought of as "soft"-coded—we can change it at will while the game is running. So, assuming some nicely formatted code, let's consider its properties: being raw C++, it is obviously extremely fast, it will handle errors without crashing, it has easy access to all the state in our AI system, it can share sub-trees as function calls, it can use all our C++ math and utility routines, we can make use of our existing debugger, we can apply our existing profiler if we need to, you can see useful diffs from source control … the list goes on. In a few lines of code you've implemented a behavior tree—in fact, an unusually fast and powerful behavior tree.

The main aspect for improvement is that of the interface for designers. Simple parameters may, of course, be exposed through XML or a GUI. In this author's experience more structural changes are best kept the responsibility of AI programmers, who often find a simple text specification better to work with than a graphical one. However, such if-else code may be very easily generated from a graphical representation should one be required, with the simple act of replacing the source file triggering runtime-compilation.

12.9.2 A Blackboard

Blackboards may be naturally represented in languages such as Lua or Python as a table of key-value pairs, comprising strings and dynamically typed values. While similar constructions are possible in C++, they represent a possible performance bottleneck. In an analogous approach to our behavior tree, we can represent our blackboards under RCC++ as simple structs—each key-value pair becoming a named member variable of appropriate type.

Reading and writing from the blackboard becomes as simple as passing its pointer to our sensory systems and to our RCC++ behavior tree. The main difficulty we must resolve is that of dependencies, as all the code that uses it must include the struct definition as a header, and must be recompiled should it change.

The header-tracking feature of RCC++ makes this simple, with a change to the include file triggering recompilation of all the dependent code. We advise using a hierarchical form of blackboards with, for example, a particular agent's full blackboard inheriting from one shared blackboard across all agents, and one shared by its species, and with separate access to any blackboard used solely by the current behavior. This approach helps ensure that only relevant AI code needs to be recompiled when the blackboard definition is changed, keeping recompiling as efficient as possible.

12.10 Crytek Case Study

Following a presentation at the Paris Game/AI conference in 2011, Crytek implemented a similar system internally which they call SoftCode. The system has been used on several game projects currently active in Crytek and has been used for systems as diverse as render effects, UI, and animation. It is most heavily employed currently on the AI system in use for *Ryse* for authoring behaviors and managing behavior selection.

SoftCode builds upon the approach of RCC++ in several interesting directions. The first is that it provides the compilation and change tracking functionality of the runtime compiler as a Visual Studio 2010 add-in, which works for 32-bit and 64-bit Windows builds as well as Xbox 360. Additionally, it generalizes the concept of the runtime object system, allowing developers to expose their own system through a type library. Thus, rather than having to derive from a single `IObject` base class, each SoftCoded type can derive from their own base interface. Like RCC++, SoftCoding has an error-handling mechanism using structured exceptions, but its lambda functions allow call state capture so that individual methods can be retried after failure. To simplify development, SoftCode types use a `SOFT()` macro to expose class member variables rather than through an explicit Serialize function, and globals can be exposed through an `SC_API` macro.

12.11 Future Work

With Mac and even Linux becoming more popular targets for games, we feel support for these platforms is a natural next step for the project. Beyond this, moving to a client/server model for the Runtime Object System and Runtime Compiler would permit further targets such as Consoles and mobile devices to be targeted.

An interesting further step would be to support a simpler interface to programming than C++ with an intermediate compiler that generates C++ code, using RCC++ to permit runtime usage. A basic graphical interface to construct object data members and function declarations with function bodies editable in a variant of C++, which limits operator arithmetic and what functions can be called, may be sufficient for many technically oriented designers. Alternatively, full blown graphical scripting methods like Unreal's Kismet or Crytek's Flow-Graph could output C++ rather than data, allowing the compiler to make optimizations where possible. A hybrid approach permitting existing building blocks to be connected together, and new ones constructed in code on the fly, seems a good solution for allowing designers freedom of expression in a safe and highly productive environment.

Meanwhile, we will continue to evolve the current codebase in our search for faster iteration times, easier development, and the potential for maximum performance. Check the author's blog at RuntimeCompiledCPlusPlus.blogspot.com for updates.

12.12 Conclusion

Our initial goals with Runtime Compiled C++ were to demonstrate that compiled code could replace scripting for iterative and interactive development of game logic and behavior, particularly in performance-critical areas of code such as AI. We believe we have not only succeeded in this goal, but have also developed a technique (and permissively licensed open source code base), which permits developers to go further and develop substantial proportions of their game code this way.

Changing behavior, fixing bugs, adding new functionality, and even optimizing are now all possible without needing to restart the process, with turnaround times on the order of a few seconds.

With special thanks to Adam Rutkowski

References

[Crytek 12] Crytek. "CryENGINE 3 AI System." http://mycryengine.com/index.php?conid = 48, 2012.

[DeLoura 09] M. DeLoura. "The Engine Survey: General Results." http://www.satori.org/2009/03/the-engine-survey-general-results/, 2009.

[Epic 12a] Epic Games. "UnrealScript." http://www.unrealengine.com/features/unrealscript/, 2012.

[Epic 12b] Epic Games. "Unreal Kismet." http://www.unrealengine.com/features/kismet/, 2012.

[Epic 12c] Epic Games. "Unreal Engine 4." http://www.unrealengine.com/unreal_engine_4, 2012.

[Fulgham 12] B. Fulgham. "The Computer Language Benchmark Game" http://shootout.alioth.debian.org/, 2012.

[Havok 12] Havok. "Havok Script." http://www.havok.com/products/script, 2012.

[Jack, Binks, Rutkowski 11] M. Jack, D. Binks, and A. Rutkowski. "Runtime Compiled C++" https://github.com/RuntimeCompiledCPlusPlus/RuntimeCompiledCPlusPlus.

[Martins 11] M. Martins. Paris Shooter Symposium 2011. Available online (https://aigamedev.com/store/recordings/paris-shooter-symposium-2011-content-access.html).

[Microsoft 10] Microsoft. "Supported Code Changes." http://msdn.microsoft.com/en-us/library/0dbey757%28v = VS.100%29.aspx, 2010.

[Shaw 10] J. Shaw. "Lua and Fable." Presentation, Games Developer Conference (GDC), 2010. Available online (http://www.gdcvault.com/play/1012427/Lua-Scripting-in-Game).

[Staheli 98] D. G. Staheli. "Enhanced Debugging with Edit and Continue in Microsoft Visual C++ 6.0." http://msdn.microsoft.com/en-us/library/aa260823%28v = vs.60%29.aspx, 1998.

[Zao 10] H. Zao. "HipHop for PHP: Move Fast." https://developers.facebook.com/blog/post/2010/02/02/hiphop-for-php—move-fast/, 2010.

13

Plumbing the Forbidden Depths
Scripting and AI

Mike Lewis

13.1 Introduction

Lurking deep in the mists of contemporary artificial intelligence work is a controversial and hotly debated technique—a "black magic" that has been rumored to accomplish fantastical things, but at perilous cost. This forbidden ability has been responsible for some of the most cherished game AI in the industry's history ... and also for some of its worst embarrassments. I speak of scripted AI.

Scripting, however, need not be feared. Like any good black art, it must be understood and mastered to be wielded safely [Tozour 02]. Here, we will explore the good, bad, and dangerous aspects of scripting as it pertains to developing game AI—all with an eye towards delivering the kind of dynamic, adaptive, challenging-but-entertaining experiences that modern gamers demand.

There are, of course, a multitude of ways to integrate scripting techniques into a game's architecture, but for the most part they comprise two basic philosophies. These rival points of view can be thought of as the "master" and "servant" ideologies. While both have their proper place, it can be tremendously useful to consider which role scripts will play in a given game's implementation. It is also of paramount importance to maintain as much adherence to that role as possible, for reasons which will be considered later.

By the same token, there is a vast spectrum of complexity in scripting systems, ranging from simple tripwire/response mechanisms to full-blown programming languages. Once again, each possible approach has its merits and drawbacks. As with any technology or tool, the situation at hand must be carefully examined and considered in order to decide how best to deploy scripting systems and what their implementations should look like.

13.2 The Master and the Servant

From the very beginning of working with an AI scripting mechanism, it is important to understand the system's place in the overall architecture of the game—not just how it interacts with other AI features, but how it will function in terms of the totality of the game's systems. Moreover, it is deeply beneficial to remain true to that decision for the duration of development. Without this discipline, scripts can quickly become unruly monsters that suck up huge amounts of debugging time, deliver subpar gameplay experiences, or even drag down development as a whole.

The most successful approaches to scripting will generally fall into one of two camps. First is the "scripts as master" perspective, wherein scripts control the high-level aspects of agent decision making and planning. The other method sees "scripts as servant," where some other architecture controls the overall activity of agents, but selectively deploys scripts to attain specific design goals or create certain dramatic effects.

In general, master-style systems work best in one of two scenarios. In the optimal case, a library of ready-to-use tools already exists, and scripting can become the "glue" that combines these techniques into a coherent and powerful overarching model for agent behavior. Even in cases where such a library is not immediately available, master scripts are often the superior approach when it is known in advance that agents must be able to fluidly transition between a number of different decision-making or planning techniques.

By contrast, servant scripts are most effective when design requires a high degree of specificity in agent behavior. This is the typical sense in which interactions are thought of as "scripted"; a set of possible scenarios is envisioned by the designers, and special-case logic for reacting to each scenario is put in place by the AI implementation team. Servant scripts need not be entirely reactive, however; simple scripted loops and behavioral patterns can make for excellent ambient or "background" AI.

Most game designs will naturally lend themselves to one side or the other of the master/servant divide. Even when the game itself does not clearly lean towards a preferred approach, the human factor almost always will. Different teams will work more effectively in one style or another, depending on any number of circumstances: the ratio of programmers to designers, relative experience of the engineers working on the AI, time and budget constraints, and so on.

One such factor worth considering is the investment required to implement either approach. A master system will tend to work best with developers who can draw upon a diverse bag of tricks to help flesh out the overall implementation of the AI. Servant systems are much easier to design and implement in terms of code, but require extra care from gameplay design to avoid falling into the classic trap of producing agents that feel like cardboard cutouts.

Alternative philosophies surely exist, but they can be difficult to tame. Interspersing "scripted" logic with other architectural approaches is often a recipe for creating exactly the kind of rigid, inflexible agents that have (rightfully) earned scripting a bad reputation. Without clear boundaries and responsibilities, different systems will begin competing for dominance—either at an abstract level in the code's design and details, or in the worst case, while the game is being played.

13.2.1 Scripts as Benevolent Overlords

The master-script philosophy derives its power from one fundamental principle: delegation. It is not the responsibility of the script to dictate every detail of how an agent behaves, or even to anticipate every possible scenario that might occur during the game experience. Instead, a good master script seeks to categorize and prioritize, and hand off responsibility for the mundane details to other systems.

Categorization is all about recognizing the nature of what is going on in the simulation at a given moment. Knowledge representation is often the key to doing this effectively; it is mandatory that agents have coherent and believable ideas about the world they inhabit so they can interpret events in a manner that is consistent with their worldview, and thereby take appropriate action. Note that it is not necessary for agents to have *accurate* or *precise* beliefs, so long as they do things which seem *sensible* from the perspective of the player. It can be tempting to build highly complex knowledge systems, but this often leads to inscrutable decision-making processes that wind up feeling arbitrary or mysterious to an outside observer.

Prioritization, on the other hand, boils down to choosing what to do with the gathered knowledge of an agent's surroundings and situation. For the master script, this is not a matter of selecting behaviors or states per se. Rather, during prioritization, the master script examines a set of lower-level control mechanisms, decides which are most appropriate for the moment, and selects one or more of those mechanisms to contribute towards the final decision-making process.

For example, consider a typical open-world role-playing game in which a large number of agents populate a town. The master script shouldn't concern itself too much with the minutiae of what an agent happens to be doing at any given moment. Instead, it acts like a sort of abstract state machine, governing which systems might control an individual agent at any point in time.

During peaceful spells, the master may choose between simple idle animation loops for a stationary blacksmith agent or perhaps it might assign a utility-based system to monitor the desires and needs of that agent and select activities based on those demands. The script might gather a group of agents to take on the role of the town militia, patrolling for nearby threats and policing the streets; these agents might be controlled using group tactical reasoning and movement systems, whereas a stray dog might simply wander around randomly and attempt to eat various things it encounters in the world.

All of this is simply prioritization. The master oversees the "peaceful" environment and delegates responsibility for agents to specific subsystems. This works elegantly alongside traditional subsumption architectures, where the details of an agent's activities are divided into increasingly abstract layers. At the highest layer, the master script plays the role of benevolent overlord, coordinating the activities of the lower-level agents and systems, and if necessary, dealing with situations that are otherwise problematic or insurmountable for the more specific layers.

Categorization enters the picture when the peaceful little hamlet becomes embroiled in a vicious battle with the local band of roving goblins. Suddenly, the master script must detect that the once-sensible actions it has been assigning to its minions are no longer appropriate. It is here that the abstract state machine makes a transition, and begins issuing a different set of prioritizations and orders.

The blacksmith, once happily pounding away on his anvil, might suddenly shift from making horseshoes to making swords. This might be accomplished by changing his idle animation, or simply adjusting the relative merits of sword-making in his utility inputs. The militia must cease worrying about pickpockets in the local market and begin establishing a line of defense against the marauding goblins; they still act as a tactical unit, but now with a very different set of priorities and behaviors that may not fit well with their peacekeeping patterns. Even the poor, mangy, stray dog must not be forgotten: instead of rooting around in the trash for scraps, he might be found behind the barred gates of the town, bristling and growling at the shadowy enemy that lurks outside.

Note that the master script need not transition to the wartime state in any particular fashion; in fact, it is precisely the freedom to choose how this transition occurs that makes scripting a powerful tool for this type of scenario. If the game leans towards the sandbox style, the master might simply examine how many goblins are near the town and trip the transition when their "threat level" exceeds some threshold. In a more narrative-driven title, the master script might simply wait for twenty minutes after the player enters the area and then initiate the invasion.

In any case, the important flexibility of master-scripting lies in the general abstractness of the script's activities. Throughout this example, the master script is rarely, if *ever*, in the position of actually controlling the blow-by-blow activities of any given agent. This is, of course, always an option, but should be used sparingly. The whole purpose of a master architecture is to enable more appropriate control schemes to come into play as necessary. It is through this philosophy that the master script evades the trap of brittle, predictable, boring behavior. Since the script is only guiding the broad strokes of the simulation, other systems retain the freedom to act in interesting and meaningful ways based on the details of that simulation.

13.2.2 Scripts as Humble Indentured Labor

It is, of course, hardly necessary for a scripting system to maintain the high-level "master" overview of how agents behave in a simulation. A perfectly viable alternative is to invert the priority hierarchy and place a traditional behavior control system in charge of the overarching flow of the simulation, while relegating scripts to handling certain particular details. This is the "servant" approach to scripting.

In this view, scripted logic is deployed only when other techniques cannot deliver the precise behavior desired in an easily configurable manner. Most commonly, servant scripts are used to plug the gaps where design requirements have asked for a very specific outcome. For instance, a standard behavior tree could be used to dictate an agent's actions for the majority of a simulation, while a script is activated at a particular node (typically a leaf node) of the tree in order to realize a step in a story progression, or a highly crafted response to a particular stimulus, and so on.

Servant scripts derive the bulk of their power from their specificity. Unlike master scripts, which aim for the exact opposite, servant scripts are generally designed to handle a narrow range of scenarios in a simulation. The "triggers" for these scripts are, for the most part, looking for very precise combinations of events or inputs, and the scripts themselves create agent reactions (or even proactive behaviors) that make sense only in that exact context.

As a tool for rounding out the suite of techniques used to create robust AI, servant scripts certainly have their place. The principal danger in using scripts in this manner lies in the fact that servant scripts are, by far, most effective when used sparingly as supplements to other behavior control systems.

From the perspective of a player, overuse of servant scripts produces brittle, predictable, and—after the first few encounters with the script—stale interactions. One commonly (and fairly) criticized use of scripting is the "tripwire" technique, where agents mindlessly repeat some particular pattern of action until the player crosses an invisible line in the sand, which switches the script to the next set of behavior.

Tripwires are of course not inherently bad; the issue is in using servant scripts in a vacuum. When there is no high-level system producing interesting behavior, scripted actions are no longer exceptional. Once scripted behavior becomes the norm in a simulation, players are likely to become frustrated or bored very quickly with the repetitive and overly patterned interactions they can have with the AI.

Heavy reliance on servant scripts requires an exacting attention to detail and an exhaustive capacity for predicting the sorts of situations players are likely to create. This is certainly possible, and a few noteworthy titles have created exceedingly memorable and believable experiences using extensive scripting. A serious risk, though, is the creation of an "uncanny valley" effect. Good scripting can produce very immersive results up until the point where a player does something the scripts could not have anticipated. At that point, the realism is shattered and the player often comes away feeling disappointed at the discontinuity of the illusion.

Much like in master scripting, it is imperative to maintain a selection of alternative techniques for producing interesting and compelling AI behaviors. The key difference between the two approaches is simply a matter of which extreme the scripts control—generalized, or specialized scenarios.

13.2.3 The Evils of Cross-Pollination

As mentioned earlier, wrangling a herd of AI scripts successfully requires consistent adherence to either of the servant or master models. Straying from these recipes can have disastrous consequences.

The reasons for this are primarily organizational. Without a clear set of guidelines about how scripts are to be deployed, it is virtually inevitable that a project will become inconsistent and variegated in its views on what exactly scripts are meant to do. As a result, different interactions with AI agents within the simulation will feel very different. Some might be highly scripted and controlled to exacting detail, while others are loose and rely on other AI techniques to be interesting.

In the best case, this haphazard use of scripts will produce a disjointed and inconsistent experience for the player. In the worst case, the confusion and wildly varying level of "quality" of interactions will render the experience painful and unpleasant.

The aforementioned uncanny valley effect is nearly certain to appear if agents have highly variable degrees of believability. Certainly, for practical reasons, we may not be able to craft every single agent's entire life in crystal-clear detail for the duration of the player's experience. Indeed, most large-scale simulations are forced to embrace the idea of "ambient" or "throw-away" agents who exist solely as background or filler and generally are low level-of-detail creatures.

However, there is a fine line between level of detail and level of fidelity. Players are, for the most part, willing to accept agents who forego excruciatingly detailed existences within the simulation. What causes problems, however, is lack of fidelity in the behaviors of those agents. A particularly egregious flaw is to intersperse carefully scripted behavior of a particular agent with other control techniques acting on the same agent, without regard to the player's perception of the changes. This is a classic recipe for ruined immersion. Agents will feel inconsistent, arbitrary, or even random in their responses to simulation stimuli, and the net effect is almost universally negative.

This is not to say that all scripting must remain at one polar extreme or the other; to be sure, it is possible to inject scripted logic at various degrees of generalized or specialized control over a simulation, which can even be done to great effect if planned carefully. The key is to remain mindful of the effect that this can have on the end-user experience. To that end, heavy design, oversight, and constant testing and iteration are essential.

13.2.4 Contrasting Case Studies: The X Series

In the "X Series" of space-simulation games by Egosoft, we used a range of scripting technologies to implement the agent AI. Across the span of three titles, the overall philosophy of scripting shifted dramatically, although it never really landed on a clear footing with regards to the master/servant paradigm.

For *X²: The Threat* agents were controlled via a haphazard blend of servant scripts. Each individual "quest" or mini-story in the game was a separate scripted encounter. Moreover, content could be implemented in any of three layers: the C++ core engine, a bytecode-based language called KC, or a third layer known only as "the script engine" which was in turn implemented on top of KC.

This rapidly created the sort of uncanny valley experience described earlier; with no consistent quality or degree of fidelity to the agents and their behavior, the game offered a typically less-than-compelling patchwork of content. As a result, players tended to gravitate towards a tiny fraction of the in-game world that had been implemented with the most attention to detail.

The game's sequel, *X3: Reunion*, saw the introduction of the so-called "God Module" which represented a shift towards master-style scripting, at least in part. The purpose of this module was to observe the state of the simulated game universe and arbitrarily introduce events which would change the world to some degree. At the most extreme, entire swaths of space stations could be built or destroyed by this master script throughout the course of gameplay.

Unfortunately, due to limitations on time, the master philosophy was not consistently applied to all AI development. Much of the old servant style remained, and a large part of the game's content again suffered from a consistent lack of quality and detail. This was addressed post-ship via a number of downloadable patches. Even after extensive updates, however, the disjointed fidelity of agent behavior remained a common complaint among players.

Finally, in *X3: Terran Conflict*, we introduced a system known as the "Mission Director." Interestingly, this represented far more of a shift back towards servant-style scripting than the name might suggest. Instead of attempting to control the experience from a high level, the Mission Director allowed developers—and, eventually, enterprising players—to write highly concise and expressive scripts using a common framework and tool set.

The net result of the Mission Director was to allow the servant philosophy to flourish. With access to rapid development tools and a unified policy for how to create new game content, *Terran Conflict* shipped with substantially more hand-crafted AI behavior and quests than any of the game's predecessors.

Ultimately, the most compelling conclusion to be drawn from this experience is that the actual selection of a design philosophy is not as important as consistent application of that decision. Once again, it is also extremely beneficial to select a design approach that fits nicely with the development resources available for a given project.

13.3 Implementation Techniques

Once a guiding philosophy for scripting's role has been chosen for a given project, it's time to begin considering implementation details. There are numerous mechanisms that could be considered degrees of "scripting" to some extent. These range from simple observation and reaction systems all the way to full-fledged programming languages embedded within the larger simulation itself.

For the most part, implementation choices are orthogonal to the philosophical choices outlined previously. Generally speaking, any of the techniques detailed in the following sections can be applied equally well to master or servant script models. There are a few exceptions to this, which will be specifically called out, but the predominant factors involved in choosing a script implementation approach pertain to the team involved more than the master/servant distinction itself.

Before embarking on the journey of building a scripting system, it is worth taking some time to evaluate the situation's particulars in order to ensure that the most appropriate techniques are selected. For example, observation/reaction systems have a distinct advantage when the majority of the simulation "script" logic needs to be emplaced by designers or nonprogrammer staff. At the other extreme, rolling a custom language is best reserved for engineers with prior language creation experience—although depending on the nature of the custom language, the audience may not necessarily need much technical programming experience, as we shall see later.

In the realm of implementation decisions, there are far more potentially profitable approaches than can be exhaustively enumerated here. Instead, we'll look at both extremes of the implementation spectrum, and then examine a happy medium that can be deployed to balance out the strengths and weaknesses of other approaches.

13.3.1 Observation and Reaction Systems

The canonical observation/reaction system is the "tripwire." This is a simple mechanism which observes the location of an agent within the simulation's world space, and when the agent enters (or exits) a particular locale, a reaction is triggered [Orkin 02].

Tripwires are trivial to implement in the context of most engines, because they rely only on testing intersection of an agent's bounding volume with some other (typically invisible) bounding volume within the simulation space. Such functionality is almost always necessary for other aspects of the simulation, such as generalized physics or collision detection and response, so very little new code needs to be written to accomplish a simple tripwire.

The simplest case of a tripwire resembles the ubiquitous automatic sliding doors found at the entrances to supermarkets; when something moves into the sensor volume, the door opens, and when nothing has moved there for a time, the door shuts again. This is fine for trivial interactions—where things get interesting with tripwires is in selective reaction.

Suppose we want to have a security system on the door, so that it only opens if someone carrying the appropriate keycard walks into the sensor volume. This can become an arbitrarily complex task depending on the nature of the rest of the simulation. Is a "keycard" just a Boolean flag on an agent, or might agents have inventories which need to be enumerated in order to find a key? To selectively activate the tripwire, it is suddenly necessary to interface with a large part of the rest of the simulation logic.

The challenge here is in providing appropriately rich tools. Those responsible for creating the AI technology must ensure that those actually using the technology have all the hooks, knobs, levers, and paraphernalia necessary for accomplishing the design goals of the project. While it can be tempting to throw in the kitchen sink, there is tremendous benefit in careful up-front design of both the game systems themselves and their interactions with the tripwire AI systems. Otherwise, the tools can become overwhelmingly complex and detailed, even to the point of obscuring the most commonly needed functionality.

Context is supremely important when making these decisions. What is appropriate for a team creating a general-purpose engine for licensing purposes will be dramatically different from what makes the most sense for a small, nimble team producing mobile titles at the rate of several per year. While the two systems may bear a striking resemblance to one another in the broad strokes, it is generally straightforward to keep the feature set of a tripwire system minimalistic if the scope of the simulation is well defined up front.

Any number of considerations may be useful for an observation/reaction system. Again, context is extremely important in selecting them. However, there are a few patterns that are so broadly applicable that they are worth considering—even if only to mutate them into something more specifically useful for the project at hand.

The first and most common consideration is **classification**. Put simply, this consideration examines the "kind" of thing that has just tripped the sensor: perhaps it only examines player agents, or only AI agents, or only agents on the Blue Team, and so forth. An even more powerful option is to allow things besides agents to trip the sensors. If a sensor volume moves along with an agent, and the volume is "tuned" to trip a response when a grenade enters it, it becomes trivial to build grenade evasion logic into an agent using nothing but observation/reaction architecture.

A sister technique to classification is **attribute checking**. An attribute check might look for the presence (or absence) of a particular inventory item, or compare values based on some threshold, and so on. Attribute checking is also convenient when needing to make decisions that are not strictly binary. For example, an attribute check might look at a player's health and ammunition levels before triggering a reaction that sends out squads of enemies in response to the perceived threat.

Another useful consideration is **sequencing**. A sequence requires that one tripwire be activated before another can become active. Sequencing allows designers to create linear flows of connected events. Combined with configurable timings, sequencing can be used to unfold entire story arcs based simply on having one event follow logically after another.

Deduplication is yet another handy technique. This is a trivial state flag which simply ensures that a particular tripwire cannot be triggered more than once, or more often than at some prescribed rate. This avoids the classic blunder of AI systems that repeatedly greet the hero as he steps back and forth across the threshold of the city gates.

It is worth noting that observation/reaction does not necessarily lead to strictly linear behavior, in contrast to the images that the term "scripted AI" typically conjures up. Branching logic can be accomplished easily with the use of attribute checks and sequences. Deduplication can be applied to ensure that logic does not become repetitively applied to the simulation. Last but not least, there is the potential for movable trigger zones to be employed, as suggested in the grenade evasion example from earlier.

If a single agent has a set of tripwires applied to itself, it can quickly become prepared to handle all kinds of contingencies in the simulation world. Indeed, the limitations are predominantly found in the foresight and creativity of the designers rather than technical details.

Obviously, however, if everything in a complex simulation is handled by tripwires of various kinds—and especially if intricate, nonlinear storytelling becomes involved—the number of tripwires required can explode exponentially very easily. This is the primary weakness of simple observation/reaction systems; since they are essentially data driven mechanisms, they scale proportionally with the number of situations that the simulation must present and/or respond to. Even if the feature set of the tripwire technology is minimalistic and elegant, the number of actual triggers needed to realize a sophisticated project might be prohibitive.

13.3.2 Domain-Specific Languages

At the opposite extreme of implementation technique lies the **domain-specific language**, or DSL. A DSL is simply some kind of tool for expressing specialized types of logic. Strictly speaking, DSLs can run the gamut from little more than textually defined observation/response systems, to intricate monstrosities that rival the complication of full-blown traditional programming languages.

As the name hopefully suggests, however, domain-specific languages should be precisely that: constrained heavily to accomplish one particular task—or *domain*. The further a language strays from this self-imposed limitation, the more likely it is to become a liability rather than an asset [Brockington et al. 02]. General-purpose languages require extraordinary amounts of effort to develop to the point where they are suitable for general-purpose tasks; rolling a custom general-purpose language almost automatically entails giving up on existing tools, programmer knowledge, and battle-tested code. As such, it pays to keep the "domain-specific" part in mind at all times.

In a nutshell, the goal of a good DSL is to allow implementers to talk (in code) about what they want to happen using the same vocabulary and mental patterns that they use to think about it. DSLs are by nature very heavily tied to their intended audience; a language for helping helicopter pilots navigate automatically is going to look very different from a language used to help physicists calibrate particle accelerator experiments.

A key realization in the creation of DSL-based AI is that it is not necessary to lump *all* functionality of the AI into a single language. In fact, it is almost universally detrimental to do so, given that such accumulation of features will by necessity cause the language to stop being specific and start being more general.

Another important thing to keep in mind is that DSLs are often most useful for people who are not primarily programmers [Poiker 02]. There is no need for a DSL to be littered with squiggly symbols and magical words; on the contrary, a good DSL will tend to resemble both the terminology and the overall structure of a design diagram of the intended logic. If the intended audience tends to use certain symbols or incantations to describe their goals, then those things should be considered perfectly at home in a DSL. However, a good language design will avoid bending over backwards to "look" or "feel" like a general-purpose programming language.

Put simply: a good DSL should not look like C++ code, nor should it require a complex parser, compiler, interpreter, virtual machine, or any other trappings of a typical general-purpose language. In fact, a simple whitespace-based tokenizer should be amply sufficient to power most DSLs. Another common option entails using existing file formats such as XML or JSON to encode the logic, and providing thin user interfaces on top of these formats for creating the actual programs in the language. End users need not write XML by hand; they can use comfortable, visually intuitive tools to craft their logic [McNaughton et al. 06]. Meanwhile, there is no need to roll yet another parsing system just to load the generated scripts. Good DSLs are about leveraging existing technologies in new ways, not reinventing wheels.

For most DSL implementations, the real work is in specifying a compact yet usable language; actually parsing and executing the code is relatively straightforward. Simple techniques include large `switch` statements, or groups of "executable" classes derived from a simple abstract base class or interface, where virtual dispatch is used to trigger the corresponding code for each language "keyword" or operation.

Of course, from a theoretical standpoint, there exists the possibility of writing an entire virtual machine architecture just for executing game logic; this has in fact been explored in numerous successful titles, including the *X Series* described earlier. However, rolling a true, custom VM is almost always a serious crime of excess when a DSL is concerned.

An effective guideline for designing DSLs is to create a language that expresses the sort of things that might be useful in a more simplistic observation/reaction architecture. All the standard considerations apply: classification, attribute checking, sequencing, and so on are all fundamental control flow techniques for the language.

In sharp contrast to a general-purpose language, DSLs need not worry about handling every contingency under the sun in terms of writing agent behavior logic. Rather, the language designers craft the vocabulary and syntax with which the AI implementers assemble the final resulting scripts—the language is the bricks and mortar, and the actual building is up to the AI programmer or designer to accomplish.

The nature of those bricks can have profound consequences for the final constructed building. As such, just as with a tripwire architecture, DSLs require a large degree of context-specific decision making to be effective. It is exceedingly unlikely that a DSL from one genre of game could be readily reused in a totally different kind of simulation experience, for example.

It is worth mentioning again that confining a game to a single DSL is usually a mistake. Even within the AI system, it can be highly effective to deploy multiple DSLs in concert. Subsumption architectures are a perfect match for this approach, and master-script systems may see tremendous benefit from deploying DSLs for various subsets of the fine-detail control mechanisms.

The basic idea is to divide up agent behavior into discrete, well-defined, compact groupings, and write a language for each grouping. Describing the behavior of an agent wandering freely about the world might require a very different linguistic framework than

Listing 13.1. This fragment of a hypothetical DSL shows how a clearly readable, minimalistic language can be used to dictate the behavior of a simple robot. The robot's basic life goal is to collect widgets until he needs to recharge his batteries, at which point he will return to the charging station and wait until he has enough power to get more widgets.

```
; Robot.dsl
set energy = get energy of robot
set mypos = get position of robot
set chargepos = get position of charger
compute homedist = distance mypos to chargepos
trigger if energy <= homedist
    path robot to chargepos
    wait until energy equals 100
trigger if energy > homedist
    set mywidget = get closest widget to robot
    set targetpos = get position of mywidget
    path robot to targetpos
    wait until mypos equals targetpos
    pickup mywidget
repeat
```

describing the exact same agent's split-second reactions during intense combat. Moreover, DSLs can even be nested—a high-level `enter combat` command in one DSL might invoke a far more detailed script implemented in a different, lower-level language.

Listing 13.1 illustrates a simple DSL fragment used to control a widget-gathering robot. For sake of brevity, the robot isn't terribly intelligent, but it should have enough basic logic to accomplish its mission and get lots of widgets. Unfortunately, it might eventually try for a widget that is too far from home, and run out of power before it can return to recharge; but extending the logic to safely avoid such widgets should be straightforward.

The key advantage of using a DSL for this logic is that any number of robot behaviors can be crafted without having to write any general-purpose control code in a more traditional programming language. As alluded to earlier, this enables a far wider audience to create AI scripts for the simulation project—a very effective force multiplier.

Note that the DSL snippet can be parsed using a trivial tokenizer; it looks readable enough, but the vocabulary is carefully chosen so that the code can be parsed and broken down into a sequence of simple command objects in program memory at runtime. For example, consider the line, `set mywidget = get closest widget to robot`. We can split this into a series of whitespace-delimited tokens using the string parsing facilities of our implementation language of choice. In most modern languages, this is no more than a line of code or a single library function call.

Next, we traverse the list from left to right. The intention is always clear without having to peek ahead to additional tokens in the stream—we want to `set` a variable called `widget`. The equals sign can be thought of as decoration to help make the program more readable. It can simply be discarded by the parser.

Once we have ascertained that the statement is a variable assignment, we proceed—again, from left to right. We determine that we will perform a lookup of some kind (`get`). This lookup should specifically find the `closest` of two entities in the simulation. Lastly, we realize that the two entities we want to look for are of type `widget` and `robot`. Each section of the phrase can be converted directly into some kind of in-memory representation for later execution without complicated parsing algorithms or nightmarish flashbacks to compiler architecture courses.

A typical approach to executing DSL code is to process the scripts once during load time and then store them in an in-memory format that is easy to handle for fast execution. If load time performance is an issue, most DSLs can be trivially preprocessed into binary formats that are faster to convert into the in-memory format.

There are many subtly different approaches to execution models, but for the most part, they boil down to a simple decision: should execution of a single instruction in the DSL code be accomplished by virtual function dispatch or by a `switch` statement? The particulars of making this decision will of course tend to vary widely between teams, levels of experience, architectural preferences and policies, and platform performance considerations.

In the virtual dispatch model, individual instructions are implemented as classes which derive from a common interface or abstract base class. During loading, instructions from the raw source are converted into instances of these classes as appropriate. During execution, the scripting engine simply stores a container of these objects and sequentially invokes a virtual function such as `Execute` on each one.

Parameters to each instruction can be stored in a variety of formats, but typically a simple typeless DSL will only need to store strings (or enumeration "tokens" for built-in strings) that represent each parameter's value. This allows each instruction to have a simple interface that accepts a generic, untyped container of parameters which it interprets according to the semantics of the instruction itself. Implementation of a full type system is certainly possible, but it is important to weigh the work of building a type system against the (typically marginal) gains that this offers for the sort of code likely to be written in the DSL.

The switch-based model is slightly more involved. Instructions are simple constant numerical values, typically stored in the host language's notion of an enumeration. Executing a stream of DSL code consists of reading an instruction value, performing the `switch` to invoke the correct functionality, and then parsing off parameters for the instruction.

This approach generally requires the notion of an explicit execution stack as well as other forms of storage. One powerful model is to have parameters to each DSL instruction passed via a stack, and other state accessible via a blackboard mechanism. The blackboard can be shared between different DSLs and even the core language of the engine, allowing seamless passing of knowledge between various AI layers. This can be especially useful if certain routines need to be implemented directly in low-level code for performance or storage reasons.

Flow control (conditions, loops, and so on) can also be more difficult in a switch-based implementation. It is generally advantageous to have assembly language experience when working with this model, as many of the same concepts are in play—explicit jumps to certain addresses for flow control, typeless storage, an execution stack, and so on.

By contrast, flow control in a virtual dispatch model is trivial: simply create an instruction class such as `loop` (for example) that stores its own container of attached instruction objects, and executes them repeatedly based on the loop conditions.

In general, virtual dispatch-based execution models are simpler to implement and maintain—particularly to extend—but come at the obvious cost of requiring virtual functions to operate. If the DSL is focused on high-level behavior rather than per-frame behavior, however, this may not be a significant loss; if an agent only needs to complete a "thought tick" every 3 seconds on average, the cost of virtual dispatch and storing the code as objects in memory is well worth it for the advantages in ease of use.

13.3.3 Integrated Architectures

Either way, though, rolling a DSL execution engine is a considerable undertaking, and should be carefully considered against other options. One particularly effective alternative is to use existing scripting engines—or even the low-level implementation language itself—in concert with specially crafted code structures that look and feel like a DSL but require none of the implementation investment.

These "integrated architectures" are built by constructing a library of classes or functions (or both) which represent the sum total of functionality that should be available to the scripted system. The "scripts" are then simply modules in the program that access only that limited subset of functionality, and nothing else.

Listing 13.2 illustrates the same robot and widget logic, implemented entirely in C++. This is the high-level "script" only—the implementation of each of the invoked functions is left up to the imagination. Obviously, some elements such as the Wait(); function would require some thought to implement successfully, but for the most part, this is simply good code architecture put into practice. There is no reaching out to the renderer, or the physics model, or even much of the world state itself. Everything is implemented in terms of simple routines that have been deemed appropriate for use by the AI.

Listing 13.2. This is the robot from Listing 13.1, reimplemented in C++ as part of an integrated architecture. Note that the logic looks very similar aside from superficial syntax differences; the idea is that the script logic is implemented in terms of lower-level functionality provided by a library.

```cpp
//Robot.cpp
while (robot.IsActive()) {
    FloatValue energy = robot.GetEnergy();
    Position mypos = robot.GetPosition();
    Position chargepos = charger.GetPosition();
    FloatValue homedist = mypos.DistanceTo(chargepos);
    if(energy <= homedist) {
        robot.PathTo(chargepos);
        while(energy < 100.0f)
            Wait();
    }
    else {
        Widget mywidget = AllWidgets.GetClosest(mypos);
        Position targetpos = mywidget.GetPosition();
        robot.PathTo(targetpos);
        while(robot.GetPosition() != targetpos)
            Wait();
        robot.PickUp(mywidget);
    }
}
```

Clearly, this is predicated heavily on programmer discipline. There is little stopping a programmer from accessing functionality directly in the rendering system, or even the operating system itself, for example. Certain measures can be taken (limiting the use of `#include` in C and C++, or `using` in C# and `import` in Java, and so on) but ultimately it is up to the leadership of the team to ensure that all code complies with the restrictions on what functionality should be used from the "script" modules.

At first blush, integrated architecture may not sound like a scripting solution at all—there is no special language in use, no external tools, and only a minimum of specially crafted logic to support the system. However, upon closer examination, integrated architectures still fit into the paradigms of master and servant architectures described earlier and can accomplish precisely the same things as a separate scripting language.

There are several major advantages to using an integrated architecture over a separate language implementation. First, it allows programmers to use their existing language knowledge and skills without much modification. Second, using an existing language opens up access to all of the existing tools for working in that language—IDEs, debuggers, compilers, profilers, and so on. Third, it removes a layer of execution abstraction between the logic and the underlying platform, which can be a substantial performance win on lower-end hardware or when the team lacks an experienced optimizations engineer to work on the scripting language implementation.

Last, but certainly not least, integrated architectures provide an illustrative method for writing almost any large-scale code. The layered approach has been heavily encouraged for decades, with notable proponents including Fred Brooks and the SICP course from MIT. Learning to structure code in this way can be a powerful force multiplier for creating clean, well separated modules for the rest of the project, even well outside the scope of AI systems.

Although the example in Listing 13.2 uses C++, it is not necessarily the most effective language for building an integrated architecture. Lua is an immensely popular option, and provides a powerful and high-performance framework on which to build scripted systems. An embedded Python implementation can use `yield` statements instead of the `Wait()` function to accomplish cooperative multitasking between agents with very little work. For programmers who happen to be familiar with JavaScript, an embedded implementation of that language can easily use a callback-oriented event model for interleaving agent processing, as used in notable stacks such as `Node.js`.

The critical tradeoff here is giving up access to existing debugging and instrumentation tool support, in exchange for a bit of extra safety (the high-level scripting language can be trivially prevented from accessing unrelated functionality such as the renderer) and a potentially large productivity boost. This is yet another judgment call that must be made on a per-team and even per-project basis, taking into account the team's skill levels, experience levels, development preferences, and so on as well as the requirements of the target platform and the scope of the project itself.

13.4 Writing the Actual Scripts

With the dominating technical issues considered, it is time to move on to actually building a complete and functional AI using the scripting technologies of choice. Although the selection of a master or servant architecture and the details of the scripting system's implementation can play a significant role in the outcome of a scripted AI, the real artistry—and the real black magic—lies in building effective scripts on top of the technical foundation.

There are a number of challenges to creating a compelling gameplay experience via scripting. First and foremost, it is important to realize that scripting cannot and should not be used for everything. Whether in a master or servant role, scripting is most effective when used in concert with other techniques, as the project in question requires.

The chief problem with overusing scripting is combinatorial explosion. Trying to anticipate every possible circumstance that needs to be scripted for is a losing proposition. Inevitably, players will encounter some situation that the AI was not preprogrammed to handle, and the immersion will be lost entirely as the AI does something incredibly stupid. Worse, the more robust the AI seems to be, the harder these failures hit when they do occur; perfection cannot be achieved, and for the most part, the closer a scripted system comes to appearing perfect, the more disappointing its shortcomings will seem.

This can be mitigated by relying on other technologies where scripting is liable to become too hard to manage manually. The selection of these supplemental techniques is highly sensitive to the demands of each individual and unique project, but the primary guideline to keep in mind is that general situations call for general solutions. Scripting is, for the most part, a highly specific and focused approach to creating agent behavior, particularly in the servant role. It is not generally all that effective at responding to an unpredictable diversity of situations. Even in the master configuration, scripting must be carefully planned to anticipate the categories of behavior to be selected, and deferring to alternative systems is advisable when the lines get fuzzy.

13.4.1 Iteration

When implementing an AI that involves heavy use of scripting, rapid iteration is vital. As the scripts take shape, there will inevitably be gaps in the range of scenarios that the scripts are prepared to handle. Moreover, there will also be discrepancies between what the player expects an agent to rationally or believably do, and what actually occurs.

Because of this, it is crucial to test and refine scripted logic as often and thoroughly as possible. Teams with work environments set up for rapid iteration will benefit greatly, as the tiny problems can be ironed out and turned into a cohesive result. Slow or nonexistent iteration is a recipe for disaster. Because of scripting's inherent tendency to slide towards hard-coded and fixed solutions, neglecting iteration will almost inevitably result in brittle and boring behavior.

The flip side of this, of course, is that once a system passes a certain degree of flexibility and adaptability, it becomes increasingly difficult to test exhaustively. Substantial changes at this point run the serious risk of introducing more potential side effects than can be reliably checked and validated. So while iteration remains important, it is also key to limit the scope of changes made in each pass, so as to avoid constantly creating wildly different experiences that are virtually impossible to test to a satisfactory degree.

13.4.2 Transitions

There are any number of transitions that may occur during the course of a simulation unfolding: transitions between behavior control systems when scripting is used in the master role, transitions between scripts in the servant approach, transitions between levels of detail when using a subsumption architecture, and so on.

All of these transitions represent a significant challenge to creating seamless and believable scripted experiences. Any time the control of an agent undergoes such a change, it opens the possibility of a discontinuity in the perception of that agent on the part of the player.

To help alleviate this, it is important to know what transitions will occur up front during the design of the AI itself. Each transition must be carefully considered to ensure that the handoff is smooth and convincing. There are a few tricks for assisting with this, such as shared knowledge systems. If both the outgoing and incoming scripts have access to the exact same set of information, it becomes simpler to ensure that they behave consistently. Another useful variant on this technique is to explicitly communicate between the two scripts, such as handing off internal state data from one to the other.

Going a step further, it can be useful to inject special-case logic for certain transitions. For example, when moving between levels of detail, there can be great gains in believability to be had by adding extra transitory levels. These exist specifically to smooth out the jump from one degree of fidelity to another; they should be designed to come and go quickly, and give way to more long-lasting levels. In general, the larger the potential discrepancy between the behavior generated by two systems, the more appropriate it can be to use interstitial logic.

13.4.3 Variety

One of the harshest but most applicable criticisms leveled against a typical scripted AI system concerns lack of variety. Overly simplistic use of tripwire systems, for example, can easily lead to this undesirable result: if the hero is hailed by another character—using the exact same dialogue—every time he walks back and forth over some invisible line, players will inevitably lose their immersion into the simulation and come away with a less than optimal impression of the AI. Larger scale examples tend to be even more disruptive to the experience.

For this reason, it is well worth spending some time up front in design to make sure that the scripted behavior can avoid feeling canned or stale. Deduplication of tripwire activations, as discussed previously, is one simple but effective technique for doing this. In general, making sure that events do not repeat (or do not repeat too often) is a good policy for improving the feel of a scripted AI system.

Of course, past a point, adding more variety to a game's content becomes a practical problem. Content is not free to produce, and the increase in required assets may be prohibitive. In this case, simple limitations on the frequency of scripted events repeating themselves can go a long way.

Another useful trick, especially with master-style control systems, is to stagger the scripts and their execution across time. In other words, rather than having all agents begin their scripts at the exact same moment, they are dropped into the action at various points midway through the script. This avoids the eerily robotic look of dozens of ambient AI agents performing the exact same routine in a sort of zombie lockstep. A great advantage of this approach is that it requires no additional content assets; just trigger behaviors on different timetables for each agent, and over time their routines will tend to spread out and form interesting emergent interactions.

Master systems tend to be a little easier to use when it comes to creating variety. Because the master script is delegating to one or more of a handful of actual control systems for agents, a natural variegation will emerge from the fact that not every agent is executing in the same control scheme at a given time. Servant style scripting can be just as diverse and interesting, but at the expense of requiring much more special-case logic and design work up front.

Either way, scripts should generally be seen as a sort of "glue" that interconnects other techniques for creating convincing agent behavior. Some game implementations may be largely constructed out of scripts, but in the end, reliance on other mechanisms becomes paramount. Even if it is as simple as delegating to steering and navigation systems, handing off control from a purely hard-wired script to another system goes a long way toward creating good variety and ensuring that different situations can be handled by the AI agents effectively.

13.4.4 Surprise

Next to variety, surprise is one of the most commonly lacking elements in a script-heavy AI. Unfortunately, it is also one of the most ethereal and subjective qualities to pursue in game creation. Creating experiences that can surprise and entertain players is a difficult design challenge, regardless of scripting's role in the project itself.

Working closely with designers and testers (for iterative feedback) is, of course, central to accomplishing this goal. However, there are a few technical decisions that can heavily affect how practical it is to create surprising and engaging encounters with a game's AI agents. For example, excessively complex scripting systems (such as entire full-blown programming languages) can cost far more in terms of implementation effort than they deliver in terms of final game quality. This is true not only of the core technology's implementation itself, but also of the scripts built using that technology.

Because of this, it is advisable to favor simple solutions that require a little bit of creativity over excessively complex and deceptively "powerful" systems. Carefully designed tripwire systems, minimalistic DSLs, and well-crafted integrated architectures can all be set up in such a way as to provide tremendous amounts of flexibility for design purposes without becoming overly complicated.

The important factor here is giving designers and script implementers the ability to efficiently handle a diverse range of possible scenarios in which the player may find herself. However, it is just as important to resist the urge to anticipate every possible situation in advance. The specifics of this depend on whether a master or servant approach is taken.

For the master ideology, it is sufficient to categorize a broad range of situations and react to them appropriately via delegation. The servant perspective requires a little more care. Generally, the goal is to avoid creating scripts for all possible scenarios, and allowing generalized behavior control schemes to dominate as much of the time as possible. This enables the AI to provide a varied and interesting experience while retaining the potential for carefully crafted encounters created via scripts.

13.4.5 Narrative

Perhaps the most effective home for scripting is in the creation of rich narrative experiences. When specific sequences of events are meant to unfold in a particular way during gameplay, scripting is the logical choice for implementing such a design. As has hopefully become clear, this is not the only venue in which scripting can be an effective tool, but it is certainly one of the most natural.

Creating a compelling interactive narrative experience is no small task. For its part, AI must be designed to help further the experience, and not fight against it [Barnes et al. 02]. Everyone has stories of watching a hapless character stoically continue their idle animations while chaos and battle rage all around them. Slightly less common but just as egregious are situations where the AI actively seems to refuse to do what it is meant to do.

A major component of creating good narrative AI is visibility. The developer must always be able to understand why the AI has done something particular. When using scripting, this often simply boils down to keeping a trace log of the steps that have been performed by the agent, and, where applicable, what branches have been selected and how often loops have been repeated. Being able to select an agent and view a debug listing of its complete script state is also an invaluable tool.

In the end, interactive narratives are most compelling when everything works together to create a harmonious gameplay experience. Careful iteration, attention to transitions, provision of variety, and the occasional surprise all play key roles in fulfilling this objective.

13.5 Conclusion

Scripting is all too often treated as a brittle, boring, and undesirable approach to creating game AI systems. Unfortunately, this stigma is largely justified by the negative experiences of players struggling to enjoy games with little depth or variety to their AI interactions. The good news is that this is not an inevitable outcome; with proper care and investment, scripting can be a very powerful tool.

To wield this tool effectively requires intimate coordination between the design and technical concerns of the project. Knowing the design plans and requirements is critical to success, as is forethought on how to accomplish those plans.

Moreover, scripting must be viewed as simply one tool in a diverse toolbox. Over-reliance on scripts is bound to wind up producing the exact brittle, boring results that we are trying to avoid. Scripts should be seen as a sort of glue that attaches various decision-making, planning, and knowledge representation systems into a cohesive and powerful whole.

By the same token, it is important to resist the urge to try to anticipate everything that a script might need to handle. Delegation to other technologies and techniques is crucial to upholding the quality of the final game experience. Whether this is done via a "master" or "servant" approach, consistency of application is also vital. Staying true to a design philosophy, chosen early on, will help guide the creation of all of the scripted logic and underlying technologies.

As is often the case in software engineering, simpler is better when it comes to script systems. Designers have a persistent knack for creatively using (some might say abusing) any tool set before them; this can be leveraged for great effect. Instead of creating overly complicated and intricate systems, focus on creating simple ones that are flexible and can be used in creative and interesting ways.

Last but not least, never ship blind. Play testing and iteration are critical to refining and drawing out the fun in a game, and this applies just as strongly to scripted AI as anything else. Always be prepared to rapidly tweak an interaction based on player feedback or design decisions, and stay nimble.

Scripts are a sharp blade. They can accomplish amazing feats, but one false move can be hazardous. There is no need to fear, however; with proper care and control, scripting remains one of the most powerful techniques available to the AI creator. Whether it is a simple looping behavior or a complex, blossoming tree of intricate narrative possibilities, scripting is everywhere.

It takes only some imagination and some discipline to unleash.

References

[Barnes et al. 02] J. Barnes and J. Hutchens. "Scripting for undefined circumstances." In *AI Game Programming Wisdom*, edited by Steve Rabin. Hingham, MA: Charles River Media, 2002.

[Brockington et al. 02] M. Brockington and M. Darrah. "How not to implement a basic scripting language." In *AI Game Programming Wisdom,* edited by Steve Rabin. Hingham, MA: Charles River Media, 2002.

[McNaughton et al. 06] M. McNaughton and T. Roy. "Creating a visual scripting system." In *AI Game Programming Wisdom 3*, edited by Steve Rabin. Charles River Media, 2006.

[Orkin 02] J. Orkin. "A general purpose trigger system." In *AI Game Programming Wisdom*, edited by Steve Rabin. Hingham, MA: Charles River Media, 2002.

[Poiker 02] F. Poiker. "Creating scripting languages for non-programmers." In *AI Game Programming Wisdom*, edited by Steve Rabin. Hingham, MA: Charles River Media, 2002.

[Tozour 02] P. Tozour. "The perils of AI scripting." In *AI Game Programming Wisdom*, edited by Steve Rabin. Hingham, MA: Charles River Media, 2002.

14

Possibility Maps for Opportunistic AI and Believable Worlds

John Manslow

14.1 Introduction

The state of a game world is the combination of the states of all the objects within it: the state of the player (his or her location, orientation, health, inventory, etc.), the states of all NPCs (nonplayer characters—their locations, emotional states, etc.), the states of inanimate objects (which doors are locked, which buildings have collapsed, etc.), and so on. Games usually simulate a game world in order to track the evolution of its state, perhaps using level-of-detail approximations for unobserved elements of game state to reduce the complexity of doing so.

This chapter will introduce the idea of maintaining probability and possibility distributions over some unobserved elements of game state rather than simulating their evolution explicitly. If such distributions are used correctly, they allow the artificial intelligence (AI) to defer decisions relating to unobserved elements of game state without the player realizing that anything unusual is happening. This makes it possible to identify opportunities for action that might otherwise have required the creation and execution of complex plans and hence to create opportunistic AI that appears much smarter than it actually is.

14.2 What Are Probability and Possibility Maps?

A probability map provides a mapping from game states to probabilities that represent the relative likelihoods of the game being in different states. For example, the location of a character in a village is part of the game state and can be approximated by discrete locations such as the character's home, the stables, the tavern, the well, the shop, and the stretches of road between them. A probability map can be used to associate these locations with probabilities so as to model the likely location of the unobserved character. The map might change with time of day so that the character is more likely to be found at home at night or in the tavern in the evening.

Possibility maps are simplified versions of probability maps that dispense with probability values and only map states to indications as to whether they are possible. A possibility map for a character in a village, for example, would be true for every location where the character could possibly be located and false everywhere else. Because possibility maps aren't concerned with the relative likelihoods of states, they are typically easier to use and better suited to applications that are concerned with creating the illusion of intelligence rather than level-of-detail approximations.

14.3 Using Possibility Maps

For an application of probability and possibility maps to be convincing, it is important that they are updated in a way that is consistent with the player's observations of the game's state. We will first consider how to do this for possibility maps because the mechanisms for updating them are easier to understand than are those for updating probability maps.

A possibility map must regularly be updated to propagate possibility information according to its propagation rules. The precise form of those rules depends on what the possibility map represents: if it represents the location of an NPC, for example, the propagation rules would reflect how the NPC moves around the environment. If an update would propagate possibility information into a state that would affect the player's observations, or the player makes an observation that determines a state that is marked as possible, the AI must immediately decide whether to put the game into that state. If it does decide to put the game into that state, all mutually exclusive states must be marked as impossible; if it decides not to put the game into that state, then that state must be marked as impossible.

The decision as to whether to put the game into a particular state is taken based on the AI's assessment of the state's desirability from a gameplay perspective except when it is the only possible state remaining, in which case the AI has no choice. A simple example of an element of game state that can usually be represented by a possibility map is the location of an NPC. Figure 14.1 shows a possibility map for the location of an NPC on a simple level where P represents the player's location, N the NPC's location, the Xs represent walls and the ?s represent possible locations of the NPC.

Initially, in Figure 14.1a, the player can see the NPC and hence there are no possible alternative locations for it. If the NPC moves east and the player remains stationary, the player loses sight of the NPC and the possibility map starts to track the NPC's possible movement, as represented by the question marks in Figure 14.1b. The progress of the question marks is determined by the map's propagation rules and, since the map represents the possible location of the NPC, the rules are simply set up to reflect its range of possible movement. Figure 14.1c shows

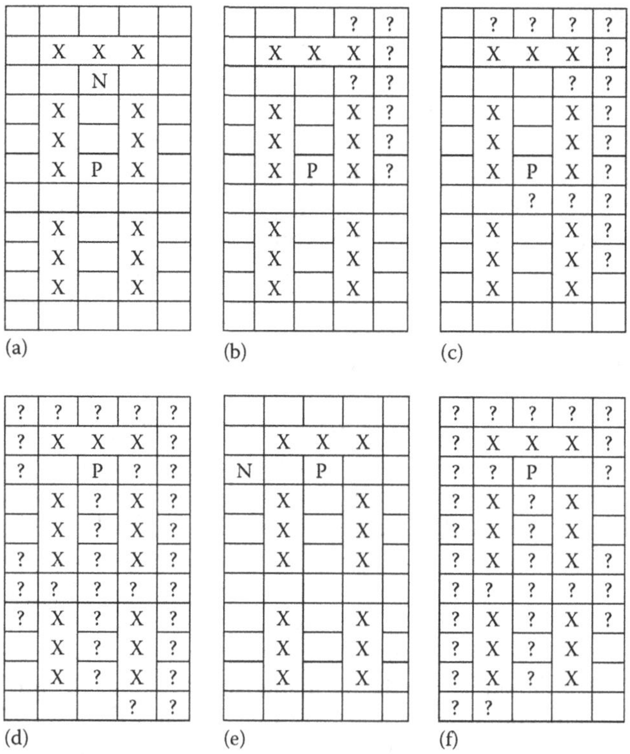

Figure 14.1

Possibility maps of an NPC's location. (a) A possibility map with a player looking north at an NPC. (b) The state of the possibility map a few seconds after the NPC moves out of sight to the east. (c) The state after a few more seconds. A melee attack from behind the player is now possible. (d) After the player moves north three squares, the AI can choose from a variety of melee and ranged weapon attacks. (e) The state of the map if the AI instantiates the NPC behind the player as the player turns to face east. (f) Possible locations for a second NPC that started in the same location as the first but moved west.

that, after several seconds, it becomes apparent that the NPC could've crept up behind the player and the AI has the opportunity to instantiate it and perform a melee attack.

If the AI chooses not to instantiate it and the player moves north three squares and starts to turn to the right, as shown in Figure 14.1d, the player will be about to observe two squares that are possible locations of the NPC. The AI must therefore decide whether to instantiate the NPC or to keep it hidden and continue propagating possibility information. It has a rich set of options if it chooses to instantiate it—it can instantiate it south of the player for a melee or ranged weapon attack, a couple of squares west of the player for a ranged weapon attack from behind, or to the east of the player for either a melee or ranged weapon attack. Figure 14.1e shows the state of the possibility map if the AI chose to instantiate it west of the player. If it chose not to instantiate it, the possibility map would look the same as in Figure 14.1d except that the two squares east of the player would be blank to indicate that the NPC cannot possibly be present at those locations.

In this example, the AI was forced to decide whether to instantiate the NPC when the player observed possible locations for it. It might also be the case that the player could infer the location of the NPC by other means, such as by hearing sounds that might be emitted when the NPC walks over noisy surfaces. If the player is out of earshot of the surfaces, then possibility information can propagate over them as if they didn't exist. If the player is within earshot, however, the surfaces block the propagation of possibility information and the AI would need to instantiate the NPC to allow it to cross. Similarly, if the NPC had no stealth capability, then the rules for propagating possibility information would've prevented locations adjacent to the player being marked as possible in Figure 14.1c and d and the AI would've needed to instantiate the NPC to get it close to the player. In general, the AI can choose to instantiate an NPC at any time though doing so prevents it from deferring decisions about the NPC's behavior and hence early instantiation is usually undesirable.

If the map in Figure 14.1 had contained two NPCs, their locations would've been represented by two independent possibility maps. The AI could create the illusion of finely coordinated movement between them by taking account of both their maps when deciding when and where to instantiate them. For example, assuming that both NPCs had started at the same location but the second moved west out of sight of the player, then the possibility map for the first NPC is as shown in Figure 14.1d, and the map for the second would be as shown in Figure 14.1f. As the player turns to the right, it is clear that the AI could instantiate an NPC almost anywhere and, in particular, could instantiate both NPCs to create the illusion of a planned coordinated attack from behind and to the side, from the front and to the side, from the front and from behind, and both from the front, both from the side, and both from behind. Note that, although the AI is technically cheating by using possibility maps, it always has to behave in a way that is consistent with the player's observations and hence a skillful player can often prevent the AI from springing these kinds of opportunistic traps by careful observation.

Figure 14.2 shows a level with a resource item—a health pack that can be used by NPCs—represented by an H. If the player initially observes the NPC, as shown in Figure 14.2a, and the NPC moves out of sight to the north, the possibility map will evolve as shown in Figure 14.2b. When it becomes possible for the NPC to have reached the health pack, the AI can either decide that the NPC should pick the health pack up immediately, in which case the possibility map is reset with the only possible location of the NPC being the location of the health

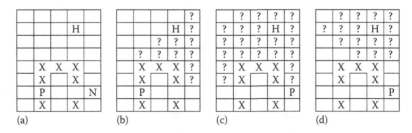

Figure 14.2

Possibility maps of an NPC's location with a health pack. (a) A possibility map with one health pack and a player facing an NPC. (b) The state of the map a few seconds after the NPC moves north out of sight of the player. (c) The state if the NPC did not pick up the health pack and the player moves three squares east. (d) The state if the NPC did pick up the health pack.

14. Possibility Maps for Opportunistic AI and Believable Worlds

pack, or the AI can defer the decision. In order to defer the decision, the AI needs to fork the possibility map into two—one for the location of the NPC with the health pack and one for the location of the NPC without. The latter is simply a continuation of the original but the former is a new map with the only possible location of the NPC being the location of the pack.

If, as the NPC possibly reaches the health pack, the player moves east three squares, the possibility map for the NPC without the health pack, which is shown in Figure 14.2c, reveals that both melee and ranged weapon attacks are possible and the possibility map for the NPC with the health pack, which is shown in Figure 14.2d, shows that only a ranged weapon attack is possible. The AI therefore has the opportunity to choose between the lower health version of the NPC performing a melee or ranged weapon attack, the higher health version performing a ranged weapon attack, and keeping the NPC hidden. If the NPC is particularly effective in melee combat or ineffective at a distance, the benefits of deferring the decision about collecting the health pack are obvious.

Forking can be used to defer decisions in relation to a wide variety of actions—should an NPC pick up a key, unlock a door, flick a switch, buy a sword, etc.? It can, however, also result in a combinatorial explosion of possibility maps if the environment contains too many opportunities for action and the AI will usually have to make some decisions earlier than is strictly necessary simply to control the number of maps. Even deferring a decision for a short time, however, can be beneficial as the AI often has more information available to it when it comes to make the deferred decision than it would've had if it had not deferred the decision at all.

14.4 Updating Probability Maps

Like possibility maps, probability maps must also regularly be updated—this time to propagate probability information according to its propagation rules. The precise form of those rules depends on what the probability map represents: if it represents the location of an NPC, for example, the propagation rules would reflect the likelihood of the NPC moving from each location to every other. If an update results in nonzero probability in a state that would affect the player's observations, or the player makes an observation that determines a state that has nonzero probability, the AI must put the game into that state with the probability indicated by the probability map. If the game is put into the state, the probabilities of all mutually exclusive states are set to zero, but if the game is not put into the state, the probability of the state is set to zero. Normalization of the probability map must be maintained at all times—that is, the sum of the probabilities of all states must always be equal to one.

Consider, for example, a guard that's controlled by a state machine with the states patrolling from point A to point B, patrolling from point B to point A, eating, sleeping, and playing solitaire. Each of those states would be assigned a probability by the probability map and the map's propagation rules would provide probabilities for transitions between states and, perhaps, minimum times that the transitions should take. Table 14.1 gives some example transition probabilities, and Table 14.2 shows how the probability map evolves after the player sees the guard patrolling from point A to point B.

If the player entered the dining hall when the probability map had the values in the second to last row of Table 14.2, the AI would instantiate the guard in the eating state with probability 0.097. If the instantiation happened, the probability of the eating state would be set to one and the probabilities of all other states would be set to zero. If the instantiation did not happen, the probability of the eating state would be set to zero and the

Table 14.1 Transition Probabilities for a Guard

		Next State				
		A to B	B to A	Sleeping	Eating	Solitaire
Current state	A to B	0.00	1.00	0.00	0.00	0.00
	B to A	0.95	0.00	0.00	0.05	0.00
	Sleeping	0.04	0.00	0.95	0.01	0.00
	Eating	0.18	0.00	0.01	0.80	0.01
	Solitaire	0.50	0.00	0.50	0.00	0.00

Table 14.2 Probability Map for a Guard

Time	A to B	B to A	Sleeping	Eating	Solitaire
1	0.000	1.000	0.000	0.000	0.000
2	0.950	0.000	0.000	0.050	0.000
3	0.009	0.950	0.001	0.040	0.000
4	0.910	0.009	0.001	0.080	0.000
5	0.023	0.910	0.002	0.064	0.001
6	0.877	0.023	0.003	0.097	0.000
6 after observation	0.970	0.026	0.003	0.000	0.001

probabilities of the other states updated so that they still sum to one, as shown in the last row. In practice, state transition probabilities usually need to vary with time of day to produce realistic behavior. For example, the probabilities of transitioning from any state to the sleep state would be very high at night for a guard that was only working the dayshift.

Probability maps provide the AI with information about the relative likelihoods of different game states and that allows it to distinguish between states that are almost certain and others that are theoretically possible but highly unlikely. In this sense, they are more powerful than possibility maps. Unfortunately, it can be difficult to come up with transition probabilities that produce sensible behavior and, if the transition probabilities vary with time, the probability map will never stabilize. This means that the AI will, in principle, need to continue to update it regardless of how long it is since it was last affected by the player. These problems can be avoided by combining probability and possibility maps using the method described in the next section.

14.5 Combining Possibility and Probability Maps

A useful approximation to a normal probability map can often be achieved by combining a static probability map and a possibility map. A static probability map assigns probabilities to states but the probabilities are not propagated across the map according to transition probabilities as they are in a normal probability map. Instead, they represent the likelihoods of observing states when no previous observations have been made and a possibility map is used to ensure that only states that are consistent with the player's observations can be instantiated.

For example, Table 14.3 shows three static probability maps for a guard, the first to be used during the working day, the second at mealtimes, and the third at night. If the player

Table 14.3 Static Probability Map for a Guard

Time	A to B	B to A	Sleeping	Eating	Solitaire
Working day	0.495	0.495	0.001	0.003	0.001
Mealtimes	0.010	0.010	0.000	0.970	0.010
Night	0.002	0.002	0.990	0.003	0.003

observes the games room, the AI checks to see whether the possibility map indicates that it's possible for the guard to be in there and, if it is, the AI instantiates the guard with the probability specified by the static probability map after it's been adjusted so that the sum of the probabilities of all possible states is one. For example, in the unlikely event that it's mealtime and the player has just observed that the guard is not in the dining hall, then the guard must either be patrolling from A to B, patrolling from B to A, or playing solitaire—hence, the probabilities of those states are all $0.010/(1 - 0.970) = 0.333$. If the player observes the games room, the AI would therefore instantiate the guard there with probability 0.333.

If the player left the area completely, it wouldn't take long for every state in the possibility map to be marked as possible, at which point, no further computation would be necessary until the player returned and made another relevant observation.

14.6 Factorizing Game State

The complete state of a game is an extremely complex multidimensional entity, and it is not realistic to expect to be able to create probability and possibility maps over the state in its entirety. Instead, it is necessary to factor the game state into independent elements and create multiple independent maps. Such elements must be independent in the sense that the state of one should not affect the probable or possible states of another. The most easily identifiable independent elements are usually the locations of NPCs, although they can become dependent when NPCs need to interact.

For example, if the guard in the earlier example had played poker rather than solitaire, then it would've been necessary for the AI to make sure that there was never only a single guard in the games room, thereby creating a dependency between the locations of guards. That problem could be solved by checking the probability and possibility maps of all guards when the player enters the games room to see if enough guards could be there for a game to be taking place and only instantiating them if that was the case. To guarantee that the AI always had a choice, however, it would need to make sure that no single guard ends up with the games room as his or her only possible location—something that could easily be achieved when deciding whether to instantiate guards elsewhere.

Shared resources create more serious dependencies. Consider, for example, a map with two NPCs and a health pack that can be taken by only one of them. As has already been described, as each NPC possibly reaches the location of the health pack, their possibility maps must fork and the game must maintain four possibility maps—two for each NPC, one to represent possible movement with the health pack and one without. When the AI decides to instantiate an NPC, it must decide whether it will be the version with the health pack or the one without and must remember that the health pack is with only one of the NPCs. The situation gets even more complicated if the health pack regenerates after a short time. In that case, it is possible for both NPCs to have picked it up but one of them could only have done so after it had regenerated. This situation can be modeled with additional forking to account for the order in which the NPCs picked up the pack and to allow for its regeneration time.

Another example of a shared resource that creates dependencies is a lift. Lifts create dependencies because, when one NPC moves the lift, it affects its availability for the others in an extremely complex way—the amount of time that an NPC's possibility map takes to propagate from one floor to the next via the lift depends on the location of the lift at the time the NPC possibly reaches it, the times other NPCs possibly reached it, and where they possibly left it—and all of that depends on deferred decisions that have not yet been made. In principle, this problem can also be solved by forking but it's probably better and certainly simpler to use an approximation such as to ignore the dynamics of the lift altogether and just propagate possibility information between floors with a slight delay.

If a suitable factorization of the game state cannot be found, a joint map can be created to model the probability or possibility of the combined state of multiple elements. This is effectively what is being done by forking; when, in the earlier example, an additional possibility map was created when the NPC could've picked up the health pack, the AI was dynamically creating a possibility map for the combined states of the location of the NPC and its health. The problem with this approach is that the number of states in a joint map grows exponentially with the number of elements of game state that it represents and hence joint maps can be excessively large and unwieldy. Some factorization is therefore always necessary for the successful application of probability and possibility maps.

14.7 Conclusion

This chapter has described probability and possibility maps and shown how they can be used individually and in combination to produce level-of-detail effects and allow the AI to defer decisions to create the illusion of highly intelligent, coordinated, and carefully planned behavior. Respect for the player's observational history ensures that this is achieved without the player noticing any inconsistencies and provides a way for players to limit the options of the AI through their own careful planning and observation.

15

Production Rules Implementation in *1849*

Robert Zubek

15.1 Introduction

This chapter presents implementation details of the production rule system used in the game *1849*. The system's main design goals were enabling quick iteration via a data-driven approach and good performance on a variety of hardware, down to significantly underpowered tablet devices.

First, we discuss the details bottom up, from the world model, through rule implementation, up to the overall rule system that manipulates them. Then, in the second half, we examine the performance consequences of these design choices, as well as lessons learned in the process of implementing the system.

15.2 Game Mechanics and Production Rules

1849 is a city building and management game for tablets, desktops, and the web. The fiction of the game is that gold has just been discovered in California, and player's task is to build gold mining towns and make money in the gold rush. The following is an overview of the game mechanics and simulation.

15.2.1 Game Mechanics

In terms of game mechanics, the game is a classic city builder, along the lines of early Impressions Games such as *Caesar* or *Zeus*. The main units of gameplay are as follows:

- *Buildings*, which the player places in town; they can be houses for residents or workplaces that produce resources or city benefits (such as fire prevention).
- *Resources* are created by buildings, either from nothing (such as farms producing wheat) or by consuming other resources (such as bakery consuming wheat and producing bread).
- *Workers* are the fuel powering all these buildings; they cannot be directly controlled by the player, but they can be influenced by providing them the resources they want.

The main feedback loops are set up such that workers power all buildings, but they are fickle and sensitive to what resources are available. As the town grows, more and more workers arrive looking for work, but they also demand more complex resources, and if they don't get what they want, they vote with their feet and leave, causing workplaces to shut down. Initially, their demands are simple, just food and drink, but soon, they start demanding increasingly processed resources, such as shoes, clothes, or newspapers. The player can either try to import those processed resources at a high cost or build out resource conversion buildings and manage their logistics. Much of the fun and difficulty of the game comes from the "spinning plates" feeling, of setting up these increasingly complicated resource production and conversion chains and then maintaining them and making sure that they are all running smoothly, that workers remain happy, and that the town's overall budget is trending in the right direction.

15.2.2 Game Simulation

The game simulation is implemented using a production rule system: all buildings run a collection of stand-alone rules that simulate the town's economy.

We can discuss them as a hierarchy of abstractions:

- Each building is a stand-alone rule executor for a set of rules.
- Each rule has some conditions that can match and produce some actions.
- Conditions typically involve queries about resources or the world, and actions typically involve resource modification and issuing side effects.
- Resource queries and modification bottom out in a data model optimized for specific types of context-sensitive access.

15.3 Rule System

Having introduced the layers of the system, let's discuss them bottom up.

15.3.1 Resources

The basic atomic unit of game economy is a *resource*. This is an <id, amount> tuple, such as "50 dollars" or "10 units of gold" or "50 units of stone." Everything that can be produced or consumed is a resource.

Most resources are concrete, like gold or stone or food. But there are also abstract resources such as people and map effects such as crime level.

When you build a house, and people move in, that's represented as the house gaining a "1 resident" resource—and later, when that resident gets a job, the workplace gains a "1 worker" resource as well (and the reverse happens when the resident moves out).

Map effects are things like crime, boredom, or fire risk. For example, every house creates a tiny amount of fire risk, say, "0.01 fire risk" per day, and this resource collects up in the world, and later causes fires, as we'll describe in a moment.

15.3.2 Resource Bins

Resources are not loose objects, rather, they're stored in bins. A resource bin contains a whole bag of resources and their amounts. There are three types of bins in the game.

First, *player's inventory* during a game session is stored in a bin. For example, the facts that I have $1000 in cash and 10 units of gold ready for trade are just two resource entries in my bin.

Second, each *board unit* (such as a building) has its own bin, which is its own inventory. For example, when a wheat farm grows wheat, it inserts a bunch of wheat units in its own bin. But those units are not yet usable by the player. There's a separate delivery step that has to happen, to deliver this wheat from the building to the player's inventory.

Finally, each *map tile* has a resource bin that's separate from any building that might sit on top of it. For one example, gold underground is represented as a gold resource inside that tile's bin, and it needs to be mined out of the ground and into the building's bin. For another example, fire hazard is a resource, conjured up and inserted into the world by wooden buildings.

15.3.3 Conditions and Actions

Since almost everything in the simulation is a resource, a lot of the game is based on resource conversions. Some simplified examples from our data definition files:

Ranch produces meat and leather, and shows an animated NPC at work:

```
"doWork":
  "outputs": ["unit 6 meat", "unit 6 leather"]
  "success": [
    "_ a-spawn-worker npc npc-farmer action ranch days 7"
  ]
```

Ranch delivers meat into storage, 20 units at a time:

```
"deliverWork":
  "frequency": "every 5 days",
  "checks": ["unit workers > 0"],
  "inputs": ["unit 20 leather"],
  "outputs": ["player 20 leather"],
  "success": [
    "_ a-spawn-walker npc npc-delivery
       to bldg-trade-store then return"
  ]
```

Cobbler brings leather from storage if it doesn't have any, consumes it, and produces shoes:

```
"bringMaterials":
  "checks": ["unit workers > 0", "unit leather < 2"],
  "inputs": ["player 8 leather"],
  "outputs": ["unit 8 leather"]
"doWork":
  "inputs": ["unit 2 leather"],
  "outputs": ["unit 3 shoes"]
```

But conversion rules don't have to be limited to just buildings bins—they also frequently interact with map tiles underneath and around:

Gold mine consumes gold from the map tiles underneath and produces gold in its own inventory, until all ground gold has been exhausted:

```
"doWork":
  "inputs": ["map 5 gold"],
  "outputs": ["unit 5 gold"]
```

Every wooden house produces a little bit of fire risk in the map tile underneath:

```
"produceFireHazard":
  "frequency": "every 7 days",
  "checks": ["map fire-hazard < 1 max"],
  "outputs": ["map 0.04 fire-hazard"]
```

Fire brigade consumes all fire risks from the map, within a given radius, using a special action:

```
"consumeMapResource":
  "frequency": "every 7 days",
  "checks": ["unit workers > 0"]
  "success": ["_ a-change-resource-in-area
              radius 5 res fire-hazard amount -1"]
```

As you can see, the fact that gold comes from underground, while food and other things are made in buildings, is not actually hard-coded anywhere in the engine. Right now, it's just a matter of convention. This means that you could rewrite the rules such that, for example, the cobbler makes shoes and inserts them underground inside the tile. You probably wouldn't want to, because nobody would be able to get at those shoes if they wanted them, but it's a possibility.

15.3.4 Rule Execution

As you can see from the previous examples, each rule consists of several elements. Here is the complete list:

- "Frequency": how often we check.
- "Checks": all of these have to be satisfied.
- "Inputs": if checks are satisfied, we check if desired inputs exist, and if so, they will be consumed.

Listing 15.1. Pseudocode for rule matching algorithm.

```
for each rule that should run at this point in time
     if all checks are satisfied
          if all inputs exist
               consume inputs
               produce outputs
               run success actions
          else
               run failedInputs actions
     else
          run failedChecks actions
```

- "Outputs": if inputs were consumed successfully, these will be produced.
- "Success": actions to run if this rule was applied successfully (neither checks nor inputs have failed).
- "FailedInputs": fallback actions to run if inputs were insufficient.
- "FailedChecks": fallback actions to run if checks failed.

The algorithm in pseudocode is listed in Listing 15.1. As we can see, "frequency" and "checks" both denote *conditions* in which the rule runs, "inputs" defines both *conditions* to be checked and related *actions* (consume inputs), while "outputs" and other fields define *actions* only. Frequency is pulled out separately as an optimization step (see next section).

15.4 Performance

Our production system is very efficient—in a town with many hundreds of entities, the rule engine's CPU consumption is barely noticeable in the profiler, even when running on rather underpowered tablets.

Most of the processing power is spent, predictably, on checking conditions. One of the design goals for this system was to make sure conditions can be checked quickly, ideally in constant or near-constant time, to help with performance.

We have three optimizations in place to help with this: flexible frequency of rule execution, a drastically simplified language for conditions and actions, and an efficient world model that is inexpensive to query.

15.4.1 Condition Checking Frequency

Production systems vary in how often the rules should be run. For example, we could run rules whenever something changes in the world, which in a game could be every frame, or maybe on a fixed schedule, such as 10 Hz, or on every game "turn" in a turn-based game.

In *1849*, the game's simulation is triggered off of game clock days (e.g., a farm produces wheat every 7 days), so we felt no need to run the rules too often. Our default frequency is once per day, and we made it easy to raise or lower the frequency as needed on a per-rule basis.

Here is an example of how frequency is specified—it's pulled out of the conditions definition into its own data field:

```
"produceFireHazard":
  "frequency": "every 7 days",
  "checks": ["map fire-hazard < 1 max"],
```

Finally, we implemented a very simple scheduler that keeps track of which rules are supposed to run when, so that they don't get accessed until their prescribed time.

15.4.2 Condition Definition Language

Many rule systems express conditions and actions in an expressive language such as predicate logic, so that the developer can make queries and assertions about entities as a class without committing to specific instances, and let the computer figure out to which entities those rules can be applied.

Here is a made-up example in a made-up predicate language:

```
If is-a(X,gold-mine) and is-a(T,map-tile) and
is-under(T,X) and contains(T,R,5) and is-a(R,gold)
=> Then increment(X,R,5) and increment(T,R,-5)
```

This kind of a rule would be very expressive and general. However, finding entities in the world that match this query can get expensive quickly: it's essentially a search problem. While numerous optimizations for inference systems are well known (e.g., the Rete algorithm [Forgy 82]), they're still not enough, given our desire to make conditions execute in constant or near-constant time.

Conditions and actions we use in our engine are not so generic. Instead, they are more contextual, which lets them be simpler. Once again, here is our gold mine example:

```
"doWork":
  "inputs": ["map 5 gold"],
  "outputs": ["unit 5 gold"]
```

Here, "map" and "unit" are like variables, in that they're not specific entities like "gold mine #52"—but they're also not free variables like X was in the previous example. Instead, they're contextually bound indexicals: "unit" refers to the entity that's currently executing this rule, "map" refers to all tiles underneath the unit, and "player" refers to the singleton entity that keeps player's city inventory.

In other words, instead of using objective representation and predicate logic, we use deictic representation [Agre 87], with variables that are already contextually bound at query time to particular entities. Game units typically only care about themselves and their immediate surroundings, so deictic representation is a perfect match.

This choice constrains our system's expressiveness, compared to a language with completely free variables and unification, but it drastically eliminates a huge search problem and associated costs.

15.4.3 Data Model

Most conditions are resource queries, and most actions are resource modifications. For example: check if there is gold underground, and if so, consume it and produce gold in my inventory; or check if I have any workers working here, and if there is gold in my inventory, and if so, deliver gold over to player's inventory, and so on.

As we described before, we store resources in resource bins, and those bins are attached to units, map tiles, and the player's data object. Each resource bin is implemented as a vector of 64 floating-point numbers, indexed by resource (because there are currently 64 resource types).

A resource query such as "unit gold > 5" then works as follows: first, we get a reference to the unit's own resource bin (via a simple switch statement), then look up resource value (an array lookup), and finally do the appropriate comparison against the right-hand side value (another simple switch statement). All this adds up to a constant-time operation. Similar process happens for update instead of a query.

A query such as "map gold > 5" is marginally more expensive, because it means "add up gold stored in all tiles under the unit and check if > 5". Fortunately, units are not arbitrarily large—the largest one is 2 × 2 map tiles—which means we execute at most four tile lookups, making it still a constant-time operation.

And as a fallback, we allow ourselves to cheat if necessary: both conditions and actions can also refer to a library of named built-in functions, and those can do arbitrary computation. For example, the fire brigade has a built-in action `a-change-resource-in-area` that consumes a pre-tuned amount of fire risk resource within its area of effect, but this operation is actually linear in map size. We use such actions rarely.

15.5 Lessons from *1849*

With the system overview behind us, we'll quickly go over what worked well in the process of building our game using this engine, and what, with the benefit of hindsight, we wish we had done differently.

15.5.1 Benefits

Performance was clearly a high point of the system, which can run cities with hundreds of active entities without breaking a sweat, even on comparatively underpowered tablet devices. We could probably push production rules even further, if the rendering subsystem had not claimed all available processor cycles already.

Also, as you can see from our examples, the rules themselves are specified in a kind of a domain-specific language, based primarily on JSON, with condition and action bodies expressed as strings with a specific syntax. They get deserialized at load time into class instances, following simple command pattern.

Exposing game rules as a DSL that can be loaded up with a simple restart, without rebuilding the game, had the well-known benefits of data-driven systems: decoupling configuration from code, increasing iteration speed, and ultimately empowering design.

15.5.2 Lessons

At the same time, we ran into two problems: one with how our particular DSL evolved over time, and one with production systems and how they matched the game's design.

The DSL was initially developed to support only queries such as "`<bin> <resource> <comparison> <value>`" or actions such as "`<bin> <resource> <delta>`".

These were appropriate for most cases, but we quickly found ourselves wanting to do more than just resource manipulation. For example, we wanted to start spawning workers to go dig up gold or carry it in wheelbarrows to the storage building—or even more mundane things, like playing sound effects or setting or clearing notification bubbles if a building is understaffed or can't get road access.

Over time, we added support for more types of actions, and a generic deserializer syntax, which supported actions such as " _ a-spawn-worker npc npc-farmer action ranch days 7". This was just syntactic sugar for a definition like {" _ type": "a-spawn-worker", "npc": "npc-farmer", "action": "ranch", "days": 7}, and that in turn just deserialized into the class ASpawnWorker and filled in the appropriate fields.

In retrospect, we should have added support for custom or one-off conditions and actions from the very beginning; that would have saved us engineering time later on reworking parts of the system. Even in the most organized system design, there will *always* be a need for one-off functionality to achieve some specific effects, and all systems should support it.

Separately from this, we also discovered a representational deficiency, which came from a mismatch between one-shot and continuous processes. This is a deficiency we failed to resolve in time for shipping.

From the earliest points in the game's design, we operated under the assumption that resource manipulation is sparse and discrete, for example, every 7 days, the wheat farm produces 6 units of wheat or the bakery consumes 3 wheat and produces 5 bread. This lent itself perfectly to a rule system that triggers on a per-rule timer.

However, fairly late in the process, we realized that this kind of a discrete system was hard for our players to understand. Whether it was because we surfaced it poorly or because their expectations were trained differently by other games, our beta players had difficulty understanding the simulation and what was actually going on, because the activities were so sparse.

When we explored this further, we found that players reacted best when buildings looked like they operated continuously, for example, wheat farm producing wheat at velocity of 0.8 per day, and when its storage fills up, the surplus gets delivered.

Ultimately, we were able to produce much of the desired user effect by essentially faking it in the UI and in how we give feedback to the player. But had this happened earlier in development, we might have rewritten all of our rules to run much more frequently, to simulate continuous production, even at the cost of spending significantly more processing time on rule checks per second. Even better, we should have considered combining it with a form of parallel-reactive networks [Horswill 00], to help represent continuous processes, and hooked that up as part of the data model manipulated by the rule system.

15.6 Related Work

On the game development side, this implementation was very directly influenced by previously published implementation details of Age of Empires (AoE) [Age of Empires 97] and of the GlassBox engine used in SimCity [Willmott 12].

AoE was one of the earliest games to expose data-driven production systems. Their syntax is based on s-expressions, and rules might look something like

```
(defrule
  (can-research-with-escrow ri-hussar)
=>
  (release-escrow food)
  (release-escrow gold)
  (research ri-hussar))
```

The AoE system plays from the perspective of the player, that is, one rule engine is active per enemy player. The GlassBox rules, on the other hand, are much more granular and run from the perspective of each individual unit, for example,

```
unitRule mustardFactory
    rate 10
    global Simoleans in 1
    local YellowMustard in 6
    local EmptyBottle in 1
    local BottleOfMustard out 1
    map Pollution out 5
end
```

We were highly inspired by the design choices from GlassBox, especially the data model that organizes resources into bins, distributes those bins in the game world, and lets production rules check and manipulate them.

Finally, the representation of conditions and actions using a contextual language like "unit gold > 5" is related to the history of work on deictic representation, such as the implementation of game-playing AI for the game Pengi by [Agre 87] or reactive autonomous robots in [Horswill 00]. In particular, we decided against inference or queries with arbitrary free variables such as "is(X,gold-mine) and has-workers(X)". Instead, we replaced them with task-relevant indexicals, which made fast queries much easier to implement. The task of binding deictic variables can then be moved to a separate subsystem that can be optimized separately (in the Pengi example, it was done by simulating a visual attention system, but in our system, it's trivially easy, based on which entity executes the rule).

15.7 Conclusion

This chapter examined the implementation details of a production rule system used in the game *1849*. We started by examining the architecture of the system, followed by details of production rules and their components. As we demonstrate, a few specific simplifications enabled a very efficient implementation, suitable even for underpowered mobile devices.

References

[Age of Empires 97] Uncredited. 1997. *Age of Empires*. Developed by Ensemble Studios.
[Agre 87] Agre, P.E. and Chapman, D. 1987. Pengi: An implementation of a theory of activity. In *Proceedings of the AAAI-87*. Los Altos, CA: Morgan Kaufmann.

[Forgy 82] Forgy, C. 1982. Rete: A fast algorithm for the many pattern/many object pattern match problem. *Artificial Intelligence* 19: 17–37.

[Horswill 00] Horswill, I.D., Zubek, R., Khoo, A., Le, C., and Nicholson, S. 2000. The cerebus project. In *Proceedings of the AAAI Fall Symposium on Parallel Cognition and Embodied Agents*, North Falmouth, MA.

[Willmott 12] Willmott, A. 2012. GlassBox: A new simulation architecture. *Game Developers Conference 2012*, San Francisco, CA.

16

Production Systems
New Techniques in AAA Games

Andrea Schiel*

16.1 Introduction

Production systems have been around since the 1940s and are now applied in a wide array of applications and ongoing research. AAA games bring a unique set of challenges to production systems; they require that AI systems be runtime efficient, deterministic, memory lean, and above all, implementable within the development cycle. Over the course of many of our titles, production systems have developed along different lines. This chapter tries to describe the majority of our more unique production systems, assuming that the reader has a basic knowledge of production systems. For readers who want to code their first production system, there is a list of references that describe basic production systems in more detail [Luger 93, Millington 09, Laird 12, Bourg 04] and these

---

* The author has worked at Electronic Arts for over 18 years on a variety of titles, in particular sports games. This chapter contains the insights from applying production systems to multiple AAA over many generations of consoles.

Table 16.1 Terms in Use in This Chapter

Term	Alternate
AI	AI agent or AI opponent system
Rule	Production, statement
LHS (left-hand side)	Precondition, conditional statement, if side
RHS (right-hand side)	Then side, action, postcondition
Rules database	Rules set, working set
Variable	Operator, assertion symbol, datum, working memory element, fact
Working memory	Input, assertion set, perceptions, knowledge, set of facts
Scripting language	Predicate logic, symbolic script
Matching stage	Rule binding, LHS evaluation, variable unification
Selection stage	Rule selection, conflict resolution
Execution stage	Act, RHS evaluation

should get you started. This chapter will step through some of the design choices you might make for a more advanced or specific system and presents some of the innovations in our AAA titles.

16.1.1 Terminology

Terminology surrounding production systems can be confusing since it varies depending on the source of the material. For clarification, Table 16.1 lists the terms in use in this chapter and some common alternate terms.

16.1.2 Design Considerations

Coding your own production system can be very rewarding but there are some choices that need to be made beforehand. Skipping one of these decisions has caused problems in development in the past and many of these can be found in postmortems on production systems:

- What decisions is the system trying to make? (scope and domain choice)
- How are rules represented? (rules representation)
- How will rules be authored?
- How does the left-hand side (LHS) evaluate? (matching systems)
- What happens if the AI fails to find a rule?
- What happens if there are multiple rules? (selection algorithms)
- Execution and the design of the right-hand side (RHS)
- How will the system be tuned?

The following sections go into more detail about each one of these points.

16.2 What Decisions Is the System Trying to Make?

Like any other architecture, production systems are good at certain tasks and not at others. If the decisions are particularly simple, a rules-based system is probably overkill. However, if the game doesn't break down into nice discrete states and the decisions need to reflect different scenarios, a production system (or variation thereof) would be appropriate. At a minimum, a production system can be used when

- AI decisions are based on a variety of factors and are not easily quantified
- The system needs to respond quickly to changes in state
- There is an *expert* with knowledge of the game that needs encoding and that knowledge doesn't break down into a nice algorithm
- The actions for the system are independent of each other

The key decision is which part of the game the production system should be applied to. For example, production systems could make decisions for only part of the AI's process: when to do a trick or execute specific plays—though even these more narrow scenarios still need to fit the aforementioned criteria. A more specific AI can help limit when the system runs, which will help contain the runtime cost, though spikes in performance can still be an issue.

Alternatively, the production system could run all of the AI's decision logic. This sort of system requires more extensive optimization, and memory may be an issue since the scope of the AI is broader. The same can be true if the AI is being used for all of the simulation. Production systems can also be used for non-AI logic—such as for a game analysis system like color commentary for a sports game or for a contextual help system. The scope of these applications are harder to determine and handling the case when no rule triggers can be critical.

Performance-wise, production systems have a heavier update cost than most decision trees or state machines. Memory is required, but not necessarily more than what might be needed for another AI system. The rules themselves tend to have a small footprint, but they do add up quickly as a *typical* AI agent can require 100–500 rules. Different applications or more narrow applications of the system may require fewer rules, of course. There is also a hidden workflow and tool development cost in that an expert needs to author the rules, be able to iterate on those rules, and debug behaviors.

16.3 Choice of Rules Representation

The way rules are described is probably the biggest difference between the way these systems are implemented in games, compared to those used in research and other industries. The actual scripting language varies between systems: in CLIPS [Riley 13], it's C; SOAR has its own symbolic language [Laird 12]; and in our games, the language is very specific for the domain that the rule is being used for. In larger production systems, the scripting language supports predicate logic and unification to allow more flexibility in deciding which rules are applicable. This is often expensive both to develop (if you're coding your own) and to run. Due to the cost of unification, there are algorithms like Rete [Schneider 02, Millington 09] that optimize the matching. The advantage of a full predicate calculus (like SOAR) is that the language is very flexible and can describe a large variety of scenarios.

In deterministic games, however, unification is often difficult to take advantage of, and when it is removed, the development of a rules representation can be simplified. Unification can make it difficult to optimize for the scale of the AI. In the majority of our games, a more custom, smaller, and specific language was used. The elements of the LHS are designed to reflect the game's perception and state variables and the RHS are called into the animation or lower systems.

Another detail we discovered is a little unusual; sometimes, designers wanted the ability to create temporary variables. These variables may not map to a variable in the perception system but are to represent some value the designers want to check, the most common being some type of counter. In systems with a working memory, this is trivial to implement, but if there isn't a working memory, a form of scratch memory or blackboard is needed to carry these temporary variables.

One caution here is that designers might attempt to use temporary variables to introduce state into the decision process itself. This should be discouraged and the solution is usually to sit down with the designer to assist them with building a better rule. Temporary variables have also been used to introduce randomness into the system—which could be another sign that the designer may need assistance with the development of the LHS of a rule (i.e., it is being selected too often or too little). Having useful operators for the LHS of rules or building in a weighting system for rule selection can help here. The types of operators (usually logical) will help determine how extensive the rules language will need to be.

16.4 Method of Rules Authoring

Full proprietary systems often support their own editor and in these cases, the authors are effectively scripting their rules. In addition, with the ability to read definitions at runtime, the evaluation of the rules can be a fantastic asset for debugging purposes. Live editing could also be possible but in one variant system we developed, the rules are recorded.

16.4.1 Recorded Rule System

Recording systems allow for rapid iteration on rules and for very quick authoring of rules. The author runs the game, puts the system into record mode, and the system will automatically record the state of the game. When the specific type of action occurs, the state of the game is associated with the action and becomes the LHS of the rule (the action is the RHS). The disadvantage of this system is that manual tweaking of the rules is limited.

For the LHS (the recorded part), the following are necessary considerations:

- What's being recorded: which game state variables are important?
- How important each game state variable is: a weight for each variable that modifies how much that variable applies when being matched. Lower weighted variables are less necessary for a match.
- The tightness of the matching for each variable: the range of values that would be tolerated for each variable.
- How far back in time is needed to be recorded to form the LHS—is it a snapshot right before the action or a time range before the action.

In our implementation, the LHS rules produce a score that is considered a match if it surpasses a given threshold value. The rules that match form the matched rules set and the rest of the system is a classic production system. That is, the actions (RHS) go through a stage of conflict resolution and whichever rules are left after selection then run their actions.

The disadvantage is that the system works best if the rules share a lot of the same LHS variables. By the same token, sharing a lot of LHS elements does make the Rete algorithm a good choice. However, since predicate calculus wasn't in use, a custom matching system was implemented.

Determining which game state variables are needed for the LHS is a challenge. Once this step is completed, the actual authoring is very quick. A useful aid here is the ability for the system to rewind and playback the rule and to identify, at runtime, which rules are being triggered, and specific for a rule, how each of the elements of the LHS matched.

16.4.2 More Typical Systems

Nonrecorded authoring utilizes a custom editor—though the best systems seem to be the ones that read in text files and effectively compile them into rules. However, this may allow for authors to create malformed rules (which they will have to correct), but it gives them the most freedom to use whichever text editor they prefer. As such, this is one of the more accessible approaches.

Alternatively, if the grammar is quite specific, a more symbolic or graphical editor can be used. In retrospect, many designers seem to dislike graphical editors but depending on the complexity, this is an option. How easy it is for designs to author the rules will have a direct impact on the efficiency of the workflow.

16.5 Choice of Matching System

On some platforms where we are constrained by runtime performance, and unification isn't being supported, optimization of the system's matching stage is required. In one case, this led to the development of a new system that is a departure from a true production system. In this variant, with a very large rules database, the matching system stops at the first rule matched. This turned the production system into a specialized rules-based system but it did open up some unique applications. This type of selection, a type of greedy selection, is described in Section 16.5.1.

16.5.1 Greedy Matching/Selection

As an example, let's start with 500 rules in our database, numbered 1–500. In any given update, the rule matching is capped at 1 ms. For up to 1 ms, process the LHS of the rules in order. If a match is made, exit early. If a match is not made, continue to the next rule. Once a match is made, selection has been effectively completed as well since there is only one rule. That rule's RHS is then executed.

This approach created the complication that the AI would always fire the same rule for the same state. This was solved by randomizing the order of the rules in the rules database. Figure 16.1 demonstrates how this works.

- *Step 1*: Rule 1's LHS is evaluated but it doesn't match. The system tries rule 2 and so forth until it matches rule 4. Rule 4's RHS is then executed. Before the next update, the rules database is randomly shuffled.
- *Step 2*: Several updates later when the same state occurs again, the database is now in a different order. The system starts with rule 300 (which doesn't match in this example). Finally, rule 87 matches/is selected. Its RHS is then executed. (This example assumes rule 4 was shuffled below rule 87).

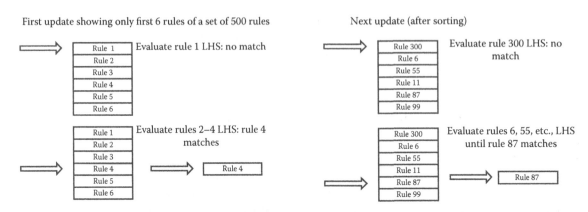

Figure 16.1

Greedy-based selection's first two updates (read left top to bottom, then right top to bottom).

This made the matching/selection processing extremely fast, allowing it to run very large rules databases on very limited platforms. In addition, we capped the matching so that only n numbers of rules were actually checked. This allows for the capping of a spike if all rules were not going to match. The capping is used because, like any list, the worst-case runtime is O(n), which, again, can be prohibitive if n is large or a rule has an expensive LHS. It's worth noting that spikes can occur during matching (even with a cap) if a rule's LHS is very expensive to evaluate. This is mitigated by optimizing the LHS variables and by limiting the number of variables allowed for the LHS of a rule.

16.6 What Happens If the AI Fails to Find a Rule?

This may seem like a simple problem, but in practice, we've run into issues with the AI stalling. The first challenge is ensuring that it's obvious when the system fails to find a matching rule. The second challenge is to determine if that's acceptable. In some games, as long as the AI already has an action, it is fine if the AI doesn't find a new rule. In other games, this can lead to an AI standing absolutely still, or a factory not producing anything, or no tricks being performed, etc. As long as this is identified, a default rule could be the solution or additional rules to fill in the missing scenarios could be authored. In one unique case, backward chaining was used. This allowed the system to work out a sequence of steps to get to a matchable state. Backward chaining is beyond the scope of this chapter, but it is possible so long as the amount of back chaining is constrained.

16.7 What Happens If There Are Multiple Rules?

When there are multiple rules—that is, when greedy matching isn't in use—the matched rules need to undergo selection. The purpose of selection or conflict resolution is to ensure that the RHS of rules do not produce actions that conflict with each other but in some cases, it is also to scope down the number of rules. For example, in one system, when the set of matched rules is very large, only the first n rules are selected and this limits the number of RHS that execute and scales down the possible conflicts. If the RHS are kept as unique as possible, then the number of conflicting rules should be reduced since all rules would be able to run. We discovered it was important to track the number of times that a rule was executed (selected) since the selection algorithm was sometimes filtering out rules to the extent that they never were selected.

One system had the problem where for a few game states, a very large number of rules were always matched. The solution was to randomly select a subset, process these for conflicts (which were minimal), and then execute the subset. The random selection prevented a bias from creeping into the system from the selection algorithm (constraining the matching in this particular situation wasn't possible).

By contrast, in another system where a large number of matches occurred on a regular basis for many rules, a form of partially supervised training was the solution. The system supports a weighting of the LHS. When a rule is successful, its LHS weight is increased. If it fails, the LHS weight is decreased. This requires a selection algorithm that selects biased on a weight, a system that monitors the results of the RHS execution, and a method for the authors to tweak the amount of negative/positive feedback for the training system. The AI is then run many times in training mode against both itself and human players. After many games, the resulting database is locked and the result is a self-tuned rules database. The rules subset selected are the first n number of rules that matched—but not a random subset. Instead, since the subset reflects the result of training, the subset is the set of higher-performing rules.

This proves to be highly successful and it allows for the weeding out of bad rules. However, you will need to manually check for rules that are too highly rated and remove low-frequency rules. Low-frequency rules won't have as much reinforcement applied to their weights and will drift to the bottom. Likewise, you can boost the weight of a rule to increase its probability of selection if the expert feels a rule is being unfairly penalized.

16.8 Execution and the Design of the RHS

The RHS is the part of the system where an action can be taken as a result. It can be a flag, a setting of a variable, a message, or an event or any other form of implementation. In general:

- The RHS should be cheap as possible to execute
- As much as possible, the RHS should not preclude other RHS actions. That is, minimize the number of conflicts between the RHS if possible
- If implementing backward chaining, the RHS should be discretely identifiable and be reusable as a variable on the LHS
- The RHS should be able to support being called multiple times without restarting on every call or the LHS will need to check if a RHS action is already running
- There should be minimal dependency between RHS. If an RHS requires that another action runs before it, the rules need to enforce this, which adds additional checks to the LHS of the rules

Authoring of the RHS can be done in the same manner as the LHS or it can be distinct. In the example that follows, the RHS is generated during a recording session.

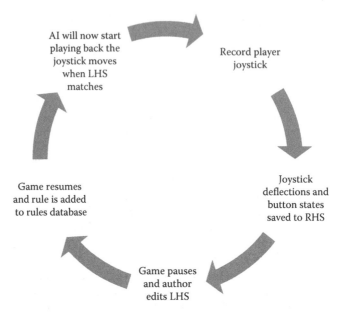

Figure 16.2

Recording the RHS.

16.8.1 More Complex RHS

One system records the joystick actions to produce the RHS of the rules, as shown in Figure 16.2. The execution for the RHS is simply a playback of the recorded joystick. This system allows a production system to be applied to a more complicated series of actions. It's very fast to author but it also requires a postediting stage so that authors can tweak the playback or discard bad recordings. Selection is also an issue since it isn't apparent when rules would be in conflict.

This is solved in two ways. In the first method, the rule is marked as unique so that if it matches, only that rule can be selected. In the second method, which applies to most of the rules, certain joystick maneuvers are identified and any rules that also hold these maneuvers are selected out. The authors could also watch the AI play, and if a rule is firing in the wrong scenario, the game can be paused, the rule opened for editing, and the LHS can be tweaked. The game then resumes but the production system reruns so that the author can ensure that their changes were appropriate. The final issue with this system is that if the player is what is being recorded, this will only work if the AI can use the data in the same way that the player uses it.

16.9 Debugging and Tuning

Several variants on how to author systems have been presented, but all of these need to be tuned and tested. Outside of the typical performance profiling, there are a couple of common key indicators that all of our systems have:

- Number of times a rule executes
- Success rate of executing the RHS

- Number of times a LHS variable matches
- List of rules that execute with a very high frequency
- List of rules that never execute

Another common debugging tool is to allow the RHS for a rule to be executed on demand—such that the behavior itself can be tuned or tweaked. Some systems support a complete reedit or rerecording of the RHS.

One implementation uses the selection step to train its AI. In training mode, the game is running with debug information available and the rules open for editing. If a rule is selected in training mode that the expert (designer) doesn't like, they can indicate that, and the system lowers the rule's weighting. Alternatively, the expert can pause the game and adjust the rule's LHS at runtime to ensure that the rule doesn't fire in that circumstance. They can likewise reward a given selection. This system requires a runtime editor for the rules and a way to reload the rules. Much more common is for production systems to log the results of matching and selection and have the *training* done offline.

In general, support for live editing can make iteration on the LHS of rules much easier. It can be difficult to author the constraints for the LHS of a rule for all possible scenarios—and having a way to edit and then rerun a scenario can help with this tuning immensely.

Logging and debug display of which rules are firing for a given AI is common. It helps to know which rules are creating the current behavior. Many systems support the graphical display for the test of the LHS variables. For example, if a variable is testing the range from one object to others, the debug might inscribe a circle to show what the radius/distance is set to.

16.10 Conclusion

Production systems have been used in a variety of published AAA titles and have proven themselves in many industries for some time now. All of the systems described are the results of the hard work of many engineers for different types of games over the course of many years. Some of these systems have evolved over time—almost all due to a practical constraint. Some are no longer production systems but all had their start with such a system and were usually developed initially over the course of 2 years.

A challenge all of these systems face is that they need to be very easy to iterate on and this has inspired new ways to author systems. Likewise, domain-specific systems have launched a variety of new ways to represent rules and to optimize matching outside of Rete and other classic algorithms. There is nothing inherently flawed with a more classic approach, but it is hoped that by presenting some of the techniques we use, readers might be inspired to think beyond the typical implementation and extend what is possible for these systems in their own games.

References

[Bourg 04] Bourg, D. M. and Seemann, G. 2004. *AI for Game Developers*. Sebastapol, CA: O'Reilly Media Inc.
[Laird 12] Laird, J. 2012. *The Soar Cognitive Architecture*. Cambridge, MA: Massachusetts Institute of Technology.

[Luger 93] Luger, G. F. and Stubblefield, W. A. 1993. *Artificial Intelligence Structures and Strategies for Complex Problem Solving*, 2nd edn. Redwood City, CA: The Benjamin/ Cummings Publishing Company Inc.

[Millington 09] Millington, I. and Funge, J. 2009. *Artificial Intelligence for Games*. Boca Raton, FL: CRC Press.

[Riley 13] Riley, G. 2013. CLIPS: A tool for building expert systems. Sourceforge. http://clipsrules.sourceforge.net/ (accessed May 27, 2014).

[Schneider 02] Schneider, B. 2002. The Rete matching algorithm. *Dr. Dobbs Journal*. http://www.drdobbs.com/architecture-and-design/the-rete-matching-algorithm/184405218 (accessed May 27, 2014).

17

Building a Risk-Free Environment to Enhance Prototyping

Hinted-Execution Behavior Trees

Sergio Ocio Barriales

17.1 Introduction

Working on game technology is an iterative process. From game to game, we try to reuse as many systems as we can, but this leaves us in a situation where few substantial changes can be made to our already proven and solid solutions. At the same time, the creative nature of games is craving for changes, prototyping and testing new ideas, many of which come during production or even near the end of a project, when the risk of breaking things is at its peak. Can we do something to offer a risk-free environment to work on those potentially game changing ideas, or should we let them go?

Hinted-execution Behavior Trees (HeBTs) try to address this problem. The technology is an extension to the traditional behavior tree (BT) model that allows developers to dynamically modify the priorities of a BT based on some high-level logic; the new layer works in a plug-and-play fashion, which means it can be easily removed, leaving the base behavior untouched. This greatly reduces the inherent risk of changes.

In this chapter, we present the technology—which is a proven solution, successfully applied to the AI in *Driver: San Francisco*—then study how it works and show how HeBTs can be applied to real-world problems.

17.2 Explaining the Problem

Video games are a type of software that benefits from changes, and prototyping is necessary to develop fun. Building such experiences is a joint effort between programmers and designers. This is a two-way process: designers come up with ideas that are transformed into technology by programmers, but this technology, at the same time, refines the original idea and converts it into something feasible. This back-and-forth iterative process shapes what is going to be in the final game.

Let us focus in the technological aspect of the process. At a high-level, programmers produce black box systems with some tweakable parameters; game or level designers will use these black boxes to build what is going to be the final game. This workflow, which is shown in Figure 17.1, is very commonly used in the industry: ideas come from designers, who request the feature from engineering; after some implementation time, the new pieces are ready to use by design.

The key property of this type of process is that designers have very little control over what the new "box" is doing. In many situations, this is desirable, as programmers are the ones with the technical capabilities and designers do not need to worry about implementation details. However, it is worth noting that going from conception to being able to use the feature can be a long process and any change to a black box will restart the loop (i.e., generate another request that engineering will process and implement). Ideally, we would like design to be able to test or prototype new ideas faster, without going through engineering.

Although this scenario mitigates the potential long delays between conception and actual availability of features in game, it will most likely not be a feasible solution in most situations. The new workflow, as shown in Figure 17.2, could require working with very

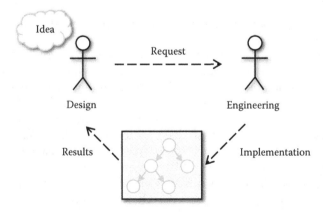

Figure 17.1

Traditional design/engineering collaboration workflow.

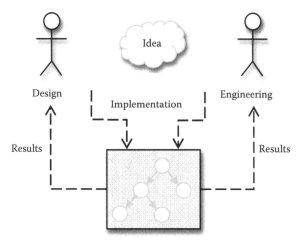

Figure 17.2

In an ideal world, both designers and engineers should have similar privileges when it comes to implementing and testing new ideas.

technical nonengineers that can manage, for example, modifying our BTs directly, which can be risky and produce more problems than benefits.

Another factor we have to take into account is that due to the complexity of video games, often new games use and improve previous games' codebases. This means we must be able to apply our solution to already existing code and technology.

The solution presented in this chapter, HeBTs [Ocio 10], is an extension to the traditional BT model. It tackles these problems and allows for fast and safe prototyping.

In the following sections, we will show how we can modify and manipulate an existing BT implementation to allow an extra high-level decision-making layer to dynamically change the priorities of certain sections of our behaviors.

17.3 Behavior Trees

The popularity of BTs has been growing steadily in the last 10 years and they have become a fundamental part of many games. In this section, we will cover the basics of what a BT is, as this knowledge is required to understand the rest of the chapter. Readers wanting to get better descriptions or some extra details about how a BT works should refer to [Isla 05, Champandard 08, Champandard 13] or the various materials available at AiGameDev.com [AIGameDev 15].

17.3.1 Simple BT

BTs are data-driven structures that can be easily represented in the form of a tree or graph. Nodes in a BT can be leaves or branches. Leaf nodes represent either an action or a conditional check, that is, nodes with a direct communication to the world. On the other hand, branch nodes do not perform any action but control the execution flow. In this category, we find nodes for control flow (selectors, sequences, parallels, etc.) or decorators.

Let us use a simple example, shown in Figure 17.3, to study how a BT works.

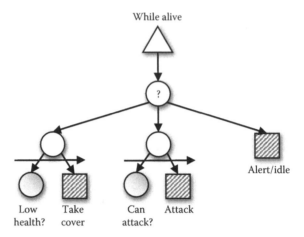

Figure 17.3

A simple BT.

In our example, we have modeled a very simple soldier behavior that will make the AI go and take cover if it is low in health, attack if it can, or just be alert (or idle) in any other case.

When a node is updated, it always returns a status value: "success," "failure," or "running." Return values are handled by parent nodes, which then decide what to do with this information. Thus, execution flow in a BT comes from its static structure (i.e., different branches will be activated in different orders all depending on what type of nodes we have used).

The most important node of the example tree is the selector (represented in the figure with a question mark). Selectors allow us to represent conditionals in a BT; translating it to what we could do in a programming language such as C++, selectors are the BT version of an "if-then-else" construction. It is this node's responsibility to decide what the AI is going to be doing at any given point. Priorities in the selector used in this example come from the order in which children of the selector are defined, that is, the leftmost node/branch is the highest priority and the rightmost, the lowest, resulting in static priorities.

Selectors try to pick the best possible child branch by testing each of them until one succeeds. In the example, we have represented two of the branches as sequences. A sequence is a special type of node that will run each of its children in order, succeeding if all the children succeed or failing otherwise. Due to this, sequences will very frequently be testing some preconditions as their first tasks and, if the preconditions pass, the actual actions can and will be run.

In the figure, our sequences have two children each: the first node is a condition node, or node that is just checking facts in the world; the second node is a proper action, or node that makes modifications in the state of the world.

Finally, we added a filter to our tree, which in the example is actually the root of the BT. The filter makes sure the behavior keeps running as long as the AI is alive.

For the sake of simplicity, we will continue using the example studied in the previous section, but the concepts presented in this chapter can be applied to BTs of any size.

17.3.2 Tree Complexity

The tree we are studying is very simple—it only has a handful of nodes—and making changes to it would be pretty straightforward. The problem is that, in a real-case scenario, trees can have dozens or hundreds of nodes and are not as easy to modify. There are some solutions to this, most of which involve having a good tool that allows us to work with the trees more easily (e.g., by expanding/collapsing branches or other UI improvements), but this does not remove the inherent complexity of the structure we are creating. Understanding the implications and side effects that a change might have in a complex tree is not trivial.

Going back to our example tree in Figure 17.3, let us say that at some point, we decide to bump the priority of the "attack" branch, because we want to model very brave (or, should we say, suicidal) soldiers that never retreat to take cover. In that situation, we would have to modify our tree, but that will make the "take cover" branch pretty much useless. What if, instead, we decide to only increase the priority of the attack in some circumstances?

Just by using the basic model, we can achieve this in a few different ways, like adding a new selector and duplicating some parts of the tree or by adding an extra precondition to the "take cover" branch, which is not that bad.

But, what if we would like the NPCs to attack for just 5 s then retreat and only do this for some specially flagged NPCs? Things can get complicated. In this case, we could end up with a tree similar to the one shown in Figure 17.4.

There are probably better ways to reorder the tree to accommodate for the new case, but the one presented in the figure is good enough to prove our point: modifying a BT to accommodate for new logic requires some thinking and always carries a risk.

In this chapter, we want to focus on a case like this one, particularly those in which we have to work with large BTs and where big changes are discouraged by deadlines or production milestones, but yet we need to keep iterating on our systems.

17.4 Extending the Model

BTs are a great technology, but they require good technical skills and hours of thinking to maintain them. The example of a change in the logic of a tree, studied in the previous section, showed how small changes in a simple tree can become difficult to understand very quickly. Logic changes are scary and, potentially, something we want to avoid, pleasing producers but hurting creativity.

In this section, we present a solution for these problems: HeBTs. The idea behind this extension is to allow extra layers of higher-level trees to run concurrently with our main tree and have the new logic dynamically modify priorities in the main BT.

17.4.1 Hint Concept

The main difference between a BT and a hinted-execution counterpart is that, while the execution flow in the former is defined by its own structure, HeBTs can reorder their branches dynamically to produce different results.

The system tries to imitate real-life command hierarchies, where lower-levels are told by higher-level ones what should be done, but, in the end, deciding how to do it is up to the individuals. In our system, the individual AI is a complex BT that controls the AI,

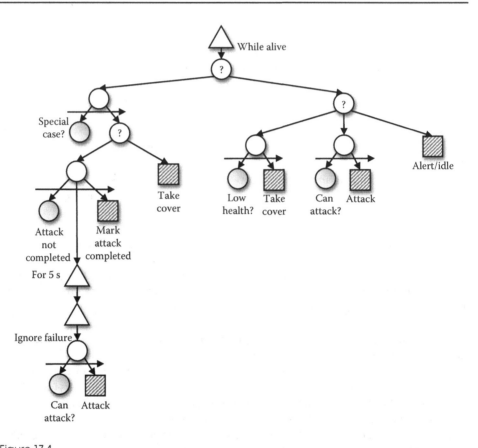

Figure 17.4

A more complex BT that adds special cases and extra checks.

so it behaves autonomously, but we want to open the higher-level layers to every member of the team, so they can test their ideas.

Nontechnical people will probably not be interested in how the AI works internally and will just want to tell it to do things (i.e., they just want to be able to order the AI to "kill an enemy," rather than "find a path to your enemy, then get closer, draw your weapon, and fire at your target, reloading your gun when you need to, etc."). These suggestions are called *hints* in the HeBT model.

A hint is a piece of information an AI can receive from a higher-level source and use it to produce an alternative behavior, as a consequence of a priority reorder. This means that an NPC, while maintaining its capability to respond properly to different situations, will take into account the requests coming higher in the command hierarchy to adapt its behavior to these petitions.

17.4.2 HeBT Selectors

Most of the decision making in a BT takes place in its selectors, which try different possibilities based on some priorities until a match is found.

17. Building a Risk-Free Environment to Enhance Prototyping

In the simplest implementation of a selector, the priorities normally come from the order in which the branches were added to the selector node. So this means all of our priorities are *static*. HeBTs allow developers to change those priorities dynamically, resorting the branches associated to their selectors based on the information that a higher-level piece of logic has passed down to them. In order to do so, HeBTs introduce a new type of selector node.

Selectors, as composite nodes, have a list of children subbranches, each of which represents a possible action that a higher-level will, potentially, want the node to choose. We will talk further about these higher levels later on. In our new selectors, branches are assigned a unique identifier, which is assigned at creation time. This allows designers/ engineers to name the branches and therefore create the hints that will favor each branch's execution.

Hints can be positive, negative, or neutral; if a hint is positive, the tree is being told to do something; if negative, it is being told not to do something; and, if neutral, the selector is not receiving the hint at all. Neutral hints are used to reset a priority to its default value.

The system works as follows: the AI is running a base BT (i.e., the one that contains all the logic for our game) and it can receive hints from a higher-level source. When a hint is received, the BT passes the information to all its selectors. The selectors will then recalculate the priorities of their branches.

For example, let us say we have a selector with five branches, named "A," "B," "C," "D," and "E." We have just implemented a HeBT system and our higher-level logic is telling us "D" and "E" are very desirable, but "A" is something we really should try to avoid. Figure 17.5 shows how the new selector would use this information.

The new selectors maintain four lists to control their children and their priorities. The first list just keeps track of the original priorities; the three extra lists store nodes that have been positively hinted (and thus, have more priority), nodes that have not been hinted (they are neutral), and nodes that have been negatively hinted (they have reduced priority). These extra lists are still sorted using the original order, so if two or more nodes are hinted, AIs will know which action is more important according to their original behavior.

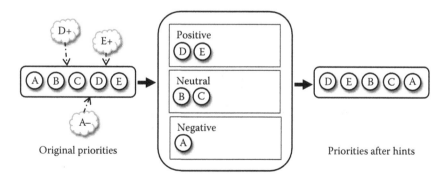

Figure 17.5

A HeBT selector sorts its children based on the hints it receives.

17.4.3 Hints and Conditions

With the modifications presented so far, we have made our trees capable of accepting hints and reordering the branches controlled by their selector nodes. It is up to tree designers to expose whatever logic they feel is important to expose to higher levels (i.e., to choose what hints the tree will accept).

As we have said, the execution flow in a BT is controlled by the type of nonleaf nodes we use and how we combine them. We can have many different type of nodes, but simplifying the traditional BT model, we could say most trees are collections of selectors and sequences, as shown in Figure 17.6.

Most of these sequences follow a basic pattern—shown in Figure 17.7—where some condition nodes are placed as the first children, followed by actual actions. This way, the actions will only get executed if these preconditions are met. If one of the conditions fails, the sequence will bail out, returning a failure, which will probably be caught by a selector that will then try to run a different branch.

This is not good for our hints in some situations, as the conditions could be making a hinted branch fail and not be executed. We can use the example shown in Figure 17.3 to illustrate this.

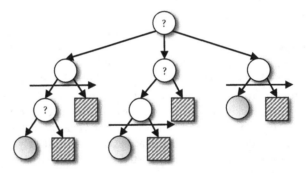

Figure 17.6

A basic BT can be seen as a series of selectors and sequences that control its execution flow.

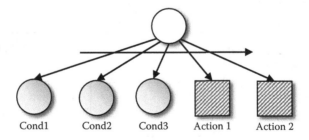

Figure 17.7

Basic sequence structure, where actions are preceded by a collection of preconditions.

17. Building a Risk-Free Environment to Enhance Prototyping

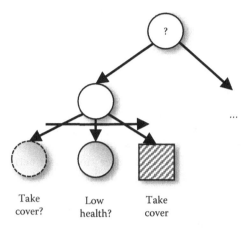

Figure 17.8

By using hint conditions, we can overcome problems caused by preconditions.

Let us say we have exposed the two first branches as hints. We will use the names "take cover" and "attack." Let us also say that we want to hint the AI to "take cover," by sending a positive hint to the tree.

The way we had defined our BT, the "take cover" branch already had the highest priority, so the selector does not really need to reorder its children (actually, it does reorder them, but this time, the order of the branches will not change). If we look closely at the first branch, we can see "take cover" is built as a sequence that checks a precondition (just as shown in Figure 17.7), called "low health?".

In the case where the AI has full health, the precondition will fail, making the sequence bail. The failure is ultimately propagated to the selector, which will run a different branch. Because we were hinting the AI to "take cover," we might be expecting it to take our suggestion into account, and not just ignore it blatantly.

So, we need a way to be able to ignore these preconditions *if that makes sense*, that is, if the condition is not really mandatory for the rest of the branch to be executed. In our example, we did not really need to be low on health to cover: this was just a design decision, probably trying to make the behavior more believable.

For that, HeBTs offer a *hint condition node*. This type of node is used to allow the BT to test if it is receiving a certain hint and what its type is (positive, negative, or neutral). We can modify our example's BT to modify the preconditions of the sequence, so our branch will look like what we show in Figure 17.8.

17.5 Multilevel Architecture

In the previous section, we introduced the concept of hints and how behaviors can be dynamically modified through them. These hints were sent to our trees by what we called "higher levels of logic."

Different approaches can be taken to implement these levels. For example, a quick and effective solution could be a layer of scripts that use the system to generate new behaviors.

However, the usage of scripts can make things harder to understand, as they normally require some technical background. A visual solution would be much more appropriate, as visualizing things is much simpler than learning a new language and its rules. Why not take advantage of the tools we have built to generate our base BTs, and expand it?

17.5.1 Behavior Controllers

BTs are constructed using a set of building blocks, among which we have actions; they are the nodes in charge of modifying the environment or the state of the AI instance itself. Depending on the granularity of the system, these actions can be more or less complex, ranging from subbehaviors, such as "take cover" to atomic actions such as "find cover spot." For users not interested in how the behaviors work—but just in the fact they do work—the coarser the granularity, the simpler the system will be for them.

Modifying a big BT can be complex and could require taking into account quite a lot of variables. Also, small changes in a tree could lead to undesirable behaviors, making AIs not work as expected. Because of this, we do not want new behaviors to be created from scratch; instead, we just want them to be flexible and malleable. So let us keep a base tree, maintained by engineers, and provide the team with the means to create new higher-level trees.

Higher-level trees use a different set of building blocks. Specifically, we will replace the action nodes with some new nodes that we call *hinters*. These nodes, as their name indicates, will send hints to the tree's immediate lower-level BT. The new trees will work on top of our base behavior, modifying it dynamically and allowing designers to prototype new ideas easily and safely, as the main BT is not modified permanently, thus reducing risks.

From now on, our AI instances will no longer be controlled by a single tree but by a number of layers of BTs. This set of trees is owned by a behavior controller. These controllers are in charge of maintaining the multiple levels of trees an AI can use and of running all of them to produce the final results.

A behavior controller works as a stack where we can push new trees. The top of the stack represents the highest level of logic, whereas the bottom contains the base BT. Every time we add a new tree, the controller informs the newly created high-level tree about what its immediate lower-level tree is, which will allow hints to be sent to the correct BT. This multilevel architecture is shown in Figure 17.9.

Once all the different trees have been created and registered with a behavior controller, it can run the final behavior. HeBTs are run from the top down, so higher levels are run first; this means that, by the time a tree is going to be executed, it would have already received all its hints, and their branches would be properly sorted. This process is shown in Figure 17.10.

By the end of each update, the AI will have run whatever action it has considered to have the higher priority, based on the information it has gathered from the environment *and* the hints it has received.

17.5.2 Exposing Hints to Higher Levels

High-level trees are built using a base BT to determine the hints that are available to them. When creating new trees, designers can name the branches of their selectors, which will

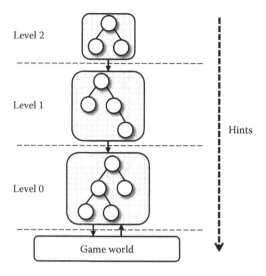

Figure 17.9

Multilevel structure of a HeBT.

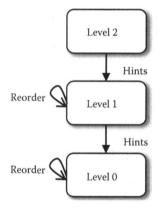

Figure 17.10

Each level in a HeBT will send hints to the level immediately below, causing the lower-level to reorder its priorities.

automatically expose the corresponding hints. In a similar way, if a condition hint is used anywhere in the low-level tree, the hint will automatically be exposed.

High-level trees cannot use actions; instead, they use hinters. Hinters allow trees to send any of the hints their lower-level trees are exposing to them, in order to produce new behaviors. Internally, they are very simple nodes: their logic is only executed once, and they bail out succeeding right after the hint has been sent.

It is important to note that hinters can send different types of hints, allowing us to send positive or negative hints. They can also set a hint back to neutral if necessary.

17.6 More Complex Example

So far, we have studied what a HeBT is and how it works internally. We have also been illustrating our exposition with a simple example. However, this example does not show the full potential of the system, so in this section, we will present an example that is closer to what we could find in a real game.

17.6.1 Prototyping New Ideas

There are many different ways to modify a behavior to obtain different responses from two AIs running the same logic. Some of them are even trivial to implement, such as the use of personality traits. However, adding more complex logic on top of an existing behavior starts getting complicated, especially if we do not want or cannot change the original BT.

In a real project, we are always subject to changes at any time, but new ideas and changes may pose a big risk to the project or require resources we cannot afford. As we saw, HeBTs allow us to generate this logic easily, just by using a high-level BT that will run on top of our base tree, guiding its normal execution toward what our new logic is suggesting should be done.

17.6.2 Base Behavior

Working on a new behavior requires that we have a base one working correctly, as it will define the way AIs in our game respond to different situations. In a real-life project, it would also have been thoroughly tested and optimized.

Let us say that for our example, our design team have decided the game needs some soldiers that

- Are able to patrol using a predefined route
- Detect the player as an enemy when they enter their cone of vision
- Attack the player once it is identified
- Try to find a cover position to keep attacking from it, if the agent takes damage

This behavior would be represented by a complex BT, and we show a simplified version of it in Figure 17.11.

Let us take a look at the base behavior. At a first glance, we can see there are three main branches controlled by a selector. We have named the branches "PATROL," "COVER," and "ATTACK;" this automatically exposes hints with the same names that can be used by a higher-level tree. The BT's root is a conditional loop that will keep the tree running until the AI is killed.

The first branch defines the agents' precombat behavior. In our case, we have chosen to have the soldiers patrol the area while they do not have an enemy. As we saw in a previous section, this condition might prevent the tree from behaving as expected when it receives the "PATROL" hint; to fix that, we have added a hint condition and put both condition nodes under a selector, which will allow us to enter the branch if either condition is true. It is also worth noting we have used a parallel node to run our conditions as an assertion (i.e., the conditions will be checked continuously to enforce they are always met); this way, the branch will be able to bail out as soon as the AI engages an enemy.

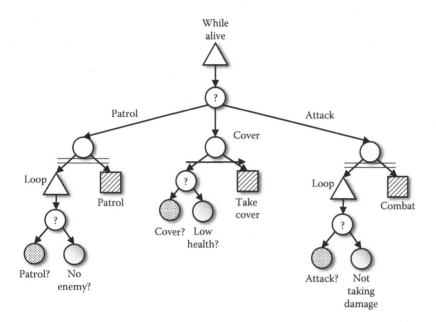

Figure 17.11

Simplified base BT our soldiers will run.

The second branch will make sure the agent takes cover when it is low on health. Similarly to the patrol branch, we have added a hint condition to make sure the tree will use hints properly.

Finally, the third branch is our combat behavior. Its structure is very similar to the "COVER" branch, with an assertion running to ensure combat is only triggered if we are not under fire (i.e., taking damage).

17.6.3 Prototype Idea

Once our AIs are able to run autonomously, in an ideal situation, most of the work for AI engineers will consist of debugging and polishing the behaviors. However, we could find ourselves in a situation when substantial changes to these behaviors are required, or maybe the team needs to keep testing new ideas to keep improving the game experience. This is where the power of HeBTs comes into play.

To demonstrate the capabilities of our new system, we will implement a "disguise" system just by adding a high-level tree to hint our base BT what should be done. The design for our feature is

- Players can wear the clothes of the enemies they kill, going unnoticed to other AIs if they do so.
- AIs should not recognize "disguised" players as enemies. However, they should react if the player damages them.

Basically, these changes would require gameplay and AI code modifications, and this new feature could not make it through to the final game. Because our game is using HeBTs, we could delegate the prototyping of new ideas to the design team or at least let them play with new thoughts with minimal technical supervision (if we have the appropriate tools for the job).

We must bear in mind that if we want to have a system that requires virtually no programming work to be extended, we must start from designing our base behaviors correctly. Also, building a complete set of tree nodes and conditions can facilitate things further down the line.

17.6.4 Creating a High-Level Tree

So, as designers, the idea behind our new system is that we want AIs to ignore players that are "in disguise." So, basically, we want to hint the base level to prefer patrolling. The first pass at the high-level tree would be very similar to the one shown in Figure 17.12.

This is, in a nutshell, what our high-level tree should look like. However, we still have to define our condition. We want to check if the player is disguised, but we do not have a condition that does that.

Our system must have defined a way for AIs to maintain some knowledge about the world. A common way to do this is by using blackboards. Let us say we do have such a system, where we can write information and from where we can get details about the state of the world. In this case, our condition would be transformed to an "is enemy in disguise?" condition that checks for that information in the blackboard. But, if we need to read this information from the blackboard, we must have set it somewhere first.

For the sake of simplicity, we will use a "broadcast" action that allows us to write a value to the system's blackboard. What we want to do is to let other AIs in the world (by adding this information to the blackboard) about the new status of the player as soon as one AI dies. Since our first pass at the high-level tree was already checking if the AI was alive, let us extend the tree to modify the blackboard properly. We show this in Figure 17.13.

The first thing we have done is add an extra sequence as the new root of our tree. The idea behind it is that we want to run the "alive branch" (on the left) first, but always have a blackboard update following it.

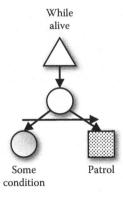

Figure 17.12

Basic idea behind the "disguise" system.

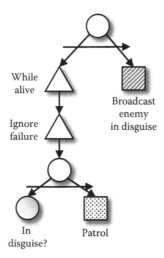

Figure 17.13

A first pass on a more complex high-level tree.

We have also added an extra decorator as a parent to our old sequence. The decorator's purpose is to ignore failures in the sequence, which will happen pretty frequently in our case (in fact, the sequence will fail every frame unless the player is in disguise); we never want the branch to fail, as it would break the root sequence.

So, with these changes, while the AI is alive, the tree will continue checking the blackboard to decide whether or not to hint the base BT to patrol; and, once the agent is dead, the blackboard will always be updated. When this happens, the remaining AIs will then have their blackboards updated, and they will start sending "PATROL" hints to their base BTs, causing those agents to ignore the player as intended.

Although this is a good first attempt at implementing the new feature, the tree is not completely correct yet, as AIs will not react to damage anymore if the player is disguised. To fix this problem, we need to clear the blackboard if an agent is under attack. The final high-level tree is shown in Figure 17.14.

In the final tree, we have added an extra selector that will catch whether the enemy has been attacked, clearing the disguise flag. The second branch of the selector is the same one our previous iteration had and, finally, the third branch is just making sure that, if nothing is going on, the "PATROL" hint is cleared.

17.6.5 Analyzing the Results

The key to this type prototyping is that the new logic is completely optional. We can just let the system know about it and see how the AI behaves with the extra feature or we can just remove the high-level tree, which will leave our original behavior untouched.

The base behavior requires minimal data changes, which are almost deactivated unless a high-level tree is used. Particularly, we have been using two types of base BT modifications: branch naming is a harmless change, as it does not affect the behavior at all; hint conditions do modify the original structure of the tree, but since they are straightforward

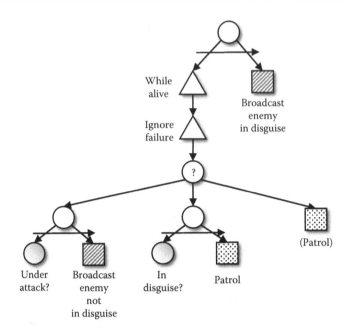

Figure 17.14

Final high-level tree that models the new feature.

flag (hint) checks, and the hints will never be enabled if a high-level tree is not present, it poses a very small risk. Hint conditions are also optional, and in some situations, we might not want to use them at all. Simply naming branches preemptively will expose dynamic priority control.

17.7 Other Applications

Over the course of this chapter, we have focused on the benefits HeBTs bring to quick and safe prototyping. These trees can also be used to help in other cases. In this section, we will present a couple of extra scenarios that can benefit from using HeBTs.

17.7.1 Adaptation

There are different ways to make our game more accessible to different types of players. Among them, we find the manual selection of a "difficulty level," which has been part of the game almost from the very beginning, or the adaptation of the difficulty level or situations to the player, which can allow us to offer a better and tailor-made experience to different groups of people.

HeBTs can help us offer different experiences to each player experience level and also allow us to modify things on the fly: we can define a different high-level tree per category and, in run-time, decide which one is most appropriate for our player. The base tree will recalculate its priorities based on the hints it is receiving and, hopefully, the player will enjoy our game better.

This is the approach Ubisoft's *Driver: San Francisco* used. In *Driver*, getaway drivers were able to adapt their route selection algorithm—which was controlled by a BT—by implementing a range of different high-level trees that could guide the route generation process [Ocio 12]. These high-level trees were called "presets," and they did things like making the route finder prefer straight routes (so casual players can catch the getaways easier) to zigzag routes or routes through dirt roads or alleyways.

17.7.2 Group Behaviors

Our hinted-execution model could also be used to create complex group behaviors based on command hierarchies. Hints would flow down the chain, allowing some AIs to have a better control over what others should do.

In a hint-based system, we would be able to create new links in our chain as high-level trees that are built on top of several base behaviors, rather than just one; in this case, each base tree would expose the orders that a particular class of AI can accept. Our higher-level tree would be able to broadcast hints to groups of AIs that are using the behaviors this level was based on.

An example of this would be a small army that has warriors, archers, and medics. A simplified version of their behaviors is shown in Figure 17.15.

We could use different generals, defining different high-level trees to create an intelligent army that obeys the orders we want to send. For instance, we could build a high-level AI that wants to attack with its archers first, holding off warriors and medics, and continuing with a melee-type attack that includes sending the medics along with the warriors to try and heal wounded units, and never allowing the units to retreat. The high-level tree that would control such behavior is shown in Figure 17.16.

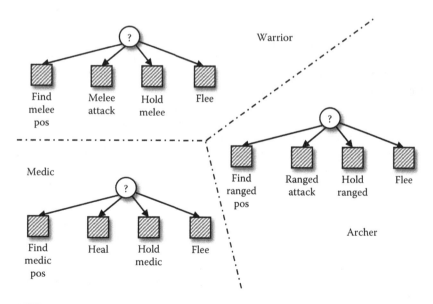

Figure 17.15

Base BTs controlling the different types of units in our army.

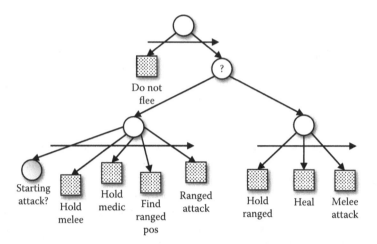

Figure 17.16

High-level tree that will define a tyrant high-level AI that never allows individuals to retreat.

Groups of units (as high-level entities) would also be controlled by HeBTs, so they could potentially receive hints too, producing a complex chain of command that can help us create more credible group behaviors.

17.8 Conclusion

BTs are a proven technology that has been used in many successful commercial games. However, as with any other technology, any change is risky, especially if these changes are made in the last stages of production.

HeBTs try to mitigate these risks by providing a way to do dynamic, revertible modifications to bigger, more complex BTs. These modifications are also controlled by another BT (that we call "high-level" BT), so we can still take advantage of the power and visual editing capabilities of the technology.

As we showed in this chapter, HeBTs help in many different problems, such as rapid prototyping, dynamic behavior adaptation, or group behaviors. In any case, risks are kept to a low, as we will never lose our base, tested behavior.

This technology is not hard to implement on top of an existing BT system and has also been used in an AAA game, *Driver: San Francisco*. HeBTs were key to the success of the game's AI, allowing its developers to adapt the behaviors of their getaway drivers to the skills of their players.

References

[AIGameDev 15] AIGameDev.com. http://www.aigamedev.com/.
[Champandard 08] Champandard, A. J. 2008. Getting started with decision making and control systems. *AI Game Programming Wisdom*, Vol. 4, pp. 257–263. Boston, MA: Course Technology.

[Champandard 13] Champandard, A. J. and Dunstan P. 2013. The behavior tree starter kit. In *Game AI Pro: Collected Wisdom of Game AI Professionals*. Boca Raton, FL: A K Peters/CRC Press.

[Isla 05] Isla, D. 2005. Handling complexity in the Halo 2 AI. In *Proceedings of the Game Developers Conference (GDC)*, San Francisco, CA.

[Ocio 10] Ocio, S. 2010. A dynamic decision-making model for game AI adapted to players' gaming styles. PhD thesis. University of Oviedo, Asturias, Spain.

[Ocio 12] Ocio, S. 2012. Adapting AI behaviors to players in driver San Francisco: Hinted-execution behavior trees. In *Proceedings of the Eighth AAAI Conference on Artificial Intelligence and Interactive Digital Entertainment (AIIDE-12)*, Stanford University, Stanford, CA.

Smart Zones to Create the Ambience of Life

Etienne de Sevin, Caroline Chopinaud, and Clodéric Mars

18.1 Introduction

To design "background nonplayer characters" that breathe ambient life into a virtual environment, we propose new concepts that facilitate the creation of *Living Scenes*. The aim is to generalize their use in video games as a way to improve the feeling of presence for the player. This chapter introduces the concept of *Smart Zones* used to design credible, consistent, and interactive ambient life, involving autonomous and adaptive NPCs.

18.2 Designing an Ambience of Life

Consider the following situation: *8 pm, the night is still young when our player arrives at a restaurant looking for his friends. As he enters the building, he sees dozens of clients eating, talking, and drinking. His friends, as they see him, made signs for him to join them. On the way, he meets a waiter asking him if he wants to order something.*

The problem we are trying to solve is how to quickly structure and design this ambience of life. Our answer: using a set of Living Scenes!

18.2.1 What Is a Living Scene?

A Living Scene is a set of nonplayer characters (NPCs) interacting with each other and with the players. Its aim is to give a feeling of life to a virtual environment, to give the player *a sense of being there*. To achieve this, the behaviors resulting from the Living Scene have to make sense in the context of the current setting, location, story, and actions of the player. Therefore, the living scene is located in the virtual environment, situated in time and reactive to the presence of the player.

Each NPC involved in a scene fulfills a *role*. Each role in the scene is defined by a set of *behaviors* that will be executed by the NPCs to achieve the scene. The behaviors assigned to the different roles are staged in order to execute the collective behavior expected for the scene.

Our aim is to split the design of ambient life in two: the individual behaviors level and the Living Scenes level. With such a distinction, game designers are able to focus separately on each level in order to create complex individual behaviors, as well as an explainable and consistent collective behavior. Furthermore, we introduce a role abstraction layer that enables reusability and allows a wide range of possible combinations.

Back to our restaurant example, we can extract three Living Scenes: the clients exhibiting behaviors related to the restaurant such as eating, talking, and drinking (Scene 1), the friends exhibiting specific reactive behaviors related to the presence of the player (Scene 2), and the waiter exhibiting an interactive behavior with the clients of the restaurant including the player (Scene 3).

In Scene 1, each NPC assumes the role of a client and has access to three individual behaviors: "eat," "talk," and "drink." These behaviors can be staged in a specific order, or chosen automatically by autonomous NPCs. In that case, the clients decide when is the best moment to drink, eat, or talk related to their current states and the global situation in Scene 1.

Scene 2 focuses on a part of Scene 1: the clients who are player's friends located at specific table in the restaurant. Each NPC in this scene assumes the same role of friend and has access to one more reactive behavior: "make a sign to the player to join them." They can also access the behaviors of a client such as "eat," "talk," and "drink."

Finally, in Scene 3, the unique NPC assumes the role of a waiter and can execute the "interact" behavior. This behavior is triggered when another NPC enters the scene (around the waiter). More precisely, when the player enters the scene, the waiter exhibits a complex interactive behavior to discuss with the player about his or her desire to drink or eat.

18.2.2 Performing Living Scenes through Smart Zones

To put a living scene into a virtual environment and to manage its execution, we propose to define a scene through a Smart Zone. A Smart Zone is a concrete representation of a Living Scene that can be located in the environment and executed in a stand-alone way to manage the lifetime of the scene. The concept of Smart Zones is inspired by *Smart Objects* [Kallmann 99], which is often used in video games for managing agent–object interaction such as in The Sims [The Sims 99].

The idea is to include the description, within Smart Zones, of all the characteristics of the Living Scenes and how the involved NPCs execute behaviors in order to play out the scene. Thus, when an NPC go into a Smart Zone, he or she has access to every characteristic of the scene, and a role is potentially assigned to the NPC, to be an actor of the scene. If required, he or she may have to execute a specific behavior according to the other NPCs playing in the scene. As Smart Objects manage the interactions between agents and objects, Smart Zones manage the individual and collective behaviors and their relation with the NPCs interacting within the zones. When the game is running, the Smart Zones will manage the "casting" from the available and skilled NPCs. Similar approaches, applying smart events to narrative for storytelling, have been described in earlier works [Stocker 10, Shoulson 11].

This approach leads to a decentralized control of the NPCs' behaviors in dedicated zones representing the Living Scenes. This is a way to reduce the complexity of the game control: it is not necessary to control the current situation as a whole; we can just focus on each Smart Zone instantiated in the environment. Moreover, because a Smart Zone embeds all the characteristics and information essential for the execution of the Living Scene, the control of the NPCs involved in a scene is easier: it is possible to assign, stage, and execute the NPCs' behaviors directly through the zone independently of the NPCs themselves.

18.3 Smart Zones in Practice

This section describes the definition and execution details of smart zones.

18.3.1 Definition of Smart Zones by Game Designers

To develop Living Scenes, game designers define Smart Zones in the game environment. Defining a Smart Zone means filling all the characteristics essential for the execution of the related Living Scene:

- The roles to be assigned to the NPCs
- The behaviors able to perform a role
- The orchestration of the scene by defining a sequence of behaviors
- The triggers for the scene activation
- The site of the scene (position, size, and shape)

The concepts of roles and behaviors are essential for the scene execution. The role is a way to assign a specific set of behaviors to an NPC that entered in a zone. A role is the main relation between an NPC and a scene. When an NPC assumes a role, he or she executes concretely the behaviors associated with the role in the scene. A behavior is a sequence of actions executed by the NPC during a given time interval. We decided to use these concepts because they are easily understandable and accessible for game designers. Moreover, these concepts are often used in storytelling and agent design in general.

In this way, the introduction of these concepts allows the design of the Living Scene in independent steps:

- The design of the individual behaviors
- The specification of the roles (defined by a set of behaviors)
- The organization of the Living Scene through the choice of the roles dedicated to the scene

Then, the most important part of the Living Scene design is the orchestration between the NPCs' behaviors in order to obtain a coherent collective behavior. Game designers can place behaviors of the NPCs into a timeline according to the roles, which leads to a sequence of behaviors for the Living Scene (or a part of the Living Scene) and describes the triggers to manage the starting of the scene.

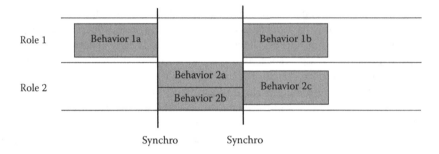

Figure 18.1

A timeline defining the orchestration of behaviors.

The timeline is organized as follows (see Figure 18.1):

- One row exists for each role.
- The behaviors are represented as boxes, and they have a beginning and an end. When several behaviors are placed at the same "time" in a single row, it means one of them will be chosen at runtime. This choice is specified by design (e.g., probability function) or automatically through the decision-making process of the NPC. This point leads to improve the variety of the observed behaviors.
- Synchronization points are used to trigger the beginning and ending of behaviors across several roles. They are added automatically after one behavior is added at the end of the timeline. However, the game designers can drag another behavior between two synchronization points to obtain specific behavioral sequences. For a given synchronization point, when all the behaviors executed by main roles end, it leads to the cancellation of the behaviors of all the other nonmain roles. For example, when the juggler finishes his or her performance, the spectators stop commenting or applauding and start congratulating (see Figure 18.6 in Section 18.4.2). If an NPC enters the Smart Zone during the execution of the Living Scene, he or she synchronizes his or her behavior with the current behavior executed by the main roles.

Finally, the game designers place the Smart Zones in the environment. The environment is considered as the "world zone" and includes all the Smart Zones. Smart Zones can overlap, in which case a priority order between the scenes must be defined. This order can be based either on the size of the zones or directly through priorities defined by the game designer.

In our example of a restaurant, each Living Scene is designed in the environment with a Smart Zone. Each Smart Zone defines the role (clients, friends, or waiter), the behaviors (drink, eat, ...), and the place of the scene in the environment. For instance, the orchestration between the behaviors in the third Smart Zone (to develop Scene 3) corresponds to a sequence of interactions between the waiter and the player in order to obtain a consistent collective behavior. The trigger of the Scene 3 consists in the entrance of an NPC in the zone. Finally, the Smart Zone to develop Scene 2 has priority on the Smart Zone to develop Scene 1.

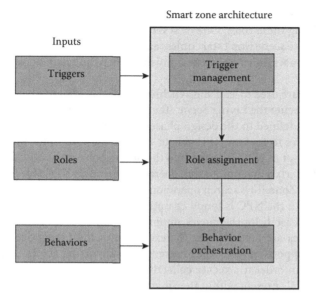

Figure 18.2

Runtime architecture of a smart zone.

18.3.2 Functioning of the Smart Zone Architecture

At runtime, when a Smart Zone is executed, it manages the lifetime of the Living Scene. In this section, we will present the runtime architecture (see Figure 18.2) for Smart Zones. It is made of several modules with different responsibilities. A Smart Zones will instantiate, start, execute, and stop a parameterized Living Scene and assign behaviors to NPCs.

18.3.2.1 Trigger Management

Triggers are a set of activation rules defining when a Living Scene should be started. Triggers can be the occurrence of a specific moment in time, the presence of a given NPC or player in a specific area, the beginning of an interaction with a particular object, or a combination of several of these rules.

This first module of the architecture aims to check whether the current situation allows the scene to be executed. The module takes as inputs the triggers defined for the scene and checks if all the trigger conditions are verified in the current situation. If that is the case, the next module steps in.

Let's consider, in our example, the waiter serving the player. The scene can start if and only if the two following trigger conditions are true: the waiter and another NPC are in the same zone at the same time, and it is after 8 pm.

18.3.2.2 Role Assignment

This module is responsible for the assignment of a role to each NPC present in the Smart Zone. An NPC has only one role in a scene. As described previously, a Smart Zone embeds a set of roles defined for the scene. In order to manage automatically the assignment of the roles, we define three subsets: main roles, supporting roles, and extras.

Main roles are essential for the execution of the scene. The scene itself revolves around characters fulfilling these roles. One or several NPCs can take main roles; they become the main actors. The scene won't start unless all the main roles are fulfilled with characters belonging to the Smart Zone. The scene is finished when the behaviors of all the main roles are finished.

The main roles are used to lead and synchronize all the collective behaviors. Main roles are essential to execute the Living Scene. The main role can be cast in two ways: either a particular NPC is defined in the design phase as a main actor for the Living Scene or the module should have to find an NPC able to endorse the role. Thus, the module chooses an NPC from the set of NPCs located into the Smart Zone. If no NPC is able to take the role, the module starts a dynamic search operation to find an NPC able to take a main role around the Smart Zone. This search operation uses an expanded zone, which is automatically extended until the NPC is found or until the expanded zone wraps the world zone. When the NPC is cast, he or she moves automatically to the Smart Zone.

Supporting roles are favorable for the execution of the Living Scene. Zero or more NPCs can take supporting roles; they become the supporting actors. They interact with the mains actors in order to execute collective behaviors. The supporting roles are first fulfilled by the NPCs present within the Smart Zone.

Finally, extra roles are optional for the realization of the Living Scene. Adding extras to a Living Scene allows the casting of numbers of nearby characters to execute "ambient" behaviors that will mostly react to the "main" set piece.

Let's illustrate these three sets of roles in a juggling show:

- The main role is the juggler; it triggers the start of the show.
- The supporting roles are the spectators.
- The extras are additional spectators as passersby, which are not mandatory for the show to be consistent, but that get involved because they are close to the show and interested from a distance.

The Role Assignment module needs to determine if a given character can fulfill a given role. This is why each created NPCs needs to be assigned a set of roles it can fulfill. The use of a role hierarchy can help to facilitate this assignment.

This role assignment step determines if the Living Scene can actually start. If at least all main roles can be cast, the runtime proceeds to the behavior orchestration. Then, each time an NPC enters the Smart Zone, the module determines if a role should be assigned to the NPC in the set of supporting or extra roles. If a supporting role is available, the role is assigned to the NPC. If all the supporting roles are fulfilled and if an extra role exists, the extra role is assigned to the NPC. If no extra role exists, the NPC does not join the Living Scene.

18.3.2.3 Behavior Orchestration

In practice, the "output" of a Living Scene is the execution of different behaviors by the involved NPCs. From the assigned role, an NPC is able to execute some behaviors defined for the role. This module is responsible for the assignment of a behavior to the NPCs, through the sequence of behaviors defined in a timeline (see Figure 18.1). The timeline orchestrates the roles of NPCs over time and synchronizes them in order to have credible individual and collective behaviors, including during a dynamic role assignment.

18.3.3 NPC Behaviors

To obtain a better ambience of life, we propose to take advantage of the principle of autonomy, by moving a part of the decision making to the NPC level.

18.3.3.1 Role Interruption

In the previous sections, we described a simple scenario where all participants of a Living Scene stay until all the main role behaviors end. The NPCs can also decide not to participate in a Living Scene according to their own goals. In this case, the Smart Zones do not entirely control the exit of the NPCs from the Living Scene, but they handle dynamic role assignments. Once more, the rules depend on the role:

- An NPC assigned to a main role can't leave the scene without stopping it if is not possible to recast the main role among other NPCs in the zone.
- When an NPC assigned to a supporting role leaves the scene, the role is cast automatically among extras and nonparticipants.
- NPCs with extra roles can leave as they wish without any incidence.

If the NPC decides to participate in a Living Scene, their behaviors are controlled by the timeline of the Living Scene. However, the selection between the NPC goals and the ones of Living Scene is based on priorities. If the priorities of goals are higher than the one of the Living Scene, the NPC can leave the scene. For example, if the hunger of a spectator is higher than its motivation of participating in the spectacle, it leaves the Living Scene and goes to eat.

18.3.3.2 Management of Overlapping Zones

As described previously, several levels of overlapping Smart Zones can result from their placement, which leads to a priority order of the scenes. The order can be defined through the relative sizes of the zones or directly by the game designers as a priority in the properties of the zones. These priorities are used by the NPCs to choose the best behaviors when they are located in several zones at the same time.

By default, the NPC chooses the behavior associated with the zone with the highest priority, but the NPC can also decide to execute a behavior from a zone with a lower priority for specific reasons, for instance:

- The behavior allows the NPC to achieve several Living Scenes at the same time
- The current internal state of the NPC allows him or her to execute the behavior but not the one from the zone with a higher priority
- The behavior allows the NPC to complete an individual goal

With such a degree of autonomy, an NPC can try to find a compromise between the roles of a scene and his or her goals.

18.4 Concrete Example

This section walks through an example scenario.

18.4.1 Scenario and the Smart Zones

The aim of this scenario example is to demonstrate how to create ambient life in a shopping street using multiple Living Scenes: "queue at the cash machine" (LS1), "spend time on a bench" (LS2), "buy interesting things at the shop" (LS3), "wait for the bus" (LS4), and "juggling show" (LS5).

The world zone is corresponding to the street, in which we define five specific Smart Zones to represent and manage these Living Scenes (see Figure 18.3):

- Smart Zone 1 (SZ1) is placed around the cash machine and triggered when an NPC enters the zone. The main role is the "cash taker" associated with the behavior "take cash" accessible when the NPC is the first in the queue. The supporting role is "queued" associated with the behavior of "wait for my turn." Several NPCs can take this role at runtime. No extra role is defined.
- Smart Zone 2 (SZ2) is placed around the bench and triggered when an NPC enters the zone. The main role is "dreamer" associated with the behavior "spend time." Several NPCs can take this role at runtime (depending on the size of the bench). No supporting or extra roles are defined.
- Smart Zone 3 (SZ3) is placed around the shop and triggered when the scenario is started. The main role is "merchant" associated with the behavior "sell things." The supporting role is "buyer" associated with the behaviors of "choose items," "buy items," and "wait for my turn." Several NPCs can take this role at runtime. No extra role is defined.
- Smart Zone 4 (SZ4) is placed around the bus station and triggered when an NPC enters the zone. The main role is "passenger" associated with the behaviors "buy a ticket," "wait for my turn," and "wait for the bus." Several NPCs can take this role at runtime. No supporting and extra role is defined.
- Smart Zone 5 (SZ5) is placed in the middle of the street and triggered every two hours. The main role is "juggler" associated with the behaviors "announce," "juggle," and "say goodbye." Only one NPC can take this role. The juggler NPC

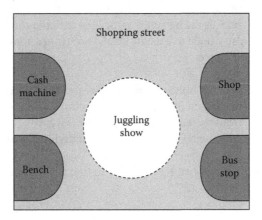

Figure 18.3

Schematic representations of the smart zones in our example.

is statically cast by the game designer before the beginning of the game. The supporting role is "spectator" associated with the behaviors "comment," "applaud," and "congratulate." Several NPCs can take this role. The extra role is "passerby" associated with the behavior "look from a distance."

By default, the NPCs that are in the world zone, take a default role of "wanderer," and can follow the default behavior of "wander" or "say hello" depending on the current situation. Thus, by default, they navigate randomly within the world zone from an activated Smart Zone to another (SZ1, SZ2, SZ3, and SZ4). To add some interaction between NPCs and the player, when an NPC meets another NPC, the behavior "say hello" can be executed.

When the first NPC enters, for example, SZ1, he or she is cast as a main role and then takes cash. Otherwise, the NPC entering in the zone is cast as a supporting role and stands in line in front of the cash machine. He or she takes cash when it is his or her turn (he or she is cast as the new main role). Similar operations occur for the other Smart Zones with the corresponding roles and behaviors.

18.4.2 Implementation in Unity3D

We have implemented the Living Scenes of the shopping street in Unity3D [Unity 14] and created the behaviors under MASA LIFE [MASA 14] using behavior trees [Champandard 08, Champandard 13]. We focus only on decisional behaviors and scene execution, and not on animation, navigation, and 3D design.

We created the roles and the associated behaviors for each Living Scene. The Smart Zones of the Living Scenes were placed in the environment of the shopping street (circles on Figure 18.4). We specified the characteristics of the Living Scenes through a dedicated

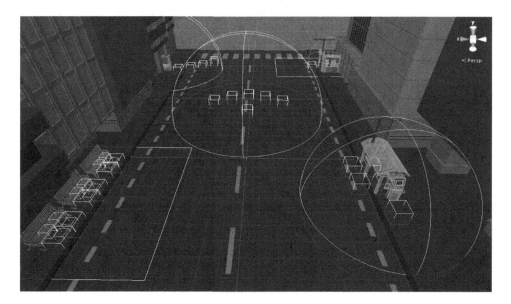

Figure 18.4

Instantiation of the shopping street example.

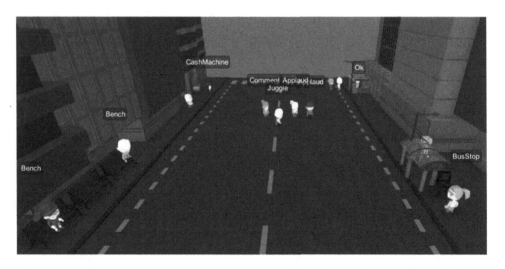

Figure 18.5

The shopping street example in Unity3D.

graphical interface in Unity3D by selecting the associated Smart Zones. Figure 18.5 illustrates the result of the Smart Zones execution in Unity3D.

Let's consider the juggling show scene. SZ5 defines five slots in which the spectators can take position to watch the show. Thus, five supporting roles are available in this specific case.

The timeline of the show defines the sequence of behaviors and their synchronization for the juggler and the spectators (see Figure 18.6). The show has three stages: announcement, juggling, and end. During the announcement, the juggler informs that it will begin the show soon (he or she executes the "announce" behavior).

The trigger for the scene is a given period. When the time comes, the juggler is automatically cast. In our example, the designer associates a particular NPC to the role of

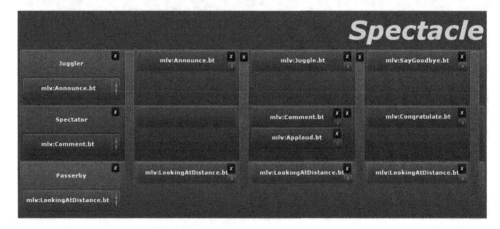

Figure 18.6

The timeline for the juggler spectacle.

18. Smart Zones to Create the Ambience of Life

juggler before runtime. The NPCs already in SZ5 when the scene is triggered are first cast as "spectators" if they can assume the role, until all the supporting roles are filled. The remaining NPCs cast as "extras" if they can assume the role. Moreover, NPCs interested in the show can go to SZ5 attracted by the announcement, and they are cast in the same way. They automatically adapt their behaviors to the corresponding stage of the show. During the juggling phase, the juggler juggles, and the spectators comment or applaud randomly. At the end of the show, the spectators congratulate the juggler, and the juggler says good-bye, and then the scene ends.

18.5 Conclusion

Living Scenes allow the execution of an ambience of life in video games with autonomous and less repetitive nonplayer characters exhibiting consistent, credible, and interactive behaviors. We propose a solution with Smart Zones to manage the NPCs' behaviors for the Living Scene execution and thus to move the complexity of the design into the zones. We implemented our solution into MASA LIFE and instantiated an example with Unity3D to test the Smart Zone concept, with positive results.

We demonstrated the prototype to game designers and their feedback is very encouraging. The model and the architecture seem to fit their needs to create ambience of life. Despite the simplicity of the scenario example presented in the previous section, the shopping street in Unity3D gives a good impression with less repetitive and more credible behaviors. Through this first implementation, we noticed that without the proposed model and architecture of Smart Zones to define and execute a Living Scene, the design of such an ambience would have been more complex.

This work is a part of the OCTAVIA Project, a research project funded by the French government (DGE). The main goal of the project is to propose an innovative tool to design and test scenes of ambient life involving interactive and autonomous nonplayer character in 3D environment. In this project, we plan to evaluate our solution design in order to validate its usability and whether our solution concretely simplifies the design of ambient life.

Although Smart Zones are an interesting and accessible approach to design Living Scenes, two main challenges need to be addressed to complete the solution: the integration of the player into a Living Scene with the impact of his or her actions on the scene; and the simplification of the design of the behaviors of autonomous NPCs in relation to Living Scenes, especially to allow NPCs to reason about Living Scenes.

Acknowledgments

This research is funded by the French government DGE within the OCTAVIA Project (PIA-FSN-2012) and supported by the cluster Cap Digital.

References

[Champandard 08] Champandard, A.J. 2008. Getting started with decision making and control systems. In *AI Game Programming Wisdom*, Vol. 4, pp. 257–264. Charles River Media, Hingham, MA.

[Champandard 13] Champandard, A.J. and Dunstan, P. 2013. The behavior tree starter kit. In *Game AI Pro: Collected Wisdom of Game AI Professionals*. A K Peters/CRC Press, Boca Raton, FL.

[Kallmann 98] Kallmann, M. and Thalmann, D. 1998. Modeling objects for interaction tasks. In *Proceedings of the Ninth Eurographics Workshop on Animation and Simulation (EGCAS)*, Lisbon, Portugal, pp. 73–86.

[MASA 14] MASA Group. 2014. MASA LIFE. http://www.masalife.net (accessed September 10, 2014).

[Shoulson 11] Shoulson, A. and Badler, N.I. 2011. Event-centric control for background agents. In *Lecture Notes in Computer Science*, Vol. 7069, pp. 193–198. Springer, Berlin, Germany.

[Stocker 10] Stocker, C., Sun, L., Huang, P., Qin, W., Allbeck, J.M., and Badler, N.I. 2010. Smart events and primed agents. In *Proceedings of the 10th International Conference on Intelligent Virtual Agents*, pp. 15–27. Springer-Verlag, Berlin, Germany.

[The Sims 99] The Sims. 1999. Electronic arts. http://www.ea.com/sims (accessed February 7, 2015).

[Unity 14] Unity Technologies. 2014. Unity 3D. https://unity3d.com/ (accessed September 10, 2014).

19

Separation of Concerns Architecture for AI and Animation

Bobby Anguelov

19.1 Introduction

There are two requirements for creating believable characters in today's games: the first is that characters need to make the correct decisions (artificial intelligence [AI]), and the second is that they need to look good when acting on those decisions (animation). With the heavy visual focus in today's games, it is fair to say that an AI system will live or die based on the quality of its animation system. Smart decisions won't matter much if the animation system can't execute them in a visually pleasing manner.

As we've improved the animation fidelity in our games, we've encountered a huge jump in the amount of content needed to achieve the required level of fidelity. This content refers to both the animation data, the data structures that reference the animation data, and the code required to control and drive those data structures. The biggest challenge facing us today is simply one of complexity, that is, how do we manage, leverage, and maintain of this new content in an efficient manner?

We feel that traditional techniques for managing this content have already reached their limits with the content volumes present in the last generation of games. Given the order of magnitude jump in memory between the last generation and the current-gen consoles, as well as the expectations of the audience, it is not unreasonable to expect a similar jump in the content volumes. As such, we need to take the time to evaluate and adjust our workflows and architecture to better deal with this increase in content and complexity.

In this chapter, we propose an architecture for managing the complexity of a modern animation system based on our experience developing for both last- and current-gen titles [Vehkala 13, Anguelov 13].

19.2 Animation Graphs

Before we discuss the higher-level architecture, it is worth giving a quick overview of modern-day animation systems. Animation graphs (animgraphs) are ubiquitous within the industry when it comes to describing the set of animations as well as the necessary chaining of these animations in performing in-game actions.

An animgraph is, in its simplest form, a directed acyclic graph wherein the leaf nodes are the animation sources (i.e., resulting in an animation pose) and the branch nodes are animation operations (i.e., pose modification such as blending). These sorts of animgraphs are commonly referred to as blend trees since they primarily describe the blends performed on a set of animations. Animation operations contained within a blend tree are usually driven through control parameters. For example, a simple blend between two animations will require a "blend weight" control parameter to specify the contribution of each animation to the final blended result. These control parameters are our primary means of controlling (or driving) our blend trees, the second mechanism being animation events.

Animation events are additional temporal hints that are annotated onto the animation sources when authored. They provide contextual information both about the animation itself and information needed by other systems. For example, in a walking animation, we might want to mark the periods in which the left or right foot is on the ground as well as when the game should trigger footstep sounds (i.e., contact period for each foot). Animation events are sampled from each animation source and then are bubbled up through the graph to the root. As these events bubble up through the graph, they can be also used by the branch nodes in their decision making, especially within state machine transitions. A simple blend tree describing forward locomotion for a character is shown in Figure 19.1, wherein we can control the direction and the speed of a character with the control parameters: "direction" and "speed."

In addition to blending, we also have the ability to select between two animations at branch nodes. For example, in Figure 19.1, we could replace the speed blend with a "select" node that will choose either the walk blend or the run blend based on the control parameter.

While a blend tree can perform all the necessary operations needed for a single action, it is extremely difficult to build a single blend tree to handle all the actions available to our characters. As such, we often wish to separate each action into its own blend tree and have some mechanism to switch between the actions. Often, these actions would have a predefined sequence as well as restrictions on which actions could

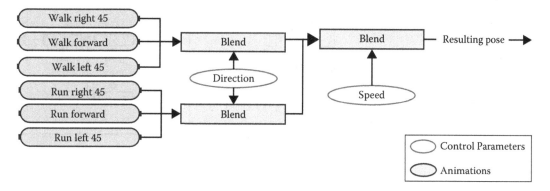

Figure 19.1

A simple blend tree describing forward locomotion.

be chained together, and so traditionally this switching mechanism between actions took the form of a state machine.

Within these state machines, the states would contain the blend trees, and the state transitions would result in blends from one blend tree to another. Each state transition would be based on a set of conditions which, once met, would allow the transition to occur. These conditions would also need to check animation-specific criteria like control parameter values, animation events, and time-based criteria like whether we reached the end of an animation. In addition, the states would also need to contain some logic for controlling and driving the blend trees (i.e., setting the control parameters values appropriately).

State machines were the final tool needed to allow us to combine all our individual actions in one system and so allow our characters to perform complex behaviors by chaining these actions together. Let's consider the simple example presented in Figure 19.1; since it only covered the forward arc of motion, we extend the direction blend to cover all directions, but we don't have any animation for when the character is idle and not moving. So we add this animation in another blend tree, which results in us needing a state machine to switch between the two blend trees. Now we realized the transitions between moving and idle don't look great, so we want to add some nice transition animations, which means that we need two more blend trees. Now we then realize that when stopping, it matters which foot of the character is planted, so we need two states to cover that and transitions that check the animation events in the walk animation. In the end, we end up with the state machine setup shown in Figure 19.2.

We can already see that for even the most basic setup, there is already a large degree of complexity present. Consider the fact that each blend tree might have its own set of control parameters that the code needs to be aware of and control, as well as all of the transition logic and state setup that needs to be created and driven. Now factor in that modern-day characters have dozens of available actions, each of which may require numerous blend trees as well as state logic for each and we now have a recipe for a complexity explosion, one which, unfortunately, has already occurred, and we now find ourselves trying to move forward through the fallout.

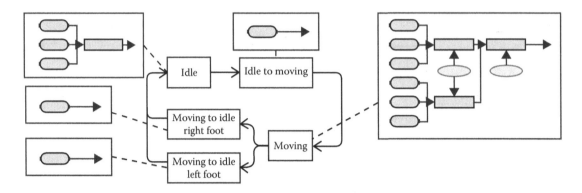

Figure 19.2

A simple animation state machine describing basic locomotion.

19.3 Complexity Explosion and the Problem of Scalability

To discuss the problem of scalability, we need to focus on the state machines described previously. Traditionally, a lot of developers would reuse the same state machine for driving both the animation and the gameplay state changes. This applies both to AI, where the state machine might take the form of a behavior tree or some other decision-making construct, as well as the player's state machine setup. We used the term state machine here, but this could be any sort of AI state change mechanic (behavior trees, planners, etc.). For simplicity's sake, from now onwards, we will use the term gameplay state machine to refer to any sort of high-level AI or player decision-making systems.

Reusing the high-level gameplay state machines for animation purposes is problematic for a variety of reasons, but the main issue is one of code/data dependency. As the blend graphs exist outside of the code base, they can be considered data and so are loaded at runtime as resources. With these blend graph resources, it is the responsibility of the game code to drive them by setting the necessary control parameters required by the graph. As such, the code needs to have explicit knowledge of these parameters and what they are used for. It is important to note that control parameters usually represent the animation-specific values (i.e., normalized blend values [0–1]), and so desired inputs need to be converted by the gameplay code into values that the animation system understands (e.g., the direction value in Figure 19.1 needs to be converted from degrees into a 0–1 blend value). In giving our code this explicit knowledge of the control parameter conversions, we've created a code/data dependency from our gameplay code to the blend tree resources meaning that whenever we change the blend trees, we need to change the code as well. The code/data dependency is pretty much unavoidable, but there is a lot we can do to push it as far away from gameplay code as possible, thereby reducing the risks resulting from it as well as allowing fast iterations.

The second biggest problem with reusing gameplay state machines is the asynchronous lifetimes of states, in that there isn't a one-to-one mapping between the gameplay states and the animation states. For example, consider a simple locomotion state from the gameplay's standpoint: a single state is usually enough to represent that a character is in motion, but on the animation side, we require a collection of states and transitions to

19. Separation of Concerns Architecture for AI and Animation

actually achieve that motion. This usually means that we end up having animation only state machines embedded within the gameplay state machines, and over the course of a development cycle, the line between the two state machines becomes blurred. In fact, this is the main concern with the code/data dependency, since if we are required to make significant modifications to the blend trees, then the code needs to be adjusted as well and, unfortunately, this could end up affecting or even breaking the current gameplay since the two systems are so intertwined. Even worse, when animation and gameplay are so closely coupled, it can be tempting for a programmer to make direct use of information from the blend tree or make assumptions about the structure of the blend trees for gameplay decisions, which in pathological cases requires large portions of the gameplay code having to be rewritten when animation changes.

The example presented in Figure 19.2 is misleading: the idle state is a separate gameplay state. So if we were to create a simple gameplay state machine for a character with some additional abilities like jumping and climbing ladders, we might end up with a state machine setup similar to that in Figure 19.3.

There is already a significant degree of complexity in Figure 19.3, but even so, it doesn't show the full picture, as now the transitions between the gameplay states also need to contain and drive animation transitions. For example, when we transition between the idle and jump states, we somehow need to let the jump state know which animation state we are arriving from, so that we can choose the appropriate target animation state. Changing or adding animation transitions means we now need to modify the gameplay transitions in addition to all of the actual gameplay code and animation logic. As our system grows, maintenance and debugging starts to become a nightmare. The costs and risks associated with adding new states can be so high that it becomes nearly impossible to justify such change late in the development cycle. The best way to move forward and avoid this situation is to work toward loosening the couplings between the systems, and this is where a separation of concerns (SoC) architecture comes in.

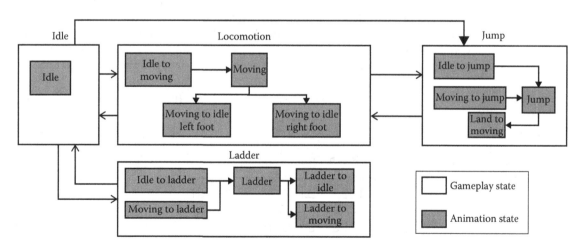

Figure 19.3

A combined gameplay/animation state machine for a simple character.

19.4 SoC

SoC is a principle that states that various systems that interact with one another should each have a singular purpose and thereby not have overlapping responsibilities [Greer 08]. It is already clear that this isn't the case for the state machine presented in Figure 19.3, as we have two distinct state machines and responsibilities intertwined together. So as a first step, we want to separate the animation state logic from the gameplay state logic. This is relatively easy, and, for many developers, this is already the case, in that their animation system supports animation state machines (e.g., *Morpheme, Mecanim, EmotionFX*). Unfortunately, the concept of animation state machines is not as common as one would imagine, and it was only in version 4 of both the Unity and Unreal engines that animation state machines were introduced. An animation state machine is simply a state machine at the animation system level, allowing us to define and transition between animation states as described in the previous sections. From this point on, we will use the term "animgraph" to refer to the combination of blend trees and state machines in a single graph.

Animation state machines can also be hierarchical in that the blend trees contained within a state can also contain additional state machines as leaf nodes. This allows for easy layering of animation results on top of one another but is not a feature that is available in all animation systems. For example, Natural Motion's *Morpheme* middleware is entirely built around the concept, while Unity's *Mecanim* only supports a single state machine at the root of an animgraph, but allows for the layering of multiple graphs on top of one another.

If we extract all the animation state machine logic from Figure 19.3, we end up with the state machine setup shown in Figure 19.4. As you can see, the animation state machine once separated out is still relatively complex but this complexity can be further simplified by making use of hierarchical state machines, with container states for each action (i.e., "jump" or "ladder"). The gameplay state machine is now free to only worry about gameplay transitions without having to deal with the animation transition, and it is now also possible, to some degree, to work on either system independently.

There is still a catch. While this initial separation goes a long way to help decouple the systems, we still have a coupling between the gameplay state machine and the animation system. We still need to have explicit knowledge of the control parameters

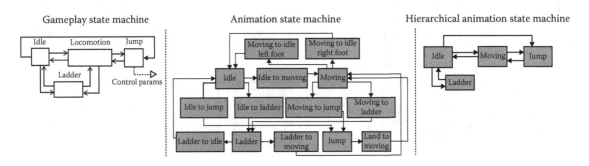

Figure 19.4

Separation of animation and gameplay state machines.

19. Separation of Concerns Architecture for AI and Animation

required to drive the state machine as well as explicit knowledge of the topology of the animgraph to be able to determine when states are active or when transitions have occurred/completed. This means that we still need a lot of code to drive and poll the animation system, and unfortunately this code still takes the form of some sort of state machine. It is surprising to note that only once we separated out the animation state machines from the gameplay state machines did we realize that we actually had three state machines that were intertwined: the gameplay state machine that controls character decision making, the animation state machine representing the states and possible transitions, and the animation driver state machine that acts as the interface between the gameplay and animation state machines. The fact that there was a hidden state machine goes a long way to highlight the danger posed by building monolithic systems.

Coming back to the animation driver state machine, its responsibilities are to inspect the animation state machine and provide that information back to the gameplay system. It is also responsible for converting from the desired gameplay control parameter values to values the animation system understands as well as triggering the appropriate animation state transitions when needed. In many cases, this driving code would also be responsible for any animation postprocessing required, that is, post rotation/translation of the animation displacement. As such, we still have a lot of different responsibilities within one system and we haven't really improved the maintainability or extensibility of our characters. To move forward, we need to pull all of this animation-specific code out of our gameplay systems, which will remove any remaining code/data dependencies we have between our animation data and gameplay code.

19.5 Separating Gameplay and Animation

To pull out the animation driving code, there are two things we can do, the first is relatively easy and goes a long way to simplify the gameplay code, while the second is significantly more invasive and time-consuming. So if you find yourself battling code/data dependencies toward the end of a project, the first technique might prove useful.

We mentioned that one of the key responsibilities of the animation driving code was to convert between high-level gameplay desires such as "move at 3.5 m/s while turning 53° to left" to the animation level control parameters, which might be something like "direction = 0.3 and speed = 0.24" (i.e., the blend weight values that will result in the required visual effect). To do the conversion between the gameplay values and the animation values, it is necessary for the gameplay code to have knowledge about the animations that are available, the blends that exist, what values drive what blends, etc. Basically, the driving code needs to have full knowledge of the blend tree just to convert a value from, for example, degrees to a blend weight. This means that if an animator modifies the blend tree, then the gameplay code might be invalidated and require code changes to restore the functionality. This means that any animgraph changes require both programmer and animation resources and a potentially significant delay before a build with both the code and data changes can be rolled out to the production team.

A simple way to get around this problem is to move all translation logic into the animgraph (i.e., directly feed in the higher-level gameplay values). Depending on your

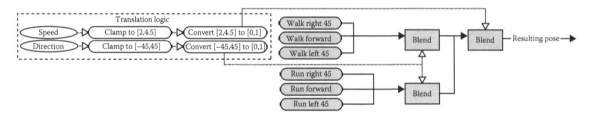

Figure 19.5

Moving control parameter translation logic to the animgraph.

animation system, this may or not be possible. For example, in Unreal 4, this is relatively trivial to do through the use of blueprints, while on Unity, there seems to be no way to perform math operations on control parameters within the graph. The benefits of moving the translation logic into the graph are twofold: first, gameplay code does not need any knowledge of the graph or the blends; all it needs to know is that it has to send a direction and speed values in a format it understands (i.e., degrees and m/s, respectively). In removing that dependency from the code and moving it into the animgraph, animators can now make drastic changes to the animgraphs without having to modify the gameplay code; in fact, they can even swap out entire graphs just as long as the inputs are the same, taking the setup shown in Figure 19.1 and moving all translation logic to the blend tree result in the setup shown in Figure 19.5.

In addition to the translation logic, we can also move a lot of other control parameter logic to the graph (e.g., dampening on input values so we get smooth blends to the new values instead of an instant reaction to a new value).

It is still important to note that gameplay code should probably be aware of the capabilities of the animation (i.e., roughly what the turning constraints are and what reasonable speeds for movement are, but it doesn't have to be explicit). In fact, it is usually gameplay that defines some of these constraints. Imagine that we have the setup in Figure 19.5 and gameplay decides we need the character to sprint; the gameplay team simply feeds in the faster velocity parameter and notifies the animation team. The animation team can now create and integrate new animations independently of the gameplay team. From a technical standpoint, moving the translation logic from the code to data removes one layer of coupling and brings us closer to the final SoC architecture we'd like.

The second thing we need to do to achieve the SoC architecture is to move all the animation driver state machine code from the gameplay state machine into a new layer that exists between the animation system and the gameplay code. In the classic AI agent architecture presented in [Russel 03], the authors separate an agent into three layers: sensory, decision making, and actuation. This is in itself an SoC design and one that we can directly apply to our situation. If we think of the gameplay state machine as the decision-making layer and the animation system as the final actuators, then we need an actuation layer to transmit the commands from the decision-making system to the actuators. This new layer is comprised of an animation controller and animation behaviors. Gameplay systems will directly interface with this new layer for any animation requests they have.

19. Separation of Concerns Architecture for AI and Animation

19.6 Animation Behaviors

An animation behavior is defined as a program that executes a specific set of actions are needed to realize a character action from a visual standpoint. As such, animation behaviors are purely concerned with the visual aspects of character actions, and they are not responsible for any gameplay state changes themselves. That is not to say they have no influence on gameplay, though. There is bidirectional flow of information between the gameplay systems and the animation behaviors, which will indirectly result in gameplay state changes, but these changes will not be performed by the behaviors themselves. In fact, we suggest the animation behaviors are layered below the gameplay systems (in your engine architecture), so that there is absolutely no way for the behaviors to even access the gameplay systems.

In describing animation behaviors, we feel it makes more sense to start at the animation system and slowly move back up to the gameplay system. As such, let's take a look at the example animgraph presented in Figure 19.6. We have a full-body animation state machine that contains all the full-body actions that our characters can perform. Within that state machine, we have a state called "locomotion," which, in turn, contains a state machine with the states necessary to perform locomotion. Each of these states represents additional blend trees/state machines.

Let's say that we wish to build a "move" animation behavior. For this behavior to function, it will need to have knowledge of the animgraph (especially the "locomotion" state machine), all the states contained within it, and the contents of each state. Once we've given the animation behavior all the necessary graph topological information, it will need to drive the state machine, which implies it requires knowledge about the needed control parameters and context thereof. With this knowledge, the animation behavior is ready to perform its task. This is achieved in three stages: "start," "execute," and "stop."

The "start" stage is responsible for ensuring that the animgraph is in a state in which the execute stage can proceed. For example, when starting to move from idle, we need to trigger the "idle to move" transition and wait for it to complete; only once that transition is complete and we are in the "move" state, we can move onto the "execute" stage. In the case of path following, we may also need to perform some pathfinding and path postprocessing here before the behavior can continue.

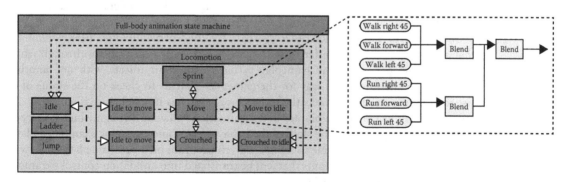

Figure 19.6

An example of a full-body animation state machine.

The "execute" stage is responsible for all the heavy lifting. It is responsible for driving the animgraph to generate the required visual result. In the context of locomotion, we would perform the path following simulation and set the direction and speed parameters needed to follow a given path. Once we detect that we have completed our task, we will transition over to the "stop" stage.

The "stop" stage is responsible for any cleanup we need to do as well as transitioning the animgraph to a neutral state from which other animation behaviors can continue. With our locomotion example, we would free the path and then trigger the "move to idle" transition in this stage and complete our behavior.

It is important to note that in the example given in Figure 19.6, the actual transition between "idle" and the "locomotion" state exists within the "full-body" state machine. This implies that both "idle" and "locomotion" need to know about the "full-body" state machine. Well, in fact, it turns out that all states in the "full-body" state machine need to know about it. This brings us to the concept of *animgraph views*. An animgraph view is an object that has knowledge of a specific portion of the graph as well as utility functions to drive that portion of the graph. From that description, animation behaviors are in fact animgraph views themselves with the exception that they have an execution flow. It is better to think of graph views as utility libraries and the animation behaviors as programs. Multiple behaviors can share and make use of a single graph view, allowing us a greater level of code reuse and helping to reduce the cost incurred when the animgraph changes. In our example, we would have a "full-body graph view" that would know about the topology of the "full-body state machine" and offer functions to help trigger the transitions between the states, for example, set full-body state (IDLE).

To execute a given task, animation behaviors require some instruction and direction. This direction comes in the form of an animation order. Animation orders are sent from the gameplay systems and contain all the necessary data to execute a given behavior. For example, if the gameplay systems want to move a character to a specific point, they would issue a "move order" with the target point, the desired movement speed, the character's end orientation, and so on. Each animation order has a type and will result in a single animation behavior (e.g., a "move order" will result in a "move behavior"). Animation orders are fire-and-forget, in that once an order is issued, the gameplay system doesn't have any control over the lifetime of the animation behavior. The only way that behaviors can be cancelled or have their orders updated is by issuing additional orders, as detailed in the next section.

In addition to the animation orders, we have the concept of *animation behavior handles* that are returned for each order issued. These handles are a mechanism through which the animation behaviors and gameplay systems can communicate with one another. Primarily, the handles are a way for the gameplay systems to check on the status of an issued animation order (i.e., has the order completed, has it failed, and, if so, why?). An animation handle contains a pointer to the animation behavior through which it can perform necessary queries on the state of the behavior. In some cases, for example, a player character, it is useful to be able to update a given program on a per frame basis (i.e., with the controller analog stick inputs that will be translated into animation control parameter settings by the behavior each frame).

We show a simple timeline representing the interaction between a gameplay system and an animation behavior for a simple "move" order in Figure 19.7. It is important to note

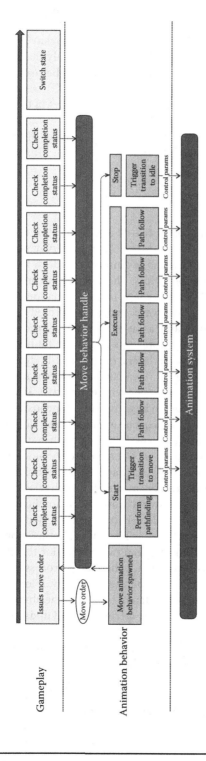

Figure 19.7

Timeline for an animation behavior.

how all communication between the animation behavior and the gameplay system occur through the animation handle.

In addition to the three update stages, animation behaviors also feature a post-animation update "postprocess" stage. This stage is mainly used to perform animation postprocessing such as trajectory warping but can also be used for post-physics/post-animation pose modification (i.e., inverse kinematics [IK]). As a note, IK and physics/animation interactions should ideally be performed as part of the animation update but not all animation systems support this.

Since we will have multiple animation behaviors covering all of a character's actions, we need some mechanism to schedule and execute them. This is where the animation controller comes in.

19.7 Animation Controller

The animation controller's main role is that of a scheduler for the animation behaviors. It is the primary interface used by the higher-level gameplay systems to issue requests to the animation system through the use of animation orders. It is responsible for creating and executing the animation behaviors. The animation controller also features animation behavior tracks (queues) used for layering of animation behaviors. For example, actions such as "look at," "reload," or "wave" can be performed on top of other full-body animations (e.g., "idle" or "walk"), and, as such, we can layer those actions on top of full-body actions at the controller level. In previous games, we found it sufficient (at least for humanoid characters) to have only two layers: one for full-body actions and one for layered actions [Anguelov 13, Vehkala 13]. We also had different scheduling rules for each track. We only allowed a single full-body behavior to be active at any given time, whereas we allowed multiple layered behaviors to be active simultaneously.

For the full-body behaviors, we had a queue with two open slots. Once a full-body animation order was issued, we would enqueue an animation behavior into the primary slot. If another full-body order was received, we would create the new animation behavior and first try to merge the two behaviors. Merging of animation behavior is simply a mechanism through which an animation order can be updated for a behavior. For example, if we issue a move order to point A, we would spawn a move animation behavior with the target A. If we then decided that point B is actually a better final position, we would issue another move order with point B as the target. This will result in another move animation behavior being spawned and merged with the original move behavior thereby updating its order; the second behavior is then discarded. Once the merge process completes, the behavior will then detect the updated order and respond accordingly. If an animation order results in a full-body animation behavior of a different type than the already queued behavior, we would have queued the new behavior to the second slot and updated it, but we would have also notified the original behavior to terminate. Terminating a behavior forces it to enter the stopping stage and complete. Once an animation behavior completes, it is dequeued and is not updated any more. This means that we can in essence cross-fade between two full-body actions allowing us to achieve greater visual fidelity during the transition.

The merging mechanism does have the requirement that all behaviors be built in a manner that supports order updating. While this manner of updating animation behaviors might seem strange at first, it has significant benefits for the gameplay code. The main one is that gameplay no longer needs to worry about stopping and waiting for animations to complete or how to transition between the different animation states, as this is all handled at the controller/behavior level. This transition micromanagement at the gameplay level is also extremely problematic when trying to delegate animation control between different systems, for example, when triggering an in-game cut scene, the cinematics system requires animation control of the character. When control is requested, the character could be in any animation state. The cinematic system needs to resolve that state in a sensible way, and this has been extremely difficult to achieve in the past without coupling unrelated systems (i.e., giving knowledge of the AI system to the cinematics system). With our approach, we can now delegate control to various systems without having to create any coupling between unrelated systems. For example, animation behaviors could be written for cinematics, and when the cinematics code takes control, it could issue those orders that would terminate existing orders and result in sensible transitions between orders. In fact, the cinematics system can even reuse the same locomotion orders that the AI is using, since they are entirely system agnostic. Imagine we needed to have an nonplayable character (NPC) climb a ladder in a cut scene. Instead of fully animating the cut scene, or trying to script the AI to climb the ladder, we could simply issue the animation order directly in the cinematics system without any knowledge of the AI or the current state of an NPC.

There is also an additional benefit of this approach on the animation side. If for whatever reason we have a barrage of orders from the gameplay systems, that is, behavior oscillation, our full-body queuing mechanism will simply overwrite/merge the queued behavior with whatever new behaviors it is ordered to perform. This greatly reduces the visual glitches that traditionally arise from these kind of gameplay bugs. On the downside, it does make those bugs harder to detect from a quality assurance (QA) perspective, as there is no visual feedback now, so we greatly recommend that you implement some sort of animation order spam detection.

When it comes to the layered behaviors, we can have any number of behaviors queued, and it is up to gameplay code to ensure that the combination makes sense. We also merge layered behaviors in the same manner as for the full-body behavior, giving us the same set of update capabilities.

There is one last thing to discuss when it comes to the scheduling of animation behaviors: behavior lifetimes. The lifetime of a behavior is not synchronous with that of the gameplay state that issued the original order. Once a behavior completes, it is dequeued, but we may need to keep the behavior since the handle may still be checked by gameplay code, which updates at a different frequency. The opposite may also be true, wherein a gameplay state issues an animation order that then completes without waiting for the order to complete. As such we decided to control animation behavior lifetime through the concept of shared ownership. A behavior is kept alive (in memory), while either a handle to it still exists or it is still on one of the animation controller update queues. This can be easily achieved through the use of an STL shared_ptr smart pointer. The final architecture across all system layers is presented in Figure 19.8. For more details on the controller/behavior architecture, readers are referred to [Anguelov 13].

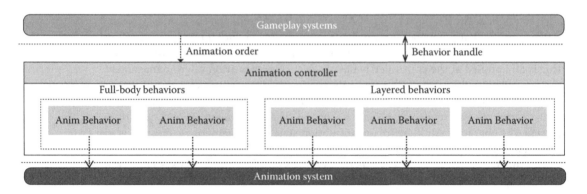

Figure 19.8

The final SoC architecture.

19.8 Benefits of an SoC Animation Architecture

Up until this point, we have discussed the SoC as a means to solving some existing problems. However, it is important to mention that there are some additional benefits in moving to an SoC architecture, which might not be immediately clear, and so we would like to highlight a few of them.

19.8.1 Functional Testing

The first clear benefit from this architecture is that systems can now be functionally tested in isolation. For example, if we wish to create some tests for the AI system, we can create a dummy animation controller that will receive orders and complete/fail them as desired without actually running any animation code. This will greatly simplify the task of debugging AI issues, as the animation code can be entirely removed from the equation. In the past with all the intertwined systems, we would never really be sure what the root cause of a bug was. This is also very true for animation testing. On a past project, we had built a stand-alone scripting system for testing the animation layer. This scripting system would issue the exact same orders as the AI, but allows us to build animation function tests in complete isolation. This was a massive win for us on previous projects when maintaining and verifying animation functionality, even across multiple refactoring phases of the gameplay code.

19.8.2 System Refactoring

Another huge benefit of this approach is that when we wish to make significant animation changes, it is much safer and easier to do so. This architecture allows us to replace character actions, one by one, without any risk of breaking the gameplay code. Furthermore, this approach allows us to perform nondestructive prototyping. When building a new version of an action, we can simply build a new behavior alongside the existing one and have a runtime switch to select between the two within the controller.

19. Separation of Concerns Architecture for AI and Animation

The beauty of this approach is that we can swap out behaviors at runtime without the gameplay code even being aware. If we combine this technique with the function testing mentioned earlier, it allows us to build a new version of an action and compare the two actions side by side (which alone is priceless), without having modified neither the original action nor the gameplay code. This allows us to rapidly prototype features with bare minimum functionality and expose them to the gameplay systems early on, all while building the final versions alongside them, allowing us to experiment and break actions without affecting the build.

19.8.3 Level of Detail

Being able to switch between behaviors at runtime without affecting gameplay allows us to leverage this to build a dynamic level of detail (LOD) system for the animation. In scenario's where the lifetime of characters is significant and AI updates are required even for offscreen characters (i.e., artificial life simulations), we require some mechanism to reduce or remove the cost of animation updates. If NPC locomotion was based on the animation (animation driven displacement), then this becomes relatively complex to achieve without a clear separation of the animation and gameplay systems.

With our approach, we can build several sets of cheap animation behaviors that can be dynamically swapped out at runtime based on a character's LOD level [Anguelov 13]. When we have an NPC at the highest LOD, we would want to run our default animation behaviors. As the character moves away and drops in LOD, we could exchange out some of the expensive layered behaviors with lightweight ones so as to reduce the cost. Once the character moves offscreen, then we can replace all animation behaviors with dummy behaviors that simply track the animation state needed to resume a high LOD behavior when needed.

For example, with locomotion, at the highest LOD, we would run the animation locomotion fully as well as having a layered footstep IK behavior enabled. At a medium LOD, we would replace the footstep IK behavior with a dummy behavior while keeping locomotion untouched. At the lowest LOD (offscreen), we would replace the locomotion with a simple time-based update on the given path, as well as estimating the velocity and state of the character (crouched, standing, etc.). Once this character comes back into view, we would simply swap back to the standard locomotion behavior and continue seamlessly. We suggest that you build separate behaviors for the different LODs, as this allows you to create "LOD sets" for different characters using various combinations of the behaviors. For example, you might not want to disable the footstep IK for huge characters even at medium LOD, since it may be more visible than for smaller characters.

19.9 Conclusion

In this chapter, we have presented an approach for decoupling your gameplay systems from your animation systems. We discussed the potential improvements to productivity and maintenance offered by this approach as well as provided advice on how to move toward a similar architecture.

References

[Anguelov 13] Anguelov, B. and Sunshine-Hill, B. 2013. Managing the movement: Getting your animation behaviors to behave better. *Game Developers Conference*. http://www. gdcvault.com (accessed May 11, 2014).

[Greer 08] Greer, D. 2008. The art of separation of concerns. Online article: The aspiring craftsman. http://aspiringcraftsman.com/2008/01/03/art-of-separation-of-concerns/ (accessed May 11, 2014).

[Russel 03] Russel, S.J. and Norvig, P. 2003. *Artificial Intelligence: A Modern Approach*, 2nd edn. Pearson Education, Englewood Cliffs, NJ.

[Vehkala 13] Vehkala, M. and De Pascale, M. 2013. Creating the AI for the living, breathing world of hitman: Absolution. *Game Developers Conference*. http://www.gdcvault.com (accessed May 11, 2014).

Optimizing Practical Planning for Game AI

Éric Jacopin

20.1 Introduction

Planning generates sequences of actions called plans. Practical planning for game artificial intelligence (AI) refers to a planning procedure that fits in the AI budget of a game and supports playability so that nonplayer characters (NPCs) execute actions from the plans generated by this planning procedure.

Jeff Orkin developed Goal-Oriented Action Planning (GOAP) [Orkin 04] as the first ever implementation of practical planning for the game [F.E.A.R. 05]. GOAP implements practical planning with (1) actions as C++ classes, (2) plans as paths in a space of states, and (3) search as path planning in a space of states, applying actions backwardly from the goal state to the initial state; moreover, GOAP introduced action costs as a search heuristic. Many games used GOAP since 2005, and it is still used today, for example, [Deus Ex 3 DC 13] and [Tomb Raider 13], sometimes with forward search, which seems easier to debug, as the most noticeable change.

In this chapter, we present how to optimize a GOAP-like planning procedure with actions as text files [Cheng 05] and forward breadth-first search (refer to Section A.2 of [Ghallab 04]) so that it becomes practical to implement planning. Actions as text files allow nonprogrammers to provide actions iteratively without recompiling the game project: nonprogrammers can modify and update the action files during game development and debugging. That is, planning ideas can be developed and validated offline. Moreover, if needed, C++ can always be generated from the text files and included in the code of your planner at any time during development.

Forward breadth-first search is one of the simplest search algorithms since it is easy to understand, extra data structures are not required prior to search, and short plans are found faster and with less memory than other appealing plan-graph-based planning procedures [Ghallab 04, Chapter 6]. Last, it is also a complete search procedure that returns the shortest plans; NPCs won't get redundant or useless actions to execute.

This chapter will first present the necessary steps before going into any optimization campaign, with examples specific to practical planning. Next, we will describe what can be optimized in practical planning, focusing on practical planning data structures that lead to both runtime and memory footprint improvements.

20.1.1 Required Background

The reader is expected to have a basic knowledge of GOAP [Orkin 04], predicate-based state and action representation [Cheng 05, Ghallab 04, Chapter 2], and basic search techniques (e.g., breadth-first search) as applied to planning [Ghallab 04, Chapter 4].

20.2 How Can You Optimize?

There are two main features to optimize in practical planning: time and memory. Ideally, we want to minimize both, but ultimately which one to focus on depends on the criteria of your game. Additionally, most algorithms can trade memory for time or vice versa.

20.2.1 Measure It!

Your first step is to get some code in order to measure both time and memory usage. The objective here is to instrument your practical planning code easily and quickly to show improvements in runtime and memory usage with respect to the allowed budgets.

Runtime measurement is not as easy as it sounds. Often, you'll get varied results even when the timings were performed under the same testing conditions. So an important aspect is to decide on a unit of time that has enough detail. Several timings under the same testing conditions should provide enough significant digits, with their numerical values being very close. If you're going to improve runtime by two orders of magnitude, you need to start with at least 4 significant digits. C++11 provides the flexible `std::chrono` library [Josuttis 13] that should fit most of your needs, but any platform-specific library providing a reliable high-resolution counter should do the job. Using microseconds is a good start.

With no (unpredictable) memory leak, memory measures are stable and must return the exact same value under the same testing conditions. The first step here is to measure memory overhead; for instance, an empty `std::vector` takes 16 bytes with Microsoft's Visual C++ 2013, while an empty `std::valarray` takes only 8 bytes if you can use it instead (they only store numeric values; they cannot grow but they can be resized), and there's no memory overhead for an instance of `std::array`, again if you can use it (they are C-style arrays: their size is fixed). The second step is to decide whether any measure is at all relevant; for instance, do you want to count distinct structures or the whole memory page that was allocated to store these structures?

Finally, you'll have to decide between using conditional compiling to switch on and off the call to measures, assuming the linker shall not include the unnecessary measurement code when switched off, or a specific version of your practical planner that shall have to be synchronized with further updated versions of the planner.

20.2.2 Design Valuable Tests!

The second step is to design a set of planning tests.

A first set of planning tests is necessary in order to confirm the planner generates correct plans, that is, plans that are solutions to the planning problems of your game. If your planner uses a complete search procedure such as breadth-first search, the correct plans should also be the shortest ones. By running your planner against these gaming problems, your objective is to show this planner can be used in your game. Do not consider only planning problems related to your game, because these problems certainly are too small to stress the full power of a GOAP-like planner. On one hand, a GOAP-like planner generates less than one plan per second per NPC on average, and on another hand, these plans are very short, say, at most four actions. Consequently, a second set of complex planning tests is needed to show any improvement in the optimization process. Runtime for such complex tests can be up to several minutes, whereas in-game planning runtime, it is at most several milliseconds. There are two kinds of complex tests: scaling tests and competition tests.

First, scaling tests provide an increasing number of one specific game object: box, creature, location, vehicle, weapon, and so forth. Solution plans to scaling tests can be short, and plan length is expected to be the same for all of the scaling tests; the idea is to provide more objects of one kind than would ever happen in a gaming situation so that the branching factor in the search space explodes, although the solution is the same. For instance, and this is valid for a forward state space GOAP-like procedure, take an in-game planning problem such that the goal situation involves only one box; assume that this box, say box-1, has to be picked up at one location and moved to another location. Then build an initial situation with increasing number of boxes: box-2, box-3, and so on, although box-1 is still the only box that appears in the goal solution. As the planner can pick up one box, it shall try to pick up and then move each box until the goal solution, which only requires box-1, is reached.

Second, competition tests are complex problems whose objective is to swallow a lot of computing resources with the help of a high branching factor and a solution with a long sequence of actions [IPC 14]. For instance, it is now time to move several boxes to the final location. This requires that you allow for picking up and moving only one box at a time and do not impose priorities between boxes. There are consequently many solutions of the exact same length. Each of these solutions reflects the order in which the boxes reach the goal location, thus entailing a huge search space.

Of course, if any updated version of the planning code shows a performance decrease against these planning problems, then this update is not an improvement.

20.2.3 Use Profilers!

There is no way to escape the use of profilers.

With the first two steps, you are able to show your practical planner is usable for your game and that your latest code update is either an improvement or else a bad idea. But how are you going to improve more, avoid bad ideas, or discover unexpected and eventually fruitful paths? Runtime and memory profilers are here to help.

On the contrary to the quick and easy first two steps that both are matters of days, this third step is a matter of weeks and months. Either you use professional tools (e.g., Intel® VTunes™ and IBM® Rational® Purify Plus that both allow to profile source code and binaries) or else you'll need to develop specific in-game profiling tools [Rabin 00, Lung 11]. Using professional tools requires mastering them, while making your own definitively requires development time. Either way, an investment of time will need to be made.

By reporting where the computing resources go, these tools tell you where to focus your improvement effort, and this is invaluable. If, on this improvement path, you reach a point where no part of your code seems to stand out as a candidate for improvement, then, beyond changing the profiling scheme and counters and running the tests again, it might be time to settle down and think of your planning data structures and your planning algorithms.

20.3 Practical Planning Data Structures

From a far viewpoint, anything can be optimized, from parsing the action text files to the data structure holding the solution to the planning problem. There is also the planning domain (how actions are encoded) and the planning problems (how states, either initial or goal, are encoded) using properties of your game world [Cheng 05, pp. 342–343]. For instance, you may not wish to represent the details of navigation from one location to another (e.g., navigating into a building, unlocking, and opening doors, avoiding obstacles) or the necessary actions to solve a puzzle in the planning problem; instead, encode only one action that magically reaches the goal location or magically solves the puzzle; then, delegate the execution of this action to a specific routine. Our focus here is different.

From a closer viewpoint, we learn from computational complexity that time complexity cannot be strictly less than space complexity [Garey 79, p. 170]; that is, at best, the computation time shall grow (with respect to a given parameter, e.g., the number of predicates) as the amount of memory needed for this computation, but never less. Consequently, you can design better algorithms to achieve better runtimes, but you can also design better data structures and start with shrinking memory: use as less memory as you can and use it as best as you can [Rabin 11].

First, make sure to choose the smallest structure that supports the features you need. Then, avoid multiple copies of these structures by storing information only once, and share it everywhere it is needed [Noble 01, pp. 182–190]. For instance, the action text files may contain several occurrences of the same identifier; when reading the first occurrence of this identifier, push it in an std::vector and share its position:

```
std::vector<Identifier> theIdentifiers;

size_t AddIdentifier(Identifier& id)
{
    size_t position = theIdentifiers.size();
    theIdentifiers.push_back(id);
    return position;
}
```

Of course, the next occurrence of `id` in the text file must not be pushed at the back of `theIdentifiers` but must be retrieved in `theIdentifiers` in order to share its position. So you may want instead to hash identifiers in an `std::unordered_map`, storing an integer value at the hashed position, and increment this value each time a new identifier is added to the table:

```
std::unordered_map<Identifier, size_t> theIdentifiers;

size_t AddIdentifier(Identifier& id)
{
    size_t position = theIdentifiers.size();
    theIdentifiers[id] = position;
    return position;
}
```

Lookup and sharing is then achieved through an `iterator`:

```
size_t shared_position;
std::unordered_map<Identifier, size_t>::iterator it;

it = theIdentifiers.find(id);
if (theIdentifiers.end() == it)
  shared_position = AddIdentifier(id);
else
  shared_position = it->second;
```

When the parsing of the action text file ends, we know exactly how many distinct identifiers are in the action text file and thus can allocate an array and move the identifiers from the hash table to their position in the array. More space can be saved as soon as we know the number of distinct identifiers: that is, use an `unsigned char`, instead of `size_t` in the aforementioned code, to share the positions when there are less than 256 identifiers for your planning problems, and so on.

Finally, consider a custom memory allocator (even for the STL [Isensee 03]) to access memory quicker than the classical memory allocation routines (e.g., `malloc`). Several high-performance memory allocators are available [Berger 14, Lazarov 08, Lea 12, Masmano 08] with various licensing schemes. Try them or any other one before embarking into developing your own.

Assuming that predicates can share their position to other planning data structures, the rest of this section discusses the use of the sharing pattern [Noble 01, pp. 182–190] to actions, plans, and states.

20.3.1 Actions

An action is made of two sets of predicates, in the spirit of IF/THEN rules [Wilhelm 08]: the set of preconditions predicates and the set of postcondition predicates (effects). A predicate can only occur in both sets if and only if it is negative (prefixed by `not`) in one set and positive in the other set. For instance, the positive predicate `hold(gun)` can appear as a precondition of the action `Drop` if the negative predicate `not(hold(gun))` is one of its effects; accordingly (i.e., symmetrically), `hold(gun)` can be an effect of the action `Take` if `not(hold(gun))` is one of its preconditions.

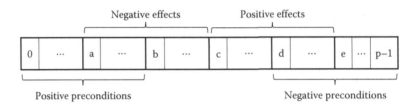

Figure 20.1

Action predicates occur only once when preconditions and effects overlap.

Assume an array of shared positions of predicates, ranging from 0 to (p − 1). Then the action predicates can be ordered in the array so that they occur only once:

- Let a, b, c, d, e, and p such that $0 \leq a \leq b \leq c \leq d \leq e \leq (p - 1)$.
- [0, a − 1] is the range of positive preconditions.
- [a, b − 1] is the range of positive preconditions that occur as negative effects.
- [b, c − 1] is the range of negative effects.
- [c, d − 1] is the range of positive effects.
- [d, e − 1] is the range of positive effects that occur as negative preconditions.
- [e, p − 1] is the range of negative preconditions.

Consequently, preconditions are in the range [0, b − 1] and in the range [d, p − 1], and effects are in the range [a, e − 1] as illustrated in Figure 20.1.

For instance, the positive predicate `hold(gun)` of the action `Drop` shall occur in the range [a, b − 1], whereas it shall occur in the range [d, e − 1] for the action `Take` (which is detailed in a following section).

Moreover, an action has parameters that are shared among its predicates; for instance, both the actions `Drop` and `Take` have an `object` as a parameter for the predicate `hold`. If we further constrain all predicate parameters to be gathered in the set of parameters of an action, then all predicate parameters only need to be integer values pointing to the positions of the parameters of their action; the type `unsigned char` can be used for these integer values if we limit the number of parameters to 256, which is safe.

20.3.2 Plans

A GOAP-like plan is a totally ordered set of actions. An action is uniquely represented by an action identifier, for example, `Drop`, and its parameters (once they all have a value), which is called the action signature, for example, `Drop(gun)`. An action signature is a good candidate for sharing its position in an array. Consequently, a plan is an array of shared positions of action signatures.

As plans grow during the search, using an `std::vector` is practical, while keeping in mind the memory overhead for `std::vectors`. Assume the 16 bytes of Visual C++ 2013, at most 256 action signatures, and a maximum plan length of 4 actions [F.E.A.R. 05]: `std::array<unsigned char,4>` (4 bytes) can safely replace `std::vector<unsigned char>` (at least 16 bytes and at most 20 bytes for plans of length 4). Assuming 65,535 action signatures and a maximum plan length of 8 actions, then `std::array<short,8>` still saves memory over `std::vector<short>`.

　　　　　　　　　　　　　　　　　　　　　　　　20. Optimizing Practical Planning for Game AI

20.3.3 States

The planning problem defines the initial and the goal states. Forward breadth-first search applies actions to states in order to produce new states, and hopefully the goal state. Indeed, if the preconditions of an action, say A, are satisfied in a state, say s, then the resulting state, say r, is obtained by first applying set difference (−) with the negated effects of A and second to s and then by applying set union (+) with the positive effects of A: r = (s − (negative effects of A)) + (positive effects of A).

States are made of predicates, and as for actions, it is obvious to substitute predicates by their shared positions.

Set operations can be easily implemented with the member operations of `std::set` or `std::unordered _ set`. The memory overhead of these STL containers is of 12 bytes for the former and 40 bytes for the latter with Visual C++ 2013; if you want to store all generated states in order to check whether the resulting state r has previously been generated, then 1000 states means 12 kb or else 40 kb of memory overhead.

Set operations can also be implemented with bitwise operations where one bit is set to 1 if the predicate belongs to the state and set to 0 otherwise. `std::bitset` provides the bitwise machinery so that a 1000 states over (at most) 256 predicates would require 32 kb.

Runtime measurement can help you make the final decision, but combining the two representations provides an interesting trade-off. For instance, you may want to use an `std::array`, which has no memory overhead, to represent a state and convert it to an `std::bitset` when computing the resulting state; then, convert the resulting state back to an `std:array`. In this case, 10 shared positions of predicates in a state on average means 10 kb for a 1000 states, which is less than 12 kb, while 32 kb would allow for the storing of more than 3000 states.

20.4 Practical Planning Algorithms

Runtime profiling should report at least the two following hot spots for forward breadth-first search with actions as text files: (1) checking which predicates of a given state can satisfy the preconditions of an action and (2) unifying the precondition predicates of an action with predicates of a given state in order to assign a value to each parameter of this action (consequently, we can compute the resulting state).

20.4.1 Iterating over Subsets of State Predicates

First, consider the following description for action `Take`, stated with simple logic expressions (conjunction and negation) and written with keywords (`:action`, `:parameters`, `:preconditions`, `:effects`), a query mark to prefix variable identifier, and parenthesis, to ease parsing and the reading of the action:

```
(:action Take
    :parameters (location ?l, creature ?c, object ?o)
    :preconditions (not(hold(?object, ?c))
                    and at-c(?l, ?c)
                    and at-o(?l, ?o))
    :effects (not(at-o(?l, ?o)) and hold(?object, ?c))
)
```

Assume the shared positions of the predicates of the action Take are the following:

Predicate	Shared Position
at-o(?l, ?c)	3
at-c(?l, ?o)	7
hold(?object, ?c)	9

If predicates are shared in the order they are read from the action file, the values of these shared positions means at-o(?l, ?o) is the third predicate that was read from the file, while at-c(?l, ?c) and hold(?object, ?c) were the seventh and ninth, respectively. With these shared positions, the array (refer to Figure 20.1) representing the 3 predicates of the action Take is shown in Figure 20.2.

Second, consider the following initial state:

```
(:initial (at-c(loc1, c1) and at-c(loc1, c2)
           and at-c(loc2, c3) and at-c(loc3, c4)
           and at-o(loc1, o1) and at-o(loc1, o3)
           and at-o(loc3, o4) and at-o(loc5, o2)
           and at-o(loc5, o5))
)
```

For instance, the action represented by the action signature Take(loc1,c1,o1) can be applied to the initial state because all its preconditions are satisfied in the initial state. But there are four more actions that can be applied to this initial state, represented by the four following action signatures: Take(loc1,c1,o3), Take(loc1,c2,o1), Take(loc1,c2,o3), and Take(loc3,c4,o4).

We can first note that each positive precondition identifier must match at least one state predicate identifier. Second, we can note that no state predicate identifier can be a negative precondition identifier. When these two quick tests pass, we can further test the applicability of an action, pushing further the use of the predicate identifiers.

To test the applicability of action Take in any state and in particular in the initial state earlier, we can sort the predicates of the state according to their identifier (refer to Figure 20.2). It is consequently possible to test only 20 pairs (4 instances of at-c × 5 instances of at-o) of predicates from the initial states instead of the 36 pairs (choosing any two elements in a set of 9 elements = (9 × 8)/2 = 36 pairs), which can be built from the initial state.

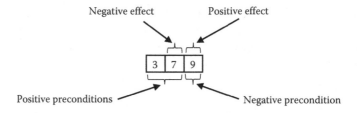

Figure 20.2

Three predicates of the action Take. Based on the key in Figure 20.1, this three-digit array can be decoded as a = 1, b = c = d = 2, and e = p = 3.

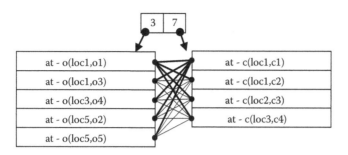

Figure 20.3

Sorting state predicates with respect to their identifiers.

In Figure 20.3, the top array containing three and seven represents the positive preconditions of action `Take`. We then iterate over the predicates of the initial state. If an initial state predicate has the same predicate identifier as a precondition predicate, then this initial state predicate is pushed at the back of the appropriate column. If the identifier of an initial state predicate does not correspond to any identifier of a precondition predicate, then this initial state predicate is ignored. Finally, iterating in both columns, we can make pairs of predicates as indicated in Figure 20.3.

Note that if the language of the actions file allows predicates with the same identifier but with a different number of parameters, then the number of parameters must also be checked to build both columns in Figure 20.3.

There are various ways of achieving the iterations over both columns. For instance, we begin by forming the two-digit number made by the size of the columns in Figure 20.3: 54. Then we start with the two-digit value 00 and increase the rightmost digit; when this value reaches 4, we rewrite the two-digit number to 10 and increase it until the rightmost digit reaches 4 again. We then rewrite this number to 20 and so on until 54 is reached. This procedure builds the following list of two-digit numbers: 00, 01, 02, 03, 10, 11, 12, 13, 20, 21, 22, 23, 30, 31, 32, 33, 40, 41, 42, and 43. Alternatively, we can start from 43 and decrease until 00 is reached, thus producing the two-digit numbers of the previous list in the reverse order. Each of these 20 two-digit numbers can be used to access a position in both columns in order to make a pair of state predicates. The iterating procedure in Listing 20.1 works for any number of positive preconditions.

20.4.2 Recording Where the Action Parameters Occur in the Action Predicates

The procedure in Listing 20.1 generates tuples such that each state predicate identifier matches the identifier of a precondition predicate. Consequently, the unification procedure need only checking whether the state predicate parameters unify with the action parameters.

We know from Figure 20.3 that the positive precondition predicate whose shared position is 3, that is, `at-o(?l,?o)`, is unified with state predicate `at-o(loc5,o5)`, and then the parameter `?l` of action `Take` gets the value `loc5`, and the parameter `?o` of action `Take` gets the value `o5`. The positive precondition predicate whose shared position is 7,

Listing 20.1. Iterating procedure to find all pairs of state predicates.

For each predicate of the current state
  Push the predicate back to the list which corresponds to its identifier
End For each;
Make the number n with as many digits as there are non-empty lists;
Set each digit of n to 0;
Repeat
  Access each of the lists with respect to the digits of n and
    make the tuple of predicates of s;
  Increase the least significant digit of n by 1;
  For each digit d of n, starting with the least significant digit,
    If the digit d is equal to the size of the dth list **Then**
      If d is the most significant digit of n **Then**
        Break the enclosing **For each** loop;
      End if;
      Reset digit d to 0;
      Increase digit (d+1) of n by 1
    Else
      Break the enclosing **For each** loop;
    End if;
  End For each;
Until the value of n is made of the size of the n lists.

that is, at-c(?1,?c), with the parameter ?1 equal to loc5, must now unify with state predicate at-c(loc3,c4). This fails because loc3 is different from loc5.

The idea is to record all the positions where an action parameter occurs in positive precondition predicates and then check that the parameters at these positions in the state predicates have the same value. For instance, the parameter ?1 of action Take occurs as the first parameter of both positive precondition predicates. If the values at these positions in the state predicates are equal (which can be trivially achieved by testing the value of the first position against all other positions), then we can check for the equality of the occurrences of the next parameter. Recording the positions can be achieved once for all when parsing the action files.

20.5 Conclusion

A Visual C++ 2013 project is available from the book's website (http://www.gameaipro. com), which implements a practical planner with the features (i.e., actions as text files and forward breadth-first search) and the data structures and algorithms described in this chapter.

Although planning is known to be very hard in theory, even the simplest planning algorithm can be implemented in a practical planner, which can be used for your gaming purposes, providing you focus on shrinking both memory and runtime requirements.

Quick runtime and memory measurement routines, as well as relevant testing and systematic profiling, can hopefully help you succeed in making planning practical for your gaming purposes.

References

[Berger 14] Berger, E. 2014. The hoard memory allocator. http://emeryberger.github.io/Hoard/ (accessed May 26, 2014).

[Cheng 05] Cheng, J. and Southey, F. 2005. Implementing practical planning for game AI. In *Game Programming Gems 5*, ed. K. Pallister, pp. 329–343. Hingham, MA: Charles River Media.

[Deus Ex 3 DC 13] Deus Ex Human Revolution—Director's Cut. Square Enix, 2013.

[F.E.A.R. 05] F.E.A.R.—First Encounter Assault Recon. Vivendi Universal, 2005.

[Garey 79] Garey, M. and Johnson, D. 1979. *Computers and Intractability: A Guide to the Theory of NP-Completeness*. New York: W.H. Freeman & Co Ltd.

[Ghallab 04] Ghallab, M., Nau, D., and Traverso, P. 2004. *Automated Planning: Theory and Practice*. San Francisco, CA: Morgan Kaufmann.

[IPC 14] International Planning Competition. 2014. http://ipc.icaps-conference.org/ (accessed May 28, 2014).

[Isensee 03] Isensee, P. 2003. Custom STL allocators. In *Game Programming Gems 3*, ed. D. Treglia, pp. 49–58. Hingham, MA: Charles River Media.

[Josuttis 13] Josuttis, N. 2013. *The C++ Standard Library*. Upper Saddle River, NJ: Pearson Education.

[Lazarov 08] Lazarov, D. 2008. High performance heap allocator. In *Game Programming Gems 7*, ed. S. Jacobs, pp. 15–23. Hingham, MA: Charles River Media.

[Lea 12] Lea, D. 2012. A memory allocator (2.8.6). ftp://g.oswego.edu/pub/misc/malloc.c (accessed May 26, 2014).

[Lung 11] Lung, R. 2011. Design and implementation of an in-game memory profiler. In *Game Programming Gems 8*, ed. A. Lake, pp. 402–408. Boston, MA: Course Technology.

[Masmano 08] Masmano, M., Ripoli, I., Balbastre, P., and Crespo, A. 2008. A constant-time dynamic storage allocator for real-time systems. *Real-Time Systems*, 40(2): 149–179.

[Noble 01] Noble, J. and Weir, C. 2001. *Small Software Memory: Patterns for Systems with Limited Memory*. Harlow, U.K.: Pearson Education Ltd.

[Orkin 04] Orkin, J. 2004. Applying goal-oriented action planning to games. In *AI Game Programming Wisdom 2*, ed. S. Rabin, pp. 217–227. Hingham, MA: Charles River Media.

[Rabin 00] Rabin, S. 2000. Real-time in-game profiling. In *Game Programming Gems*, ed. M. DeLoura, pp. 120–130. Boston, MA: Charles River Media.

[Rabin 11] Rabin, S. 2011. Game optimization through the lens of memory and data access. In *Game Programming Gems 8*, ed. A. Lake, pp. 385–392. Boston, MA: Course Technology.

[Tomb Raider 13] Tomb Raider—Definitive Edition. Square Enix, 2013.

[Wilhelm 08] Wilhelm, D. 2008. Practical logic-based planning. In *AI Game Programming Wisdom 4*, ed. S. Rabin, pp. 355–403. Boston, MA: Course Technology.

21

Modular AI

Kevin Dill and Christopher Dragert

21.1 Introduction

Repetition is everywhere in AI. The same patterns, the same fragments of code, the same chunks of data, the same subdecisions get used over and over again in decision after decision after decision. As a general rule, when we as software engineers see repetition we try to encapsulate it: put it in a procedure, put it in a class, or build some abstraction so that there is only a single instance of that repeated pattern. This encapsulation can now be reused rather than rewriting it for each new use-case. We see this approach throughout software engineering: in procedures, in classes, in design patterns, in C++ templates and macros, and in data-driven design—to name just a few examples.

Reducing repetition has numerous advantages. It decreases the executable size. It decreases the number of opportunities to introduce a bug, and increases the number of ways in which the code is tested. It avoids the situation where you fix a bug or make an improvement in one place but not others. It saves time during implementation, allowing you to write new code rather than rewriting something that already exists. It allows you to build robust, feature-rich abstractions that can perform complex operations which would take too much time to implement if you were only going to use them once. Beyond all of these incremental advantages, however, it also offers something fundamental. It allows you to take a chunk of code in all of its nitty-gritty, detail-oriented glory, and wrap it up into a human-level concept that can be reused and repurposed throughout your project.

It allows you to work closer to the level of granularity at which you naturally think, and at which your designers naturally think, rather than at the level which is natural to the machine. It changes, for example:

```
d = sqrt(pow((a.x - b.x), 2) + pow((a.y - b.y), 2));
```

into:

```
d = Distance(a, b);
```

The challenge with AI, however, is that while there are often aspects of a decision that are similar to other decisions, there are also invariably aspects that are quite different. The AI might measure the distance between two objects both to determine whether to shoot at something and to determine where to eat lunch, but the objects that are evaluated and the way that distance is used in the larger decision is certain to be different (unless you are building a nonplayer character (NPC) that likes to shoot at restaurants and eat its enemies). As a result, while the distance function itself is a standard part of most math libraries, there is a much larger body of code involved in distance-based decisions that is more difficult to encapsulate and reuse.

Modular AI is fundamentally about this transition. It is about enabling you to rapidly specify decision-making logic by plugging together modular components that represent human-level concepts. It is about building up a collection of these modular components, where each component is implemented once but used over and over, throughout the AI for your current game, and on into the AI for your next game and the game after that. It is about enabling you to spend most of your time thinking about human-sized concepts, to build up from individual concepts (e.g., distance, line of sight, moving, firing a weapon) to larger behaviors (taking cover, selecting and engaging a target) to entire performances (ranged weapon combat), and then to reuse those pieces, with appropriate customization, elsewhere. It is an approach that will allow you to create your decision-making logic more quickly, change it more easily, and reuse it more broadly, all while working more reliably and generating fewer bugs because the underlying code is being used more heavily and thus tested more robustly, and also because new capabilities added for one situation immediately become available for use elsewhere as part of the reusable component they improved.

This chapter will first discuss the theoretical underpinnings of modular AI and relate them to broadly accepted concepts from software engineering, and then describe in detail the Game AI Architecture (GAIA). GAIA is a modular architecture, developed at Lockheed Martin Rotary and Mission Systems, that has been used to drive behavior across a number of very different projects in a number of very different game and simulation engines, including (but not limited to) both educational games and training simulations. Its roots go back to work on animal AI at Blue Fang Games, on boss AI for an action game at Mad Doc Software, and on ambient human AI at Rockstar Games.

21.1.1 Working with this Chapter

This chapter goes into great depth, and different readers might be interested in different aspects of the discussion. If your primary interest is in the big ideas behind modular AI and how the modular pieces work together, your focus should be on Sections 21.2, 21.5, and 21.6. If you are interested in an approach that you can take away right now and use in an existing architecture, without starting over from scratch, then you should consider implementing just considerations (Sections 21.5.1 and 21.6). Finally, if you are interested in a full architecture that can be reused across many projects, across many game engines, and which allows you to rapidly configure your AI in a modular way, then the full chapter is for you!

21.2 Theoretical Underpinnings

Modular AI, and modular approaches in general, seek to raise the level of abstraction of development. Rather than focus on algorithms and code, a good modular solution leads to a focus on AI behaviors and how they fit together, abstracting away the implementation details. The question is how this can be done safely and correctly, while still giving designers and developers the fine-grained control needed to elicit the intended behaviors.

Success in modular AI development is driven by the same principles found in good software development: encapsulation, polymorphism, loose coupling, clear operational semantics, and management of complexity. Each of these familiar concepts gains new meaning in a modular context.

Modules themselves encapsulate a unit of AI functionality. Good modules follow the "Goldilocks Rule": not too big, not too small, but sized just right. Large modules that include multiple capabilities inhibit reuse—what if only part of the functionality is needed for a new AI? Modules that are too small do not do enough to raise the level of abstraction. The goal is to capture AI functionality at the same level that a designer uses to reason about NPCs in your game. Then, the development problem shifts to selecting and integrating the behaviors and capabilities needed for a new NPC, rather than implementing those capabilities from scratch, which is a highly appropriate level of abstraction.

Using modules in this fashion requires that module reuse to be safe. For this, module encapsulation must be strictly enforced. Preventing spaghetti interactions between modules ensures that each module can run correctly in isolation. This is essential for reuse—even subtle dependencies between modules quickly become problematic.

Encapsulation leads naturally to the creation of a module interface. Much like an API, a module interface describes exactly how to interact with that module. It shows the inputs that it can accept, the outputs that it provides, and details the parameters that are exposed for customization of module behavior when applied to a specific AI. With an explicit interface, handling dependencies between behaviors becomes a much simpler problem of connecting the inputs and outputs needed to properly express the behavior. Since each module is properly encapsulated, the results of adding and removing new modules become predictable.

Polymorphism arises as a result of this loose coupling. Imagine a module tasked with fleeing from an enemy. As a bite-sized module, it could perform the checks and tests needed to find an appropriate flee destination, and then send off a move output. The module that receives this output no longer matters. One AI can use a certain type of move module, while a different AI can use another. The exact type of move module should not matter much. Complicating factors, like "is my NPC on a bicycle," or "is she on a horse," and so on, can all be handled by the move module, or by other submodules. This keeps each module cleanly focused on a single functional purpose while ensuring that similar behaviors are not repeated across modules.

21.3 GAIA Overview

GAIA is a modular, extensible, reusable toolset for specifying procedural decision-making logic (i.e., AI behavior). GAIA emphasizes the role of the game designer in creating decision-making logic, while still allowing the resulting behavior to be flexible and responsive to the moment-to-moment situation in the application.

Taking those points more slowly, GAIA is:

- A library of tools that can be used to specify procedural decision-making logic (or "AI behavior").
- Focused on providing *authorial control*. In other words, the goal of GAIA is not to create a true artificial intelligence that can decide what to do on its own, but rather to provide a human author with the tools to specify decisions that will deliver the intended experience while still remaining flexible enough to handle varied and unexpected situations.
- *Modular*, meaning that behavior is typically constructed by plugging together pre-defined components. Experience has shown that this approach greatly improves the speed with which behavior can be specified and iterated on.
- *Extensible*, making it easy to add new components to the library, or to change the behavior of an existing component.
- *Reusable*, meaning that GAIA has been designed from the ground up with reuse in mind. This includes reuse of both code and data, and reuse within the current project, across future projects, and even across different game engines.

GAIA is data driven: behavior is specified in XML files and then loaded by the code at runtime. This chapter will generally refer to the XML as the *configuration* or the *data* and the C++ as the *implementation* or the *code*. For simplicity, this chapter will also use the term *NPC* to denote GAIA-controlled entities, *PC* to denote player-controlled entities, and *character* to denote entities that may be either NPCs or PCs.

21.3.1 GAIA Control Flow

GAIA makes decisions by working its way down a tree of decision makers (*reasoners*) that is in many ways similar to Damian Isla's original vision of a Behavior Tree (BT) (Isla 2005). As in a BT, different reasoners can use different approaches to decision-making, which gives the architecture a flexibility that is not possible in more homogenous hierarchical approaches (e.g., hierarchical finite-state machines, teleoreactive programming, hierarchical task network planners, etc.).

Each reasoner picks from among its *options*. The options contain *considerations*, which are used by the reasoner to decide which option to pick, and *actions*, which are executed if the option is selected. Actions can be *concrete*, meaning that they represent things that the controlled character should actually do (e.g., move, shoot, speak a line of dialog, cower in fear, etc.), or *abstract*, meaning that they contain more decision-making logic.

The most common abstract action is the `AIAction_Subreasoner`, which contains another reasoner (with its own options, considerations, and actions). Subreasoner actions are the mechanism GAIA uses to create its hierarchical structure. When an option that contains a subreasoner is selected, that subreasoner will start evaluating its own options and select one to execute. That option may contain concrete actions or may, in turn, contain yet another subreasoner action.

Options can also contain more than one action, which allows them to have multiple concrete actions, subreasoners, or a combination of both, all operating in parallel.

21.3.2 GAIA Implementation Concepts

Reasoners, options, considerations, and actions are all examples of *conceptual abstractions*. Conceptual abstractions are the basic types of objects that make up a modular AI. Each conceptual abstraction has an *interface* that defines it, and a set of *modular components* (or just *components*) that implement that interface. As discussed above, there are multiple different types of reasoners, for example, but all of the reasoners—that is, all of the modular components that implement the reasoner conceptual abstraction—share the same interface. Thus the surrounding code does not need to know what types of components it has. The reasoner, for example, does not need to know what particular types of considerations are being used to evaluate an option, or how those considerations are configured—it only needs to know how to work with the consideration interface in order to get the evaluation that it needs. This is the key idea behind modular AI: identify the basic parts of the AI (*conceptual abstractions*), declare an interface for each abstraction, and then define reusable *modular components* that implement that interface.

Modular components form the core of modular AI reuse—each type of component is implemented once but used many times. To make this work, each type of component needs to know how to load itself from the configuration, so that all of the parameters that define the functionality of a particular instance of a modular component can be defined in data.

Continuing with the distance example from the introduction, GAIA makes distance evaluations reusable by providing the `Distance` consideration. The configuration of a particular `Distance` consideration specifies the positions to measure the distance between, as well as how that distance should be evaluated (Should it prefer closer? Farther? Does it have to be within a particular range?). For example, a sniper selecting a target to shoot at might use a `Distance` consideration to evaluate each potential target. This consideration might be configured to only allow the sniper to shoot at targets that are more than 50 m and less than 500 m away, with a preference for closer targets. This consideration could then be combined with other considerations that measure whether the prospective target is friend or enemy, how much cover the target has, whether it is a high-value target (such as an officer), and so on. What is more, the consideration does not work in isolation—it makes use of other conceptual abstractions in its configuration. For instance, the two positions are specified using *targets*, and the way the distance should be combined with other considerations is specified using a *weight function*. Targets and weight functions are two of the other conceptual abstractions in GAIA.

One advantage of this approach is that it is highly extensible. As development progresses and you discover new factors that should be weighed into a decision, you can create new types of considerations to evaluate those factors and simply drop them in. Because they share the same interface as all the other considerations, nothing else needs to change. Not only does this make iterating on the AI behavior much faster, it also decreases the chance that you will introduce a bug (because all changes are localized to the consideration being added, which can be tested in isolation). Consequently, it is safer to make more aggressive changes later in the development cycle, allowing you to really polish the AI late in development once gameplay has been hammered out and QA is giving real feedback on what you have built.

This ability to rapidly specify and then easily reuse common functionality greatly reduces the amount of time it takes to specify behavior, generally paying back the cost of implementation within weeks. We have used modular AI with great success on several projects where there were only a few months to implement the entire AI—including one game whose AI was implemented in less than 4 months that went on to sell millions of copies.

21.3.3 An Example Character: The Sniper

Throughout this chapter, we will use as our example a sniper character that is based on, but not identical to, a character that was built for a military application. Broadly speaking, the sniper should wait until there are enemies in its kill zone (which happens to be an outdoor marketplace), and then take a shot every minute or two as long as there are still enemies in the marketplace to engage, but only if (a) it is not under attack and (b) it has a clear line of retreat. If it is under attack then it tries to retreat, but if its line of retreat has been blocked then it will start actively fighting back, engaging targets as rapidly as it can (whether they are in the kill zone or not). The overall structure for this configuration is shown in Figure 21.1.

At the top level of its decision hierarchy, our sniper has only four options to choose between: snipe at a target in the kill zone, retreat, fight back when engaged, or hide and wait until one of the other options is available. The decision between these options is fairly cut-and-dried, so a fairly simple reasoner should work. GAIA includes a `RuleBased` reasoner that works much like a selection node in a BT—that is, it simply evaluates its options in the order in which they were specified and takes the first one that is valid given the current situation. In this case, a `RuleBased` reasoner could be set up as follows:

- If the sniper is under fire and its line of retreat is clear, retreat.
- If the sniper is under fire, fight back.

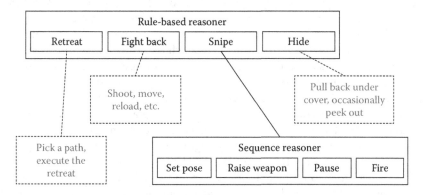

Figure 21.1

Overall structure for a sniper AI. Aspects of the AI that are not fully defined are shown with dotted lines.

- If the sniper's line of retreat is clear, there is a valid target in the kill zone, and a minute or two has elapsed since the sniper's last shot, snipe.
- Hide.

None of those options are likely to contain concrete actions. Retreat, for example, will require the AI to pick a route, move along that route, watch for enemies, react to enemies along the way, and so forth. Fight back requires the AI to pick targets, pick positions to fight from, aim and fire its weapon, reload, and so on. Hide requires it to pull back out of sight and then periodically peer out as if checking whether targets have become available. Thus, once the top-level reasoner has selected an option (such as Snipe), that option's subreasoner will evaluate its own options. In Figure 21.1, we see that the Snipe option, for example, uses a `Sequence` reasoner to step through the process of taking a shot by first getting into the appropriate pose (e.g., the "prone" pose), then raising its weapon, pausing (to simulate aiming), and finally firing.

21.4 GAIA Infrastructure

Before delving into the different conceptual abstractions and modular components, it is helpful to have an understanding of the surrounding infrastructure. This section provides an overview of the major singletons, data stores, and other objects which, while not themselves modular, support evaluation of and communication between the modular components.

21.4.1 The `AIString` Class

Strings are tremendously useful, but they also take up an unreasonable amount of space and are slow to compare. Many solutions to this problem exist; GAIA's is to use the djb2 hash function (http://www.cse.yorku.ca/~oz/hash.html) to generate a 64 bit hash for the strings and then to keep a global string table that contains all of the raw strings (as `std::strings`). This lets GAIA do constant time comparisons and store copies of strings in 64 bits. It also lets GAIA downcase the string when it is hashed, so that comparisons are case insensitive (which makes them much more designer friendly). On the other hand, it has an up-front performance cost and makes a permanent copy of every string used (whether the string itself is temporary or not), so GAIA still uses `char*` and `std::string` in places where the `AIString` does not make sense (such as debug output).

Of note, no hash function is a guarantee. If you do take this approach, it is a very good idea to have an assert that checks for hash collisions; simply look in the string table each time you hash a string and ensuring that the stored string is the same as the one you just hashed.

21.4.2 Factories

GAIA uses factories to instantiate all of the modular objects that make up the AI. In other words, the portion of a configuration that defines a consideration, for example, will be contained within a single XML node. GAIA creates the actual C++ consideration object by passing that XML node (along with some supporting information, like a pointer to the NPC that this configuration will control) to the `AIConsiderationFactory`, which instantiates and initializes an object.of the appropriate type. GAIA's factory system was the topic of an earlier chapter in this book, so we will not repeat the details here (Dill 2016).

21.4.3 The `AIDataStore` Base Class

Data stores are `AIString`-indexed hash tables that can store data of any type. GAIA uses them as the basis for its blackboards and also all of its different types of entities. As a result, individual modular components can store, share, and retrieve information to and from the blackboards and/or entities without the rest of the AI having to know what is stored or even what type the information is. This allows data to be placed in the configuration that will be used by the game engine if an action is executed, for instance, or even for the game engine to pass data through to itself. Of course, it also allows AI components to share data with one another—we will see an example of this in the sniper configuration, below.

There are many ways to implement this sort of hash table, and GAIA's is not particularly special, so we will skip the implementation details. It is worth mentioning, however, that since the data stores are in essence of global memory, they run the risk of name collisions (that is, two different sets of components both trying to store data using the same name). With that said, experience has shown that as long as you have a reasonably descriptive naming convention, this is not normally a problem. Nevertheless, GAIA does have asserts in place to warn if the type of data stored is not the expected type. This will not catch every possible name collision, but it should catch a lot of them.

GAIA currently has two types of blackboards and three types of entities, described as follows.

21.4.3.1 The `AIBlackboard_Global` Data Store

The game has a single *global blackboard*, which can be used as a central repository for information that should be available to every AI component, regardless of what character that component belongs to or what side that character is on.

21.4.3.2 The `AIBlackboard_Brain` Data Store

Every AI-controlled character also has a blackboard built into its brain. The *brain blackboard* allows the components that make up that character's AI to communicate among themselves.

21.4.3.3 The `AIActor` Data Store

Every NPC is represented by an *actor*. The game stores all of the information that the AI will need about the character (e.g., its position, orientation, available weapons, etc.), and AI components can look that information up as needed. The actor also contains an `AIBrain`, which contains the top-level reasoner and all of the decision-making logic for that character.

On some projects, actors are used to represent every character, whether AI controlled or not. In these cases, actors that are not AI controlled may not have a brain or, if they switch back and forth between AI and player control, they will have a brain but it will be disabled when the AI is not in control.

21.4.3.4 The `AIContact` Data Store

As hinted above, there are two ways to keep track of what an NPC knows about the other characters in the game. The first is to use actors to represent every character and give the AI components in each NPC's brain direct access to the actors for other characters.

This works, but it either means that all NPCs will have perfect information, or that every AI component has to properly check whether they should know about a particular piece of information or not. Furthermore, even if the AI components make these checks, it still means that everything that they know is correct. This makes it much more difficult to, for example, allow the AI to know that an enemy exists but have an incorrect belief about its location.

The alternative is to have each NPC create a *contact* for every other character that it knows about, and store its knowledge of that NPC on the contact. Thus the contacts represent what the NPC knows about other characters in the game, whether that knowledge is correct or not. For example, imagine an RPG where the player steals a uniform in order to sneak past hostile guards. The guards would each have a contact that stores their knowledge of the player, and if the guards are fooled then that contact would list the player as being on their side even though he or she is actually an enemy. This allows each NPC to have its own beliefs about the characters that it is aware of, but it also means that the AI has to store a lot of redundant copies of the information for each character.

There is no single right answer here, which is why GAIA supports both approaches—the best one is the one that best supports the needs of the individual project. Using actors to represent all characters is simpler and more efficient when there is little uncertainty in the environment (or the behavior of the characters is not greatly affected by it), while using contacts is better when imperfect situational awareness plays an important role in the behavior of the NPCs.

21.4.3.5 The `AIThreat` Data Store

Threats represent things that an NPC knows about and should consider reacting to. They can include enemy characters (whether represented as actors or contacts), but may also include more abstract things such as recent explosions, or locations where bullets have impacted. This enables characters to react to the impact of a sniper's shot even if they do not actually know about the shooter, or to break out of cover based on where rounds are impacting rather than where they are being fired from, for example. Like contacts, threats are not used by every project, and are stored on the brain blackboard.

21.4.4 Singletons

Singletons provide managers that are globally accessible. You can access a singleton from anywhere in the codebase by simply calling the static `Get()` function for that class. You can also replace the default implementation of any singleton with a project-specific version (which must be a subclass) by calling `Set()`.

21.4.4.1 The `AIManager` Singleton

The *AI manager* is responsible for storing all of the actors. It also has an `Update()` function that the game should call every tick in order to tick the actors, and thus their brains.

21.4.4.2 The `AISpecificationManager` and `AIGlobalManager` Singletons

As we have said, GAIA is data driven. All of the decision-making for an NPC is stored in its configuration, in XML. The *specification manager* is responsible for loading, parsing, and storing all of the configurations. Then, when the game creates an NPC's brain, it specifies the name of the configuration that character should use.

Duplication can happen in data as well as in code. GAIA partially addresses this by allowing configurations to include *globals*, which are component specifications that can be reused within a configuration or across all configurations. The globals are stored by the *global manager*. Globals were discussed in the earlier chapter on factories (Dill 2016).

21.4.4.3 The `AIOutputManager` Singleton

Good debug output is critical to AI development. GAIA has the usual mix of log messages, warnings, errors, and asserts, along with "status text," which describes the current decision (and is suitable for, for example, displaying in-engine next to the NPC in question). The *output manager* is responsible for handling all of those messages, routing them to the right places, enabling/disabling them, and so forth.

21.4.4.4 The `AITimeManager` Singleton

Different game engines (and different games) handle in-game time in different ways. The *time manager* has a single function (`GetTime()`), and is used throughout the AI to implement things like cooldowns and maximum durations. The built-in implementation just gets system time from the CPU, but most projects implement their own time manager that provides in-game time instead.

21.4.4.5 The `AIBlackboard_Global` Singleton

As described above, the global blackboard is a shared memory space that can be used to pass information between the game and the AI, and/or between AI components. It is a singleton so that it will be globally accessible, and also so that projects can implement their own version which is more tightly coupled with the data being shared from the game engine if they wish.

21.4.4.6 The `AIRandomManager` Singleton

Random numbers are central to many games, both inside and outside of the AI. The *random manager* contains functions for getting random values. The default implementation uses the dual-LCG approach described by Jacopin elsewhere in this volume (Jacopin 2016), but as with other singletons individual projects can replace this with a custom implementation that uses some different RNG implementation if they so desire. For example, we have a unit test project whose RNG always returns 0, making it much easier to write deterministic tests.

21.5 Modular AI: Conceptual Abstractions and Modular Components

Conceptual abstractions define the base class types that the architecture supports. In other words, these abstractions define the interfaces that the rest of GAIA will use. A modular component is the counterpart, with each component providing a concrete implementation for a conceptual abstraction. This approach, where objects interact through well-defined interfaces, allows GAIA to provide an environment that supports loosely coupled modular composition untethered from specific implementations. The developer is free to think about types of abstractions that will produce desired behaviors, and then configure the implementation by reusing and customizing existing modular components, or by creating new components as necessary. This section will describe the major conceptual abstractions used by GAIA, provide examples of their use, and give their interfaces.

21.5.1 Considerations

Considerations are the single most useful conceptual abstraction. If you are uncertain about building a full modular AI, or are just looking for a single trick that you can use to improve your existing architecture, they are the place to start.

Considerations are used to represent each of the different factors that might be weighed together to make a decision. At the core, each type of consideration provides a way to evaluate the suitability of an action with respect to the factor being considered. Listing 21.1 shows the consideration interface in full.

Listing 21.1. The consideration interface.

```
class AIConsiderationBase
{
public:
    // Load the configuration.
    virtual bool Init(const AICreationData& cd) = 0;

    // Called once per decision cycle, allows the
    // consideration to evaluate the situation and determine
    // what to return.
    virtual void Calculate() = 0;

    // These are GAIA's weight values. They return the
    // results computed by Calculate().
    virtual float GetAddend() const;
    virtual float GetMultiplier() const;
    virtual float GetRank() const;

    // Certain considerations need to know if/when they are
    // selected or deselected.
    virtual void Select()   {}
    virtual void Deselect() {}
};
```

To understand how these work in action, let's take a look at the sniper's decision to snipe at an enemy. It will only select this option if:

- The line of retreat is clear.
- There is a target in the kill zone.
- It has been "a minute or two" since the last time the sniper took a shot.

Building the configuration for this option requires three considerations: one for each of the bullet items above. Each one is a modular component that implements the consideration interface.

First, an `EntityExists` consideration is used to check whether there are any enemies in the area that the sniper will retreat through. The `EntityExists` consideration goes through all of the contacts (or all of the actors, or all of the threats, depending on how it is configured) to see whether there is at least one which meets some set of constraints. In this case, the constraints are that the entity must be an enemy and that it must be inside the area that the sniper plans to escape through. That area is defined using a region, which is another conceptual abstraction (described below). This first consideration vetoes the option (i.e., does not allow it to be picked) if there is an enemy blocking the line of retreat, otherwise it allows the option to execute (but the other considerations may still veto it).

Next, the sniper needs to pick a contact to shoot at, and for this a second `EntityExists` consideration is used. The contact must be an enemy and must be in the kill zone. Other constraints can easily be added—for example, the sniper could be configured to prefer contacts that are closer, those that have less cover, and/or those that are high-value targets (such as officers). The consideration is configured to use a picker (discussed in a later section) to select the best target and store it on the brain's blackboard. If the option is selected then the Fire action will retrieve the selected target from the blackboard, rather than going through the process of selecting it all over again. As with the escape route, this consideration will veto the option if no target is found, otherwise it has no effect.

Finally, an `ExecutionHistory` consideration is used to check how long it has been since the sniper last fired a shot. This consideration picks a random delay between 60 and 120 seconds, and vetoes the option if the time since the last shot is less than that delay. Each time the option is selected (i.e., each time the reasoner picks this option and starts executing it) the consideration picks a new delay to use for the next shot.

Considerations are the single most powerful conceptual abstraction, and can be used with or without the other ideas described in this chapter. They are straightforward to implement (the only slightly tricky part is deciding how to combine them together—that topic is discussed in detail later in this chapter), but all by themselves allow you to greatly reduce duplication and increase code reuse. Once you have them, configuring a decision becomes a simple matter of enumerating the options and specifying the considerations for each option. Specifying a consideration is not much more complex than writing a single function call in code—it typically takes anywhere from a few seconds to a minute or two—but each consideration represents dozens, or often even hundreds of lines of code. From time to time you will need to add a new consideration, or add new capabilities to one that exists—but you only need to do that once for each consideration, and then you can use it again and again throughout your AI.

As considerations are heavily reused, they also allow you to take the time to add nuance to the decision-making that might be difficult to incorporate otherwise. `EntityExists` is a good example of how complex—and powerful—considerations can become, but even a very simple consideration like `ExecutionHistory` can make decisions based on how long an option has been executing, how long since it last ran, or whether it has ever run at all. This allows us to implement things like cooldowns, goal inertia (a.k.a. hysteresis), repeat penalties, and one-time bonuses with a single consideration (these concepts were discussed in detail in our previous work [Dill 2006]). It can also support a wide range of evaluation functions that drive decision-making based on that elapsed time—for example, by comparing to a random value (as we do in this example) or applying a response curve (as described in Lewis's chapter on utility function selection and in Mark's book on Behavioral Mathematics [Lewis 2016, Mark 2009]). Having a single consideration that does all of that means you can reuse it in seconds, rather than spending minutes or even hours reimplementing it. It also means that when you reuse it, you can be confident that it will work because it has already been heavily tested and thus is unlikely to contain a bug.

One issue not discussed above is how the reasoners actually go about combining considerations in order to evaluate each option. This is a big topic so we will bypass it for now (we devote an entire section to it below) and simply say that considerations return a set of *weight values* which are combined to guide the reasoner's decisions.

21.5.2 Weight Functions

While considerations do a lot to reduce duplication in your code base, there is still a lot of repetition between different types of considerations. Consequently, many of the remaining conceptual abstractions were created in order to allow us to encapsulate duplicate code within the considerations themselves. The first of these is the *weight function*.

Many different types of considerations calculate a floating point value, and then convert that single float into a set of weight values. The weight function abstraction is responsible for making that conversion. For example, the `Distance` consideration calculates the distance between two positions, and then uses a weight function to convert that floating point value into a set of weight values. Some games might use a `Health` consideration, which does the same thing with the NPC's health (or an enemy's health, for that matter). Other games might use an `Ammo` consideration. The `ExecutionHistory` consideration that we used on the sniper is another example. It actually has three weight functions: one to use when the option is selected, one to use if it has never been selected, and one to use if it was previously selected but is not selected right now.

Of course, not all considerations produce a floating point value. The `EntityExists` consideration, for example, produces a Boolean: TRUE if it found an entity, FALSE if it did not. Different instances of the `EntityExists` consideration might return different weight values for TRUE or FALSE, however. In the sniper example, one `EntityExists` consideration vetoes the option when an entity was found (the one that checks line of retreat) while the other vetoes the option if one is not found (the one that picks a target to shoot at). This is done by changing the configuration of the weight function that each one uses. Other considerations might also produce Boolean values—for instance, some games might have a `LineOfSight` consideration that is TRUE if there is line of sight between two characters, FALSE if there is not.

There are a number of different ways that we could convert from an input value to a set of weight values. For floating point numbers, we might apply a response curve (the `BasicCurve` weight function), or we might divide the possible input values into sections and return a different set of weight values for each section (e.g., veto the Snipe option if the range to the enemy is less than 50 m or more than 300 m, but not if it is in between—the `FloatSequence` weight function), or we might simply treat it as a Boolean (the `Boolean` weight function). We might even ignore the input values entirely and always return a fixed result (the `Constant` weight function)—this is often done with the `ExecutionHistory` consideration to ensure that a particular option is only ever selected once or that it gets a fixed bonus if it has never been selected, for example.

The consideration should not have to know which technique is used, so we use a conceptual abstraction in which the conversion is done using a consistent interface and the different approaches are implemented as modular components (the `BasicCurve`, `FloatSequence`, `Boolean`, or `Constant` weight functions, for example). The interface for this conceptual abstraction is given in Listing 21.2.

Listing 21.2. The weight function interface.

```
class AIWeightFunctionBase
{
public:
    // Load the configuration.
    virtual bool Init(const AICreationData& cd) = 0;

    // Weight functions can deliver a result based on the
    // input of a bool, int, float, or string. By default
    // int does whatever float does, while the others all
    // throw an assert if not defined in the subclass.
    virtual const AIWeightValues& CalcBool(bool b);
    virtual const AIWeightValues& CalcInt(int i);
    virtual const AIWeightValues& CalcFloat(float f);
    virtual const AIWeightValues& CalcString(AIString s);

    // Some functions need to know when the associated option
    // is selected/deselected (for example, to pick new
    // random values).
    virtual void Select()    {}
    virtual void Deselect()  {}
};
```

Coming back to the sniper example, both of the EntityExists considerations would use a Boolean weight function. The Boolean weight function is configured with two sets of weight values: one to return if the input value is TRUE, the other if it is FALSE. In these two cases, one set of weight values would be configured to veto the option (the TRUE value for the escape route check, the FALSE value for the target selection), while the other set of weight values would be configured to have no effect on the final decision.

The ExecutionHistory consideration is a bit more interesting. It has three weight functions: one to use when the option is executing (which evaluates the amount of time since the option was selected), one to use if the option has never been selected (which evaluates the amount of time since the game was loaded), and one to use if the option has been selected in the past but currently is not selected (which evaluates the amount of time since it last stopped executing). In this instance, when the option is selected (i.e., when the sniper is in the process of taking a shot) we use a Constant weight function that is configured to have no effect. We also configure the weight function for when option has never been selected in the same way—the sniper is allowed to take its first shot as soon as it has a target. The third weight function (which is used if the option is not currently selected but has been executed in the past) uses a FloatSequence weight function to check whether the input value is greater than our cooldown or not, and returns the appropriate result. This weight function is also configured to randomize the cooldown each time the option is selected.

21.5.3 Reasoners

As discussed in previous sections, *reasoners* implement the conceptual abstraction that is responsible for making decisions. The configuration of each reasoner component will specify the type of reasoner, and also what the reasoner's options are. Each option can contain a set of considerations and a set of actions. The considerations are used by the reasoner to evaluate each option and decide which one to select, and the actions specify what should happen when the associated option is selected. The interface for this abstraction is given in Listing 21.3.

Listing 21.3. The reasoner interface.

```cpp
class AIReasonerBase
{
public:
    // Load the configuration.
    virtual bool Init(const AICreationData& cd);

    // Used by the picker to add/remove options
    void AddOption(AIOptionBase& option);
    void Clear();

    // Enable/Disable the reasoner. Called when containing
    // action is selected or deselected, or when brain is
    // enabled/disabled.
    void Enable();
    void Disable();
    bool IsEnabled() const;

    // Sense, Think, and Act.
    // NOTE: Subclasses should not overload this. Instead,
    // they should overload Think() (ideally they shouldn't
    // have to do anything to Sense() or Act()).
    void Update();

    // Get the current selected option, if any. Used by the
    // picker.
    AIOptionBase* GetSelectedOption();

    // Most reasoners are considered to be done if they don't
    // have a selected option, either because they failed to
    // pick one or because they have no options.
    virtual bool IsDone();

protected:
    void Sense();
    virtual void Think();
    void Act();
};
```

GAIA currently provides four different modular reasoner components:

- The Sequence reasoner, which performs its options in the order that they are listed in the configuration (much like a sequence node in a BT). Unlike the other types of reasoners, the sequence reasoner always executes each of its options, so it ignores any considerations that may have been placed on them.
- The RuleBased reasoner, which uses the considerations on each option to determine whether the option is valid (i.e., whether it should be executed, given the current situation). Each tick, this reasoner goes down its list of options in the order that they are specified in the configuration and selects the first one that is valid. This is essentially the same approach as that of a selector node in many BT implementations.

- The FSM reasoner, which allows us to implement a finite-state machine. For this reasoner, each option contains a list of *transitions*, rather than having considerations. Each transition specifies a set of considerations (which determines whether the transition should be taken), as well as the option (i.e., the state) which should be selected if the transition does fire. The reasoner uses a picker (described in Section 21.7, below) to pick from among the transitions.
- The DualUtility reasoner, which is GAIA's utility-based reasoner. The dual utility reasoner calculates two floating point values: the *rank* and the *weight*. It then uses these two values, along with the random number generator, to select an option. Dual utility reasoning is discussed in our previous work (Dill 2015, Dill et al. 2012) and also in Section 21.6.2.

Of course, a modular architecture does not need to be limited to only these approaches to decision-making. For example, we have often considered implementing a Goal-Oriented Action Planner (GOAP) reasoner (for those cases when we want to search for sequences of actions that meet some goal). Like the FSM reasoner, this would require a bit of clever thinking but should be quite possible to fit into GAIA by implementing a new type of reasoner component.

21.5.4 Actions

Actions are the output of the reasoner—they are responsible for sending commands back to the game, making changes to the blackboard, or whatever else it is that the reasoner has decided to do. Their interface is given in Listing 21.4.

Listing 21.4. The action interface.

```
class AIActionBase
{
public:
    // Load the configuration.
    virtual bool Init(const AICreationData& cd) = 0;

    // Called when the action starts/stops execution.
    virtual void Select()   {}
    virtual void Deselect() {}

    // Called every frame while the action is selected.
    virtual void Update()   {}

    // Check whether this action is finished executing. Some
    // actions (such as a looping animation) are never done,
    // but others (such as moving to a position) can be
    // completed.
    virtual bool IsDone()   { return true; }
};
```

As discussed above, actions can either be abstract or concrete. Abstract actions are actions which exist to guide the decision-making process, like the subreasoner action. Other abstract actions include the Pause and SetVariable actions. The Pause action delays a specified amount of time before marking itself as complete. It is commonly used in the `Sequence` reasoner, to control the timing of the concrete actions. The `SetVariable` action is used to set a variable on a data store (most often the brain's blackboard).

Concrete actions, by their very nature, cannot be implemented as part of the GAIA library. They contain the game-specific code that is used to make NPCs do things. Common concrete actions include things like `Move`, `PlayAnimation`, `PlaySound`, `FireWeapon`, and so on. Our factory system handles the task of allowing the developer to inject game-specific code into the AI (Dill 2016).

21.5.5 Targets

Targets provide an abstract way for component configurations to specify positions and/or entities. For example, the `Distance` consideration measures the distance between two positions. In order to make this consideration reusable, GAIA needs some way to specify, in the configuration, what those two positions should be. Perhaps one is the position of the NPC and the other is the player. Perhaps one is an enemy and the other is an objective that the NPC has been assigned to protect (in a "capture the flag" style game, for instance). Ideally, the distance consideration should not have to know how the points it is measuring between are calculated—it should just have some mechanism to get the two positions, and then it can perform the calculation from there. Similarly, the `LineOfSight` consideration needs to know what positions or entities to check line of sight between, the `Move` action needs to know where to move to, the `FireWeapon` action needs to know what to shoot at, and so on.

GAIA's solution to this is the *target* conceptual abstraction, whose interface is shown in Listing 21.5. Targets provide a position and/or an entity for other components to use. For example, the `Self` target returns the actor and position for the NPC that the AI controls. The `ByName` target looks up a character by name (either from the actors or the contacts, depending on how it is configured).

Listing 21.5. The target interface.

```
class AITargetBase
{
public:
    // Load the configuration.
    virtual bool Init(const AICreationData& cd) = 0;

    // Get the target's position. If the target has an
    // entity, it should generally be that entity's
    // position.
    virtual const AIVectorBase* GetPosition() const = 0;

    // Not all types of targets have entities. If this one
    // does, get it. NOTE: It's possible for HasEntity() to
    // return true (i.e. this type of target has an entity)
    // but GetEntity() to return NULL (i.e. the entity that
    // this target represents doesn't currently exist). In
    // that case, HasEntity() should return true, but
    // IsValid() should return false.
    virtual AIEntityInfo* GetEntity() const { return NULL; }
    virtual bool HasEntity() const         { return false; }
```

(Continued)

```
    // Checks whether the target is valid. For instance, a
    // target that tracks a particular contact by name might
    // become invalid if we don't have contact with that
    // name. Most target types are always valid.
    virtual bool IsValid() const          { return true; }
};
```

All targets can provide a position, but some do not provide an entity. For example, the
`Position` target returns a fixed (x, y, z) position (which is specified in the target's configuration), but does not return an entity. The person writing the configuration should be aware
of this and make sure not to use a target that does not provide an entity in situations where an
entity is needed, but GAIA also has checks in place to ensure that this is the case. In practice
this is really never an issue—it simply would not make sense to use a `Position` target in a
situation where an entity is needed, so why would a developer ever do that?

As with all conceptual abstractions, some types of targets can be implemented in GAIA,
while others need to be implemented by the game. For example, some games might add a
`Player` target which returns the contact (or actor) for the PC. For other games (such as
multiplayer games, or games where the player is not embodied in the world) this type of
target would make no sense.

21.5.6 Regions

Regions are similar to targets, except that instead of specifying a single (x, y, z) position
in space, they specify a larger area. They are commonly used for things like triggers and
spawn areas, although they have a myriad of other uses. The sniper configuration, for
example, would use them to specify both the kill zone (the area it should fire into) and the
line of retreat (the area it plans to move through in order to get away).

Regions are a conceptual abstraction because it is useful to supply the AI designer with
a variety of ways to specify them. Implementations might include a circular region (specified as a center position—or a target—and a radius), a parallelogram region (specified as
a base position and two vectors to give the length and angle of the sides), and a polygon
region (specified as a sequence of vertices). Similarly, some games will be perfectly happy
with simple 2D regions, while others will need to specify an area in all three dimensions.
The interface for this abstraction is given in Listing 21.6.

Listing 21.6. The region interface.

```
class AIRegionBase
{
public:
    // Load the configuration.
    virtual bool Init(const AICreationData& cd) = 0;

    // Test if a specified position is within the region
    virtual bool IsInRegion(const AIVector& pos) const = 0;
```
(Continued)

```
        // Set the outVal parameter to a random position within
        // the region
        // NOTE: IT MAY BE POSSIBLE FOR THIS TO FAIL on some
        // types of regions. It returns success.
        virtual bool GetRandomPos(AIVector& outVal) const = 0;
};
```

21.5.7 Other Conceptual Abstractions

Conceptual abstractions provide a powerful mechanism that allows us to encapsulate and reuse code which otherwise would have to be duplicated. The abstractions discussed above are the most commonly used (and most interesting), but GAIA includes a few others, including:

- Sensors, which provide one mechanism to pass data into the AI (though most projects simply write to the data stores directly).
- Execution filters, which can control how often reasoners and/or sensors tick.
- Entity filters, which are an alternative to pickers for selecting an entity that meets some set of constraints.
- Data elements, which encapsulate the things stored in data stores.
- Vectors, which abstract away the implementation details of how a particular game or simulation represents positions (it turns out that not every project uses (x, y, z)).

Furthermore, as GAIA continues to improve, from time to time new conceptual abstractions are found and added (vectors are the most recent example of this). GAIA includes a system of macros and templatized classes that allow us to create most of the infrastructure for each conceptual abstraction, including both their factory and the storage for any global configurations, by calling a single macro and passing in the name of the abstraction (Dill 2016).

21.6 Combining Considerations

Considerations are the single most important type of modular component. They are, in many ways, the key decomposition around which GAIA revolves. In general terms, they are the bite-sized pieces out of which decision-making logic is built. They represent concepts like the distance between two targets, the amount of health a target has left, or how long it is been since a particular option was last selected. Reasoners use the considerations to evaluate each option and select the one that they will execute—but how should reasoners combine the outputs of their considerations?

Over the years we have tried a number of different solutions to this problem. Some were quite simple, others were more complex. This chapter will present one from each end of the spectrum: a very simple Boolean approach that was used for a trigger system in an experimental educational game (Dill and Graham 2016, Dill et al. 2015) and a more complex utility-based approach that combines three values to perform the option's evaluation (Dill 2015, Dill et al. 2012). While the latter approach might initially seem too hard to work with, experience has shown that it is both extremely flexible and, once the basic conventions are understood, straightforward to use for both simple and complex decisions.

21.6.1 Simple Boolean Considerations

The simplest way to combine considerations is to treat them as Booleans. Each option is given a single consideration, which either returns TRUE (the option can be selected) or FALSE (it cannot). Logical operations such as AND, OR, and NOT can be treated as regular considerations, except that they contain one or more child considerations and return the combined evaluation of their children. Thus an option's single consideration will often be an AND or an OR which contains a list of additional considerations (some of which may, themselves, be Boolean operations).

This approach was used for the trigger system in *The Mars Game*, which was an experimental educational game, set on Mars, that taught topics drawn from ninth and tenth grade math and programming. An example of a *Mars Game* trigger is shown in Listing 21.7 (specified in YAML). This particular trigger waits 15 seconds after the start of the level, and then plays a line of dialog that gives a hint about how to solve a particular challenge in the game, and also writes a value on the blackboard indicating that the hint has been played. However, it only plays the hint if:

- The hint has not already been played during a previous level (according to that value on the blackboard).
- The player has not already started executing a Blockly program on their rover.
- The player's rover is facing either south or west (i.e., 180° or 270°), since the hint describes how to handle the situation where you start out facing the wrong way.

Listing 21.7. Trigger a hint.

```
playHint_2_9_tricky:
  triggerCondition:
  - and:
    - delay:                     # Wait 15 seconds after the
      - 15                       #   start of the level.
    - not:
      - readBlackboard:          # Check the blackboard and
        - thisOneIsTrickyHint    #   only play it once.
    - not:                       # Don't play it if the player
      - isBlocklyExecuting:      #   has already started their
        - rover                  #   program.
    - or:
      - hasHeading:              # Only play it if the rover
        - rover                  #   is facing south or west.
        - 180
      - hasHeading:
        - rover
        - 270
  actions:
  - playSound:                   # Play the hint dialog.
    - ALVO37_Rover
  - writeToBlackboard:           # Update the blackboard so
    - thisOneIsTrickyHint        #   that it won't play again.
```

This approach has the obvious advantage of great simplicity. Most developers—even game designers—are comfortable with Boolean logic, so it is not only straightforward to implement but also straightforward to use. It works quite well for things like trigger systems and rule-based reasoners that make decisions about each option in isolation, without ever needing to compare two options together to decide which is best. It suffers greatly, however, if there is ever a case where you do want to make more nuanced decisions—and those cases often pop up late in a project, when the designer (or QA, or the publisher, or the company owner) comes to you to say "what it does is mostly great, but in this one situation I would like it to…"

With that in mind, most projects will be best served by an approach that allows Boolean decisions to be specified in a simple way, but also supports complex comparisons when and where they are needed—which brings us to dual utility considerations.

21.6.2 Dual Utility Considerations

Dual utility considerations are the approach used by GAIA. Each consideration returns three values: an *addend*, a *multiplier*, and a *rank*. These three values are then combined to create the overall *weight* and *rank* of the option, which are the two utility values that give this approach its name.

21.6.2.1 Calculating Weight and Rank

Taking those steps one at a time, the first thing that happens is that the addends and multipliers are combined into an overall weight for the option (W_O). This is done by first adding all of the addends together, and then multiplying the result by all of the multipliers.

$$W_O = \left(\sum_{i=1}^{n} A_i \right) \cdot \left(\prod_{i=1}^{n} M_i \right) \tag{21.1}$$

Next, the option's overall rank (R_O) is calculated. This is done by taking the max of the ranks of the considerations.

$$R_O = \text{Max}_{i=1}^{n} \left(R_i \right) \tag{21.2}$$

There are other formulas that could be used to calculate weight and rank, and GAIA does support some alternatives (more on this in a later section), but the vast majority of the time these two formulas are the ones that we use.

21.6.2.2 Selecting an Option

Once the weight and rank have been calculated, the reasoner needs to use them to select an option. Exactly how this is done depends on the type of the reasoner, but all are based on the dual utility reasoner.

The idea behind dual utility reasoning is that the AI will use the rank to divide the options into categories, and then use weight-based random to pick from among the options in the highest ranked category. In reality, there are actually four steps to accomplish this:

1. Eliminate any options that have $W_O \leq 0$. They cannot be selected in step 4 and will make step 2 more complicated, so it is best to eliminate them up front.

2. Find the highest *rank* from among the options that remain, and eliminate any option with a rank lower than that. This step ensures that only options from the highest ranked category are considered.
3. Find the highest *weight* from among the options that remain, and eliminate options whose weight is "much less than" that weight. "Much less than" is defined as a percentage that is specified in the reasoner's configuration—and in many cases the reasoner is configured to skip this step entirely. This step makes it possible to ensure that the weight-based random will not pick a very low weight option when much better options exist, because doing so often looks stupid—the option was technically possible, but not very sensible given the other choices available.
4. Use weight-based random to select from among the options that remain.

A couple things are worth calling out. First, notice step 1. Any option can be eliminated simply by setting its weight to 0, no matter what the weights and ranks of the other options are. What is more, looking back at Equation 21.1, any consideration can force the weight of an option to 0 (i.e., *veto* it) by returning a multiplier of 0, no matter what the values on the other considerations. Anything times 0 is 0. This provides a straightforward way to treat dual utility options as if they had purely Boolean considerations when we want to. We say that an option is *valid* (which is to say that it is selectable) if it has $W_O > 0$ and *invalid* if it does not. The rule-based reasoner works by checking its options in order, and selecting the first valid one, regardless of rank.

21.6.2.3 Configuring Dual Utility Considerations

The key to implementing dual utility considerations is to provide default values that ensure that even though the system is capable of considerable complexity, the complexity is hidden when configuring a consideration unless and until it is needed. This section will discuss the default values, naming conventions, and other tricks that GAIA uses to accomplish this. Along the way, it will give examples that might be used by our sniper AI to pick a target.

In GAIA, the most basic way to specify weight values is to simply specify the addend, multiplier, and/or rank as attributes in the XML. Any of the three values that are not specified will be set to a default value that has no effect (i.e., an addend of 0, a multiplier of 1, and a rank of –FLT_MAX, which is the smallest possible floating point value). Thus the developer who is configuring the AI only needs to specify the values that he or she wants to change.

As an example, a good sniper should prefer to shoot at officers. In order to implement this, the game can place a Boolean "IsOfficer" value on each contact (remember that contacts are data stores, so we can store any value that we want there). This value would be true if the NPC believes that contact to be an officer (whether or not the belief is true), false otherwise. Then, in the configuration, we use a BooleanVariable consideration to look up this value from the PickerEntity target (the picker entity is the entity that we are considering picking). The consideration uses a Boolean weight function to set the multiplier to 10 if the value is true, otherwise it does nothing (i.e., returns default values). Assuming that there are about 10 enlisted enemies (each with a weight of roughly 1) per officer (with a weight of roughly 10) this means that, all other things being equal, the sniper will shoot at an officer about half of the time. This consideration's configuration is shown in Listing 21.8.

Listing 21.8. A consideration that prefers to pick officers.

```
<Consideration Type="BooleanVariable"
               Variable="IsOfficer"
               DataStore="Target">
  <DataStoreTarget Type="PickerEntity"/>
  <WeightFunction Type="Boolean">
    <TrueWeights Multiplier="10"/>
  </WeightFunction>
</Consideration>
```

In some cases, a consideration wants to prevent its option from being selected no matter what the other considerations say. For example, when the sniper is picking its target we might want to ensure that it only shoots at entities that it thinks are enemies. This could be implemented by storing the "Side" of each contact as an `AIString`, with possible values of "Friendly," "Enemy," or "Civilian." If the "Side" is not "Enemy," then the sniper should not select this target no matter where it is or whether it is an officer or not. This could be configured by specifying a `multiplier` of 0, but configurations should be more explicit and easier to read. With this in mind, rather than specifying an `addend`, `multiplier`, and `rank`, weights can specify a Boolean `veto` attribute. If `veto` is true then, under the covers, the `multiplier` will be set to 0. If it is false, then the default values will be used for all three weight values.

The resulting consideration for the sniper would look like Listing 21.9. This consideration is much like the one in Listing 21.8, except that it looks up a string variable rather than a Boolean one, and passes the result into a `String` weight function. The string weight function tries to match the string against each of its entries. If the string does not match any of the entries, then it returns the default values. In this case, that means that if the string is "Enemy," then the consideration will have no effect (because when `veto` is false it returns the default values), otherwise it will set the `multiplier` to 0 (because `veto` is TRUE) and thus make the option invalid.

Listing 21.9. A consideration that vetoes everything other than enemies.

```
<Consideration Type="StringVariable"
               Variable="Side"
               DataStore="Target">
  <DataStoreTarget Type="PickerEntity"/>
  <WeightFunction Type="String">
    <Entries>
      <String Value="Enemy" Veto="False"/>
    </Entries>
    <Default Veto="True"/>
  </WeightFunction>
</Consideration>
```

As an aside, the considerations in Listings 21.8 and 21.9 do a nice job of showing exactly why modular AI is so powerful. These considerations evaluate the value from a variable on a data store. It could be any variable on any data store. In this particular case the data store is specified using a target (rather than being, say, the NPC's actor or the brain's blackboard), which again could be any type of target that specifies an entity. Once the consideration has looked up the value for the variable, it passes that value to a weight function to be converted into weight values. Without the ideas of considerations, and data stores, and weight functions, we would have to write a specialized chunk of code for each of these checks that is only used inside of the sniper's target selection, and is duplicated anywhere else that a Boolean data store variable is used. Furthermore, that code would be dozens of lines of C++ code, not a handful of lines of XML. Most importantly, though, the values being specified in the XML are for the most part the sorts of human concepts that we would use when describing the logic to a coworker or friend. What should the AI evaluate? The target that it is considering shooting (the `PickerEntity` target). How should it evaluate that target? By checking whether it is an enemy, and whether it is an officer. What should it do with this evaluation? Only shoot at enemies, and pick out the enemy officers about half the time.

There is one other detail to configuring considerations that has not been discussed yet. In order to be selected, every option needs to have a weight that is greater than 0, but the default addend for all of the considerations is 0. If we do not have at least one consideration with an addend greater than 0 then the overall weight is guaranteed to be 0 for the same reason it is when we set the multiplier to 0—anything times 0 is 0. Furthermore, we would like the default weight for all options to be something reasonable, like 1.

We address this problem with the `Tuning` consideration, which is a consideration that simply returns a specified `addend`, `multiplier`, and `rank`, and which has a default `addend` of 1. The option's configuration can (and often does) specify a `Tuning` consideration, but if it does not then a default `Tuning` consideration with an addend of 1 will automatically be added.

21.6.2.4 Changing Combination Techniques at Runtime

Up until now, we have said that the option owns the considerations, and is responsible for combining them together for the reasoners. This is actually slightly inaccurate. The option has an `AIConsiderationSet`, which in turn contains the considerations. The consideration set is responsible for combining its considerations and returning the overall weight and rank, and it can also return the combined addend and multiplier for its considerations without multiplying them into an overall weight. Its interface is shown in Listing 21.10. This distinction is important, because it means that we can place flags on the consideration set to specify that the considerations in that particular set should be combined with different rules. What is more, there is a special type of consideration that contains another consideration set (called the `AIConsideration_ConsiderationSet`). This makes it possible to have different rules for some of the considerations on an option than for the others.

The most commonly used alternate approaches for combining considerations are ones that apply different Boolean operations to the weights. By default, if any consideration vetoes an option (i.e., returns a multiplier of 0) then that option will not be selected. This is in essence of a conjunction (i.e., a logical AND)—all of the considerations have to be "true" (i.e., have multiplier greater than 0) in order for the option to be "true" (i.e., valid). In some cases, rather than an AND, we want a logical OR—that is, we want the option to be valid as long as at least one consideration does not have a multiplier of 0. This is implemented by having the consideration set ignore any consideration with a multiplier less than or equal to 0, unless every consideration has a multiplier that is less than or equal to 0. Similarly, NOT is implemented by having the consideration replace any multiplier that is less than or equal to 0 with 1, and any multiplier that is greater than 0 with 0.

Listing 21.10. The `AIConsiderationSet` interface.

```
class AIConsiderationSet
{
public:
    bool Init(const AICreationData& cd);

    // Evaluate all of the considerations and calculate the
    // overall addend, multiplier, weight, and rank.
    void Calculate();

    // Sets the best rank and weight currently under
    // consideration. These don't change the calculated
    // values, but they will change the values returned by
    // GetRank() and GetWeight().
    void SetScreeningWeight(float bestWeight);
    void SetScreeningRank(float bestRank);

    // Get the rank and weight. GetWeight() returns 0 if
    // the screening rank or screening weight checks fail.
    float GetWeight() const;
    float GetRank() const;

    // Get the raw values, unscreened.
    float GetAddend() const;
    float GetMultiplier() const;
    float GetWeightUnscreened() const;
    float GetRankUnscreened() const;
};
```

GAIA also supports different approaches for combining the ranks: rather than taking the max, it can take the min or add all of the considerations' ranks together to get the overall rank. All of these changes are configured just like everything else—which is to say that there is an attribute that tells the consideration set which calculation method to use, and the defaults (when the attribute is not specified) are to use the standard approaches.

More techniques for configuring dual utility considerations and for working with utility in general can be found in Dill (2006), Dill et al. (2012), Lewis (2016), and Mark (2009).

21.7 Pickers

The last topic that we will cover in this chapter is *pickers*. Pickers use a reasoner to go through a list of things (typically either the list of contacts, actors, or threats, but it could also be the list of transitions on an FSM option) and select the best one for some purpose (e.g., the best one to talk to, the best on to shoot at, the best one to use for cover, etc.). There are slight differences between the picker used by the `EntityExists` consideration (which picks an entity) and the one used by an FSM reasoner (which picks a transition), but the core ideas are the same; in the interests of brevity, we will focus on picking entities.

While most reasoners have all of their options defined in their configuration, a picker's reasoner has to pick from among choices that are determined at runtime. For example, we might use a picker to look through our contacts to pick something to shoot at, or to look through our threats to pick one to react to, or to look through nearby cover positions to pick one to use (although the game would have to extend GAIA with support for cover positions to do this last one). The `EntityExists` considerations in our sniper example use pickers to pick something to shoot at, and also to check for an entity that is blocking its line of retreat. The first picker should use a dual utility reasoner, because it wants to pick the best entity. The second one might use a rule-based reasoner, because it just needs to know whether such an entity exists or not.

Picker options are created on-the-fly by taking all of the entities in some category (for instance all of the actors, or all of the contacts, or all of the threats), and creating an option for each one. Each of these options is given the same considerations, which are specified in the configuration. The considerations can access the entity that they are responsible for evaluating by using the `PickerEntity` target. For example, the picker that is used to pick a sniper's target might have considerations that check things like the distance to the target, whether it is in the kill zone, how much cover it has, whether it is an enemy, whether it is an officer, and so forth. The picker that checks line of retreat would simply check whether each entity is an enemy, and whether it is in the region that defines the escape route.

Putting everything together, a simple option for the sniper that considers taking a shot might look like Listing 21.11. This option uses an `EntityExists` consideration to pick a target, and then stores the selected target in the `SnipeTarget` variable on the brain's blackboard. The picker has two considerations—one to check that the target is an enemy, and the other to check that it is between 50 m and 300 m away. It uses a `Boolean` weight function to veto the option if a target is not found. If a target is found, it uses the `Fire` action to take a shot. In reality, we would probably want to add more considerations to the picker (to make target selection more intelligent), but the key ideas are shown here.

Listing 21.11. An option for the sniper, which picks a target and shoots at it.

```
<Option Type="ConsiderationAndAction">
  <Considerations>
    <!-- Look through the contacts, pick a target, store it
         on the brain's blackboard as SnipeTarget. -->
    <Consideration Type="EntityExists"
                   Location="Contacts"
                   Variable="SnipeTarget">

      <Picker>
        <!-- This picker uses a dual utility reasoner because
             it wants to pick the *best* target. A picker
             that just wants to check whether any entity
             meets some set of constraints (like the one for
             checking line of retreat) would likely use a
             rule-based reasoner instead. -->
        <Reasoner Type="DualUtility"/>
```

(Continued)

```
        <Considerations>
          <!-- Only targets between 50m and 300m away -->
          <Consideration Type="Distance">
            <FromTarget Type="Self"/>
            <ToTarget Type="PickerEntity"/>
            <WeightFunction Type="FloatSequence">
              <Entries>
                <Entry Exact="50" Veto="true"/>
                <Entry Exact="300" Veto="false"/>
              </Entries>
              <Default Veto="true"/>
            </WeightFunction>
          </Consideration>

          <!-- Only enemies -->
          <Consideration Type="StringVariable"
                         Variable="Side"
                         DataStore="Target">
            <DataStoreTarget Type="PickerEntity"/>
            <WeightFunction Type="String">
              <Entries>
                <String Value="Enemy" Veto="False"/>
              </Entries>
              <Default Veto="True"/>
            </WeightFunction>
          </Consideration>

          <!-- Other considerations (like the one to prefer
               officers, or one to check that the target is
               in the kill zone) could be added here. -->

        </Considerations>
      </Picker>

      <!-- Use a default Boolean weight function - that is,
           veto if a target is not found -->
      <WeightFunction Type="Boolean"/>
    </Consideration>

    <!-- The considerations to check line of retreat and time
         since the last shot would go here. -->
    ...

  </Considerations>

  <Actions>
    <!-- Fire at the target the picker picked -->
    <Action Type="Fire">
      <Target Type="DataElement_EntityList"
              Variable="SnipeTarget"/>
    </Action>
  </Actions>
</Option>
```

21.8 Conclusion

Modular AI is an approach to AI specification that draws heavily on principles from software engineering to dramatically reduce code duplication and increase reuse. It allows the developer to rapidly specify decision-making logic by plugging together modular components that represent human-level concepts, rather than by implementing code in C++. Because these components are implemented once and then widely reused, they become both more robust (i.e., more heavily tested) and more feature laden (i.e., capable of more subtle nuance) than would be feasible if each component were only ever used once. What's more, because most of the work consists of invoking code that has already been written, AI specification can be done much, much faster than would otherwise be possible. Modular AI has been used with success on several projects that were only a couple months long, including one game that sold over 5,000,000 copies in which we implemented all of the boss AI, from scratch (including implementing the architecture), in less than 4 months.

This chapter presented a full modular architecture (GAIA), which uses a variety of different types of modular components. Of all of those conceptual abstractions, considerations are by far the most powerful. For those who are constrained to work within an existing architecture, it is very possible to get much of the benefit of modular AI even within an existing architecture, simply by implementing considerations and allowing them to drive your evaluation functions. We took this approach on another best-selling game with great success.

References

Dill, K. 2006. Prioritizing actions in a goal based RTS AI. In *AI Game Programming Wisdom 3*, ed. S. Rabin. Boston, MA: Charles River Media, pp. 321–330.

Dill, K. 2015. Dual utility reasoning. In *Game AI Pro 2*, ed. S. Rabin. Boca Raton, FL: CRC Press, pp. 23–26.

Dill, K. 2016. Six factory system tricks for extensibility and library reuse. In *Game AI Pro 3*, ed. S. Rabin. Boca Raton, FL: CRC Press, pp. 49–62.

Dill, K., B. Freeman, S. Frazier, and J. Benito. 2015. Mars game: Creating and evaluating an engaging educational game. *Proceedings of the 2015 Interservice/Industry Training, Simulation & Education Conference*, December 2015, Orlando, FL.

Dill, K. and R. Graham. 2016. Quick and dirty: 2 lightweight AI architectures. *Game Developer's Conference,* March 2016, San Francisco, CA.

Dill, K., E.R. Pursel, P. Garrity, and G. Fragomeni. 2012. Design patterns for the configuration of utility-based AI. *Proceedings of the 2012 Interservice/Industry Training, Simulation & Education Conference*, December 2012, Orlando, FL.

Isla, D. 2005. Handling complexity in Halo 2 AI. http://www.gamasutra.com/view/feature/130663/gdc_2005_proceeding_handling_.php (accessed June 26, 2016).

Jacopin, É. 2016. Vintage random number generators. In *Game AI Pro 3*, ed. S. Rabin. Boca Raton, FL: CRC Press, pp. 471–478.

Lewis, M. 2016. Choosing effective utility-based considerations. In *Game AI Pro 3*, ed. S. Rabin. Boca Raton, FL: CRC Press, pp. 167–178.

Mark, D. 2009. *Behavioral Mathematics for Game AI*. Boston, MA: Charles River Media.

22
Overcoming Pitfalls in Behavior Tree Design

Anthony Francis

22.1 Introduction

Unless you have been living under a rock, or are new to the game industry, you have probably heard of behavior trees (Isla 2005, Champandard and Dunstan 2012). Behavior trees are an architecture for controlling NPCs based on a hierarchical graph of tasks, where each task is either an atomic, a simple behavior an agent can directly perform, or a composite, a behavior performed by a lower level behavior tree of arbitrary complexity. As they provide a cleaner decomposition of behavior than alternatives such as hierarchical finite-state machines—and because of the many good reports from people who have successfully used them—behavior trees are increasingly used to allow large software teams to collaborate on complex agent behaviors, not just in games but in the robotics industry. But there are a few key choices in their implementation, which can either make them much harder to architect than they need to be—or much more flexible, easy to extend, and easy to reuse.

I found this out the hard way. By a weird trick of fate, I have implemented behavior trees five times, including three systems in Lisp similar to the architecture that later got the name behavior trees as part of the *Halo 2* AI, and more recently two behavior tree implementations in C++ for robots at Google. Along the way, I have learned some of the things to NOT do when creating a behavior tree—including needlessly multiplying core primitives, inventing a whole programming language for control, and jumping the gun on routing all communication through "proper" channels like a blackboard—and I have developed specific recommendations on how to create a system which avoids these pitfalls, especially if licensing or interoperability concerns prevent you from building on existing commercial or open-source solutions.

22.2 What Makes Behavior Trees Work

Ideas like behavior trees were around long before *Halo*. Hierarchical decompositions of behavior into tasks were pioneered in particular by reactive action packages, or RAPs (Firby 1987): high-level RAPs get decomposed into low-level RAPs, ultimately bottoming out in leaf skills used to directly control real and simulated robots (Bonasso et al. 1997). My TaskStorm architecture is even closer to modern behavior trees, integrating hierarchical task decomposition directly into a blackboard system encapsulating the agent state, enabling cognitive operations to be time sliced with each other over the course of behavior (Francis 2000).

Although these systems are *functionally* similar to behavior trees, the key insight that Damian Isla added is a software design focus on simplifying the code needed to generate behaviors (Isla 2005). Isla argues that four key features made it possible to create the *Halo 2* AI and its successors at large scales: customizability, explicitness, hackability, and variability. Behavior trees are customizable because behaviors are decomposed into smaller components, which can be individually changed or parameterized; they are explicit because the things that an agent does can be represented as distinct behavior nodes, and the whole behavior as a graph; they are hackable because the radical decomposition of behaviors makes it easy to replace nodes with custom versions, and they allow variability because the control algorithms themselves are represented as nodes.

In my experience, it is easy to get lost building functionality that you think you will need and in the process lose sight of this simplification focus. A system which functionally breaks behaviors into atomic behaviors orchestrated by trees of composite behaviors may act like a behavior tree, but it will not be customizable or hackable if behaviors are too tightly coupled, nor will it be explicit or variable if the nodes are too large. What is worse, architectural constraints to enforce these features can become a cure worse than the disease, making the overall system harder to maintain. Although some of these problems are unavoidable, other pitfalls are easy enough to avoid if we are careful about how we design our behavior trees.

22.3 Pitfalls in Behavior Tree Design

A behavior tree runs as a decision-making component within a larger structure—a game engine, a robot operating system, or a cognitive architecture—and it is tempting to design something that serves all the needs of the parent system. But software components work better when they have clearly defined responsibilities and clear separation of concerns, and making your behavior tree too much can, perversely, leave you with something that does too little. Three of these pitfalls are

1. Adding too many kinds of classes to the decision architecture of your behavior tree.
2. Building a complete programming language into your behavior tree before you need it.
3. Forcing all communication to route through the blackboard as a point of principle, rather than when required by the needs of the application at hand.

If you are on a large project and have a clear specification for (or experience with) what you need, (2) and (3) may not apply to you; but if you are on a smaller or novel project, simpler structures may work for you.

22.3.1 Pitfall #1: Creating Too Many Organizing Classes

Occam's Razor gets reduced to "Keep It Simple, Stupid," but originally stated, translated more like "Do not multiply entities needlessly"—which is more on point for understanding a pitfall of behavior tree architecture: creating a separate architectural category for every kind of thing that your system needs to do. This, perversely makes it harder to develop the features you need.

For example, in addition to atomic behaviors that perform actions and composite behaviors which orchestrate them, your characters may need low-level "skills" that directly manipulate your animation system or your robot controllers, or high-level "modules" that manage the resources provided by your game engine or your robot operating system. But it is probably a mistake to have a separate architectural category for each of these—that is root classes for Behaviors, Composites, Skills, and Modules. Behavior trees already provide low-level and high-level constructs, and with the addition of an external memory store, their decision-making power is Turing-complete. So why not just use behaviors?

Many of the prehistoric behavior tree-like systems, described earlier, made distinctions between concepts like skills, tasks, task networks, or modules—and created classes or modules to implement each. This approach got the job done, and maybe was a fine way to do things in the bad old days of Lisp hacking—but this multiplication of entities introduces pitfalls in modern C++ development, which often depends on having smaller numbers of classes to enable quicker refactoring.

For example, one behavior tree we developed for an internal Google robotics project had both `Modules`, which talked to the robot operating system via `Contexts`, and `Tasks` that made up the behavior tree themselves, which communicated to agents indirectly through thin wrappers called `AgentHandles` that hid the underlying communication protocols. But as the architecture of the system evolved, every simple refactoring affected both trees of classes—`Modules` and `Tasks`—and more complex new functionalities affecting things like the blackboard system had to be developed for and woven into both since their features were not quite in parity.

The converse of creating too many kinds of organizing abstractions is to use just one: tasks. We have yet to be burned by thinking of everything we can do in a behavior tree as creating a new kind of task. Performing an atomic action? A task. Grouping several actions? Another kind of task. Accessing system resources? A task. Running an entire behavior tree script? Yet another kind of task. We ultimately adopted a mantra "It's Tasks, All the Way Down."

When we ported this behavior tree to a new robotic platform, everything became a task. Well, technically, not everything—resources from the robot operating system were provided uniformly by `ExecutionContext`, but all classes responsible for behaviors—Modules, things like the old `AgentHandles`, and scripts—were implemented as children of a single task, the `SchedulableTask`, shown in Listing 22.1; this class provides an interface for a single decision-making step, given a particular `ExecutionContext`.

Forcing all these different types into a single model did not hurt us; on the contrary, the result was that our new behavior tree became a system with a single responsibility—decision-making—whose API had just two points of external contact: the `ExecutionContext`

Listing 22.1. The root of our behavior tree system: the `SchedulableTask`.

```
class SchedulableTask {
 public:
  SchedulableTask(
    const string& name,
    ExecutionContext* execution_context);
  virtual ~SchedulableTask() = default;
  virtual TaskStatus Step();
  // More member functions relevant to our use case ...

 private:
  string name_;
  ExecutionContext* execution_context_;
  TaskStatus status_;
};
```

provided at the top or custom code in leaf tasks at the bottom. This simpler design enabled us to build out functionality in weeks where the old system had taken us months.

22.3.2 Pitfall #2: Implementing a Language Too Soon

A behavior tree is a decision-making system, which means that the behavior nodes that make up the tree need two separate properties: a node needs both the ability to run a behavior and to decide whether to run it. This raises the question of whether the behavior tree system itself should implement a condition language.

You can do a lot with a little; even very simple decision-making structures are Turing-complete: you can perform virtually any computation with just NANDs or NORs. Therefore, you can implement sophisticated control behaviors with very few node types. Tests can be implemented by atomic actions that simply succeed or fail; if–thens can be implemented by composites like Selectors that execute the first nonfailing action, and blocks of code can be implemented by Sequences that execute all their nonfailing actions or Parallel nodes, which allow multiple actions to be executed concurrently (Champandard and Dunstan 2012).

But implementing complicated behaviors out of very simple components, Tinkertoy-style, can lead to a lot of boilerplate—so it is tempting to add more control constructs. A Decorator task that wraps other tasks enables the creation of Not that inverts the significance of failures; a subclass of a Sequence can create an And task that succeeds only if all its tasks succeed, and so on, and so on. Soon you find yourself developing a whole programming language, which enables you to parsimoniously represent character logic.

Perhaps surprisingly for a "pitfalls" section, I am not recommending that you do not implement a whole programming language (how is that for a double negative); if your behavior tree gets a lot of usage, you probably do want to implement a language. But I have implemented these kinds of languages in two different ways: driving from the top–down from language concerns and driving from the bottom up based on an understanding of the problem domain, and the latter is a much more effective strategy.

There are an enormous number of possible language constructs—Not, And, Or, If-Then-Else, Cond, Loop, For, While, Repeat-Until, Progn, Parallel, Any, All, Try-Catch-Except—one or more of which you may have fallen in love with when learning your favorite programming language (which may not be the C++ you are forced to program in). The logic for most of these constructs is very clear, so it is easy to build up a large library for any possible need.

The problem is, much of this logic is better implemented using just standard behavior tree nodes—`Actions`, `Decorators`, `Sequences`, `Parallels`, and `Selectors`. (I challenge you to find a meaningful difference between a Selector and a Cond). The best case scenario is that you end up with a node with a nonstandard name. A worse scenario is that you code functionality you do not need. The actual worst-case scenario is that you end up with duplicated logic between very similar nodes that you actually need but now have trouble maintaining as your API evolves.

A better approach is to begin with the standard set of behavior tree nodes—Actions, Decorators, Sequences, Parallels, and Selectors—and to push these as far as you can for your problem domain. If you are implementing it yourself, each behavior tree will have slightly different semantics for task execution, failure and success, and logical tests. Once you understand what patterns you need for your problem domain, you can then expand out your language— often by specializing an existing construct for a new need. This will result in less duplicated, easier to maintain code—and a library of constructs driven by what is useful for your game.

This is easy to see for structural features like object containment; for example, if the `SchedulableTask` has `GetChildren` and `AddChild` to manage its children, these should be overridden differently in atomic leaf tasks with no children and in composite tasks which have children. For almost all of the different kinds of containers in our use case, one high-level class, the `ContainerTask` shown in Listing 22.2, suffices to handle all these implementation details.

Listing 22.2. Expanding `SchedulableTask` to support `ContainerTask`.

```cpp
// Expanded SchedulableTask definition ...
class SchedulableTask {
 public:
  // ... previously declared member functions
  virtual std::vector<SchedulableTask*> GetChildren() = 0;
  virtual bool AddChild(std::unique_ptr<SchedulableTask> child) = 0;
  ...

// ContainerTask definition ...
class ContainerTask : public SchedulableTask {
 public:
  ContainerTask(
    const string& name,
    ExecutionContext* execution_context);
  ~ContainerTask() override = default;

  std::vector<SchedulableTask*> GetChildren() override;
  bool AddChild(
      std::unique_ptr<SchedulableTask> child) override;

 private:
  std::vector<std::unique_ptr<SchedulableTask>> children_;
};
```

This is bread and butter class design, so I will assume you have no trouble carrying forth the implementation of this class, or of its counterpart, the `AtomicTask`. Virtually every composite task we have inherits from `ContainerTask`; the only departures we have from this pattern are certain kinds of queues that do not inherit from a vector.

But we have an even better opportunity for reuse in the area of behavior. Rather than simply implementing each task's Step member function separately, we should decompose the Step member function and expose the innards of the stepping API to subclasses through the class's protected interface, shown in Listing 22.3.

Listing 22.3. Implementing stepping.

```
// Expanded SchedulableTask definition ...
class SchedulableTask {
 public:
  // ... previously defined member functions
  virtual TaskStatus Step();
  virtual bool IsFailure() const;
  virtual bool IsTerminated() const;
  virtual TaskStatus GetStatus() const;
  // More member functions for our use case ...

 protected:
  virtual TaskStatus PerformAction() = 0;
  virtual void SetStatus(TaskStatus status);
  // More member functions for our use case …
  ...

// Expanded SchedulableTask implementation ...
TaskStatus SchedulableTask::Step() {
  if (!IsTerminated()) {
    SetStatus(PerformAction());
  }
  return GetStatus();
}
```

Using these protected member functions, the `Step` member function is implemented in `SchedulableTask` in a way which looks almost trivial. But by defining this (and similar member functions) near the top of the tree, we define the execution model for tasks, so all that we really need to know about a task is how it differs from the norm. The `ContainerTask` we have already shown just holds tasks; it does not have execution semantics. But at the very next level of the tree appear tasks like `ParallelTask` or `SequenceTask`, which do override these protected methods, as shown in Listing 22.4.

The meat of an actual `SequenceTask` can be fairly simple, encoded in its `PerformAction` member function. But we did more than just implementing this member function; we exposed some of its innards in the protected API as well, including `HandleChildFailure` and `AdvanceToNextChild`.

Listing 22.4. Implementing stepping in SequenceTask.

```cpp
// SequenceTask definition ...
class SequenceTask : public ContainerTask {
 public:
  SequenceTask(string name,
                ExecutionContext* execution_context);
  ~SequenceTask() override = default;

 protected:
  uint current_task_;
  TaskStatus PerformAction() override;
  virtual bool AdvanceToNextChild();
  virtual TaskStatus HandleChildFailure(
      TaskStatus child_status);
  // More member functions related to our use case ...
};

// SequenceTask implementation ...
TaskStatus SequenceTask::PerformAction() {
  if (GetStatus() == WAITING) {
      SetStatus(STEPPING);
      current_task_ = 0;
  }

  TaskStatus child_status{STEPPING};
  auto child = GetCurrentChild();
  if (child != nullptr) {
    // Step the child unless it has stopped.
    if (!child->IsTerminated()) {
      child->Step();
        }

    // Now check for and handle completed children.
    if (child->IsTerminated()) {
      if (child->IsFailure()) {
         // Propagate child failure up
         child_status = child->GetStatus();
      } else {
         // Move to next task
         AdvanceToNextChild();
      }
    }
  }

  // Now check for and handle failed children.
  if (IsStatusFailure(child_status)) {
    SetStatus(HandleChildFailure(child_status));
  } else if (current_task_ >= GetChildren().size()) {
    SetStatus(SUCCESS);
  }
  // Propagate status up the API.
  return GetStatus();
}
```

(Continued)

```
bool SequenceTask::AdvanceToNextChild() {
  // Advance until we run out of children.
  current_task_++;
  return HasCurrentChild();
}

TaskStatus SequenceTask::HandleChildFailure(
    TaskStatus child_status) {
  // Propagate failure up to parent.
  return child_status;
}
```

We chose to do so by looking at the actual decision-making use cases of our robot application, where we wanted finer-grained control on how the tasks responded to various circumstances without making the actual `SequenceTask` very complicated.

For example, we wanted a `TryTask` which tried tasks in sequence but did not fail itself if a child failed. By exposing `AdvanceToNextChild` and `HandleChildFailure` in the protected API, we were able to write a `TryTask` with (essentially) half a page of code, shown in Listing 22.5.

Listing 22.5. Implementing a `TryTask`—essentially, the whole thing.

```
// try_task.h
// Header includes omitted ...
class TryTask : public SequenceTask {
 public:
  TryTask(const string& name,
          ExecutionContext* execution_context);
  ~TryTask() override = default;
 protected:
  TaskStatus HandleChildFailure(TaskStatus_) override;
};

// try_task.cc
// More header includes omitted ...
TaskStatus TryTask::HandleChildFailure(TaskStatus _) {
  // Ignore failures, continue until we are done.
  return AdvanceToNextChild() ? STEPPING : SUCCESS;
}
```

The only member function we needed to override was `HandleChildFailure`, and that override itself was very simple. This made developing and testing this class easy; we could rely on the containment and stepping logic of the parent class, and focus our testing on `HandleChildFailure` and its impact on, well, child failure.

This design breaks behavior tree down based on a class hierarchy with overridable member functions. In C++, this can be less efficient than carefully written code specialized to the use case at hand. The chapter on the Behavior Tree Starter Kit in the first volume of *Game AI Pro* describes a series of these tradeoffs, which you could consider in more detail (Champandard and Dunstan 2012).

For our use case, this explicit breakdown of behavior was appropriate for a robot whose top-level decision-making cycle needed to run no more than 30 hertz. This may not necessarily work for a game that needs to optimize every cycle, but we were able to run a behavior tree step for a simple benchmark at 60 million hertz on a not too beefy computer. So you may want to begin with a clean breakdown, which is easily extensible and return to optimize it later as your benchmarks, profiling, and the needs of your game demand.

22.3.3 Pitfall #3: Routing Everything through the Blackboard

Previously, BT-like systems were designed to break cognitive tasks apart into small parts (Francis 2000), so the thinking that the system did could be interleaved with the system's memory retrieval processes; for that memory retrieval to work, virtually all the data that the system manipulated needed to be exposed in the system's blackboard. A robot control system where multiple independent processes communicate, like ROS (ROS.org 2016), has similar constraints, and the first version of Google's robotics behavior tree supported close interaction between the system blackboard and the behavior tree. Although not a required part of the system, this enabled us to specify a behavior tree and its data at the same time.

Similar concerns operate in games with characters that need sensory models, like stealth games (and many other modern shooters), but it is probably a mistake to tie the overall behavior tree logic too closely to the logic of the blackboard—and even more of a mistake during prototyping to make simple tasks dependent on a blackboard for communication. Coding all tasks to use a system blackboard or sensory manager, while providing many advantages as systems grow larger and more complicated, is much more complex than using native language features for communication—and is often less reliable, unless you are enough of a C++ template wizard to create a fully typesafe blackboard (and if so, more power to you).

In the prototyping phase, doing things "right" this way can actually interfere with exploring the design space of your behavior trees and perfecting their logic. For our first behavior tree, the blackboard and the behavior tree were designed together to complement each other. Unfortunately, this meant a change to the API of one affected the other—particularly in how the hierarchy of tasks referred to the hierarchy of the blackboard, and vice versa. On at least two separate occasions, a lower level API change led to a month or more work rewiring the tasks and the blackboard so that all the data were available to the right tasks.

The alternative is to strongly decouple the behavior tree from the blackboard. The same behavior tree logic should work with a complicated hierarchical blackboard with a rich knowledge representation—or with a simple C++ plain old data structure (POD), or even with no explicit blackboard at all, and communication performed ad hoc between cooperating tasks. Using ad-hoc communication can make it more difficult to build a full data-driven behavior tree, but for many problems, it is sufficient. For example, one machine learning system that successfully learned better-than-human behavior trees for controlling an unmanned aerial vehicle used a C++ POD containing only a handful of values as its "blackboard."

When we reimplemented our behavior tree for a new robot platform, we temporarily abandoned the blackboard in favor of ad-hoc communication, which had two benefits. First: we were able to complete and test the logic of the blackboard to a very high degree; second, when we made the decision to abandon a low-level API, only two leaf tasks needed to be changed. We still have a use case for the old blackboard in the new behavior tree—but the clean separation of concerns from the old blackboard means we have a behavior tree which is reliable, well tested—and can work with a variety of communication mechanisms.

I cannot as cleanly show you this difference between these two approaches using just code—the old blackboard is a lot of code, and the new communications mechanisms are peculiar to their use case—but if your behavior tree is properly architected, you should be able to use the same core decision logic in both a small toy example whose "blackboard" is a C++ POD and whose decisions are made by C++ lambdas and a full system that has a distributed blackboard and a complete behavior tree condition system that is purely data driven.

22.4 Conclusion

I have slogged through creating many, many behavior trees and BT-likes, and it is really easy to get bogged down. But the pattern I am outlining above is simple: figure out what you need to do, don't jump the gun on building too much of it until you have a good idea of what you need, and refine your abstractions until the complexity is squirreled away in a few files and the leaves of your functionality are *dead bone simple*. This approach can be applied everywhere, and when you do, it can radically improve your development experience.

I could preach about how test-driven development and continuous integration made this easier, or how refactoring tools help (and what to do when you cannot use them; sed, awk, and shell scripting are your friends). But the major point I want to make is that behavior trees can be surprisingly complicated—and yet surprisingly regular in structure—and it is very important to look carefully at the places you are repeating work and to aggressively seek ways to eliminate them using judicious use of class hierarchies.

Our first shot at creating a behavior tree had too many concepts, too much repeated code, and too much boilerplate. Through the process of reducing the number of entities, looking at the needs of our application domain, and *corralling* complexity into carefully chosen superclasses and support files, we not only radically reduced the amount of similar code we had to maintain, but the actual code we needed often collapsed to a single page—or occasionally a single line. When you have done that, and you can benchmark your system to show it is still efficient, you have done your job architecting your behavior tree right.

References

Bonasso, R. P., Firby, R. J., Gat, E., Kortenkamp, D., Miller, D. P., and Slack, M. G. 1997. Experiences with an architecture for intelligent, reactive agents. *Journal of Experimental & Theoretical Artificial Intelligence* 9(2–3):237–256.

Champandard, A., and Dunstan, P. 2012. The behavior tree starter kit. In *Game AI Pro*, ed. S. Rabin. Boca Raton, FL: CRC Press, pp. 73–95.

Firby, R. J. 1987. An investigation into reactive planning in complex domains. *AAAI* 87:202–206.

Francis, A. G. 2000. Context-sensitive asynchronous memory. PhD diss. Georgia Institute of Technology. Available online http://dresan.com/research/publications/thesis.pdf (accessed June 8, 2016).

Isla, D. 2005. Handling complexity in the Halo 2 AI. *2005 Game Developer's Conference.* Available online http://www.gamasutra.com/view/feature/130663/gdc_2005_proceeding_handling_.php (accessed June 8, 2016).

ROS.org. 2016. Powering the world's robots. Available online http://www.ros.org (accessed June 8, 2016).

From Behavior to Animation
A Reactive AI Architecture for Networked First-Person Shooter Games

Sumeet Jakatdar

23.1 Introduction

First-person shooters (FPS) are a very specific and popular genre of video games. Many of the general AI principles and techniques are applicable for FPS AI, but they need to be modified to cater to the needs of fast-paced action. The challenge lies in selecting, modifying, and combining algorithms together efficiently, so that AIs can react quickly to player actions. For an AAA FPS game with strict deadlines, the AI system needs to be ready early in the development cycle, allowing content creators to start using it. The system also needs to be simple to use, data driven, and flexible enough to be able to support creating a variety of AI archetypes. The system also needs to support networked gameplay without needing any extra effort from design and animation teams.

This chapter will provide a high-level and simple overview of an AI system that could be used for a networked FPS game. We will look into modifications to well-known AI algorithms such as behavior trees (BTs) and animation state machines (ASMs), which were made to suit specific needs of the game. We will discuss ways to keep the BT simple but still reactive to high-priority events by introducing a concept called *interrupts*. Furthermore, we will touch upon animation layers that are designed to handle aiming and shooting animations independent of the BT. Here, we will discuss modifications to traditional ASMs to help network animations, allowing cooperative or competitive gameplay across the internet.

We will also look into a Blackboard system to solve behavior and animation selection problems. Here we will introduce techniques that will help keep the Blackboard attributes up-to-date by using a *function-based* approach.

Whenever applicable, we will provide pseudocode and real examples to better explain the concepts presented. Many of you probably know these techniques individually. Hopefully, by reading this chapter, you will get an idea of how they can work together for networked FPS games.

23.2 Client-Server Engine and AI System

We will assume that our game engine is built using a client-server paradigm, where the server is authoritative in nature. This means that server dictates the position, orientation, and gameplay logic for all game entities.

From time to time, the client receives a *network snapshot* from the server for all of the entities. While processing this snapshot, each entity's position and orientation will be corrected to match the server. The frequency of these snapshots depend upon the network bandwidth and CPU performance requirements of the game. Between network snapshots, the client interpolates entities for smoother 60 fps gameplay. It is important to keep the size of the network snapshots (measured in bits) small to support hundreds of entities and to avoid packet fragmentation. The upper limit for network snapshots is usually referred to as the *maximum transmission unit* (MTU), and the recommended size is approximately 1200–1500 bytes for Ethernet connections. To be able to achieve the smallest possible MTU, we will look for opportunities to infer logic on the client side by sending across minimalistic information about entities.

The AI system is just one part of this engine. In addition, the server is responsible for handling many other systems, such as controller logic, player animation, physics, navigation, and scripting. Similarly, the client is responsible for handling effects, sounds, and most importantly rendering.

Figure 23.1 shows a high-level overview of the system and important AI modules in the engine. The BTs are responsible for choosing behavior using the knowledge stored in the Blackboard (a shared space for communication). The ASM is responsible for selecting animations and managing the animation pose of the AI. The client-side ASM has the same responsibilities as the server, but the implementation is slightly different from the server, as it does not make any decisions but merely follows the server. We will explore the details of the ASM further in this chapter.

At first, we will concentrate on the AI system on the server side. After we are done with the server, we will move on to the client side. We will finish by looking at the networking layer between the server and client AI systems. The pseudocode provided in this chapter will look very similar to C, but it should be fairly easy to translate these concepts in an object-oriented coding environment.

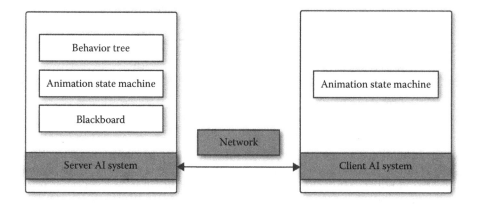

Figure 23.1

Client-server engine and AI system.

23.3 The AI Agent

Before moving on to create various AI modules, we will define the `AIAgent` structure that lies at the core of our AI system, as shown in Listing 23.1. All three of our AI modules will be contained within this structure. Both server and client will have their own representation of the `AIAgent`.

Listing 23.1. Defining `AIAgent`.

```
struct AIAgent
{
    // Blackboard
    // Behavior Tree
    // Animation State Machine
    // ...
};
```

23.4 The Blackboard

The Blackboard holds key information about the AI agent, which can be manipulated and queried by other AI modules for choosing behaviors, animations, and so on. In some cases, the Blackboard is also used as a communication layer between modules.

Our implementation of the Blackboard will support three different types of variables; strings, floats, and integers. We will call them *value-based* variables. We will also support a special variable, referred in this chapter as *function-based*.

23.4.1 Value-Based Variables (Strings, Integers, and Floats)

Table 23.1 creates four Blackboard variables for the human soldier archetype. From the first three Blackboard variables, we can infer that the human soldier is currently *standing*.

Table 23.1 Sample Blackboard for the Human Soldier Archetype

Variable	Type	Current_value	Update_function
Weapon	string	rifle_longrange	null
Number_of_bullets	int	50	null
Stance	string	stand	null
Angle_to_player	float		getangletoplayer

He or she is holding a weapon, a *long range rifle* with *50 bullets* in its magazine. There is no specific range, or possible set of values associated with these variables. So, for example, the number of bullets can be negative, which might be illogical. In such cases, it is the responsibility of other AI logic to handle that situation gracefully. However, adding support for ranges or enums should be fairly straightforward and is recommended in a final implementation.

23.4.2 Function-Based Variables

The first three Blackboard variables in Table 23.1 will be modified by external systems. For these variables, the Blackboard can be considered as some form of storage. But sometimes, we need the Blackboard to execute logic to calculate the latest value of a given variable. This is the purpose of the `update _ function`.

When a human soldier needs to turn and face the player, it will query the Blackboard to get the latest value of the `angle_to_player`. In this case, the Blackboard will execute the `getangletoplayer` function and return the latest yaw value. We call these types of variables *function-based*, as a function is executed when they are requested.

23.4.3 Implementation of the Blackboard

Let us look at some implementation details for our Blackboard. Listing 23.2 shows the implementation for `BlackboardValue`, which will essentially hold only one of the three types of values: a string, float, or integer. We have also created an enum to indicate the type of Blackboard variable and use it in the `BlackboardVariable` structure. Remember, the `update_function` is only defined and used for *function-based* Blackboard variables.

Listing 23.2. Definition of `BlackboardVariable` and `BlackboardValue`.

```
struct BlackboardValue
{
    union
    {
        const char* stringValue;
        int intValue;
        float floatValue;
    };
};
```

(Continued)

```
enum BlackboardVariableType
{
    BLACKBOARD_INT,
    BLACKBOARD_FLOAT,
    BLACKBOARD_STRING,
};
typedef BlackboardValue
    (*BlackboardUpdateFunction)(AIAgent *agent);

struct BlackboardVariable
{
    const char* name;
    BlackboardValue value;
    BlackboardVariableType type;
    BlackboardUpdateFunction updateFunction;
};
```

The `Blackboard`, in Listing 23.3, is essentially a collection of many `Blackboard Variable` structures stored as a fixed-size array. We also add `numVariables` to easily keep track of the actual number of variables in use. Finally, a Blackboard is added to the `AIAgent` definition. When an AI agent spawns, a script is responsible for populating and assigning default values to the AI agent's blackboard.

Listing 23.3. Setting up the Blackboard for the `AIAgent`.

```
struct Blackboard
{
    BlackboardVariable variables[MAX_BLACKBOARD_VARIABLES];
    int numVariables;
};

struct AIAgent
{
    // AI agent's blackboard
    Blackboard blackboard; }
```

Listing 23.4 shows an example of creating one of the Blackboard variables for a human soldier.

Listing 23.4. `BlackboardVariable` example for human soldier.

```
BlackboardValue value;
Value.name = "weapon";
value.stringValue = "rifle_longrange";
value.type = BLACKBOARD_STRING;
value.updateFunction = null;
```

23.5 The Behavior Tree

At the core of an AI agent's behaviors is a way to select various actions. A BT consists of many of these actions arranged in a tree format and inherently provides priority in its hierarchy. Every action will have prerequisite conditions, which are needed to be satisfied for that action to be chosen. If you need to get familiar with the basics of BTs, please refer to chapters in earlier *AI Game Pro* and *AI Game Programming Wisdom* books (Isla 2005, Champandard 2008, Champandard and Dunstan 2013). You can also refer to the many online articles available at *AiGameDev.com* (AiGameDev 2015) and *Gamasutra.com*. Here, we will focus on some specific modifications to known BT paradigms.

Our AI agent is going to have many behaviors. Every behavior will consist of one or more actions. However, it is important to understand that only one action will be active at a given time. For example, the human soldier behavior for suppressing the enemy can be composed of two actions; first the *throwing grenade* action and then the *charging toward the player* action. We will design the BTs with this consideration in mind.

23.5.1 Creating a Behavior Tree for the AI Agent

We will start by defining a `BehaviorTree`, and then look at the `BehaviorTreeNode` definition.

Listing 23.5. Setting up `BehaviorTree` for `AIAgent`.

```
struct BehaviorTree
{
    const char* name;
    BehaviorTreeNode nodes[MAX_BT_NODES];
    int numNodes;
};

struct AIAgent
{
    // AI agent's own blackboard
    Blackboard blackboard;
    // pointer to behavior tree definition
    const BehaviorTree *behaviorTree;
    //...
}
```

As seen in Listing 23.5, the `BehaviorTree` itself is just a fixed-size array of `BehaviorTreeNode` nodes. This size depends upon the complexity of various AI agent's behaviors, but generally it is a good idea to keep the size under 1000 nodes. If the tree gets bigger than this, then it might be worth looking at the granularity of condition nodes and finding opportunities to consolidate them.

We add one more variable, `numNodes`, to easily keep track of number of nodes used in a `BehaviorTree`. Another important assumption made here is that the "root node" will always appear first, at the 0th index of the nodes array. Each BT also has a unique name, which is used only for debugging purposes.

You would have noticed that there is only one definition for nodes, `BehaviorTreeNode`. In the next section, we will explore how it is used for supporting different types of nodes.

We saw earlier that, every AI agent stores its own copy of the Blackboard, but this is not the case with a BT. At runtime, only one, nonmodifiable copy will reside in memory for a given BT definition. Every AI agent who uses this BT will store a pointer to this definition and refer to it time and again to choose an action.

23.5.2 Behavior Tree Nodes

Now that we have represented the BT in the `BehaviorTree` structure, let us move on to representing actual BT nodes, as shown in Listing 23.6.

Listing 23.6. Implementing Behavior Tree nodes.

```
enum BTNodeType
{
    BT_NODE_ACTION,            // action
    BT_NODE_CONDITION,         // condition
    BT_NODE_PARALLEL,          // parallel
    BT_NODE_SEQUENCE,          // sequence
    BT_NODE_SELECTOR,          // selector
    //...
};

enum BTNodeResult
{
    BT_SUCCESS,
    BT_FAILURE,
    BT_RUNNNING,
    //...
};

typedef BTNodeResult(*BTFunction)
    (AIAgent *agent, int nodeIndex);

struct BehaviorTreeNode
{
    const char* name;
    // type of the node
    BTNodeType type;
    // parent node index
    int parentNodeIndex;
    // children nodes
    int childrenNodeIndices[MAX_BT_CHILDREN_NODES];
    int numChildrenNodes;

    // condition node attributes
    BTFunction condition;
    // action node attributes
    BTFunction onActionStart;
    BTFunction onActionUpdate;
    BTFunction onActionTerminate;
};
```

We start by specifying the types of BT nodes we want to support using the `BTNodeType` enum. Typically, a BT supports conditions, actions, parallels, selectors, and sequences. You can add support for additional nodes, but the core idea of the implementation remains the same.

As we have only one definition for all of the nodes, the type will be used to figure out how the node is processed during the BT evaluation.

The child and parent relationship of a `BehaviorTreeNode` is defined by storing `parentNodeIndex` and an array of `childrenNodeIndices`. This setup is going to make it easy to traverse up and down the tree. It is possible that certain types of nodes are not allowed to have any children at all. In our implementation, the leaf nodes, action, and conditions are not allowed to have children. If we need to have a condition to be successful before executing further, then we can just use the sequence node with that condition as its first child. Similarly, two actions can be put together under one sequence if one action needs to follow another action, only if the first one was successful. This approach helps keep the tree simple and readable, and we always know to reevaluate the tree from the root if an action fails.

Actions and conditions can only be part of a composite node in our BT, which guarantees that there will not be any logical issues with our tree. Allowing conditions to have children adds ambiguity about the nature of that node. Unless we add more attributes to the condition, it will be difficult to decide if the condition node needs to be treated as a sequence or a parallel. We rather choose to do it in more elegant way by using the composite nodes.

Only the composite node types such as selectors, parallels, and sequences are allowed to have children. So, if we need to create a behavior consisting of one condition and one action, then it would be represented using a sequence or a parallel node. Listing 23.7 shows an example of a sequence node for a human soldier.

Listing 23.7. Turn behavior for a human soldier.

```
{
    "name": "turnBehavior",
    "type": "sequence",
    "children":
    [
        {
            "type": "condition",
            "name": "turnCondition",
            "condition": "isPlayerBehind"
        },
        {
            "type": "action",
            "name": "turnAction",
            "onActionStart": "sayDialogue"
        }
    ]
}
```

It is worth mentioning that there is only one parent for a node in our implementation. We will validate all these requirements while populating BTs at runtime.

Just knowing the relationship between BT nodes is not enough. We need to be able to associate some logic to nodes, so that we can execute that logic and find out the result. This is where `BTFunction` comes in handy. To start with, we only need functions for two types of nodes: conditions and actions. For action nodes in particular, we need three functions: `onActionStart`, `OnActionUpdate`, and `onActionTerminate`.

23. From Behavior to Animation

These functions can be used to execute additional gameplay logic when an action is active. If any one of these functions returns BT _ FAILURE, then we will have to reevaluate the tree.

To explain this a little better, we go back to the human soldier example again. Let us say that one of the behaviors for our human is a *Turn Behavior*. If the player is behind, our agent will turn to face the player and say a line of dialogue while turning. For this behavior, we will need three nodes in our BT. Listing 23.7 shows a raw behavior tree asset that we will use to populate the human soldier's BT at runtime. Many of you might recognize the JSON format. If you plan to write your own tools to create and edit BT, then a format like JSON is worth considering as there are many available parsers and editors available which might save you time.

The isPlayerBehind condition will make use of the Blackboard variable angle _ to _ player to decide if the player is behind. If the condition is successful, then the sequence will continue and select turnAction and call the sayDialogue function once, as the action starts.

23.5.3 Handling Parallel Conditions

The only node in our BT that will last for a longer period of time is the action node. In our case, an action will continue while the corresponding animation state is active. We will look into animation states a little later in this chapter.

For some actions, it is important that all of the prerequisite conditions remain valid for the duration of the action and not just at the start. We will achieve this by using parallel nodes. Let us say our human soldier has another behavior called *Relaxed Behavior*. He or she continues to remain relaxed until he or she sees a threat and then switches to another behavior. So, when he or she is relaxing, we need a way to continue to make sure that there is no threat.

In Listing 23.8, notice that the relaxedBehavior node is a parallel node. This node will act exactly the same as a sequence node while evaluating the tree to find an action.

Listing 23.8. Relaxed behavior for a human soldier using parallel nodes.

```
{
    "name": "relaxedBehavior",
    "type": "parallel",
    "children":
    [
        {
            "type": "condition",
            "name": "checkThreat",
            "condition": "noThreatInSight"
        },
        {
            "type": "action",
            "name": "relaxedAction"
        }
    ]
}
```

Although, once the `relaxedAction` is chosen and started, the parallel node will be used to populate all of the conditions that are needed to remain valid throughout this behavior.

In a full-blown BT, there will be many parallel nodes active for a given action. We will need a way to store all active parallel nodes for every AI agent independently, so we can execute them every frame and make sure that they are valid to continue executing the current action.

Listing 23.9 extends the `AIAgent` definition to support active parallel nodes. Once the action is chosen by the BT, then the `PopulateActiveParallelNodes` function will be called to generate the list of all parallel nodes that were executed on the way to the current action nodes. This is achieved by traversing back up the tree, all the way to the root node. We make use of `parentNodeIndex` to quickly traverse back up the tree. While updating the action, the BT logic will go through all the active parallel nodes and process their children condition nodes. If any of those conditions are invalid, then the action is

---

Listing 23.9. Extending `AIAgent` to support parallel conditions.

```
struct AIAgent
{
    // AI agent's own blackboard
    Blackboard blackboard;
    // pointer to behavior tree definition
    const BehaviorTree *behaviorTree;
    // active parallel conditions
    int   activeNodes[MAX_ACTIVE_PARALLELS];
    int   numActiveNodes;

    //...
}

void PopulateActiveParallelNodes
    (AIAgent *agent, int actionNodeIndex)
{

    const BehaviorTreeNode* btNode
        = &agent->behaviorTree->nodes[actionNodeIndex];
    agent->numActiveNodes = 0;

    while(btNode->index != 0)
    {
        int parentNodeIndex = btNode->parentNodeIndex;
        btNode
            = &agent->behaviorTree->nodes[parentNodeIndex];

        if(btNode->type == BT_NODE_PARALLEL)
        {
            agent->activeNodes[agent->numActiveNodes]
                                    = btNode->index;
            agent->numActiveNodes++;
        }
    }
}
```

---

considered to be invalid. At this time, the BT will be reevaluated from root node to find a new, more suitable action.

This approach helps to create an extremely efficient BT, as we do not evaluate the complete tree every frame. It also keeps the reactiveness of the tree intact. However, extra care has to be taken while designing the tree, so that all the possible conditions are accounted for. This is a tradeoff that we could live with, as efficiency is very important.

Sequence nodes can be handled in very similar fashion with a small implementation difference. There is no need to store any active sequences, as we are only interested in advancing the immediate parent sequence when an action is complete.

23.5.4 Handling Interruption Events in the Behavior Tree

After implementing the behavior tree architecture, we still have one more problem to deal with. We need a way to forcefully reevaluate the tree for certain key events, which can happen any time. In the case of a human soldier, *damage* is a high-priority event. Most of the time, we want humans to immediately react to *damage*.

To ensure that the AI will always react to *damage,* we found ourselves duplicating the same parallel condition for most of our actions. This approach works, but it is not ideal as it makes the tree unnecessarily complex. To handle this problem, we will introduce a new concept called interrupts.

Interrupts are basically events that will force the behavior tree logic to immediately invalidate the current action and initiate a full reevaluation of the tree. Interrupts themselves know nothing about AI behaviors in the tree at all. They usually last only until the next update of the BT.

When an interrupt occurs, the full reevaluation update should lead us to an action that was meant to be chosen when this interrupt is present and other conditions are met. Hence, some condition nodes need to have additional parameters so that they will only be valid during an interrupt. To achieve this, we need to add another attribute to the condition nodes, as shown in Listing 23.10.

Listing 23.10. Adding support for interrupts to `BehaviorTreeNode`.

```
struct BehaviorTreeNode
{
    //...
    // only used by condition nodes
    const char* interrupt;
};
```

The `interrupt` attribute is optional and only used by condition nodes. However, if it is specified for a condition node, then that node will only be evaluated when the specified interrupt event is being processed.

This simple modification helps reduce the complexity of the tree greatly. This approach works well when there are only handful of interrupt events associated with the behavior tree. It is possible that interrupt events are not mutually exclusive and may occur on the same frame. This problem can be solved by having a predefined priority list of interrupt events and only processing the highest interrupt event on that list.

A good optimization is to ignore an interrupt if none of the nodes in a BT refer to it. For this to work, you can populate a separate list of referenced interrupts while creating the tree at runtime.

23.6 Animation State Machine

Now that we have a system to choose an action, it is time to figure out how our AI agent will be animated. Let us look at two basic types of animations we need to support for our AI agents in our ASM.

A *full-body* animation forms the base pose of the AI. In most cases, an AI agent needs to only play one *full-body* animation. This is not a limitation of the animation system but rather a choice we made to keep things simple. Then comes the *additive* animation type, which modifies the base pose. Contrary to the *full-body* animation, an AI agent can play multiple additive animations at a time. In fact, we will make use of *additive* animations to allow our agents to aim and shoot at the player. Let us start with the problem of selecting animations.

23.6.1 Animation Tables

The most important job of the ASM is to select animations, and it does so by using Animation Tables (ATs).

ATs can be thought of as a simple database of all possible animations, given a set of pre-defined conditions. These conditions are nothing but Blackboard values we defined earlier in our system. In our ASM, every animation state will have one or more ATs associated with it.

Table 23.2 shows one of the ATs for our human soldier. We will use this table to find one *full-body* animation when the human soldier is in an idle animation state. There are two types of columns for ATs. One is an *input column*, and another is *output column*. *Input columns* are helpful to form a query of Blackboard variable values. This query is then used to find a *first fitting row* by matching the value of each variable against that row. Once a row is found, the AT will return the corresponding entry in its animation column.

For example, if a human soldier is `crouching` and holding a `shotgun` in his hands, then the AT will end up choosing the `shotgun _ crouch _ idle` animation by selecting row number 1. It is that simple!

You might have noticed the "–" symbol in Table 23.2. This dash signifies that the value of that Blackboard variable can be ignored while evaluating that row. This is very useful, as we can always have a fallback row, which will make sure that we always find an animation to play. In this example, the fifth row is a fallback row. We also have an explicit column for *row numbers*. This column is actually not stored as part of the ATs, but it is there to explain another concept later in this chapter (so for now, let us ignore it).

Table 23.2 Sample "Idle" Animation Table for Human Soldier

Row	Stance	Weapon	Animation
0	stand	shotgun	shotgun_stand_idle
1	crouch	shotgun	shotgun_crouch_idle
2	–	shotgun	shotgun_prone_idle
3	prone	–	prone_idle
4	crouch	–	crouch_idle
5	–	–	stand_idle

Table 23.3 Aim Table for the Human Soldier

Row	Weapon	anim_aim_left	anim_aim_right	anim_aim_up	anim_aim_down
0	shotgun	shotgun_aim_left	shotgun_aim_right	shotgun_aim_up	shotgun_aim_down
1	–	rifle_aim_left	rifle_aim_right	rifle_aim_up	rifle_aim_down

As shown in Table 23.3, ATs can have multiple *input* and *output columns*. In fact, we use this to return more than one animation for the aiming and shooting of *additive* animations. In the case of the *Aim Table*, the AT will return *left*, *right*, *up*, and *down* animations. It will be the responsibility of ASM to figure out the blend weights for these animations to achieve the desired aiming pose.

Let us look at how we can implement ATs in our AI system, as shown in Listing 23.11.

Listing 23.11. Animation Table column and row definitions.

```
enum AnimationTableColumType
{
    AT_COLUMN_INPUT,
    AT_COLUMN_OUTPUT
};

struct AnimationTableColumn
{
    const char* blackboardVariableName;
    BlackboardValue expectedValue;
    AnimationTableColumType type;
};

struct AnimationTableRow
{
    AnimationTableColumn columns[MAX_COLUMNS_PER_ROW];
    int numColumnsInUse;
};

struct AnimationTable
{
    const char* name;
    AnimationTableRow rows[MAX_ROWS_PER_TABLE];
    int numRowsInUse;
};
```

Essentially, `AnimationTableColumn` stores a Blackboard variable name that it refers to and an `expectedValue` of that variable to compare against. We can easily look up the type of Blackboard variable in the `blackboard` array in our `AIAgent` definition. In the final implementation however, it is ideal to use hashes to avoid string comparisons. The structure `AnimationTableRow` is a collection of columns, and finally `AnimationTable` is a collection of rows.

Depending on the number of AI agents alive, the amount of queries can be a performance concern. To help improve performance, we can also implement a caching mechanism for the results.

23.6.2 Animation States

As mentioned earlier, every animation state is responsible for finding and applying one *full-body* animation. If it cannot find one, then there is a bug that needs to be fixed.

Depending on the state, we also need *additive* animations to modify the base pose. *Additive* animations are optional and may not be used by every animation state. In this chapter, we will assume that there are only two possible *additive* animations per animation state. One for aiming and another for the shooting animation.

To achieve this, we will need to refer to three different ATs in our animation state, as shown in Listing 23.12.

Listing 23.12. `Animation State` definition.

```
struct AnimationState
{
    const char* name;
    const AnimationTable *fullBodyTable;
    const AnimationTable *aimTable;
    const AnimationTable *shootTable;
};
```

23.6.3 Choosing the Animation State for an AI Agent

For a given action, we need to choose an animation state. We could infer the animation state by using the Blackboard variables alone, but this approach is complex and potentially unreliable. However, this approach is successfully used in many other games, and it does work very well. Keeping up with the theme of simplicity, we opt for another, rather easy solution. In our system, the BT action is responsible for choosing the corresponding animation state.

As shown in Listing 23.13, we added an animation state index to the `BehaviorTreeNode` definition. When an action is selected by the BT, a corresponding animation state will be requested by the BT and then immediately processed by the ASM.

Listing 23.13. Animation state for the current BT action.

```
struct BehaviorTreeNode
{
    // ...
    // used by action nodes to request animation state
    int animationStateIndex;
};
```

23.6.4 Managing Animations with the ASM

Given an animation state, we are now equipped to find animations. Although, once they are found, we will need to apply those animations to our agent. In the case of aiming with the given aim animations, we would need to calculate blend weights based on the direction to the player. In the case of shooting, we would need a way to select one of the animations based on the weapon agent is holding. We will achieve this by adding three functions to our ASM definition. These functions will query the ATs when the animation state is changed. They will also manage blend weights for the selected animations based on specific gameplay logic.

Listing 23.14. Definition of the ASM.

```
typedef void(*ATFunction)(AIAgent *agent, AnimationTable* table);

struct AnimationStateMachine
{
    AnimationState states[MAX_ANIMATION_STATES];
    int numAnimationStatesInUse;

    ATFunction fullBodyAnimUpdate;
    ATFunction aimAnimUpdate;
    ATFunction shootAnimUpdate;
};
```

As shown in Listing 23.14, we have created an `AnimationStateMachine`, which is essentially a collection of many animation states. We have also added three functions for managing animations for all three different animation tables.

Listing 23.15. Storing current animations and Animation State for an `AIAgent`.

```
struct AIAgent
{
    //...
    AnimationStateMachine *animationStateMachine;

    int currentStateIndex;
    int currentFullBodyRowIndex;
    int currentAimRowIndex;
    int currentShootRowIndex;
    //...
};
```

Finally, in Listing 23.15, we add a reference to the ASM. Additionally, we store the indices of the current rows we got our animations from in `currentStateIndex`. This will come in handy when we look at networking AI animations later in this chapter.

23.6.5 Transitions

It is trivial to add the concept of a transition to our ASM. Transitions are very similar to the animation states, except they are not requested specifically by a BT action. They are chosen by the ASM while transitioning from one animation state to a state requested by the BT. The BT itself is unaware of transitions and leaves this responsibility to the ASM completely. The transition can have their own *full-body, additive* layers, and related ATs. While searching for an animation in an AT for a transition, it is acceptable if no fitting animation is found. In that case, the ASM will just blend animations from the previous to next state directly. This helps the animation team, as they only add transition animations where they fit and rely on animation blending in other cases.

23.6.6 Aiming and Shooting

While designing the ASM in the earlier section, we gave the responsibility of managing the aiming and shooting logic to the ASM. In our case, using the logic in `ATFunction`, the ASM will decide to aim and shoot independent of the BT action based on the existence of tables and their respective functions. This is where our FPS version of the ASM is slightly different from traditional state machines.

This method helps to keep our BT simpler, as it will not have to worry about managing shooting and aiming. The BT can still influence animation selection for aiming and shooting by changing Blackboard variables. We can also disable the aiming and shooting logic completely if needed. In the case of an FPS game, whenever possible, the AI agents shoot the players, or choose to perform melee combat at a close range. This solution solves the problem in the ASM instead of the BT, making it easier for the BT to handle high-level logic.

In some games, shooting needs to be controlled as a behavior in the BT. In such cases, this approach may not be suitable as it does not give fine-grain control over shooting using behaviors. One suggestion is to split the shooting and aiming logic into another, lightweight state machine. Then this state machine can be controlled independently by adding more attributes and logic to the BT actions.

23.6.7 Animation Alias Tables

So far, whenever we referred to an animation in an AT, we were actually referring to an Animation Alias. An AT is purely a one-to-many mapping, responsible for choosing one of the many variations of a given animation. This simple table empowers animators to create a lot of animation variety by truly staying independent of AI logic and behaviors. Table 23.4 shows an example of an AAT for a human soldier.

We complete our `AIAgent` definition by adding a reference to an `AnimationAlias Table` in Listing 23.16.

At runtime, we can allow switching between different AATs. In fact, we can use them to change the AI's look and feel in order to make them more interesting. For example, when a human soldier is shot, we can switch to another AAT with wounded animations. This is achieved by using one default AAT and another override AAT, as seen in Listing 23.16.

Table 23.4 Example of Animation Alias Table for a Human Soldier

animation_alias	variation 0	variation1	variation2
rifle_idle	rifle_idle_lookaround	rifle_idle_smoke	rifle_idle_checkgun

Listing 23.16. Adding Animation Alias Tables (AATs) to an `AIAgent`.

```
struct AIAgent
{
    //...
    AnimationAliasTable *aliasTableDefault;
    AnimationAliasTable *aliasTableOverride;
    //...
};
```

23. From Behavior to Animation

We also allow multiple active layers of tables and search for animations starting with the `aliasTableOverride` table first. If no override animation is found, then we will fall back to the `aliasTableDefault` table. This allows creating smaller batches of animation variations.

It is important to validate all of the animations within one `AnimationAlias` to ensure that they are compatible with one another. Some of the validations include animation length, animation event markers, and most importantly positions of certain key bones relative to the root bone.

23.7 Networking AI

Players connect to the game as clients, and all of the systems we have created so far work only on the server side. At this point, we need to add a network component to our AI system to see the AI in action on the client. As mentioned earlier, we will assume that an entity's position and orientation are already parts of the general network layer. In the AI system, we are more concerned about animations as no generic animation networking layer exists in the engine otherwise.

To be able to achieve this, we will need to send across enough information to the client so that it can replicate the animation pose of the AI. This is where the ASM and ATs come in very handy, as the definitions for both are available on the client as well.

Table 23.5 lists the minimized `AIAgent` data that are sent over to the client, which is used to choose the same animations as the server. First is `currentStateIndex`, which allows the client to use the same animation state as the server. Now, the client can refer to the same AT tables as the server though the selection animation state, but it does not have any ability to choose animations yet.

On the server, ATs choose animations using a query of Blackboard variables. Unfortunately, there is no Blackboard available on the client, as our server handles all the decision-making authoritatively. If we could somehow tell the client the row number in the table, then we can look up the animation directly without needing a Blackboard at all. This is exactly why we send over row indices for all three ATs to the client: *full-body*, *additive* aim, and shoot.

With this setup, it is guaranteed that the client will always choose the same animations as the server. We need to run the same `ATFunction` on the client to be able to apply the chosen animations in the same way as server. Mostly, the server and client versions of `ATFunction` are very similar to each other in this case.

Using the row indices, we are merely choosing animation aliases and not actual animations. It is critically important that both server and client choose the same animation variation for a given animation alias. If this does not work properly, then the server and client may generate a different animation pose which can result in bugs. Let us take an example of a player

Table 23.5 Animation State Machine Data Sent Over the Network to the Client AI System

Data	Number of Bits
currentstateindex	8 bits (up to 256 states)
currentfullbodyrowindex	7 bits (up to 128 rows)
currentaimrowindex	4 bits (up to 16 rows)
currentshootrowindex	4 bits (up to 16 rows)

shooting and damaging the AI. The bullet collision will be performed on the server using the animation pose on the server. If the animation chosen is different on the client as compared to server, then sometimes players might see that they are clearly hitting the AI on client, but in fact, on the server they are not. We will have to make sure that this never happens.

We could send an extra couple of bits for animations to solve this problem, but a more optimal solution is using a deterministic random seed, which results in the same variation on both ends.

23.8 Conclusion

Presented in this chapter is a basic AI system which supports a variety of behaviors, animations, and networked gameplay. There are many more aspects to this system that we could not discuss in this chapter, but hopefully you now have a solid idea of the foundation that can be extended to match your own needs.

Let us quickly recap what we covered in this chapter. We started with laying down the design and technical requirements and then moved on to implement a Blackboard system. In addition to basic *value-based* variables, the Blackboard supported *function-based* variables to calculate up-to-date values. We used BTs as our behavior selection algorithm and also looked at how parallel conditions can be implemented to incorporate reactivity without complete evaluation of the tree every frame. We also introduced *interrupts* to handle some common high-priority events.

Then we moved on to Animation Tables, which are smart animation databases capable of selecting animations based on Blackboard variables. We also added support for selecting more than one animation and used it for shooting and aiming animations. Next up was the ASM, which made use of Animation Tables to network AI animations. Finally, we created an `AIAgent` definition that keeps track of all these systems for every AI in the game. At this time, we considered our basic AI system complete and ready for prime time.

Although there are a myriad of AI architectures and techniques available, it is important to choose appropriate ones by keeping simplicity and flexibility of a system in mind, at least in the early stages of development. Once you choose the right architecture, you can always add more paradigms to your system as you go. Usually the best approach is to start with proven, simple AI techniques and mold them to your needs in order to get something working quickly. Then you can iterate based on feedback from the team and the changing needs of the game.

References

Champandard, A. J. 2008. Getting started with decision making and control systems. In *AI Game Programming Wisdom*, ed. S. Rabin. Boston, MA: Course Technology, Vol. 4. pp. 257–263.

Champandard, A. J. and Dunstan P. 2013. The behavior tree starter kit. In *Game AI Pro: Collected Wisdom of Game AI Professionals*, ed. S. Rabin. Boca Raton, FL: A K Peters/CRC Press.

Champandard, A. J. 2015. Behavior Trees for Next-Gen Game AI AiGameDev.com. 2015. http://www.aigamedev.com/.

Isla, D. 2005. Handling complexity in Halo 2 AI. In *Proceedings of the Game Developers Conference* (GDC), San Francisco, CA.

24

A Character Decision-Making System for *FINAL FANTASY XV* by Combining Behavior Trees and State Machines

Youichiro Miyake, Youji Shirakami, Kazuya Shimokawa, Kousuke Namiki, Tomoki Komatsu, Joudan Tatsuhiro, Prasert Prasertvithyakarn, and Takanori Yokoyama

24.1 Introduction

Behavior trees and state machines were originally separate techniques—each with their own positive and negative points. The intent behind behavior trees is to make a series of character behaviors, whereas the intent behind finite-state machines (FSMs) is to make a stable cycle of character actions (Miyake 2015a, Miyake 2015b). For *FINAL FANTASY XV* shown in Figure 24.1, we have developed a new decision-making system that combines behavior trees and state machines into a single structure using the LUMINOUS STUDIO (SQUARE ENIX's game engine). This system has both the flexibility of behavior trees and the strict control of state machines as well as giving scalability to the development of a character decision-making system (Figure 24.2). This new decision-making system, which we call the AI Graph, extends the node formalism to enable sharing nodes between FSMs and behavior trees, provides advanced techniques for code reuse using trays that organize code reuse and behavior blackboards, and also provides many features for integrating with detailed low-level character behavior (Miyake 2016a).

Level designers can make a multilayered decision-making system for each character by using a visual node graph tool called the AI Graph. For example, for the first step, a level designer makes a top-layer state machine with several states by setting and connecting state machine nodes. Then the level designer can make a new state machine as a substate of one or more of the top-level states, or the designer can also make a new behavior tree inside any of the top-level states. Furthermore, the level designer can then make new state machines or behavior trees inside each subsequent substates. In this way, the level designer can make a hierarchical structure of state machines and behavior trees by simply editing nodes on the tool.

Each layer of the AI Graph also has a blackboard system by which the designer can register variables used in the game. By connecting the blackboards of separate nodes, the different layers can share and use these variables.

Figure 24.1

FINAL FANTASY XV screenshot.

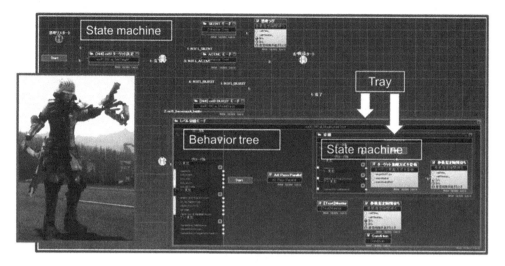

Figure 24.2

AI Graph image.

The AI Graph system has a real-time debug system that connects to and communicates with the game's run-time. Active nodes are highlighted on the decision graph tool as they are executed. During development, this makes finding any problems in the decision graph much easier. AI Graph maintains scalability, variation, and diversity in character AI design through the course of development because of its data-driven approach. In this chapter, we will explain the AI Graph structure, operation principle, and examples from *FINAL FANTASY XV*.

FINAL FANTASY XV is an RPG game in which a player travels in a large open world with three buddies while they fight with monsters and enemies in real time (Figure 24.1). All characters have intelligence to make their decisions by themselves. Also for the player character, AI supports the player character's behaviors.

24.2 AI Graph Structure and Operation Principles

AI Graph is a node-based graph system in which it is possible to make a hierarchical structure with a GUI-based node graph tool. The tool works both offline and while the game is running.

By using the AI Graph tool, a user can make a state machine or behavior tree for each layer (Figure 24.3). To make the next layer, a user can select one node and make a state machine or behavior tree in it. In this way, AI Graph makes a hierarchical nested structure. As requirements change, the hierarchical nested structure allows developers to make as many layers as they want. Finally, the AI Graph generates the data to be executed by the AI program.

The hierarchy executes in the following manner. When a node in the state machine or behavior tree contains another layer, it immediately executes that next layer. The process continues executing nodes until it cannot go to a deeper layer. It then returns to a higher layer after finishing a lower layer.

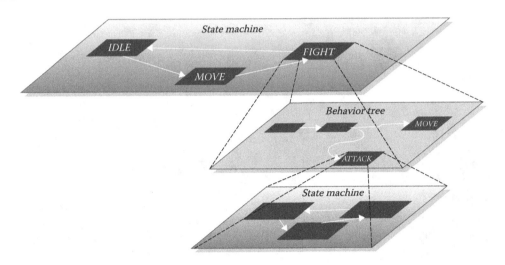

Figure 24.3

AI Graph model.

When a state machine's transition happens in an upper layer, the state currently executing lower layers must be finished. In this case, after all processing of lower layers has finished, the transition occurs. (See Section 24.5.3 for dealing with interruptions.)

24.3 AI Graph Tool

AI Graph tool is one part of the SQUARE ENIX game engine used to make a character's AI. It has three regions (Figure 24.4). The center of the screen is a field to build a state machine and behavior tree graph by connecting nodes. The left vertically long window

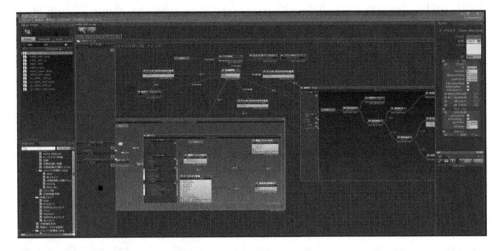

Figure 24.4

AI Graph tool screenshot.

24. A Character Decision-Making System for *FINAL FANTASY XV*

shows variables and nodes that are already made and can be reused. The right vertically long window shows properties for customizing a node and is called the property window. A node can be connected with another node by an arc. In a state machine, a node denotes a state, and an arc indicates transition of the state. In a behavior tree, a node denotes a behavior or operator of the behavior tree, and an arc is used to express the behavior tree structure.

A tray is used to enclose a state machine or a behavior tree. This enables a user to move one entire state machine or behavior tree by moving the tray, and it is also easy to see the layered architecture through the tray hierarchy.

24.4 Implementation Techniques of the AI Graph Node

In the AI Graph, all nodes are reused. For example, a node that can be used in a state machine can also be used in a behavior tree. But ordinarily, the execution method of state machines and behavior trees is different. To make it possible for an AI node to be executed in both a state machine and behavior tree, each AI Graph node has four methods:

1. Start process (when a node is called)
2. Update process (when a node is executed)
3. Finalizing process (when a node is terminated)
4. A condition to signal termination

For both a behavior tree and state machine, the start process, the finalizing process, and the update process are necessary to begin to execute, finalize, and execute a node. The difference between them is what causes stopping a node. For a behavior tree, a node terminates itself by judging an internal terminate condition, whereas a state machine node is terminated by an external transition condition. Thus if a node has these four components, it can be executed in both behavior trees and state machines.

24.5 AI Graph Features

The following describes features of the AI Graph.

24.5.1 The Blackboard within the AI Graph

Variables can be shared via a blackboard consisting of two types (Figure 24.5). One is a local blackboard, which belongs to a tray. Variables of a local blackboard can be shared only in that local blackboard. The other is the global blackboard. Variables of the global blackboard can be shared with the game and all characters' individual AIs. In the AI Graph tool, both blackboards are shown on the left side. In Figure 24.5, you can see there are several variables listed. In the tool, two connected blackboards can share variables.

These variables are used to describe the properties of a node, the transition conditions of a state machine, and so on. For example, the global variable "IS_IN_CAMERA" means whether an actor is in camera or not, and this variable can be used to describe a transition condition inside a state machine contained in a tray.

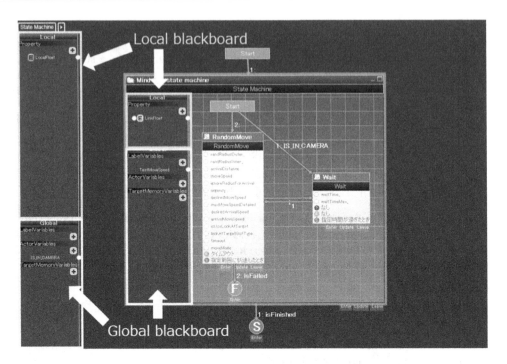

Figure 24.5

Blackboard architecture.

24.5.2 Parallel Thinking within the AI Graph

For some situations, a character must think about two things at a time. The AI Graph allows a character to have two concurrent thinking processes, and it is better to make two simple graphs rather than one big complex graph (Figure 24.6).

For example, one thinking process is a simple state machine to set a character behavior, and the other is a simple state to cause the character to look at a target that suddenly appears. The one state machine begins from a "START" node, and the other state machine begins from "PSTART" node.

The two state machines are executed concurrently. So the character can look around and search for a new target while it keeps attacking. Further, a behavior tree can execute two processes by a parallel node. For example, one behavior is to decide on a target and the other is to approach and attack.

24.5.3 Interrupting the Thinking Process

Often, a character will need to interrupt its current execution and execute another specific action. An interrupt node interrupts a process in the AI Graph when an interrupting condition is satisfied, and it executes the node linked to the interrupt node. For example, when a new game mission starts, monsters must rush to a player. After rushing toward a

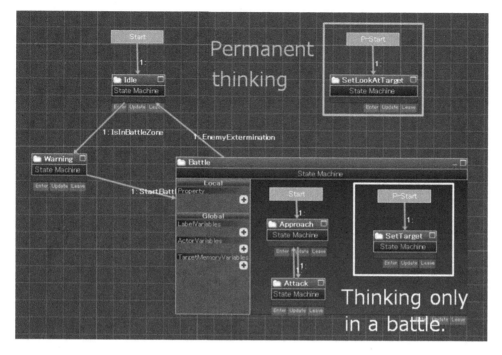

Figure 24.6

Parallel thinking.

player's position, they begin their original thinking process. In this case, two AI Graphs are prepared. One AI Graph includes an interrupt node (Figure 24.7). It causes the current tray to stop and the other tray process to start when the transition condition connected to the interrupt node is satisfied. And after the tray process finishes, the process returns to the original process.

24.5.4 Data and Overrides

An AI Graph can be saved as an asset file. If an AI Graph is fundamental for a character, it is repeatedly called and used. But an AI Graph often requires changes, because it needs to be specialized for each character. For example, when a state machine is saved as an asset file, a user might change a state of the state machine to customize the behavior. In this case, a function to change a node is called an "override," much like in C++.

In *FINAL FANTASY XV*, there are many different types of monsters. For all monsters, the top layer is set through a common template, but their fighting states are different. Therefore, the fighting state is overridden for each monster. Furthermore, a monster's AI Graph can be created by overriding the graph repeatedly from the common logic to monster battle logic (Figure 24.8). In this way, overriding methods make the AI Graph development easier and more effective.

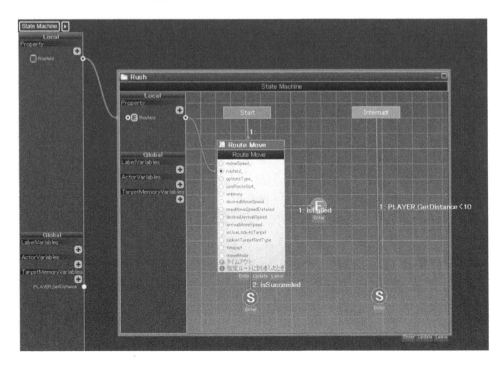

Figure 24.7

Interrupting an AI Graph.

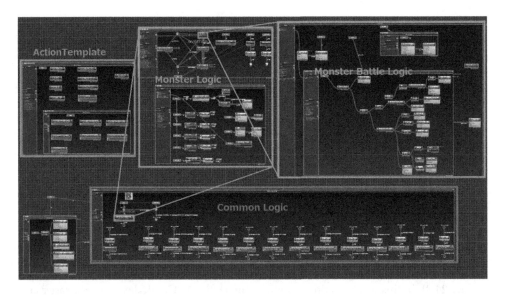

Figure 24.8

Overriding a monster's AI Graph.

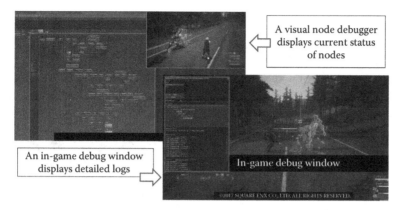

A visual node debugger displays current status of nodes

An in-game debug window displays detailed logs

In-game debug window

Figure 24.9

Visual node debugger (a) and in-game debug window (b).

24.6 Debugging with the AI Graph

For AI development, fast iteration is one of the most important features to keep the AI improving until the end of development. As such, a user should be able to reload an AI Graph without compiling when they want to make a change. In our AI Graph Editor, an AI Graph can be compiled in the Editor independently from other systems' code. This is an example of a data-driven system.

There are two debug windows (Figure 24.9). While a game program runs, an AI Graph keeps a connection with the program. This is called the visual node debugger. In this debugger, the active node currently being executed is highlighted in green. This enables a user to trace the active node in real time.

The other debug window is in a game window. The window displays detailed logs that are generated from a character's AI Graph and AI Graph variables.

24.7 Extracting Animation Parameters through Simulation

In the early stages of development, some monsters' attacks could not reach a player because the attack distance was not large enough. Our solution was to simulate a monster's attack motion, measuring and storing the exact attack distance for each move.

During development, many spheres were distributed around a monster to find the orbit of the monster's attack motion (Figure 24.10). If the motion hits a sphere, the sphere is marked. All marked spheres show the orbit region of the monster's motion. Then the region can be approximated by simple solid figures such as a sphere and sector, and parameters such as the attack distance and attack angles are extracted. These parameters are assigned to an attack node of the AI Graph as the attack parameters. When the node is executed, these new parameters are used when a monster attacks a player.

Manually adjusting AI parameters would have taken too much time during development. This method of analyzing the motion through simulation adjusts the AI parameters automatically and reduces development time.

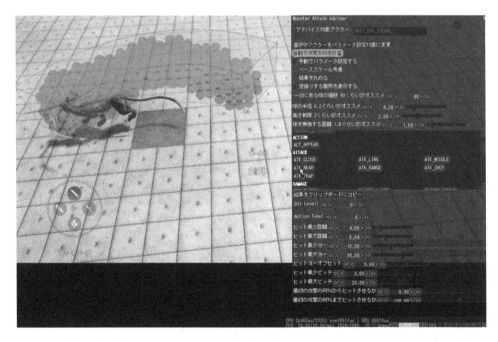

Figure 24.10

Attack motion analysis in simulation.

24.8 Cooperation of Characters via "Meta-AI"

Our meta-AI (more commonly called an AI Director) is an AI that monitors the game and dynamically changes the situation by giving characters orders (Miyake 2016b).

In *FINAL FANTASY XV*, the meta-AI arranges battle sequences. It monitors a battle situation and each character's behavior. When a player or the buddies get into danger, the meta-AI will select one of the buddies who is most appropriate to help (e.g., the nearest buddy who is not attacking). The meta-AI gives the selected character an order to go help the character in danger (Figure 24.11). Buddies' decision-making always depends on the AI Graph. But when a buddy receives an order from the meta-AI, it must stop its AI Graph and obey the meta-AI's order.

In a battle, the meta-AI can give four kinds of orders as follows:

1. Save a player or a buddy in danger.
2. When a player is surrounded by enemies, allow a player to escape.
3. Follow an escaping player.
4. Obey the team tactics.

By using these orders, a meta-AI can tighten a battle flow and can control a player's tension and relaxation.

Figure 24.11

Meta-AI gives an order to save a player to a buddy.

24.9 Sensors

A monster's visual sensors consist of two fan-shaped regions (Figure 24.12). One is a wide fan-shaped region, and the other is a narrow fan-shaped region to detect enemies more precisely. When enemies are in these regions, they will be assigned to a target list.

Figure 24.12

Monster sensor system consisting of two fan-shaped regions.

There is a node to select a target in the AI Graph. In this node, a user can select a targeting mode which is a way to select one target from a target list. Such a target mode can be customized by parameters such as min distance, max distance, min angle, max angle, and priority setting. A priority setting is the parameter type used to decide an enemy's priority in a target list.

24.10 Rule-Based AI System and the AI Graph

For some monsters, a rule-based system and AI Graph are combined. For these monsters, an AI Graph for the top layer is fixed. But there is an independent rule-based system, which includes many rules. It always checks which rule can be fired. Then it selects one of the rules, which calls a corresponding AI Graph template. This is a very simple system with the benefit that one rule condition perfectly corresponds to a single AI Graph to be executed. Although the degree of freedom is partly limited, simplicity of data and the ease of maintenance are clear benefits in our case.

24.11 Body State Machine and the AI Graph

In our game, a character system consists of three layers: an AI layer, a body layer, and an animation layer. These three modules send messages to each other and share variables via blackboards. The AI Graph does not directly initiate animation data. The AI Graph sends a message to the animation layer via a body layer, which consists of a state machine. Especially for shooting and damage behavior, the AI Graph calls the special control nodes within the body layer.

This three-layered architecture separates the roles to control a character, separating concerns between intelligence and animation. It also avoids increasing the size of an AI Graph (Figure 24.13).

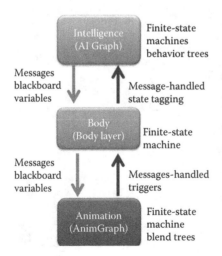
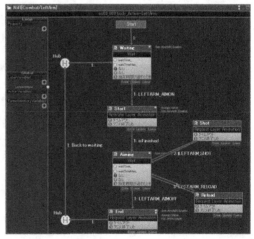

Figure 24.13

Three-layered character system.

A body layer represents a character's body as a node of a state machine. For example, a character's body state is expressed as running, jumping, or climbing a ladder.

A body layer has two roles:

1. Restricting character's actions, a body state can prohibit some actions in this state. For example, while a character is climbing a ladder, it cannot shoot using its hands.
2. Informing a change of body state to the AI layer. Sometimes a character body takes a reactive action to external force or damage. When a reactive action happens, only the body layer knows the information. Then it must send the information by a message to the AI layer. The AI layer will use it for decision-making.

24.12 Conclusion

As game environments and rules become more complex, a character is required to behave more smoothly and intelligently. When development for a next-gen AI began, we realized that it was critical to improve our AI tools. After many discussions within the team, the idea to combine state machines and behavior trees was agreed upon. This allows our developers to leverage both techniques in a nested hierarchical node structure, enabling a very flexible architecture. We called this tool the AI Graph Editor, and it was critical to completing *FINAL FANTASY XV*, which was released in 2016. Additional videos for each technical topic are available in PDF form (Shirakami et al. 2015).

All figures ©2016 SQUARE ENIX CO., LTD. All Rights Reserved. Main character design by TETSUYA NOMURA. All other trademarks are the property of their respective owners.

References

Miyake, Y., 2016a. A multilayered model for artificial intelligence of game characters as agent architecture, in *Mathematical Progress in Expressive Image Synthesis III, Volume 24 of the series Mathematics for Industry*, pp. 57–60. http://link.springer.com/chapter/10.1007/978-981-10-1076-7_7.

Miyake, Y., 2016b. Current status of applying artificial intelligence in digital games, in *Handbook of Digital Games and Entertainment Technologies*, Springer, 2016, http://link.springer.com/referenceworkentry/10.1007/978-981-4560-52-8_70-1.

Miyake, Y., 2015a. Current status of applying artificial intelligence for digital games, *The Japanese Society of Artificial Intelligence*, 30(1), 45–64. doi:10.1007/978-981-4560-52-8_70-1.

Miyake, Y., 2015b. AI techniques for contemporary digital games, *SA '15: SIGGRAPH Asia 2015 Courses*, November 2015, http://dl.acm.org/citation.cfm?id=2818164.

Shirakami, Y., 2015. Miyake, Y., Namiki, K., and Yokoyama, T., Character Decision Making System for FINAL FANTASY XV -EPISODE DUSCAE-, CEDEC 2015, In SQUARE ENIX PUBLICATIAONS, http://www.jp.square-enix.com/tech/publications.html, http://www.jp.square-enix.com/tech/library/pdf/2015cedec_FFXV_AI_English_part1.pdf, http://www.jp.square-enix.com/tech/library/pdf/2015cedec_FFXV_AI_English_part2.pdf

25

A Reusable, Light-Weight Finite-State Machine

David "Rez" Graham

25.1 Introduction

Finite-state machines are an architectural structure used to encapsulate the behavior of discrete states within a system and are commonly used in games for AI, animation, managing game states, and a variety of other tasks (Fu 2004).

For example, consider a guard character that can walk to different waypoints. When he or she sees the player, he or she starts shooting. The guard can be in one of the two states: patrol or attack. It is easy to expand on this behavior by adding more states or tweaking existing ones.

State machines are great for composing behaviors because each state can be parameterized and reused for multiple different characters. For example, you could have a state for attacking the player with each type of enemy determining the attack animations to run, how close they need to be, and so on. The biggest advantage of state machines is that they offer a lot of flexibility while still being extremely simple to implement and maintain. Due to this simplicity, this architecture is best suited for games with smaller AI needs.

Going back to the guard example, one common place for parameterization is the vision cone for the guard. How close does the player have to be before the guard sees him or her?

You could have different kinds of guards with different capabilities. For instance, an elite guard may have a bigger vision cone than a regular guard.

One decision you need to make when building a state machine is how to organize the states and where to put the transition logic. This chapter will discuss how to use transition objects to create encapsulated, reusable objects for managing transitions. This allows designers to compose the overall behavior of an enemy by selecting the appropriate states, choosing transitions for those states, and setting the necessary parameters.

The biggest difference between a traditional state machine and the one presented in this chapter is that this state machine can monitor and change states as necessary. In a traditional state machine, state changes come externally.

The techniques in this chapter were used in the platformer game *Drawn to Life: The Next Chapter* for the Wii, developed by Planet Moon Studios, to handle all of the enemy AI.

25.2 Finite-State Machine Architecture

The driver of the state machine is the `StateMachine` class. This class is owned by the intelligent `GameObject` and manages the behaviors for that object. It owns a list of every possible state the object can be in as well as a pointer to the current state the object is in right now.

The state machine is updated periodically (either every frame or on a cadence that makes sense from a performance point of view) and has an interface for setting the state. The states owned by the state machine are handled with a `State` base class. There are virtual functions for handling the entering and exiting of states, as well as a function to be called on periodic updates. All of the concrete states used by the system will inherit from this class and will override the appropriate methods.

The third major component of this architecture is the `StateTransition` class, which is also owned by the state machine. This class has a `ToTransition()` virtual function that returns a Boolean for whether or not the transition should occur. Much like states, every possible transition in the game is a subclass of `StateTransition`. Figure 25.1 shows a diagram of this architecture.

The states owned by the state machine are handled with a `State` base class, shown in Listing 25.1.

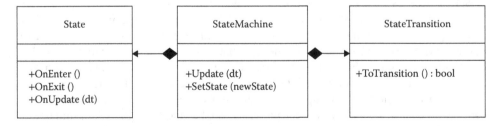

Figure 25.1

State machine architecture.

Listing 25.1. Base class for a single state.

```
class State
{
    GameObject* m_pOwner;

public:
    State(GameObject* pOwner)
        : m_pOwner(pOwner)
    { }
    virtual ~State() { }
    virtual void OnEnter() { }
    virtual void OnExit() { }
    virtual void OnUpdate(float deltaTime) { }

protected:
    GameObject* GetOwner() const { return m_pOwner; }
};
```

It is important to note that state instances live for the entire lifetime of the state machine, so it is important for OnEnter() or OnExit() to handle resetting the state.

25.3 State Transitions

The key to this architecture lies in the transition objects and the way that the state machine is updated. Every possible state inside the state machine is linked to a sorted list of transition/state pairs. Listing 25.2 shows a partial definition for the StateMachine class to illustrate this data structure.

Listing 25.2. StateMachine class.

```
class StateMachine
{
    typedef pair<Transition*, State*> TransitionStatePair;
    typedef vector<TransitionStatePair> Transitions;
    typedef map<State*, Transitions> TransitionMap;

    TransitionMap m_transitions;

    State* m_pCurrState;

public:
    void Update(float deltaTime);
};
```

The variable m_transitions holds the network of transitions for this state machine and defines how the game object will move from state to state. These are typically read from data and built at initialization time, which we will address later in this chapter.

During every update, the state machine checks to see if there are any transitions for this state. If there are, it walks through the list of those transitions and checks to see if it is time to move to another state. If it is, the transition occurs. Listing 25.3 shows the code for this update.

Having no transitions for a state is perfectly valid. For instance, you might not want to allow an enemy to transition out of the death state, or you might have a state that you want to be permanent until some outside force causes the state to manually change via a call to StateMachine::SetState().

Listing 25.3. State machine update.

```cpp
void StateMachine::Update(float deltaTime)
{
    // find the set of transitions for the current state
    auto it = m_transitions.find(m_pCurrState);
    if (it != m_transitions.end())
    {
        // loop through every transition for this state
        for (TransitionStatePair& transPair : it->second)
        {
            // check for transition
            if (transPair.first->ToTransition())
            {
                SetState(transPair.second);
                break;
            }
        }
    }

    // update the current state
    if (m_pCurrState)
        m_pCurrState->Update(deltaTime);
}
```

Using this technique, the states are completely decoupled from each other. Ideally, only the state machine cares about the states, and it never has to know which specific state a character is in.

The transition class itself is trivial and defined in Listing 25.4.

Listing 25.4. Transition class.

```cpp
class Transition
{
    GameObject* m_pOwner;

public:
    Transition(GameObject* pOwner)
        :m_pOwner(pOwner)
    { }

    virtual bool ToTransition() const = 0;
};
```

25. A Reusable, Light-Weight Finite-State Machine

Each `Transition` holds a reference to the owning game object and declares a pure virtual `ToTransition()` function, which is overridden in the subclass.

States will often need the ability to end naturally and transition into another state. A good example of this is a state that handles pathing to a location. It will naturally end once the game object reaches its destination and needs to move to another state.

One way of doing this is to define a transition that asks if the current state is finished. If it is, the transition occurs and moves to the new state. This keeps all the transition logic in the same place (the transition map) while still allowing natural transitions.

25.4 Hierarchies of State Machines and Metastates

One way to expand this state machine system is to add hierarchy to state machines through metastates. A metastate is a state that contains its own state machine, which has multiple internal states. The simplest way to manage this is by having a special `MetaState` subclass that internally has its own state machine. It would be tuned just like any other state machine and could reuse any existing states.

To illustrate this concept, let us go back to the guard example from the beginning of the chapter where we had a guard that could patrol and attack. Both of these are metastates. The patrol metastate has a transition that tests to see if the player is within the guard's vision cone. The attack metastate has a transition that tests to see if the player is outside of a large radius, which is when we consider the guard to have lost the player. So far, there is nothing special or different. As far as the root system is concerned, there are two states with simple transitions.

Inside of the attack metastate, there are two states. The initial state is an alert state that plays an alert animation. It transitions to the shoot state after a few seconds as long as the player remains in the vision cone. The shoot state will transition back to alert if the player steps out of the vision cone.

The important thing to note is that every active state machine is getting its update, which means that any state can transition at any moment. If the attack state suddenly transitions to the patrol state, it will immediately end whatever state the attack metastate was in. This allows you to treat that entire branch as self-contained.

The addition of metastates adds more complexity but also allows considerably more flexibility. You can create a metastate tree as deep as you wish. One interesting side effect with this kind of system is that it can make going from initial prototype to final implementation a little easier. For example, when implementing the above guard character, the attack and patrol states could start as regular states just to test the concepts and see how they feel in game. Once the character was locked in with animation and a full design, those states could be broken into metastates to manage the low-level nuts and bolts of the AI.

Although you do get a considerable amount of flexibility with a hierarchical approach, it is often not needed. For *Drawn to Life*, we did not find this complexity necessary at all.

25.5 Data-Driving the State Machine

One of the most important things to get right is how to drive this whole system from designer-authored data. Specific implementations are beyond the scope of this chapter and would not be useful since every project will have different needs. The original code on *Drawn to Life* used Lua tables for data. Similar solutions have been implemented in

Unity using C#, which used Unity's inspector and C# reflection for the data. These state machines and transition maps have also been built using XML.

Regardless of which solution you choose, there are several considerations for how to organize this data. The most important is to allow your states and transitions to be parameterized from data. Ideally, you should only have a handful of generic states and transitions, each of which can deliver different behaviors based on those parameters.

For example, consider the AI of a shopkeeper who needs to tend their shop. He or she might wipe down the counter, sweep the floor, tend to shelf of goods, or wait patiently at the shop counter. These all may seem different, but they really are not. At their core, each one paths to a specific target and runs an animation. That is it.

You could take this even further and have this generic state send an optional event to the target. This would allow you to reuse the same state for things like opening windows, restocking inventory, or even striking someone by sending a damage event. This same state could optionally change the internal state of the NPC, so our shopkeeper could eat when hungry. While eating, their hunger needs are fulfilled.

This is the power of data-driving this system. Designers will come up with dozens (or hundreds) of more cases for the simple state described above. Listing 25.5 shows an example of a data-driven `RunAnimationState`.

Listing 25.5. Generic state for running an animation.

```
class RunAnimationState : public State
{
    AnimationId m_animToRun;

public:
    RunAnimationState(GameObject* pOwner)
        :State(pOwner)
    { }

    // Function to load the state definition from XML, JSON,
    // or some other data system. This will fill all the
    // internal data members for this state.
    virtual bool LoadStateDef(StateDef* pStateDef)override;

    virtual void OnEnter() override
    {
        GetOwner()->RunAnimation(m_animToRun);
    }
};
```

25.6 Performance and Memory Improvements

The performance and memory footprint of this system can definitely be improved, and in this section, we will discuss a few of these improvements.

The simplest performance improvement is to time-slice the state machine update by limiting how often the state machine is updated, and how many game objects can update in a single frame. This can be done with an update list where every state machine is put into a list, and the game only allows a certain amount of time to be dedicated to the AI updates. As long as the transition map stays static during a frame, there is no reason you could not time-slice in the middle of an update either.

Another performance improvement would be to remove state updates entirely and make the whole thing event driven. This is a bit trickier to implement, but it is worth it if the performance of this system is a huge concern. In this version, states have no `OnUpdate()` function, only an `OnEnter()` and `OnExit()`. `OnEnter()` will spin up a task if necessary and will wait for a notification of completion. For example, say you have a `GoToObject` state. The `OnEnter()` function would tell the pathing system to find a path and then do nothing until the path was complete.

This system works well if many of your states do not require an update, or you can easily fit it within an existing system. At the very least, it can help eliminate a few virtual function calls.

On the memory side of things, one big issue is that the state machine class proposed above can be very wasteful if it exists on multiple game objects. For example, say you have a dozen orc enemies, and they all have the same behavior. All twelve of those orcs would be duplicating a lot of data.

One solution here is to split `StateMachine` into two different classes, one for handling the static data that never change at run-time and the other to handle the volatile data that does. The class with the volatile data is given a reference to the static data class. This would not even require a change to the interface. This is effectively the Flyweight design pattern (Freeman-Hargis 2006).

The specific choices of what data to pull out of the run-time class will depend on your game. For example, on *Drawn to Life* the transition maps never changed during run-time, so pulling those into a data class would be perfectly fine.

Along these same lines, you could pull out all of the run-time data from each state instance and store it in a state blackboard. States would be parameterized through this blackboard, allowing you to have only a single instance for each state in your system. Transitions could work the same way; all run-time data would exist on a blackboard for that character so only one instance would be required per class.

25.7 Conclusion

This chapter has only touched on the surface of this kind of architecture. It is very simple and light-weight, yet flexible enough to allow a considerable amount of power and control. This architecture can be applied directly to your AI needs, but there are a few takeaways that can apply to any architecture.

The power of the transition objects to decouple the states from one another comes from a common programming design pattern called the strategy pattern (Gamma et al. 1997). The basic idea is to wrap up an algorithm into a self-contained class so that several such algorithms can be composed at run-time to change behavior. It is very good for data-driven systems since these objects can be instantiated with a factory and composed into a data structure (the transition map in our case) to determine the final behavior. You can even change these at run-time, significantly altering behavior by swapping a few objects.

This system can also be used in conjunction with other systems. For example, you might have a `UtilityTransition` class that scores its target state to see if it is something the character wants to do. You could have a decision tree as your transition logic, using states only to manage their actions.

Either way, hopefully you see the power and flexibility of this kind of architecture.

References

Gamma, E., R. Helm, R. Johnson, and J. Vlissides. 1997. *Design Patters: Elements of Reusable Object-Oriented Software*. Upper Saddle River, NJ: Addison-Wesley.

Freeman-Hargis, J. 2006. Using STL and patterns for game AI. In *AI Game Programming Wisdom 3*, ed. S. Rabin. Newton, MA: Charles River Media, pp. 13–28.

Fu, D. and Houlette, R. 2004. The ultimate guide to FSMs in games. In *AI Game Programming Wisdom 2*, ed. S. Rabin. Newton, MA: Charles River Media, pp. 283–302.

26

Choosing Effective Utility-Based Considerations

Mike Lewis

26.1 Introduction

Theatrical actors are (perhaps stereotypically) known for asking the pointed question, "What's my motivation?" AI designers and implementers often must ask the same thing on behalf of their digital creations. In fact, entire systems of AI architecture center on that very idea: why would a creature or NPC do some specific action at a given moment in time?

In particular, *utility theory* offers a powerful and compelling model for game AI (Graham 2014). In a nutshell, available decisions are scored using some mathematical formulas, and the agent selects a course of action from among the best-scoring options. There are several available models for utility-based architectures described in existing literature and lectures (Dill 2015, Mark 2013).

Interestingly, most of the resources available until now have focused on the architectural side. The specifics of building decision-making systems are often left as a proverbial exercise to the reader, often with vague allusions to "game-specific" details.

Throughout the next several pages, we will explore some of those specific details, taking a tour of some of the decisions available to NPCs in *Guild Wars 2: Heart of Thorns*. Each decision will be broken down into the *considerations* that affect whether or not the decision is considered optimal at any given point in time. From there, we will look at the rationale for choosing each specific consideration. We will conclude with a series of general-purpose tips that can be applied to consideration selection in any utility-based architecture.

26.2 Architecture

The *Heart of Thorns* AI implementation is modeled on the Infinite Axis Utility System (Mark 2013). A major guiding principle of the design is that the AI should be data driven as much as possible. This allows for maximum flexibility and configurability, while simultaneously easing the load on engineers and empowering the design team (Lewis and Mark 2015).

To this end, AI characters are allotted a certain selection of *decisions*—actions which the AI can take at various points in time. Different archetypes or "species" of character may have very different sets of available decisions. Each possible action for a given AI agent is mapped to a decision score evaluator, or DSE. During a think cycle, each DSE for an agent is scored, and the best-scoring option determines the action the AI takes for that think cycle.

The scoring of a DSE consists of accumulating all the scores of the considerations assigned to that DSE. Each consideration is essentially a raw numeric input, normalized to the interval [0, 1]. This score is processed through a *response curve*, which remaps the original number to a final score, again normalized. These scores are then multiplied together to obtain the overall score of the DSE itself.

Suppose a DSE has two considerations: distance to target and health of the target. Health can be a simple fraction, abstracting away the detail of "hit points" or other mechanics that describe the healthiness of the target. Distance can be normalized by providing "bookends"—so, for example, a distance of 100 m might be "maximum," and 0 m might be "minimum." The normalization process will take any distance between 0 and 100 m and map it onto a score of 0–1. Any distance above the maximum automatically scores 1.

The next step is to process these raw numbers via the response curves. In this case, imagine that closer targets are more appealing than distant ones. Given a target at 25 m, the "raw" consideration score would be $25/100 = 0.25$. Passed through a suitable function, however, 25 m might score as, say, 0.95. This remapped score allows the designer fine-grained control over the relative importance of each consideration. As the setup of the response curve (as well as the choice of input that is fed into it) is entirely data driven, there is no engineering burden for modifying the preferences of an AI character.

A key trait of this design is that any consideration can disqualify an entire decision from being selected simply by scoring zero. As soon as a consideration drops the decision score to zero, the system stops processing further considerations and early-outs, moving on to the next decision. This makes it trivial to encode rules for when a decision is absolutely not supposed to be used. Additionally, it allows AI designers to optimize the decision evaluation process itself, since cheaper considerations can be ordered first and early-out to avoid processing more expensive ones.

Given these building blocks, the real art of building a character's AI lies in selecting considerations and pairing them with appropriate response curves. To properly explore the nuances of this process, let us take a closer look at some DSEs used in *Heart of Thorns*.

26.3 Tactical Movement

A considerable portion of the combat-related work that went into *Heart of Thorns* focused on the moment-to-moment, "tactical" positioning and maneuvering of individual NPCs. Many characters have an archetypical "style" or "flavor" that they represent, and the choices driving the movement of those characters on the battlefield have a substantial impact on how well the designer's intent is actually conveyed during gameplay.

However, there are also common and widely used sorts of movement—the type of things that basically every reasonably intelligent character is expected to do during a fight. A perfect example of such a common movement is "Evade Dangerous Areas." This DSE examines the environment for magical spells, mechanical traps, and other hazards created by players as well as hostile NPCs. If the AI character is too close to such a danger zone, they will rapidly exit the area, often playing a specific "dodge" animation and momentarily avoiding any incoming attacks.

26.3.1 Evade Dangerous Areas

The DSE for this action is relatively simple but highly instructive. There are only six considerations used. The first two are binary on/off switches that prevent the action from being chosen in the middle of another decision, or if the character has been prevented from moving by, say, a rooting spell. Virtually all DSEs use basic switches like these to help ensure that the AI does not do something ridiculous, like trying to move while frozen in place.

It would of course be possible to hard-code these switches into *every* DSE—and indeed there are a small number of other control factors which are hardwired into the engine. However, we chose to simply prepopulate newly created DSEs with a few commonly required switches. The more hard-coded logic that gets added, the more brittle the system becomes when exceptions are desired. Inevitably, someone will think of a good use case for bypassing those switches. When that day comes, it is beneficial to be able to simply omit a consideration versus having to add *more* hard-coded logic for bypassing the *first* bit of hard-coded logic.

Moving on, the third consideration on the Evade Dangerous Areas DSE is the real workhorse. This consideration uses an *infinite-resolution influence map* to detect nearby dangerous activities and locales (Lewis 2015). The influence map is populated every few frames with data on all potential hazards. Creating more hazards in a particular location results in a higher score for that area.

The input from this consideration is mapped through a response curve that effectively amplifies the perceived danger of moderately dangerous areas, while simultaneously squelching the perceived danger of unimportant hazards. The goal of this is to ensure that characters on the fringes of a hazard will still get out of the way, whereas characters will stay put if they are *near* a hazard but not *inside* its effective radius. The graph of the response curve is shown in Figure 26.1.

Coming in fourth and fifth are a pair of considerations designed to break cycles of repetitive behavior. They are termed *runtime* and *cooldown*, respectively. Runtime's job is to guarantee that the decision will stop being chosen after a certain number of repetitions. In this case, a response curve is used to drop the score of the consideration (and therefore

Figure 26.1

Response curve for influence map filtering on Evade Dangerous Areas.

the decision as a whole) to zero after a short time. This ensures that, even if the decision is otherwise valid, it will not be chosen too many times back-to-back. This mechanism is extremely useful for avoiding edge cases where the character constantly evades and becomes impossible to hit.

Cooldown is a standard timer that forces the decision to score zero (or nearly zero) until a given delay has elapsed. This is useful for avoiding strobing between two otherwise competing decisions and also helps ensure that a single decision is not selected too frequently. The response curve on cooldowns returns very small scores until near the end of the cooldown period, at which time the score spikes back up to its full potential (subject, of course, to the other considerations on the decision). Graphs of the standardized runtime and cooldown response curves can be seen in Figure 26.2.

The final consideration for Evade Dangerous Areas is based on the health value of the character itself. It simply dials back the score of the DSE if the character has plenty of health to absorb the damage of whatever hazard it may be standing in. This mechanism lends a bit of flavor and personality to the AI characters, since they will become willing to withstand some pain in order to, say, land a blow on an enemy player. Moreover, the same characters will become more conservative as they take damage and lose health.

26.3.2 Close to Melee when Invisible

Much like its Evade Dangerous Areas counterpart, Close to Melee When Invisible is a DSE that attempts to move a character into a more advantageous position on the battlefield. However, it is much less widely applicable; only a few characters can be invisible at all, and not all of them want to get *closer* to their enemies when they are hidden from view.

As before, the DSE begins with two switch considerations that prevent the decision from activating for immobilized or otherwise occupied characters. The third consideration

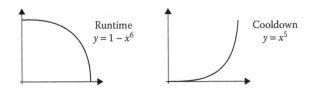

Figure 26.2

Runtime and cooldown response curves.

simply queries the game rules to see if the character is presently invisible to its target. It, too, is a binary on/off switch, rendering the decision unavailable if the AI is not in fact invisible.

Where things get interesting is the fourth consideration. This factors in the distance between the AI and its target, and elects to move closer to the target *if and only if* it can reach the target before regaining visibility. (In truth this is a constant time value, but the time was deliberately chosen to attain this effect. More complex queries may be warranted if the design rules are more sophisticated, but this was sufficient for our purposes.) The approximation for this is handled quite easily by a single response curve, which tapers off at the extreme long-range end.

The next consideration is again based on health, making the decision score lower if the AI does not have enough health to justify a sneaky attack maneuver. Finally, there is a runtime limitation of a few seconds to avoid traveling extreme distances while invisible—something which could be confusing and frustrating to players.

Overall, the effect of these considerations is striking. AI characters might engage in relatively standard combat behavior for a time, then suddenly cloak themselves and vanish from sight. As the bewildered player tries to figure out where his or her foe disappeared to, the AI is making a mad dash toward the player. Once within striking distance, the AI reappears and delivers a surprise volley of damage to the unsuspecting target.

During prototyping on *Heart of Thorns*, this behavior (among others) was used to illustrate the power of carefully chosen considerations. A stealthy predator, an assassin, and even a cheeky thief could all use the basic pattern constructed here to great effect. Such predefined patterns proved so handy during implementation that over one hundred of them were made and used in the final game. The *a la carte* power of the architecture allowed designers to mix and match ready-made behaviors and preference patterns into new creatures in a mere handful of minutes (Lewis and Mark 2015).

26.4 Skill Selection

In addition to tactical movement, characters in *Heart of Thorns* have access to an array of "skills"—abilities that are typically combat focused, aiming to deal damage to enemy targets or reinforce allies. Selection of considerations for these skills is worth exploring in its own right, since the various types of offensive and defensive abilities often require specially tailored scoring to be effective.

For the sake of increased modularity and ease of reuse, skill-related DSEs can be assigned to premade sets of considerations. This allows related skills to reuse the same decision scoring logic across the game. In addition to making the AI more discoverable and recognizable to the player, this dramatically cuts down on the number of custom-tuned DSEs that must be created during the design process.

26.4.1 Charge Attacks

The skill DSE for a basic rushing or charging attack begins with two familiar faces: considerations to avoid using the attack in the middle of another activity and while unable to move. The third consideration looks at the distance to the target. This particular consideration carries a special response curve, which scores higher for targets at moderate range; it does not make sense to burn a rush attack skill on a target which is already within easy striking distance, for example. By the same token, it makes no sense to use the charge if the actual attack will not reach the target at all.

An interesting new consideration on this DSE examines the influence map to see if there are already a reasonable number of allies in the area of the target. This is designed to ensure that players are not overwhelmed by enemy characters. A player already fighting two opponents should not need to worry about a third suddenly charging in and piling on. This is a fantastic example of a design constraint that can be easily expressed using utility AI and supporting modular AI information systems.

The next consideration simply prefers the attack to be used when the character's health is at least moderately high. It does not usually look good to charge into a horde of enemies when near death, so this consideration helps maintain some sensibility in the character's behavior. Of course, a more reckless, even suicidal type of enemy might find that the opposite is true—deploying an attack into a nearby group of enemies at low health may be just the thing for that character. This is trivial to accomplish by tweaking the response curve on the health consideration.

Another new consideration is the *relative direction* check. This is tuned for charge attacks in such a way as to prefer to charge at targets that are mostly in front of the AI. By imposing this limitation, we avoid ugly animation snaps and directional flip-flopping. The AI will not choose to charge at something behind itself, because that looks bad and typically does not make as much sense to the observing player.

Bringing up the rear is a simple line-of-sight consideration. This is another on/off switch that avoids deploying the charge attack at something that cannot be directly reached. Of course due to the limited nature of line-of-sight, it is possible for the AI to "see" a target but not be able to navigate to it on the navmesh. In *Heart of Thorns*, we mostly ignored this restriction, because of processing power limitations—it was too expensive to compute paths to all targets all the time, and the edge cases where it made a visible difference were mercifully rare.

26.4.2 Side and Rear Attacks

As a variant on the usual frontal assault style of combat, some characters in *Heart of Thorns* prefer to be a little sneakier, attacking primarily when their target is facing away from them. For melee attacks, this is handled largely by a single skill DSE. Remember that the same DSE can be used for many different skills, allowing designers to create consistent mechanics without duplicated data.

The flanking/backstab attack DSE is similar to most others in that it starts with an early-out switch to prevent the skill from being used if another action is already running for that AI character. However, unlike DSEs that involve movement, this one does not turn off for immobilized characters. This is a great example of why hard-coding the rules can be a net negative; instead of having to wire in some logic to allow this particular skill DSE to activate on rooted AIs, we simply omit the consideration that would otherwise turn it off.

As such, the second consideration on this DSE checks to make sure that the target is facing away from the AI character. This is done by checking the normalized facing direction of the target and taking the dot product of that vector by the normalized vector from the target to the AI. The closer this dot product is to 1, the closer the target is to pointing directly at the AI character. Therefore, the response curve for this consideration simply tapers off as the dot product's value reaches 1. The net result is that the character will score targets facing perpendicularly (or completely away) more highly.

The next consideration limits the DSE to avoid making flanking attacks when the character is badly wounded. Accomplishing this with a response curve is trivial: simply keep the curve value high until some arbitrary health value threshold, then drop off quickly as health continues to decline to zero.

Following the health check, there are three prioritization considerations that are used to help determine which targets are most eligible for the attack. All other things being equal, the DSE will prefer closer targets, weaker (lower health) targets, and targets that are in the AI's cone of vision.

Checking for closer targets is as simple as looking at the distance to a prospective target and scoring lower as the distance increases. By contrast, the enemy health check uses a gradual tapering effect to *diminish* the priority of full-health targets but not *zero* it.

For prioritizing targets in front of the AI (or, roughly speaking, in its vision cone), there is again a directional check. This time, however, the check looks at the AI's facing direction and compares it to the offset vector pointing toward the target. As a result, the score will drop off toward zero the more the character is looking *away* from the target.

Finally, the DSE finishes off with a simple line-of-sight check, which operates much the same as the one used for charge attacks and other skills. The order of this is actually significant, since the raycast used for the check is fairly expensive; if we can early-out from the DSE before having to do an actual check here, so much the better. This sort of optimization is a large part of what made the *Heart of Thorns* AI sufficiently performant.

26.5 Guiding Principles

On a general level, the considerations we have seen can be broken down into three basic categories. There are those which are mandatory for a decision to function at all; those which distinguish the decision from other, similar behavioral patterns; and those which mostly affect balance and the "feel" of the AI.

Mandatory considerations are the easiest to select from the toolbox. The commonly used switches and toggles enumerated earlier are all mandatory—things like "don't interrupt a running action" or "don't move when immobilized." When building a utility-based AI, it is immensely helpful to know what considerations absolutely must be in place in order for the logic to operate correctly.

Many of these rules can be hard-coded into the game rather than data driven; however, as remarked upon before, it is often beneficial *not* to hard-code mandatory considerations on the chance that someone will want to bypass or circumvent them as part of a design.

Distinguishing one behavioral pattern from another is typically a matter of tapping into game rules. For *Heart of Thorns*, there are numerous status flags ("buffs") that can be applied to a given character. As we saw with the Close to Melee When Invisible example, a consideration that looks at these buffs or status flags can go a long way.

Balance and "feel" considerations are probably the trickiest to get right. Selecting a response curve can be difficult. Within the *Heart of Thorns* architecture, it is common place to use runtime and cooldown considerations to control the timing and repetition of decisions. All of these considerations use standardized response curves to simplify the design process.

As a matter of fact, the vast majority of the response curves used in the game are chosen from a small palette of preset curves. Permitting arbitrary curves is immensely powerful but has the substantial drawback of being intimidating and possibly even unintuitive. When using an architecture that permits this sort of configurability, it is worth hiding it behind an "advanced mode" and favoring preset curves for the majority of use cases.

26.5.1 Selecting Consideration Inputs

Before reaching the point of building a response curve (or other general scoring function), it is important to gather a list of the input factors that might contribute to making a particular decision.

Some generic inputs that are broadly applicable to most AI simulations include distance (both straight-line and pathfinding distance can be useful), time, relative direction/heading, line-of-sight, and so on. These are nearly universal concepts that can be applied to most decisions in some way. Moreover, they are conceptually portable between game applications and even into nongame AI usage.

More game-specific ideas may include things like health, mobility, special status effects, relative proximity of other characters, and so on. Feeding these sorts of considerations with game data is typically straightforward and can yield remarkable results. An especially useful approach is to adapt the data from other game systems via a translation layer that converts game rules into consideration inputs. Coupled with parameters on the considerations themselves, this layer helps keep the AI data-driven and flexible without requiring huge amounts of code for each unique type of character.

As one example of pulling data from the game itself, *Heart of Thorns* uses influence maps heavily, as noted earlier. There are several common queries that extract useful AI decision-making data from those influence maps. The presence or absence of allies and enemies can be obtained individually or even combined to yield a metric that estimates how much conflict is present at a given location (Mark 2015). Environmental hazards and artificial danger zones (spells, traps, etc.) are also represented in the influence map.

When building a DSE, it is important to consider all the relevant inputs so that the character will ultimately make the "right" decisions. Some inputs may also need further parameterization, such as distance ranges, time limits, which in-game status effects to query, and so on. Although the options may seem overwhelming at first, it helps to do a little bit of applied role-play.

Suppose the character is a thief who wishes to stealthily approach targets and pickpocket them, avoiding overt combat as much as possible. Put yourself in the character's shoes, so to speak, and think about *why* you would (or would not!) want to decide to do a particular action. Distill these reasons into concrete metrics. Deciding to approach a mark should probably be based on considering things like the perceived value of the target, relative distance, whether they are facing away from the thief, and so on.

Once a variety of input factors have been identified, it is time to score the decision based on the relative importance of each factor. This is where finely tuned scoring functions come in—in the case of *Heart of Thorns*, we used response curves.

26.5.2 Constructing Response Curves

Even if most response curves used by the engine are presets, it can be very helpful to follow a few simple guidelines for choosing which curve makes the most sense. To that end, there are essentially three characteristics of the curve to consider.

An *increasing* curve tends toward higher y-values as the x-value increases, while *decreasing* curves do the exact opposite. This can be thought of as whether the curve climbs or dips as it moves to the right on a graph. Increasing curves make a decision *more relevant* toward the upper end of the input range, whereas decreasing curves will make the same decision *less relevant*.

Once the overall direction of a curve is established, the next characteristic is whether the curve is *monotonic* or not. An increasing curve is monotonic if it never "turns around" and begins decreasing instead. Recall that we only care about the response curve's behavior in the domain [0, 1] and the range [0, 1]—that is, the square from the origin to (1, 1) on the coordinate plane. Therefore, many simple monomial functions (for example) can be considered monotonic *on the relevant interval* even though they are strictly speaking not monotonic in the domain of the reals.

Monotonicity is important because it greatly simplifies the process of understanding how a consideration's score works. Most response curves in *Heart of Thorns* are monotonic, although it is occasionally useful to use nonmonotonic curves to get specific effects. A great example is keeping an enemy at arm's length. Using a distance consideration and an upside-down U-shaped response curve, we can make a character approach its enemy only if the enemy is not already too close or too far away.

The last characteristic to consider is the curve's *endpoints*. The endpoints of the curve are simply the function's values at $x = 0$ and $x = 1$. These points describe the score of the consideration at the minimum and maximum of the input range, respectively. For monotonic curves, these will also correspond to the minimum and maximum scores of the consideration. An increasing, monotonic curve will score its minimum value at $x = 0$ and its maximum at $x = 1$. By contrast, a decreasing monotonic curve will score its maximum at 0 and its minimum at 1.

Selection of response curves can make or break a utility-based AI. Broadly speaking, the scoring function (whether using a response curve or a more general function) is the heart and soul of how the AI will decide to do one thing versus another. A simple checklist can be invaluable for choosing an appropriate scoring function.

The first key question is to determine what input is being scored. For each input type, decide on bookends for the input—a clamped range that controls what input value carries a significance of 0, and what input value translates to 1 on the x-axis.

Given a well-defined range of input to work with, the next key component is the slope of the curve. Does the importance of making this decision *increase* as the input nears 1, or does it *decrease* instead? For a thief considering the perceived wealth of a target, an increasing curve makes sense. The same thief thinking about the distance to a target will probably favor a decreasing curve for that consideration—the farther away a mark is, the more danger is involved in reaching them, and therefore the less opportune that target will be.

Monotonicity is generally preferable for a response curve unless some specific behavior is needed. Think carefully about whether there should be an artificial "high point" or "low point" to the consideration's score *in between* the input extremes of 0 and 1. Configure this peak or valley such that it corresponds to the appropriate input value.

Finally, it is important to plan out the endpoints of the scoring curve. As noted earlier, these correspond to the consideration's score at the low and high ends of the input range. Endpoints have a strong influence on the decision's overall score when the inputs are at extremes. Should the score drop to zero when an input reaches minimum/maximum? Or should it simply *deprioritize* the decision instead of invalidating it altogether?

Most of the time, it is simplest to have a minimum/maximum input correspond to a consideration score of 1. In other words, if a consideration is in a perfect situation, it should yield a perfect score—subject of course to the scores of other considerations for the same decision. The primary exception is when considering the interplay of multiple decisions with similar considerations. However, there are many factors to take into account for this scenario.

26.5.3 Interleaving Decision Scores

A commonly referenced strength of utility-based systems is their organic, fluid nature. As scores rise and fall in the heat of the moment, the AI will always pick something sensible from the list of options—even if it is just doing *something, anything* rather than stand still. In practice, this is a powerful tool for ensuring robust behavior, but it can also be a double-edged blade.

Done carefully, interleaving decision scores can produce interesting effects. For example, creating a *sequence* of decisions is as simple as setting up cooldowns, and then having each subsequent decision weighted slightly lower than the prior action. As successive actions are chosen by the AI, they will enter cooldown, leaving the AI to choose the next best thing—which, by construction, is the next action in the sequence.

One scenario where decisions can clash is when the considerations and response curves happen to generate very similar scores for different decisions. Even if the absolute best-scoring decision is always selected (highly recommended), the two may oscillate or ping-pong as their respective scores rise and fall. There are a few ways to combat this: give a "commitment bonus" (small score boost factor) to the last-chosen decision, increasing the odds of it being chosen again; add weights to each decision so that their total score could be, say, 3 or 4 instead of just 1; and make judicious use of runtime and cooldown considerations.

Unfortunately, all of these methods (useful as they are) share a single common drawback. In effect, they do not eliminate the possibility of two decisions oscillating—they simply shift *where* the scores will land when the oscillation happens. It could be that those scores land far enough away from the problem zone that the oscillation is irrelevant or easily dominated by other scores in the mix. But it can also happen that scores will continue to compete in harder and harder to recognize ways.

The simplest fix to this issue is to add another consideration to one of the decisions. Although it may be counterintuitive, this will add more variation to the overall scoring process, increasing the chances that the competing decision will consistently win (or lose)—thereby eliminating the oscillation.

However, there may be situations where design constraints simply do not allow for any other consideration to "make sense." This is readily encountered when working with highly specialized set pieces and other similar sorts of AI characters. If another suitable consideration cannot be found, the next best thing is to adjust the involved response curves to minimize the zone of oscillation.

Although most of the time there is a closed-form, analytical solution to the problem, it is often not worth the effort to solve the equations on paper. Instead, it is much more effective to build a tool that allows AI developers to manipulate the various inputs for a consideration using simple sliders. Providing a visual mechanism for experimenting with considerations (and, by extension, multiple competing decisions) can radically improve the accessibility and discoverability of any utility-based AI system.

26.6 Choosing Effective Considerations

We can use the rules discussed thus far as a starting point for defining how considerations should factor into making a decision in a utility-based AI model. But even before the selection and tuning of scoring functions (such as response curves), it can be tricky to determine which specific inputs should be used at all.

Broadly speaking, answering this question requires getting into the mind of the AI agent itself, and thinking in terms of what would motivate (or deter) that agent with regards to the particular decision being modeled. Many inputs—like distance, speed, relative directions, health, and so on—are fairly easy to take into account. But what about the case where a decision is nuanced, complex, possibly expensive to evaluate, and hard to capture in a single equation?

Recall the example from earlier with the invisible character trying to get into melee range of a target before its invisibility wears off. This could be done by modeling the duration of invisibility explicitly in the model, measuring the relative velocities of the invisible agent and the target, and so on. However, we preferred a simple and elegant *proxy variable*, which is just a time constant.

In practice, the difference between the explicit, detailed model of "before invisibility wears off" and the simplified proxy time is visible only extremely rarely. When the differences *are* visible, the player herself actually offers the best solution to explaining away the problem. Players will, in general, be eager to add their own narrative reasons for why AI does what it does. As a result, there will almost always be a tiny story in the player's mind about what happens when the time constant is too short or too long.

We can extrapolate from this example to general-purpose consideration design. Always be on the lookout for situations where a complex or hard-to-capture metric can be substituted for a proxy variable. Moreover, keep in mind that the best proxy may not even be the same kind of metric.

The first question to ask is "why would I do (or not do) this action?" Once a list of potential motivations is amassed, the next order of business is to look for what data are available (or can be readily made available) that best match those abstract motivations. Look for proxy variables that can capture multiple considerations at a time, such as modular influence map combinations (Mark 2015). Lastly, consider the relative importance of each input and design a suitable scoring function or response curve.

26.7 Conclusion

Utility theory offers a compelling model for building AI agents. Yet even with a robust architecture for utility-based AI in hand, it is not always immediately apparent how to actually create good decision-making and behavior. Seeking to address this, we explored some of the specifics of how decision modeling was done for *Guild Wars 2: Heart of Thorns* and a set of general principles that should hopefully carry forward to any project using utility-based AI.

References

Dill, K. 2015. Dual-utility reasoning. In *Game AI Pro Vol. 2*, ed. S. Rabin. Boca Raton, FL: CRC Press, pp. 23–26.

Graham, R. 2014. An introduction to utility theory. In *Game AI Pro Vol. 1,* ed. S. Rabin. Boca Raton, FL: CRC Press, pp. 113–126.

Lewis, M. 2015. Escaping the grid: Infinite-resolution influence mapping. In *Game AI Pro Vol. 2*, ed. S. Rabin. Boca Raton, FL: CRC Press, pp. 327–342.

Lewis, M. and Mark, D. 2015. Building a better centaur: AI at massive scale. *Lecture, Game Developers Conference 2015.* http://gdcvault.com/play/1021848/Building-a-Better-Centaur-AI (accessed May 24, 2016).

Mark, D. 2013. Architecture tricks: Managing behaviors in time, space, and depth. *Lecture, Game Developers Conference 2013.* http://www.gdcvault.com/play/1018040/Architecture-Tricks-Managing-Behaviors-in (accessed May 9, 2016).

Mark, D. 2015. Modular tactical influence maps. In *Game AI Pro Vol. 2*, ed. S. Rabin. Boca Raton, FL: CRC Press, pp. 343–364.

Combining Scripted Behavior with Game Tree Search for Stronger, More Robust Game AI

Nicolas A. Barriga, Marius Stanescu, and Michael Buro

27.1 Introduction

Fully scripted game AI systems are usually predictable and, due to statically defined behavior, susceptible to poor decision-making when facing unexpected opponent actions. In games with a small number of possible actions, like chess or checkers, a successful approach to overcome these issues is to use look-ahead search, that is, simulating the effects of action sequences and choosing those that maximize the agent's utility. In this chapter, we present an approach that adapts this process to complex video games, reducing action choices by means of scripts that expose choice points to look-ahead search. In this way, the game author maintains control over the range of possible AI behaviors and enables the system to better evaluate the consequences of its actions, resulting in smarter behavior.

The framework we introduce requires scripts that are able to play a full game. For example, a script for playing an RTS game will control workers to gather resources and construct buildings, train more workers and combat units, build base expansions, and attack the enemy. Some details, such as which combat units to build and where or when to expand, might be very dependent on the situation and difficult to commit to in advance. These choices are better left open when defining the strategy, to be decided by a search algorithm which can dynamically pick the most favorable action.

In this chapter, we chose to represent the scripts as decision trees because of the natural formulation of choice points as decision nodes. However, our approach is not limited to decision trees. Other types of scripted AI systems such as finite-state machines and behavior trees can be used instead by exposing transitions and selector nodes, respectively.

27.2 Scripts

For our purposes, we define a script as a function that takes a game state and returns actions to perform now. The method used to generate actions is unimportant: it could be a rule-based player hand coded with expert knowledge, or a machine learning or search-based agent, and etc. The only requirement is that it must be able to generate actions for any legal game state.

As an example, consider a *rush*, a common type of strategy in RTS games that tries to build as many combat units as fast as possible in an effort to destroy the opponent's base before he or she has the time to build suitable defenses. A wide range of these aggressive attacks are possible. At one extreme, the fastest attack can be executed using workers, which usually deal very little damage and barely have any armor. Alternatively, the attack can be delayed until more powerful units are trained.

27.2.1 Adding Choices

Figure 27.1 shows a decision tree representing a script that first gathers resources, builds some defensive buildings, expands to a second base, trains an army, and finally attacks the enemy. This decision tree is executed at every frame to decide what actions to issue. In a normal scripted strategy, there would be several hardcoded constants: the number of defensive buildings to build before expanding, the size of the army, and when to attack. However, the script could expose these decisions as choice points, and let a search algorithm explore them to decide the best course of action.

When writing a script, we must make some potentially hard choices. Will the AI expand to a new base after training a certain number of workers or will it wait until the current bases' resources are depleted? Regardless of the decision, it will be hardcoded in the script, according to a set of static rules about the state of the game. Discovering predictable patterns in the way the AI acts might be frustrating for all but beginner players. Whether the behavior implemented is sensible or not in the given situation, they will quickly learn to exploit it, and the game will likely lose some of its replay value in the process.

As script writers, we would like to be able to leave some choices open, such as which units to rush with. But the script also needs to deal with any and all possible events happening during the strategy execution. The base might be attacked before it is ready to launch its own attack, or maybe the base is undefended while our infantry units are out looking for the enemy. Should they continue in hope of destroying their base before they raze ours? Or should they come back to defend? What if when we arrive to the enemies' base, we realize we do not have the strength to defeat them? Should we push on nonetheless? Some, or all, of these decisions are best left open, so that they can be explored and the most appropriate choice can be taken during the game.

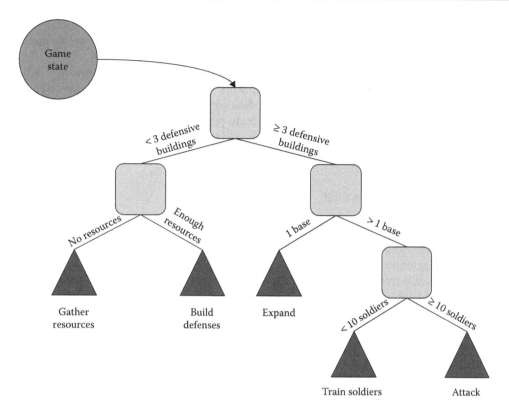

Figure 27.1

Decision tree representing script choices.

The number of choice points exposed can be a configurable parameter with an impact on the strength and speed of the system. Fewer options will produce a faster but more predictable AI, suitable for beginner players, while increasing their number will lead to a harder challenge at the cost of increased computational work.

27.3 Adding Search

So far we have presented a flexible way to write AI scripts that include choice points in which multiple different actions can be taken. However, we have not mentioned how those decisions are made. Commonly, they would be hardcoded as a behavior or decision tree. But there are other techniques that can produce stronger AI systems without relying as heavily on expert knowledge: machine learning (ML) and look-ahead search.

An ML-based agent relies on a function that takes the current game state as input and produces a decision for each choice in the script. The parameters of that function would then be optimized either by supervised learning methods on a set of game traces, or by reinforcement learning, letting the agent play itself. However, once the parameters are learned, the model acts like a static rule-based system and might become predictable. If the system is allowed to keep learning after the game has shipped, then there are no guarantees on how it will evolve, possibly leading to unwanted behavior.

The second approach, look-ahead search, involves executing action sequences and evaluating their outcomes. Both methods can work well. It is possible to have an unbeatable ML player if the features and training data are good enough and a perfect search-based player if we explore the full search space. In practice, neither requirement is easy to meet: good representations are hard to design, and time constraints prevent covering the search space in most games. Good practical results are often achieved by combining both approaches (Silver et al. 2016).

27.3.1 Look-Ahead Search

To use look-ahead search, we need to be able to execute a script for a given timespan, look at the resulting state, and then go back to the original state to try other action choices. This has to happen without performing any actions in the actual game, and it has to be several orders of magnitude faster than the real game's speed because we want (a) to look-ahead as far as possible into the future, to the end of the game if feasible and (b) to try as many choice combinations as possible before committing to one.

This means we need to be able to either save the current game state, copy it to a new state object, execute scripts on the copy, and then reload the original, or execute and undo the actions on the original game state. The latter approach is common in AI systems for board games, because it is usually faster to apply and undo a move than to copy a game state. In RTS games, however, keeping track of several thousand complex actions and undoing them might prove difficult, so copying the state is preferable.

When performing look-ahead, we need to issue actions for the opponents as well. Which scripts to use will depend on our knowledge about them. If we can reasonably predict the strategy they will use, we could simulate their behavior as accurately as possible and come up with a best response—a strategy that exploits our knowledge of the enemy. For example, if we know that particular opponents always rush on small maps, then we will only explore options in the choice points that apply to rushes to simulate their behavior, while fixing the other choices. If the script has a choice point with options (a) rush; (b) expand; and (c) build defenses, and a second choice point with the type of combat units to build, we would fix option (a) for the first choice point and let the search explore all options for the second choice point. At the same time, we will try all the possible choices for ourselves to let the search algorithm decide the best counter strategy.

However, the more imprecise our opponent model is, the riskier it is to play a best response strategy. Likewise, if we play against an unknown player, the safest route is to try as many choices for the opponent as for ourselves. The aim is to find an equilibrium strategy that does not necessarily exploit the opponent's weaknesses, but cannot be easily exploited either.

27.3.2 State Evaluation

Forwarding the state using different choices is only useful if we can evaluate the merit of the resulting states. We need to decide which of those states is more desirable from the point of view of the player performing the search. In other words, we need to evaluate those states, assign each a numerical value, and use it to compare them. In zero-sum games, it is sufficient to consider symmetric evaluation functions `eval(state, player)` that return positive values for the winning player and negative values for the losing player with

```
eval(state, p1) == -eval(state, p2).
```

The most common approach to state evaluation in RTS games is to use a linear function that adds a set of values that are multiplied by a weight. The values usually represent simple features, such as the number of units of each type a player has, with different weights reflecting their estimated worth. Weights can be either hand-tuned or learned from records of past games using logistic regression or similar methods. An example of a popular metric in RTS games is lifetime damage, or LTD (Kovarsky and Buro 2005), which tries to estimate the amount of damage a unit could deal to the enemy during its lifetime. Another feature could be the cost of building a unit, which takes advantage of the game balancing already performed by the game designers. Costlier units are highly likely to be more useful, thus the player that has a higher total unit cost has a better chance of winning.

A somewhat different state evaluation method involves Monte Carlo simulations. Instead of invoking a static function, one could have a pair of fast scripts, either deterministic or randomized, play out the remainder of the game, and assign a positive score to the winning player. The rationale behind this method is that, even if the scripts are not of high quality, as both players are using the same policy, it is likely that whoever wins more simulations is the one who was ahead in the first place.

If running a simulation until the end of the game is not feasible, a hybrid method can be used that performs a limited playout for a predetermined amount of frames and then calls the evaluation function. Evaluation functions are usually more accurate closer to the end of a game, when the game outcome is easier to predict. Therefore, moving the application of the evaluation function to the end of the playout often results in a more accurate assessment of the value of the game state.

27.3.3 Minimax Search

So far we have considered the problem of looking ahead using different action choices in our scripts and evaluating the resulting states, but the fact that the opponent also has choices has to be taken into account. Lacking accurate opponent models, we have to make some assumptions about their actions. For simplicity, we will assume that the opponents use the same scripts and evaluate states the same way we do.

To select a move, we consider all possible script actions in the current state. For each, we examine all possible opponent replies and continue recursively until reaching a predefined depth or the end of the game. The evaluation function is then used to estimate the value of the resulting states, and the move which maximizes the player-to-move's score is selected. This algorithm is called Negamax (CPW 2016b)—a variant of the minimax algorithm—because in zero-sum games, the move that maximizes one player's score is also the one that minimizes the other player's score. The move that maximizes the negated child score is selected and assigned to the parent state, and the recursion unrolls, as shown in Figure 27.2. Listing 27.1 shows a basic implementation returning the value of the current game state. Returning the best move as well is an easy addition.

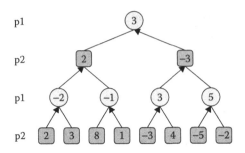

Figure 27.2

Negamax search example.

Listing 27.1. Negamax implementation in Python.

```python
def negaMax(state, depth, player):
    if depth == 0 or terminal(state):
        return evaluate(state, player)
    max = -float('inf')
    for move in state.legal_moves(player):
        childState = state.apply(move)
        score = -negaMax(childState, depth-1, opponent(player))
        if score > max:
            max = score
    return max

#example call
#state: current game state
#depth: maximum search depth
#player: player to move
value = negaMax(state, depth, player)
```

A modification is needed for the minimax algorithm to work in our scripted AI. The moves in an RTS game are simultaneous, so they need to be serialized to fit the game tree search framework. Randomizing the player to move or alternating in a p1-p2-p2-p1 fashion are common choices to mitigate a possible player bias (Churchill et al. 2012). The resulting algorithm is shown in Listing 27.2.

In Listings 27.1 and 27.2, Negamax takes as an input the height of the search tree to build, and being a depth-first algorithm, it only returns a solution when the tree has been fully searched. However, if the computation time is limited, we need an *anytime* algorithm that can be stopped at any point and returns a reasonable answer. The solution is to search a shallow depth, 2 in our case, and then iteratively deepen the search by two levels until time runs out. At first it might look like a waste of resources, because the shallower levels of the tree are searched repeatedly, but if we add a *transposition table*, the information from previous iterations can be reused.

In this chapter, we use the Negamax version of the minimax algorithm for simplicity. In practice, we would use AlphaBeta search (CPW 2016a), an efficient version of minimax that prunes significant parts of the search tree, while still finding the optimal solution.

AlphaBeta is more efficient when the best actions are examined first, and accordingly, there exist several move-ordering techniques, such as using *hash moves* or *killer moves*, which make use of the information in the transposition table (CPW 2016c).

Listing 27.2. Simultaneous Moves Negamax.

```
def SMNegaMax(state, depth, previousMove=None):
  player = playerToMove(depth)
  if depth == 0 or terminal(state):
    return evaluate(state, player)
  max = -float('inf')
  for move in state.legal_moves(player):
    if previousMove == None:
      score = -SMNegaMax(state, depth-1, move)
    else
      childState = state.apply(previousMove, move)
      score = -SMNegaMax(childState, depth-1)
    if score > max:
      max = score
  return max

#Example call
#state: current game state
#depth: maximum search depth, has to be even
value = SMNegaMax(state, depth)
```

Another class of algorithms that can be used to explore the search tree is Monte Carlo Tree Search (MCTS) (Sturtevant 2015). Instead of sequentially analyzing sibling nodes, MCTS randomly samples them. A sampling policy like UCT (Kocsis and Szepesvári 2006) balances exploration and exploitation to grow the tree asymmetrically, concentrating on the more promising subtrees.

27.4 Final Considerations

So far, we have introduced scripts with choice points, a state evaluation function, and a search algorithm that uses look-ahead to decide which choices to take. Once the search produces an answer in the form of decisions at every choice point applicable in the current game state, it can be executed in the game. Given enough time, whenever the AI system needs to issue actions, it would start the search procedure, obtain an answer and execute it. However, in practice, actions have to be issued in almost every frame, with only a few milliseconds available per frame, so this can be impractical. Fortunately, as the scripts can play entire games, a previous answer can be used as a standing plan for multiple frames. The search can be restarted, and the process split across multiple frames until an answer is reached, while in the meantime, the standing plan is being executed. At that point, the new solution becomes the standing plan. The search can be started again, either immediately, or once we find the opponent is acting inconsistently with the results of our search.

Experiments using *StarCraft: Brood War* have shown good results (Barriga et al. 2015). A script with a single choice point that selects a particular type of rush was tested against state-of-the-art *StarCraft* bots. The resulting agent was more robust than any of the individual strategies on its own and was able to defeat more opponents.

One topic we have not touched on is fog-of-war. The described framework assumes it has access to the complete game state at the beginning of the search. If your particular game does not have perfect information, there are several choices. The easiest one is to let the AI cheat, by giving it full game state access. However, players might become suspicious of the unfair advantage if the AI system keeps correctly "guessing" and countering their surprise tactics. A better option is to implement an inference system. For instance, a particle filter can be used to estimate the positions of previously seen units (Weber et al. 2011), and Bayesian models have been used to recognize and predict opponent plans (Synnaeve and Bessière 2011).

27.5 Conclusion

In this chapter, we have presented a search framework that combines scripted behavior and look-ahead search. By using scripts, it allows game designers to keep control over the range of behaviors the AI system can perform, whereas the adversarial look-ahead search enables it to better evaluate action outcomes, making it a stronger and more believable enemy.

The decision tree structure of the scripts ensures that only the choice combinations that make sense for a particular game state will be explored. This reduces the search effort considerably, and because scripts can play entire games, we can use the previous plan for as long as it takes to produce an updated one.

Finally, based on promising experimental results on RTS games, we expect this new search framework to perform well in any game for which scripted AI systems can be built.

References

Barriga, N.A., Stanescu, M. and Buro, M. 2015. Puppet search: Enhancing scripted behavior by look-ahead search with applications to real-time strategy games. *Proceedings of the Eleventh Annual AAAI Conference on Artificial Intelligence and Interactive Digital Entertainment* November 14–18, 2015. Santa Cruz, CA.

Chess Programming Wiki. 2016a. Alpha-beta. http://chessprogramming.wikispaces.com/Alpha-Beta (accessed February 8, 2017).

Chess Programming Wiki. 2016b. Minimax. http://chessprogramming.wikispaces.com/Minimax (accessed February 8, 2017).

Chess Programming Wiki. 2016c. Transposition table. http://chessprogramming.wikispaces.com/Transposition+Table (accessed February 8, 2017).

Churchill, D., Saffidine, A. and Buro, M. 2012. Fast heuristic search for RTS game combat scenarios. *Proceedings of the Eighth Artificial Intelligence and Interactive Digital Entertainment Conference*, October 8–12, 2012. Stanford, CA.

Kocsis, L. and Szepesvári, C. 2006. Bandit based Monte-Carlo planning. *17th European Conference on Machine Learning*, September 18–22, 2006. Berlin, Germany.

Kovarsky, A. and Buro, M. 2005. Heuristic search applied to abstract combat games. *Proceedings of the Eighteenth Canadian Conference on Artificial Intelligence*, May 9–11, 2005. Victoria, Canada.

Silver, D., Huang, A., Maddison, C.J., Guez, A., Sifre, L., Van Den Driessche, G., Schrittwieser, J., Antonoglou, I., Panneershelvam, V., Lanctot, M. and Dieleman, S. 2016. Mastering the game of Go with deep neural networks and tree search. *Nature*, 529, 484–489.

Stanescu, M., Barriga, N.A. and Buro, M. 2017. Combat outcome prediction for RTS games. In *Game AI Pro 3: Collected Wisdom of Game AI Professionals*, ed. Rabin, S., Boca Raton, FL: CRC Press.

Sturtevant, N.R. 2015. Monte Carlo tree search and related algorithms for games. In *Game AI Pro 2: Collected Wisdom of Game AI Professionals*, ed. S. Rabin. Boca Raton, FL: CRC Press, pp. 265–281.

Synnaeve, G. and Bessière, P. 2011. A Bayesian model for plan recognition in RTS games applied to StarCraft. *Proceedings of the Seventh Artificial Intelligence and Interactive Digital Entertainment Conference*, October 10–14, 2011. Stanford, CA.

Weber, B.G., Mateas, M. and Jhala, A. 2011. A particle model for state estimation in real-time strategy games. *Proceedings of the Seventh Annual AAAI Conference on Artificial Intelligence and Interactive Digital Entertainment*, October 10–14, 2011. Stanford, CA.

Printed in the United States
by Baker & Taylor Publisher Services